THE

CITY-COUNTY CONSOLIDATED

By

JOHN A. RUSH, A.B., A.M., L.L.B.

Member of The
State Bar of California

With an Introduction by
BENJAMIN C. HILLIARD
Chief Justice of Supreme Court of Colorado
1940

NINETEEN HUNDRED FORTY-ONE
Published by the Author
LOS ANGELES

PRESS OF

U C P Co.

LOS ANGELES

Affectionately Dedicated

To My Wife

ELSIE DODD RUSH

And To Our Sons

John L. and Robert

"The *state may mould* local institutions according to its views of policy and expediency; but local government is matter of absolute right; and the state cannot take it away. It would be the *boldest mockery* to speak of the city as possessing municipal liberty where *the state not only shaped* its government, *but at discretion sent in its own agents to administer it.*"

(Judge Cooley in the *Hurlbut* case, 24 Mich. 44.)

THE

CITY-COUNTY CONSOLIDATED

THE AUTHOR'S BACKGROUND

Member of the Denver Charter Convention, 1898; State Senator from Denver, 1901-1905; Author of Constitutional Amendment creating the consolidated City and County of Denver, 1902; Vice-President of first Charter Convention of the City and County of Denver, 1903; District Attorney of the City and County of Denver, 1913-1917; Vice-Chairman of Citizens' Committee on Governmental Reorganization, Los Angeles, 1935-1936. ("Who's Who In America"—Vol. 21, p. 2242.)

CONTENTS

Contents

CONTENTS

CONTENTS

Contents

CONTENTS

INTRODUCTION
BY CHIEF JUSTICE HILLIARD

This book gripped my attention when I first read it in manuscript form. I regard it as a masterly production by a real student of the problems about which it speaks. The author puts the facts in straightforward language and deduces his conclusions logically. It makes the book all the more interesting because it is written from the view-point of a lawyer of long experience who has taken active part in the creative and administrative field of an actual city-county consolidated. During his twenty-eight years in Denver he was a leader in movements for civic betterment. He framed the constitutional amendment which created the consolidated City and County of Denver with one set of officers in place of the two sets which we had theretofore endured. He is well equipped to write on his subject.

Lawyers and judges alike may well read this book with profit. They may not all agree with what it says, but then they quite frequently disagree even among themselves. It is well to recall the fundamental statement by Judge Cooley, eminent jurist and text writer, that: "The state may mould local institutions according to its view of policy and expediency; but local government is a matter of absolute right; and the state cannot take it away. It would be the boldest mockery to speak of a city as possessing municipal liberty where the state not only shaped its government, but at discretion sent in its own agents to administer it." The author has adopted this logical and sensible view and has pointed

out how departure from it has caused much grief to many of ou
larger cities.

Educators and students in the field of municipal governmen
will undoubtedly find in this book much of educational value. T
read of the uniformly satisfactory experience of cities in Grea
Britain and in America as set forth therein should stimulate con
sideration of what form of government is best for our urban cen
ters. Already the bulk of population in this country is in ou
cities and there can be no greater work than to aid in simplifyin
their government, thus lessening their tax burdens. It would seem
quite proper that educators and also public officials should acquain
themselves fully concerning the known advantages of the city
county consolidated. It has proven eminently satisfactory in my
city,—The City and County of Denver.

It is an unusual pleasure for me to write the introduction t
this book whose author has been my personal friend since we firs
met when he came to Denver in 1893. He did a splendid work
here and he has performed a real public service in writing this
book. I feel that it will receive a welcome from a wide circle o
readers.

Supreme Court Chambers,   BENJAMIN C. HILLIARD
Denver, Colorado,
December 30, 1940.

AUTHOR'S FOREWORD

The purpose of this book is to tell of that important system of municipal government known in England as "Counties of Cities" and as "County Boroughs," and in America as THE CITY-COUNTY CONSOLIDATED. While this form of government is not new, yet it has reached its highest development only in recent years.

A half century has elapsed since my study of this interesting form of municipal government began, yet I have found no book which treats the subject commensurate with its importance. The most that has been done is to make mention of it rather incidentally. To my mind its importance has thus been largely lost sight of. This book is intended to fill what appears to be an omission in the historical, substantive and legal treatment of the subject.

It was the year after the Act of Parliament was adopted in 1888 creating the English county boroughs that this form of municipal government came to my attention during my collegiate work at the University of Kansas and again later in a post-graduate course taken there in political science for a masters degree, coupled with a study of municipal corporations in my law course. England was not alone in that movement, for Germany was developing a somewhat similar system. At that time, also, several American cities had become more or less city-county consolidated types.

Arriving in Denver in 1893 to practice law I found the people of that progressive city greatly exercised over the law of 1889 creating a board of public works for Denver and another of 1891 cretaing a fire and police board for that city, whose members were appointed by the governor. Up to this time my interest had been only that of a student but now I became seriously engaged in the actual creation of a city-county consolidated. The political party of which I was the county chairman in 1896, elected its ticket under the slogan of "Home Rule for Denver." Membership in the Denver charter convention of 1898 spurred my interest, so that upon my election to the state senate in 1900 I drafted the constitutional amendment, submitted to and adopted by the people of Colorado in 1902, which created the consolidated "City and County of Denver" with one set of officers performing both city and county functions. Writers generally agree that it is the best plan yet drawn. In the ensuing litigation in which I took an active part, and as a member of the first charter convention of the new city-county, and as its district attorney (1913-1917), opportunity was afforded for first hand observation of the operation of public affairs under this consolidated system. The results were most gratifying. It was a great step in advance and gave and still gives general satisfaction to the people of that city. Upon coming to Los Angeles in 1921 a new field presented itself. My appointment by Mayor Shaw of that city as a member of the Citizens Committee on Governmental Reorganization in 1935 led me into further research which has resulted in the preparation and publication of this book.

Necessarily in treating this advance in municipal government the difficulties that have beset it had to be noted. Legislatures and courts have many times stood in the way of the people of our largest cities in their attempts to regain or to retain the right of selecting their own officers instead of having officers foisted upon them by the governor of the state. Examples are met with from the time of Charles II who commanded his appointed tools on the bench to declare forfeited the charter of London because the people of that great city would not surrender to his dictation, down to the decisions of American courts which, unfortunately, have swerved from the path of judicial rectitude in order to bolster up subversive ws enacted by termite politicians to deprive our cities of the ghtful power of selecting their own officers. It will be seen that England no autocratic sovereign ever interfered with the right the boroughs to govern themselves under officers of their own loosing but that he was ultimately brought to book. Yet in free merica there was originated by the courts the legal fetish that le legislature may create and destroy municpialities at will, and om that sprang the reactionary doctrine that their people may be eprived of their age-old right of selecting their own officers. This erversion of the law has greatly hindered efforts of the people consolidate, simplify and make more economical their form of overnment in our cities. These court decisions have necessitated onsideration at some length. Since courts have disagreed among lemselves concerning very simple and fundamental principles of overnment, evidently they are not sacrosanct and I have not hesilted to speak strongly about those which have made themselves ubject to merited criticism.

Wherever feasible the language of a text or of a court decision given, rather than to give a mere opinion concerning it or of its urported meaning. This affords the reader his right to draw his wn conclusions. Parts of quotations appear in italics. Generally peaking they do not thus appear in the original. I have italicized hem in order to emphasize the point under discussion. I have een much disturbed in reading a book to have my attention disracted by references to notes appearing at the bottom of the page r at the end of the book. Therefore, I have avoided this so far s possible and have placed in the text itself the name of the author nd of his book, and the style of a decided case and where it can e found.

In addition to my personal experiences upon which this book is artially based, I have profited from a recent survey of the law pplicable to the subject and have listed under "Legal Authoriies and Cases" at the end of this book those found helpful. The Bibliography" there lists the texts which I have consulted with

profit and I thank the publishers for permitting quotations there
from. Under the heading of "Those Who Have Helped" appea
the names of educators, public officials and others to whom I ar
indebted.

I am deeply gratified that Chief Justice Hilliard did me th
signal honor of writing the "Introduction" to this book.
acknowledge the kindly services of Dr. William B. Munro, note
author and educator, now Professor of History and Governmen
at the California Institute of Technology, and of Dr. Charles H
Titus, Professor of Political Science at the University of Califor
nia, and also of my long time friend William Allen White, note
editor and author, who gave their time in reading my manuscrip
and encouraged me by recommending that it be published. I tak
especial pleasure in expressing my deep appreciation to Sir Harr;
G. Pritchard, Secretary of the Association of Municipal Corpora
tions, Westminster, England, for valuable information which h
has furnished to me concerning the consolidated county boroug]
system in that country as set forth in Chapter III.

I am mindful, too, of the valuable legal aid in the Denver lit;
gation over the "Rush Bill' rendered by United States Senator
Thomas M. Patterson and Charles S. Thomas, and of J. Warne
Mills, W. H. Bryant, Guy LeRoy Stevick, John H. Gabriel anc
George F. Dunklee (now judge), and to the loyal support given b;
the *Rocky Mountain News* and the *Denver Post*.

In the half century which has elapsed since I began the stud;
of the subject of "The City-County Consolidated" I have activel;
lived with it and as a part of it and have continuously observe
it at first hand with increasing interest, and have noted with satis
faction the benefits derived from the operation of this form of gov
ernment. And so my thought has been that by writing this bool
I might perform a further service.

John A. Rush

CHAPTER I.

GENESIS OF CITY-COUNTY CONSOLIDATED

The marked characteristic of the city-county consolidated is that it has but one set of officers performing
both city and county functions, with resultant governmental simplification, elimination of overlapping jurisdiction, economy of management, and efficiency of administration. In its true form it is a municipality in which
all governmental functions not affecting equally the
people of the entire state are performed within a specific
territory by officers selected by its own people. It is self-
contained. It is self-governed. It is an autonomous
consolidated city and county.

The roots of this governmental entity, consolidated in
form and autonomous in character, run back to the earliest days of history. They are found in the development
of civilization itself. Historians generally agree that
first came the family in which the patriarch was the head.
Next came the clan or kinsmen with its "head-men" and
its "eldermen" selected by its members. Then came the
tribe composed of many families not necessarily related,
the members of which selected their own chief and their
own councillors. Whether housed in caves or in rude
bark or grass huts, under patriarchs or under self-
selected chiefs, the rule was the same. As barbaric sav-
agery was curbed and predatory instincts were brought
in leash, men abandoned their nomadic habits and settled
down with their families in fixed habitations. Protection
from forays, and enlarged opportunity for barter and

trade, induced these families in time to join together into
communities, and these grew into villages and in turn
into independent cities. H. G. Wells in his "Outline of
History" says: "The civilization of Egypt, Sumeria,
China and no doubt North India, all began in a number
of independent city states, each one a city with a few
miles of dependent villages and cultivation around it,
but out of this phase they passed by process of coales-
cence into kingdoms and empires." (v. II, p. 307.)

These ancient city states were not confined to Asia
and Africa. In the early Hellenic civilization the city
was the state, governed in general by the whole body of
the free citizens of the city who met together to discuss
and settle all questions of public policy and to select
those of their number who were to carry out that policy.
The outstanding example was Athens. The history of
Rome is simply an account of the greatest municipal
corporation the world has ever known. In *State v.
Parker,* 116 Iowa, 96, the court said: "The Roman republic took its origin from the Tiber, and was but a development and extension of that city." The city of
Rome, for years a republic and later even under the
early emperors, was quite autonomous in character and
practice. As other towns developed they were given
like status. The *municipium* was a town out of Rome,
more particularly in Italy but not confined thereto, which
not only possessed the right of Roman citizenship but
also enjoyed the right of self-government. It was a free,
or privileged town: one that had the right of being governed by its own laws and customs, under officers locally
selected by its own people, as said by Breasted, "In The
Conquest of Civilization." (p. 628.) It cherished with
pride the dignity of being a free city. There were a
thousand of these city states in the Roman Empire. During the Roman occupation of Britain, York was the provincial capital. It had many of the attributes of a city
state, and so had London which, with slight interruption,
has always maintained practical freedom from outside

interference. As said by Wells: "In England the Royal City of Westminster on the Thames stood cheek by jowl with the walled city of London, into which the king came only with ceremony and permission." (v. II, p. 182.)

Even after the downfall of the Roman Empire many of the Italian cities retained their status of city states. Despite feudalism and the usurpation of power by nobles and lords elsewhere, such cities as Genoa, Florence, Milan, Pisa and Venice, maintained their independence. The latter was a free republic like that of the former Athenian free republic. In Germany there was formed and for years existed that remarkable group of free cities under the name of the Hanseatic League. During its most flourishing period the League embraced ninety towns, scattered over the whole length and breadth of Germany, including Holland. They owed but slight allegiance to the emperor. They were city states. They framed their own laws and ordinances. They selected their own officers. They were self-governed.

There is this distinction to be kept in mind, however, that these city-states often extended their authority over territory beyond their municipal limits, in some instances covering great areas and populations, while the counties of cities and the county boroughs in England and the city-county consolidated in America have been confined to the area within their respective boundaries.

It will be observed that none of these cities was the creature of the state. They were created by their own people, just as we shall now see that the boroughs of England were created by their own inhabitants unhampered originally in the exercise of self-government and in the local selection of their own officers. These rights were, and should always have been declared to be, inalienable notwithstanding the holding of some courts to the contrary. English history furnishes strong denial of any basis for the contention that the state at will may create and destroy cities and foist its appointees upon their people. Despite the years during which autocratic

rulers usurped for a time the exercise of some of their
rights the cities, in the main, have clung to their old liberties and freedom and have gradually swung back
toward the status of the old city-state in a modified form,
as evidenced more concretely by the "counties of cities"
and the "county boroughs" in England and by the "city-
county consolidated" in America. It is fitting, therefore,
first to consider that development which has come about
in England.

CHAPTER II.

BOROUGHS AND COUNTIES IN ENGLAND

There is no authentic history of Britain prior to its invasion by Julius Ceasar in 54 B. C. The Britons at that time were a semi-barbarous people, living in mean huts scattered through the wilds of a practically uncultivated and unimproved land, with no cities worthy the name. Rome brought to this new province the benefits of its civilization. It built roads throughout the length and breadth of the land. It fostered trade and commerce under the security afforded by its rule. Former little villages grew into sizable towns governed by their own municipal officers with powers of self-government somewhat like those of the Roman *municipium*. London became the chief port in the south, with Bath as the principal town in the southwest, and Lincoln in the east. York, in the north, became the capital of the province, with its massive walls which served as protection against raids of the Scots from Wales on the west and of the Picts from Scotland on the north.

But when the Roman legions were called home in 410 A.D., to defend Italy from the incursion of the Goths who streamed down from the North, all this advance in Britain was lost. Internecine strife then sprang up between the tribes in Britain which weakened them and thus was opened the door to the conquest in 449 A.D., by the Angles, the Saxons and the Jutes, — as fierce a band of freebooters as ever scuttled a ship or scourged a

coast. They came, in the first instance, at the invitation
of the Britons to help defend against the incursions of
the Picts from Scotland. However, they did not long
behave themselves as guests should, but proceeded to
take over everything in most ruthless fashion. They
did a very thorough job of it.˙ When they got through
there were but few of the Britons left, and that remnant
was reduced to slavery. Thus the Britain of the Britons
disappeared. It became Anglo-Saxon England. Nearly
all the advance in trade and commerce and city growth
was lost, for the newcomers disliked cities. Under them
London became almost a deserted town. York, with its
great encompassing walls, was practically abandoned.
But it must be noted that the democratic principle of
local self-government in the Roman *municipium* survived
in, or rather was succeeded by, the "folk-moot" of the
Anglo-Saxons.

While the newcomers had such a forbidding back-
ground, yet to them civilization is indebted for those
systems of free government now enjoyed by democratic
nations, and for those fundamentals of liberty upon
which our American institutions rest. Their origins are
of interest. About the time Caesar invaded Britain he
came into belligerent contact with the Teutonic tribes
which he called *Germani*. They inhabited the vast Her-
cinian Forest then extending from the Black Forest on
the west across the whole of Germany of today. The
three tribes, the Angles, the Saxons, and the Jutes, occupied the northern part of that country. The northern-
most were the Jutes, whose name is preserved in the
peninsula of Jutland. To their south were the Engle, or
English, folk who occupied much of what are now the
German districts of Hanover and Oldenburg. Then to
their south and west came the Westphalian Saxons whose
district reached from the Rhine on the west to the Weser
on the east, and to the east of the latter came the East-
phalian Saxons whose district stretched from the Weser
east to the Elbe. These three powerful tribes were re-

lated by blood ties, and their customs, usages and forms
of government were practically the same.

In his "Commentaries," Caesar describes the *Germani* as being clad in skins, very warlike, living largely
from hunting and from their herds, but giving enough
attention to agriculture so that the land was allotted
each year by the elected magistrates, under the rule that
the allotees were required, at the beginning of the ensuing year, to move elsewhere lest by the acquisition of
permanent estates the weaker might be disadvantaged,
or that a desire for wealth might cause discords and divisions, and that thereby the people might be kept in a
contented frame of mind when each saw his means placed
on an equality with the others. Those entitled to participate in the annual allotment of land were vested with
the power of government. This coupling of an interest
in land with the right of suffrage and the right to participate in the functions of government was basic. Later,
when private ownership of land came about, this right
was limited to the landowner or the rentpayer, and it
has been only in the last hundred years that this limitation has practically been swept away in England and in
America.

Under this early Teutonic rule these land allottees
were the "freemen" of the "burgh" who had the right
to participate and vote in its "moot" or meeting of the
"folk." Thus assembled they administered justice, determined the policies to be pursued by the community
and elected the officers to administer and enforce them.
When war came they met in tribal assembly, either for
invasion or for defense, and there selected leaders to
conduct it. But when peace came the functions of the
leaders ceased. The officers of each burgh, even during
war, administered its affairs without any outside interference or control.

Tacitus, the great Roman historian, was a young
man when his father was Roman procurator of *Gallia
Belgica* (now Belgium), whose eastern boundary was the

Rhine just across that river from the Westphalian Saxons on the east. From that vantage point he gathered the material for his "Germania" (83 A. D.) in which he points out that kingship was infrequent among the German tribes and emphasizes their democratic form of government; that only in time of war were leaders selected, usually because of acknowledged ability or of renowned valor; and that when war ended the administration of affairs reverted solely to the burghs whose freemen met together to administer justice, determine policies, and elect officers, after free and full discussion. At the annual spring meeting allotment of the land was made in accordance with the respective needs of the inhabitants. There is much here to remind the reader of the New England town-meeting of seventeen hundred years later where the American pioneers met together to decide upon public policies, elect officers to carry them out, and then allot the land among the people for the ensuing year.

It seems hardly necessary to remind the reader that the basis of our American institutions, the very beginnings of our system of self-government, have come down to us from these Teutonic tribes. Green, in his "Short History of the English People," speaking of the Anglo-Saxons of the early days, says: "Of the temper and life of the folk in this older England we know little. But from the glimpses we catch of them when the conquest brought them to the shores of Britain, their political and social organization must have been that of the German race to which they belonged. The basis of their society was the free man. He alone was known as the 'free man' or 'the churl;' and two phrases set his freedom vividly before us. He was 'the free-necked man,' whose long hair floated over 'a neck that had never bent to a lord.' " (p. 2.) No more striking language could depict his freedom. His settlements were those of kinsmen. Green continues: "As they fought side by side on the field, so they dwelled side by side on the soil. Harling abode by Harling, and Billing by Billing; and each 'wick' or 'ham' or 'stead' or 'tun' took its name from the kinsmen who dwelt together in it. The home or 'ham' of the Billings would be Billingham, and the 'tun' or township of the Harlings would be Harlington." (p. 3.) These family communities isolated themselves from like neighboring communities except in case invasion or defense called them together for war. They grouped their homes in their burgh for mutual protection and went out therefrom to till their neighboring fields. Each was a separate independent little "farmer commonwealth," self governing and free.

That very eminent writer, former President Wilson, in his "The State," says: "The Teutonic family was the unit of government. Kinsmen, fellow tribesmen, were grouped in villages, and each village maintained without question its privileges of self-government, legislating upon its common affairs and administering its common property in village meeting. Its lands were the property, not of individuals, but of the community; but they were allotted in separate parcels to the freemen of the community, upon would-be equitable principles, to be cultivated for private, not for communal profit. Chiefs there were who exercised magisterial powers, but these chiefs were elected in village meeting. They did not determine the weightier questions of custom, in the administration of justice: that was the province of the village meeting itself." (1898 ed. p. 163.)

It will be noted that the administration of justice was the province of the village meeting itself. It proceeded, as of old, first hand, from the meeting of the village freemen. In primitive days each man had been his own avenger. Then the family had taken over that function. Later it was the community—the burgh—which administered justice with all the freemen sitting together in judgment. The accused was thus given the right of trial by jury before his peers, a right to which the Anglo-Saxon people have clung as a cornerstone of their criminal jurisprudence. Furthermore, the administration of justice was lodged in and exercised by the home-folks and not until comparatively recent years has it been taken over by outside appointees under the usurped authority of the sovereign.

Thus was transplanted to England by the Anglo-Saxons that rule of self-government which they held as a basic tenet of their faith and practice. As said further by Green: "Little knots of kinsfolk drew together in "tun" and "ham" beside the Thames and the Trent as they had settled beside the Elbe and the Weser, not as kinsfolk only, but as dwellers in the same plot, knit together by their common holding within the same bounds. Each little village-commonwealth lived the same life in Britain as its farmers had lived at home. Each had its moot hill or sacred tree as a centre, its 'mark' as a border; each judged by witness of the kinsfolk and made laws in the assembly of its freemen, and chose the leaders for its own governance, and the men who were to follow headman or ealdorman to hundred-moot or to war." (p. 15.)

These little village commonwealths were self constituted. They were not created by any outside power. Speaking of the early English boroughs, Finer, in his "English Local Government," says: "As units of government they spontaneously arose out of the local needs of an aggregation of people, for organized satisfaction of those needs. They were not the creation of a central authority, though they came to be regulated and given legal form by it. A nucleus of people in a surrounding sparsity developed a sentiment of community, proud, restricted, and independent. * * * The whole conception is one of men congregating *closely*—closely, that is, when compared with the sparsity of the rest of the land. Naturally, strategic centres, seaports, fishing villages, markets, industrial groupings, and ecclesiastic *foci,* produced boroughs. The means of livelihood and the stratification of society produced by one's station in agriculture, craft, buying and selling, determined rights to participate in government. * * * They (the boroughs) possessed common property, particularly in land; they governed tillage and pasture; they regulated manufacture, qualities, buying and selling, fisheries and harbors, sanitary nuisances, and they had the policing of morals and peace." (p. 59.) In boroughs thus constituted each had its own borough-moot, where the freemen gathered to discuss and settle matters of community concern and to select those who should conduct the local government. It should especially be noted that originally the boroughs were "spontaneous organizations," that "they were not the creation of a central authority," and that "they had the policing of their own morals and peace."

For five hundred years, sporadically interrupted by Danish invasions, this system of local self-government prevailed in England, although it became impaired more and more during the later years of that period. The cause of this deterioration was that the Anglo-Saxon tribes fought for forty years to subdue the Britons and then fought fiercely among themselves for dominance, except when occasionally they had to join together to repel the Danes. The result of these continuous wars was the breaking down of much of the independent spirit of the people and a considerable loss of that liberty which they had enjoyed for centuries. The tribal chieftains under whom they fought gradually usurped greater and greater power at the expense of the people. They assumed the prerogatives of petty kings over the several divisions of the country now serving largely as the territorial basis of the present counties. They raised their leading warriors to noble rank. Theretofore the land had been the common property of all, subject to allotment for annual use. Now these petty kings seized and divided up a part of that common land among the thegns but, running true to form, the king took the bulk of it for himself as his royal domain. It was also decreed that every man must have his lord to whom he was subject in field and in war. While feudalism thus placed its heavy hand on the people by reducing the freeholders to the status of tenants, or of feudal serfs or villains who, as regarded their lord, were practically slaves in the required performance of labor and of military service, yet, in their relations with their fellow men, they were free. In the boroughs they still followed their age old usages and customs, with the exception that the king, sometimes the neighboring lord, especially as to boroughs that were ports, sent in a new officer—the port-reeve or magistrate—who summoned together the borough-moot, presided over it, and administered justice in it. He collected the port dues, the fines and forfeitures, and the rentals payable to the king from the royal domain. But when that was done the burghers were practically free. In their borough-moot they had the right of free speech and free deliberation and free choosing of all the other officers. Even during the disheartening days of the Dark Ages the burghers, especially in the more important centers of trade, managed to retain the right of selecting their own aldermen in the several wards or quarters and gradually took to themselves the right of selecting their own mayor.

When the Danes finally took possession of the country they imposed peace upon the warring tribes. King Cnute (1013) adopted the system of government which he then found in force, except that he ousted the Anglo-Saxon lords and the petty kings from their landholdings and distributed them in part to the Danish nobles but the most part he kept for himself as the royal domain. When William the Conqueror (1066) took possession of England he, in turn, dispossessed the Danish landholders and parcelled out to his barons territories for strategic defense but he too kept the royal domain. He was the greatest landowner in his realm. The former Anglo-Saxon lords and the former Danish thegns thus were pushed from their high places and sank into a middle class which later became a strong support in regaining to the people their former liberties. Already most of the rural serfs had been lifted into almost complete freedom and William practically completed their manumission. Slavery was abolished. The burghers of the towns exercised their right of self-government, of free speech, of popular assembly, of common deliberation and the choosing of their own officers. Dr. Munro, in his "The Government of European Cities," says: "The chartered borough of the Middle Ages possessed the right to select its own executive officials without outside interference, to collect taxes from its citizens through its own taxgatherers, and to set up and maintain its own borough courts." (p. 211.) Even when the Conqueror came to the throne it was upon election by vote of the people assembled at Westminster, though that vote with military accompaniment smacked much of the Hitler and Stalin and Mussolini election methods of today. He reaffirmed the recognition made by the last of the Saxon kings of the ancient liberties of London under which its people had retained and maintained their proud independence of self-government.

But William was not one to brook opposition to his will in matters affecting his realm. He and his barons had quarreled over their prerogatives in Normandy. As a precautionary measure he settled land upon them in England largely along the frontiers where they had to fight in self-protection against any invasion. He compelled them and the Church as well to pay into his exchequer such royal revenues as he arbitrarily fixed. Smarting under his exactions they joined in an uprising but were subdued by him. His profligate and less able son continued these oppressive measures and added thereto the seizure of the revenues from the abbeys. When Henry I came to the throne in 1100 the opposition of the barons and the clergy became so strong that he was compelled to grant a charter in which he renounced the plundering of the church, and substituted customary fees to be paid by the baronage instead of the unlimited demands theretofore arbitrarily imposed. This same system was soon followed in making collection of the royal revenue from the boroughs. On the other hand the charter required the barons to do justice to their undertenants and to renounce tyrannical exactions from them. This worked to the great advantage and advancement of the boroughs. The king quickly realized that as the trade and commerce of the boroughs increased so would his revenues from them grow larger, since nearly all of them were on the royal domain. Furthermore, in casting about for support against the barons he fostered the growth of the boroughs as a counterpoise. Even under the peace enforced by the Danes and the resultant re-awakening of trade and commerce in the boroughs they were still generally mere villages, none of them having more than five thousand inhabitants excepting London alone. Their fairs, their markets and their ports were conducted by them. As trade and commerce increased the burghers became rich. And Henry was shrewd enough to recognize the importance of their friendship and at the same time quick enough to grasp the opportunity of replenishing his generally needy exchequer. So he granted charter after charter to the boroughs for a financial consideration. Later when Richard, the Lion Heart, sought funds for his part in the Crusades, and then for ransom required for his release from captivity, he sold borough charters for what he could get. These charters had little to do with the rightful powers of self-government which the boroughs had exercised for centuries. They related almost solely to matters of revenue. The boroughs had been disturbed by the king sending in his port-reeve to collect the royal rents, the port dues, the fees and tolls from the fairs and the markets. By these charters the burghers were lifted from the position of mere traders into the position of customary tenants on the basis of making annual payment to the king of a fixed rental. The port dues, the fees and tolls from the markets and fairs were also placed on a customary basis.

But the collection of these revenues was still made by the representative of the king and resulted in friction and dissatisfaction. So the boroughs next sought and regained in these charters their old rights of fixing and collecting these dues, fees and tolls, and of free control of their ports, markets and fairs, upon the annual payment of a fixed sum into the king's exchequer. And in addition the boroughs obtained in these charters exemption from payment of royal rentals to the king's collector and in lieu thereof paid to the king a fixed sum annually. After the Norman conquest the royal dues were collected by the local authorities instead of by the sheriff. Then the boroughs levied and collected their own taxes, dues, fees and tolls and from them made the annual payments to the crown in a lump sum. They not only continued to exercise their right of self-government but they also had thus regained their right to administer the borough business freed from arbitrary exactions or control. As Dr. Munro, in his "Municipal Government and Administration," says: "It is not to be understood that these charters in all cases made wholly new concessions. Very often the townsmen had already assumed their rights without explicit grant; *the charters merely gave formal recognition to the accomplished facts and confirmed to the townsmen privileges already possessed by them.*" (v. I, p. 48.)

These charters of Henry served as a direct precedent for the Magna Charta wrested from reluctant King John at Runnymede in 1215. He had arrogantly violated the rights of the barons and of the clergy and of the burghers. So he was brought to book by armed force and was compelled to sign that historic document. By it the sale or denial of justice was forbidden. The right of trial by one's peers was restored. The little coterie of sycophants with which the king had surrounded himself was displaced by the Great Council to which prelates and the greater barons were to be summoned. The under-tenants and farmers were protected against law-

less exactions of their lords just as the barons were protected from like exactions of the king. The boroughs
were safeguarded from arbitrary taxation, from interference with their own regulation of trade, and they
were secured in their rights of justice and in the enjoy-
ment of self-government. In that charter it was specifically provided, among other things, as follows: "Let
the city of London have all its old liberties and its free
customs, as well by land as by water. Besides this, we
will and grant that all other cities, and boroughs, and
towns, and ports, have all their liberties and free customs * * * (and that) those liberties were all connected
with and dependent upon the right to choose their own
officers and regulate their own local concerns." They
were exempted from the jurisdiction of all courts but
their own.

As said by Green: "In the silent growth and elevation of the English people the boroughs led the way;
unnoticed and despised by prelate and noble they had
preserved and won back again the full tradition of Teutonic liberty. The rights of self-government, of free
speech in free meeting, of equal justice by one's equals,
were brought safely across the ages of tyranny by the
burghers and shopkeepers of the towns." (pp. 92-93.)

Under Dane and under Norman the Anglo-Saxon
language, with its strong one-syllabled words, remained
as the firm foundation of the English tongue. The centuries-old Anglo-Saxon usages and customs of self-government were firmly embedded in the hearts of the people. The love of liberty, of free assembly and of free
speech by that virile race survived. The roots of popular rule and selection of their own local officers, although
at times seemingly dormant, sprang again into active
life. It was the reawakening of what had always been.
History shows that these rights were inherent in the
people themselves. Certainly, if not inherent, these
rights had become theirs by prescription, since they had
been exercised by them practically without interference

and without interruption from a time "whereof the memory of man runneth not to the contrary," save during comparatively short periods of lawless usurpation which could never ripen into legality. And yet too often these historical facts concerning the very foundation of our democratic institutions seem to have been carelessly overlooked, or to have been purposely ignored, by judges who have owed their office and their tenure to some autocratic monarch, or who have bowed supinely to the dictation of some political boss, or who, by training or environment, had become impregnated with the virus of the destructive doctrine that all power of government comes down from above and is the God-given right of the elect, especially as it affects municipal corporations.

In plain English the provisions of the Great Charter applied to "all the cities, boroughs, towns and ports" of the realm, and confirmed in them "all their liberties and free customs" and also "those liberties (which) were all connected with and dependent upon the right to choose their own officers and regulate their own local concerns." As has been shown, not one of them was the creature of the crown. As Finer says, *supra,* "as units of government they spontaneously arose * * *; they were not the creation of a central authority." In these charters the kings had made solemn acknowledgment of that historic fact. They had not created these units of government. No Parliament had created them, — indeed, no Parliament was yet in existence. There was nothing yet upon which to predicate the claim that any city or town, even though it had a royal charter, was a creature of the state, or that the state in the legal exercise of its sovereignty might foist officers selected by it upon a city or town instead of those selected locally by its own people. Whenever this power had been usurped time had brought its return to the people. That pernicious doctrine, fondly embraced and announced by some American courts but vigorously denounced by others, will be noted in later pages of this book.

John, in his charter, had agreed that he would rule in conjunction with the Great Council to be summoned by him from the nobles and the prelates. The shires and the boroughs were given no representation. They attended to their own local government. In most cases they made annually a lump sum payment to the crown in full of the royal revenues due from them. In order to fix the amount of this lump sum payment, as early as 1254 knights of the shire, selected by the minor gentry, the freeholders and the village elders of the shire, were summoned to Westminster to testify to the taxable capacity of the shires and the boroughs, and thus to ascertain how much fleecing the people could bear. Thirteen years later twenty-one cities and boroughs had bought from the crown the right to send their own representatives, as burgesses, to Westminster. Later that right was extended to about a hundred cities and boroughs. Under the parliamentary plan of Edward I (1272-1307) the Parliament consisted of four divisions, the clergy, the barons, the knights of the shire, and the burgesses from the boroughs. They made their grants apart from each other. The knights and the burgesses soon found that their interests were quite mutual and often adverse to those of the lords spiritual and temporal and so, in 1332, they drew together and formed themselves into the House of Commons, and the clergy and the barons formed the House of Lords. This parliamentary body at no time had granted, and for five hundred years thereafter had not granted, a single borough charter, — and not granting them had no power to alter or to destroy them. Indeed, the House of Commons, thus composed and imbued with the spirit of local self-government, had no desire or intention of doing any such thing. On the other hand the aristocratic and ecclesiastical House of Lords stood with the king in a mutual purpose to exalt their own power and to increase the royal revenues. This was opposed by the members of the House since their constituents had to foot the bill. The king, usually pro-

fligate and extravagant, sought means to replenish his
exchequer. He did not have the votes in the House necessary to the passage of his revenue bills. His demands
for oppressive taxes were refused. He could not coerce
its members, for John had solemnly covenanted against
it. So the crown hit upon the unscrupulous plan of increasing the number of its tools in the House by creating
new boroughs, — many of them in the royal domain
owned by the king since the days of the Norman conquest. Prior to that time charters to boroughs had never
been granted except upon the petition and request of a
respectable number of inhabitants of an established borough, who sought a charter simply to confirm in writing
their rightful powers. But the Tudors, and later the
Stuarts, without any such petition or request, created
new boroughs out of almost uninhabited areas in the
royal domain, and granted charters for them to little
hand-picked coteries of the king's henchmen. So as to
take no chances the king named these stool-pigeons of
his own choosing as life members of the first council with
full power of self-perpetuation in the filling of vacancies
in their membership for like term. Thus was created
the close municipal corporation, conceived in iniquity
and born in sin, which some courts have falsely held up
as a legitimate exercise of sovereign power. These
abortive charters, spawned by the corrupt favor of the
English kings, naturally fell into the hands of the aristocracy and great landholding interests which complai-
santly returned to Parliament borough representatives
safely subservient to the crown. Prior to the reign of
Henry VIII this illegal packing of Parliament had come
into wide use and, under that monarch of the roving eye,
it was enlarged in scope. Edward VI and Mary created
additional close corporation boroughs for the same purpose. Under Elizabeth the number of burgesses returned
to Parliament from such packed boroughs was sixty-
two. But it was James I who, in 1604, struck a deadly
blow to popular control of Parliament when he an-

nounced the doctrine of the "divine right of kings," and
the fawning bishops and clergy of the Established
Church bawled from their pulpits their approval. They
solemnly asserted that sovereignty in its origin was the
prerogative of birthright, that the sovereign was the son
of God, and that disobedience of the king's will was not
only religious heresy but was treason to the state. James
said: "Kings are not only God's lieutenants upon earth
and sit on God's throne, but even by God himself they
are called Gods." In vigorous protest the Pilgrim Fathers advocated separation of church and state, while the
Puritans, the Presbyterians, and the Quakers, strenu-
ously insisted upon their right to worship God according
to the dictates of their own conscience, and for that they
were harried from their native land. Charles I carried
out this preposterous doctrine of "divine right" to its
ultimate conclusion when he ruled England for eleven
years by royal decree, without any Parliament, until an
outraged people chopped off his head.

Under Cromwell some of the wrongs were righted,
but he was too busily engaged in quelling royalist dis-
turbances at home and in putting down the rebellion in
Ireland to uproot the bad conditions that prevailed in
many of the boroughs. When Charles II came to the
throne he created but one new borough, but he hit upon
a new plan for packing Parliament. By this time the
corporation had come into use for borough organization.
Prior thereto borough charters had run, not to the boroughs but to individuals, like the mayor, the aldermen
and the comminalty. Under them the inhabitants had
no fixed or defined status, and relied largely upon custom
and usage established by prescription. Interference
therewith by the crown in several instances led many of
the boroughs voluntarily to seek the corporate form since
it afforded them a legal status with their rights fixed in
a written charter, while perpetual existence with a corporate seal placed them in better position to handle the
common property of the borough and to safeguard it

from spoliation. At first these corporate charters did
not infringe upon the right of the burghers to select
their representatives in the House of Commons. In-
sidiously, by promise of royal favor, or even by force or
threats, some of the boroughs were induced to surrender
their ancient charters and to accept new ones in which
the king sought to influence the selection of the burgesses
sent to the House. But while these corporate provisions
insisted upon by the crown in these new charters tended
to undermine the vigorous independence of the boroughs,
yet, in many cases, their burgesses stood fast in Parliament in the interest of their constituents against the
extortionate demands of the king. So Charles hit upon
a cunning plan to coerce recalcitrant boroughs to send
up representatives to Parliament who would be his subservient tools. He caused suits in *quo warranto* to be
instituted before his hand-picked judges upon trumped-
up charges that such boroughs had violated their charters, and requiring them to show by what warrant they
operated under them. His sole purpose in these infa-
mous proceedings is well known. When he had secured
a decision by his packed court against the City of London, adjudging its charter forfeited on baseless grounds,
he offered, under Lord Keeper North, to respite the
judgment if that city would give him such right of control over its selection of burgesses as would enable him
to exclude persons not acceptable to the crown. (8 State
Trials, 1281; Lives of Lord Chancellors, Vol. 4, 316-319.)
This ignoble offer was indignantly refused. But this
and like suits frightened many boroughs into surrender-
ing their charters and accepting new ones giving more or
less control to the king in the selection of their burgesses
to the House. Charles II used forfeiture and the surrender of charters and the replacing of them with new
ones as a means of bolstering up the Established Church,
while James II used the same device in attempting to
restore Roman Catholicism, in addition to increasing
the royal revenues. The latter, while he did not, like

his father, have his head cut off yet he did lose his throne. Mary and the early Georges created more new boroughs so as to supplement their strength in Parliament. George III did not lose his throne, but in his bull-headed arrogance he lost England's greatest colony when America declared its independence in 1776.

No one will deny that this interference by the king with the age-old rights of the boroughs, and his creation of these new boroughs for ulterior political purposes, was illegal. And it is equally clear that the snatching of existing charters by the king through *quo warranto* was a piece of judicial jugglery. In plain English the king stole those charters through pliant judges appointed by him to the bench, or by threats and cajolery. Laymen as well as judges know well that thievery cannot create title and that possession of stolen goods never ripens into ownership. Yet truculent judges in America have cited this usurped exercise of power as justification and precedent for holding that the sovereign may alter and even destroy the centuries-old right of municipal corporations to select all their own officers. (Further on this point see Chapters VI and VII.)

Coupled with this creation of subservient new corporations was the deplorable fact that many of the old boroughs had fallen into decay, "so that a place like the Old Sarum, which consisted of only the ruins of an old castle, sent two members to Parliament (since a non-resident of the borough could be elected by non-residents), while the great manufacturing towns like Manchester and Birmingham were absolutely without representation. Not only the rotten boroughs, as these decayed constituencies were called, but also in many cases the towns, in which the right of suffrage belonged to a small number of freeholders, were practically in the hands of a single family (called pocket boroughs), and in this way a few great houses—Norfolk, Bedford, Devonshire, and the Pelhams, etc.—commanded more than 100 seats in Parliament. For the few places that were in the hands of the independent voters a shameless system of bribery existed, in spite of the prohibitory laws, and the prices of votes were generally known: a seat for a small place cost about $25,000." (*The Americana,* title, "Great Britain.") At the time of William and Mary, Locke wrote: "We see the bare name of a town, of which there remains not so much as the ruins, where scarce so much as a sheep-cote, or more inhabitants than a shepherd is to be found, sends as many representatives to the grand assembly of law makers as a whole county, numerous in people and powerful in riches. This strangers are amazed at."

In the old Saxon days the borough council was unknown. The qualified burghers themselves met together to transact the borough business. This was practicable because no borough, except London, in those days had a population in excess of three or four thousand. With increase in population resulting from growth of trade and commerce the freemen adopted the procedure of electing, annually, a representative borough council generally of twelve members to have charge of the borough business. This degenerated into the practice of selecting borough councillors from the wealthy class because they received no pay, and, through apathy, they were re-elected from year to year. At first the right of the freeman to attend the borough moot and there cast his vote was highly prized, especially as it had coupled with it the right to participate in the annual allotment of the land. But when the land had been seized by the king and his nobles, and the right of suffrage was coupled with onerous duties to be performed, many surrendered that right. Later, under the guild system the members of the craft guilds and of the merchant guilds entitled to vote selfishly limited their membership and this cut down the number of electors. Gradually the right of suffrage had been limited until the fact of birth, or of guild membership, or of rank conferred by the borough, or of freehold ownership, determined it. In the free boroughs the

burghers thus limited in number as to the suffrage continued to elect their own officers. But in the close corporation boroughs the people had no right of suffrage.
They elected no officers. The incorporators named by
the king in the first instance, and their self-perpetuating
successors, constituted the borough government. They
held their meetings in secret, made no accounting of their
doings to the burghers, and handled the borough property as if it were their own and for their own profit. By
1830 in fifty boroughs the corporators numbered less
than an average of thirty, while in one hundred and sixty
others the average number was but one hundred and
fifty. In some instances the corporate powers were exercised by non-residents, and the burgesses sent up to
the House were also non-residents. Under Henry V an
act was passed which required the burgesses to be residents of the borough which they represented but since
Elizabeth it had been habitually disregarded and in 1777
it was repealed.

It seems strange that the people of England should
have endured these intolerable conditions for more than
two hundred years after its first colonists to America
had fled from their homeland to escape from this and
other like despotism, before they did anything about it.
However, a gradually increasing body of protest accu-
mulated and demanded needed reforms, and especially
that the right of suffrage be broadened. Especially was
this true as to the close corporation boroughs. Dr.
Munro, in his "Municipal Government and Administration," says: "The middle classes knocked at the door of
the close corporation and demanded a part in the local
government. The radical sentiment did not care so
much whether the government was good or bad, but the
fact that the officers were not elective or were self-perpetuating was very objectionable. In 1832, when steps
were taken to correct abuses, Liverpool had a voting
population of about 5,000 freemen in a total of 165,000,
and Portsmouth had but 102 out of 46,000. This small

category of burghers, many of whom were non-resident, elected all town officials and chose the borough's representatives in Parliament." (v. I, p. 78.)

Year after year commissions had been appointed to investigate these conditions and to suggest how they could be remedied. The Royal Commission reported in 1832 that "the municipal corporations of England and Wales neither possess nor deserve the confidence or respect of British subjects." Time after time bills were passed by the House of Commons to reform these conditions, but always the Tories and the landed aristocracy in the House of Lords defeated them. Finally, under Prime Minister Grey, William IV was forced to create enough additional peers to pass the reform measure through the House of Lords and the bill became a law. It had been a long and arduous struggle by the boroughs to get back their rightful powers which had been filched from them by the crown. The Reform Bill of 1832 made sweeping changes in borough government. Fifty-six rotten boroughs were entirely disfranchised, and thirty were deprived of one member each in Parliament as being excessive. This cut out eighty-six seats in Parliament that were illegitimate. Of the important and populous boroughs then not having any representation at all twenty-two were given two members each and twenty were given one member each. The close corporations were shorn of their oligarchic power and their officers were made elective by the people instead of being self-perpetuating. The qualifications of voters were made somewhat uniform and even women who paid taxes were enfranchised in certain cases. The government of the boroughs was brought back largely to the burghers where it always had rightfully belonged. Once more they selected their own officers in the exercise of their rightful powers, and no longer were they stool-pigeons selected for them by the crown.

The Municipal Corporations Act of 1835 went still further. It enumerated one hundred and eighty-one boroughs and cities that were brought under its provisions. It provided that in the future the crown should charter boroughs only in accordance with the actual requirements of their people, and that every application for a borough charter should be considered solely upon its individual merits and not be granted for political purposes. With the exception of the City of London which had clung steadfastly to its ancient liberties and to its liberal charter, the boroughs were remodeled on a practically uniform plan, with provision made for stamping out corruption in their government. Prior to 1835 the number of freemen in the boroughs had been comparatively few. For instance, Plymouth had a population of 75,000 of which but 437 were freemen and 145 of them were non-resident, while in Ipswich less than two per cent of the inhabitants could vote and a large number of them were paupers. But by the Act of 1835 the franchise was extended and in 1867 all householders who had resided in the borough for eight months and had paid poor rates and all lodgers who had occupied for a like period lodgings of the yearly value of $50 unfurnished, were given the right to vote at borough elections. By the Act of 1882 the structure of the boroughs was standardized and their powers were regulated. Each inhabitant of the borough who had paid certain rates for three consecutive years was given the right to vote at all local elections, and all borough officers were made elective or appointive locally. Today, at borough elections, every man or woman over twenty-one years of age who has occupied, as owner or tenant, any land or premises in the electoral area during the required period, may register and vote. The burghers elect only the councillors and two of the auditors. The mayor appoints a third auditor, but this method of electing auditors has now been largely superseded by the alternative procedure of using professional firms of accountants appointed by the council. The councillors are elected for three year terms, staggered so that one third of them retire annually. The number of councillors varies. In some boroughs they are elected at large, while in others they are elected by wards. In the latter case the number of councillors representing each ward is divisible by three and one-third of them retires annually. Originally borough aldermen were elected by the councillors together with the mayor and aldermen, but in 1910 this was changed so that now the councillors alone elect the aldermen one-third in number of the former for six year terms, one-half of their number retiring every third year. All retirements above mentioned are by rotation. The councillors and the aldermen together annually elect the mayor for a one year term, who, during his term and one year thereafter, is *ex officio* a justice of the peace. He and the councillors and the aldermen sit together and constitute the borough council, and he presides over its meetings. The council elects a town clerk, an office of great antiquity, who is the chief executive officer of the borough and who acts as a sort of chief of staff not only of the council but for the other borough officers and commissions, all of whom are appointed by the council. There is a borough treasurer, a borough surveyor, a medical officer of health, a sanitary inspector, and others deemed necessary. The council has the sole power over the property of the borough, its police, its street lighting and other publicly owned utilities, its markets and harbors, and the levying and collecting of rates from which the borough expenses are met. It performs both the legislative and the administrative functions of the borough.

So far as the administration of justice within the borough is concerned it has been noted that the mayor is *ex officio* a justice of the peace during his term and for one year thereafter. In the smaller boroughs he, with at least two other justices of the peace, constitute the court which handles all juridical matters of a local character. In boroughs of more importance there is a separate commission of the peace consisting of several justices but no court of quarter sessions. In many, in addition to a commission of the peace, the borough has its own court of quarter sessions presided over by an officer called the recorder who must be a barrister of at least five years standing. All the boroughs of any size or importance are exempted from the jurisdiction of the county justices.

In England it is fundamental that every citizen is bound to participate in the preservation of the peace and the suppression of disorder. In the early days upon hue and cry by the constable in the county, and by the watch in the borough, each able-bodied man had to respond without pay. During the eighteenth century the larger towns gradually obtained special acts of Parliament for the creation of a paid force of watchmen, and in 1835 every borough was required to have a paid police force. It is under the sole control of the borough. There is no direct interference whatever by the central authority, but annually the various forces are reviewed by royal inspectors who report to the Home Secretary and only if their report is favorable as to equipment, training, grading and pay does the nation contribute to the expense by grants of aid. A considerable area lying just outside the City of London is a metropolitan police district under the control of the Home Secretary with headquarters at Scotland Yard, but the City of London is not a part of the district and has its own police. Otherwise there is no police force in all of England except the local forces appointed, maintained and controlled by the localities they serve.

Parliament has made uniform the governmental structure of the boroughs, has prescribed their general powers, and has furnished a code under which they shall transact their municipal business. In addition thereto the borough council may make its own standing orders to be observed by itself and by its committees and by the borough officers. The council is authorized to make by-laws "for the good rule and government" of the borough and "for prevention and suppression of nuisances therein." Such by-laws concerning sanitary matters must first be confirmed by the Minister of Health. In case a by-law enlarges the general powers of the borough it must first be confirmed by the Home Office. But there is no interference by the central government in the naming of any borough officer or appointee or employee. Except during the reign of Charles II and James II the boroughs have been independent of the central government. The Harts, in "An Introduction to the Law of Local Government and Administration" say: "After the Revolution of 1688 it had become an axiom that there should be no interference in, or control of, local affairs by the central government * * * liberalism demanded popularly elective bodies." (pp. 18 and 21.) As Finer says, *supra,* the boroughs were not created by the central authority, they simply "came to be regulated and given legal form by it." Not having been created by it there was no legal power in it to destroy them or to impair their inherent right of administering their affairs under their own locally selected officers.

Even when the charter of the City of London was declared forfeited by the lickspittle judges of Charles II, that did not destroy it as a borough. It continued its existence as before and administered its own affairs under its own officers, harassed somewhat by the minions of the king for a short while until Parliament set aside that forfeiture. That was probably the first time that Parliament had taken a direct hand in the matter of borough charters. Later, in 1832, it deprived fifty-six rotten boroughs of their illegal representation in Parliament, but that did not interfere with their existence as boroughs, and when in that year the "Representation of the People Act" ousted the royal stool pigeons in power and compelled the local election of borough officers, that did not destroy or impair the boroughs, but simply restored to their people their rightful powers. The usurped borrough control by autocratic kings was swept away. The illegitimate forms of government imposed on many of the

boroughs by the crown were replaced by general rules
and regulations under which they were to administer
their own affairs under their own elected officers, and
the age-old principles of Anglo-Saxon self-government
were restored. During the troublous years that autocratic monarchs and oligarchic coteries had flouted or
disparaged these principles they did not die. In any
form of government worth while they were bound to sur-
vive. And so in England the boroughs have come through
perilous times triumphant until today they enjoy undis-
turbed their ancient freedom in the administration of
their own affairs under officers of their own choosing.

Before describing how a great number of these boroughs, eighty-eight in England and Wales, and one hundred and eighty-four in Scotland, have become "Counties
of Cities" or "County Boroughs" in the former, and
"Royal and Parliamentary 'Burghs' " in the latter,
quite like the "City-County Consolidated" in America,
it seems well to speak briefly of the English counties or
shires, although they have a comparatively small bearing
upon the subject of this book. For it will be found that
the controlling factor in the creation of the consolidated
county boroughs was an evolution of the boroughs themselves and the gradual taking over by them of county
functions which they originally had exercised.

Today there are fifty-two counties in England and
Wales, forty in the former and twelve in the latter. In
the last seven hundred years their boundaries have been
practically the same. But in the seven hundred years
preceding that period there were many changes. Mention has already been made of the loose form of tribal
government prevalent among the Teutonic tribes and
undoubtedly it was brought to England but changes were
caused by conditions there arising. During the forty
years of war waged by the Angles and Saxons to con-
quer the Britons, shires were established with varying
boundaries to conform to the changing situation. In
the following five hundred years of internecine strife

between the conquering tribes for dominance among themselves these boundaries shifted from time to time as the tide of battle ebbed and flowed. In accordance with the ancient Anglo-Saxon usage, in each shire the freemen assembled in their moot to select their leader in the war. Each shire was divided into "hundreds" comprising a hundred families having able bodied men, and the hundreds were subdivided into "tythings" comprising ten families having able bodied men. Thus the shire in the early days was largely a military organization. Because of almost continuous war the shire leader thus chosen to conduct it grew more and more powerful until, in many instances, he assumed the dignity of a petty king. Shires like Kent, Sussex, Essex, Middlesex and Surrey finally had little kings but they interfered scarcely at all with the exercise of self-government by the freemen. However, the king, as usual, was interested in getting revenue and to insure its collection he appointed a shire-reeve (sheriff) to preside over the shire-moot and to enforce payment of the royal dues.

When the Danes took possession of England in 1016 these petty kings were ousted and the country was divided into four great earldoms, each having its "ealdorman" who was made the leader of the king's military forces in his district. When the Normans came into power in 1066 the four great earldoms were abolished, the shires had their name changed to counties, the shire-moot became the county court (similar to the board of county commissioners in America) presided over as formerly by a sheriff appointed by the king, and each hundred retained its court presided over by a bailiff appointed by the sheriff. At first appointed annually the sheriff gradually achieved a life tenure and in some instances claimed the office as hereditary. Occasionally he became powerful enough to challenge the king's prerogatives, until in 1170 Henry II dismissed all the sheriffs in England and replaced them with others. To further curb the sheriffs the king created the position of lord lieutenant in each county to whom was entrusted the former military duties of the sheriff. In 1194 the freemen of the shire joined in this movement to limit the latter's powers by electing in their county court from two to ten coroners in each county to keep the pleas of the crown. But by 1689 the coroners had sunk to mere holders of inquests and the sheriff had been restricted almost wholly to serving process of the courts and to handling prisoners.

Originally every freeman of the shire was entitled and was bound to attend the shire-moot generally held twice each year, and for failure to attend he was made subject to a fine. If elected to an office in the shire he received no salary and was fined if he failed or refused to serve. To escape these burdens many of the freemen voluntarily renounced their rights as such so that gradually the great landowners took over the shire government. Furthermore, long before the Normans came the right of every freeman to participate in the shire-moot had been restricted to the free landowners. Under them the general assembly in the shire-moot was superseded by a form of representative government under which each hundred selected twelve members of the county court. In the early days that court had but few administrative duties to perform other than to provide for the revenues required for carrying on the wars. The county proper was sparsely settled and the greater part of local government was exercised by the borough-moots, both of an administrative and of a judicial character. Gradually, however, the county court assumed jurisdiction in all important criminal cases for all men of the county and the hundred court was relegated to matters of minor importance.

In the seventh century, following the advent of Christianity, a new governmental agency, the ecclesiastical parish, was created originally interested in church matters and in caring for the poor and the unfortunate. The parish gradually became responsible for the preser-

vation of the peace within its borders, for the maintenance of its highways, and for the care of the needy and
the insane. At the annual meeting of the parish its
people elected the churchwarden, the surveyor of highways, the overseer of the poor, and by prescription took
over the election of the constable although by common
law his election had been by the local criminal court.
Thus in the county there were four governmental entities,
viz.: the boroughs with their moots where the inhabitants elected their own officers and administered their
own justice, and each had its own watch committee with
police powers; the parish with its annual meeting where
its people elected the constable, the surveyor of highways, the overseer of the poor, and the churchwardens;
the hundred with its court which handled matters of
minor importance; while the county court composed of
representatives from the various parts of the county
selected the county officers except the sheriff who was
still an appointee of the king.   The people chafed
under the injection of the sheriff into county affairs and
objected to him acting as president of the county court.
He was generally a great landowner appointed by the
king to carry out the latter's will with slight regard for
the interests of his own people. He collected the royal
revenues too often unjustly so that the people of the
counties demanded the right to make payment in a lump
sum and to make their own collections just as the boroughs had gained the right to do. Likewise the people
of the counties began a fight for the right to elect their
own sheriff. After a long struggle Edward I in 1300
conceded the demand, but shortly after his death in
1305 it was withdrawn by Edward II.

The course of events as to governmental affairs in
the county closely parallels what has already been described as having occurred in the boroughs. On the one
hand the people strove to retain their inherent rights of
self-government under officers of their own selection,
while on the other hand the king and his aristocratic and

titled followers were assiduously engaged in trenching upon those rights or in filching them bodily. Already noted was the exercise in the early days of unrestricted power of local self-government and of judicial administration in the boroughs and later in the shires. In order to bring the local authorities under his control the king adopted a system of inspection under itinerant justices first commissioned in 1166 by Henry II. This was the beginning of the use of the courts by the sovereign to coerce and control the local authorities, later used by Charles II, as has been mentioned, against the boroughs by his pliant tools on the bench. These early itinerant justices, appointed by the king, visited the county and called before them the sheriff, the representatives of the counties and of the hundreds and the officers of the boroughs, with their rolls and records to be submitted for judgment of approval or disapproval. But this occasional supervision did not satisfy the king. To tighten his hold on the counties Richard I in 1195 began commissioning justices of the peace in them, consisting of men of great wealth and of the landed gentry, who gradually made themselves dictators. In 1360, under Edward III, they were given power to decide criminal cases. They sat singly in ale house or in parlor in minor matters, two or more sat together in more important matters, while in 1388, under Richard II, all began sitting together in quarter sessions where the affairs of the county were subjected to their inspection and supervision. Following the example of the itinerant justices they haled before themselves the officers of the county, of the hundreds and of the parishes, and issued orders to them as to how they should perform their official duties, under penalties prescribed for failure or refusal to obey. If the court decided a bridge should be repaired, or sanitary services should be provided, or poor houses or lunatic asylums should be constructed, it not only ordered that it be done but it also fixed the rate and ordered the collection of taxes to provide the necessary funds. By the issuance of writs of injunction they prevented action by the local authorities and by writs of mandamus they compelled action to be taken by them, upon pains and penalties of contempt of court. Hundreds and tythings were practically rendered helpless and the county court was shorn of its independence. The justices of the peace in quarter sessions not only administered justice but they also licensed public houses, controlled the county constabulary, the administration of the poor laws, the building and repair of roads and bridges, the management of prisons and houses of correction, and ordered the assessment and collection of local taxes. The age old, communal courts of the shire and of the hundred were reduced in judicial matters to cases brought for collection of petty debts. Halevy, in "A Century of Municipal Progress," says: "Theoretically the justices of the peace were appointed by the crown; but the king always appointed them upon the recommendation of the lord lieutenants, who themselves never consulted the king without having first consulted the leading justices of the peace of the county,—so that, in fine, it was one of co-option rather than central appointment. * * * The justice of the peace was rich and unpaid, a man of leisure,—and thus did England 'govern herself.' "(p. 18.)

The counties had thus fallen under the rule of a judicial oligarchy, just as we have seen that the close corporation boroughs had been placed under the absolute domination of the king's favorites. Both were governed by men sitting in secret, keeping no permanent records, issuing arbitrary orders, lining their pockets with ill-gotten gains at the public expense, converting public property and the income therefrom to their own individual uses. For nearly five hundred years the people struggled against these conditions and sought return to themselves of their former rights of self-government. Halfway measures were adopted from time to time to lighten this situation and to meet the more modern requirements of a rapidly increasing population both in the counties and in the boroughs. With the beginning of the 19th century Parliament began passing local acts creating improvement districts, each with its special board, for lighting, paving, sewers, highways and bridges, elementary education, and for care of the needy and unfortunate. By 1835 six hundred of these improvement districts had thus been created, taking from the justices of the peace a great part of their administrative functions. However, the result was not encouraging, for these commissions were controlled by men not always selected for ability. In many cases they were illiterate, ignorant and venal, not residents of their districts, nor subject to the people living therein, and were under the thumb of the central authority. Government of that kind can never be satisfactory or efficient. It cannot endure.

The boroughs, other than those of the close corporation class, steadfastly stood against any control over their affairs. Dr. Jennings in his discussion of this situation states that they regarded their corporate property, their markets, their tolls, their fines and fees, their exemptions and privileges, as outside any jurisdiction other than their own. Their administration of justice was subject to no control except that of the superior courts. They had regained the right to levy and collect all taxes. They opposed any interference by outside commissions. It has been noted how the Reform Act of 1832 and the Municipal Corporations Act of 1835 had abolished the close corporation boroughs and had liberated all boroughs. But these Acts gave but little relief to the counties, save the extension of the right of suffrage. The justices of the peace were still left supreme. It was not until 1888 that the Local Government Act stripped them of all administrative functions and relegated them solely to the performance of judicial duties, except that in an administrative county the police functions are administered by a body known as the "Standing Joint Committee" one-half of whose members are elected by the county council and the other half by the justices. The Act of 1888 replaced the county quarter sessions by a county council locally elected, as to all administrative functions. This council elects its chairman, a body of aldermen, its own committees and the other county officers, for the transaction of all county business, much in the same manner as is done by the boroughs under the Act of 1835. The county council exercises no judicial functions, but must pay for the administration of justice in its area. Every county is required to keep up its highways, bridges, jails, houses of correction, and usually a shire hall, at county expense. The Local Government Act of 1929 abolished all special boards or commissions of the various districts above referred to and transferred to the county councils and to the borough councils, appropriately as to their respective functions, all their powers, duties, assets and liabilities. Finer, in "A Century of Municipal Progress," says that "the Act of 1888 put the county police under elected county councils—and fifty years shows efficiency and reliability." (p. 283) However, the Home Office has the power to approve or disapprove the appointment of the chief constable, the number and pay of the county force; to promulgate rules for its government, and to make a grant of one-half of the police expenses. This power of the purse obviously gives an opportunity for interference, although it does not appear to have been abused.

The foregoing description of the Teutonic burgh and of the English borough covering a period of more than nineteen hundred years,—reaching from the time when Caesar contacted the *Germani* in 56 B. C. down to 1888 A. D. when Parliament created eighty-three county boroughs in England and Wales,—makes clear the fundamental facts to be kept in mind when reading the succeeding chapters that these burghs and these boroughs (1) were self-constituted and were not created by any

higher power; (2) administered their own affairs under
officers of their own choosing; (3) held their own elections with their own officers conducting them; (4) generally selected their own magistrates and had their own
courts; (5) always had their own police; (6) with slight
exception no officer was appointed by the state or by the
sovereign to meddle in their affairs; (7) that the granting of charters to them by the king created no rights
but simply ratified those long existing, issued generally
to make certain the collection of his revenues, and that
when the king ventured, for a time, to control their
representation in Parliament one lost his head and another his crown.

Years of struggle did not beat down the Anglo-Saxon
spirit of liberty. The right of self-government was maintained in the boroughs. As they grew in population, industries and wealth, their political power increased. They
repelled the sporadic invasion of king and aristocracy
questing and greedy for ruthless power. Early in the
Middle Ages this virility of the boroughs resulted in the
formation and the later development of a new and improved form of local government, or rather a return to
the original burgh,—the "counties corporate," or boroughs that were "counties in themselves" and known as
"counties of cities," as governmental and political entities separate and distinct from their respective counties,—similar to the "city-county consolidated" in America.

CHAPTER III.

THE CITY-COUNTY CONSOLIDATED IN ENGLAND

In England the "City-County Consolidated" is generally called a "County Borough." It bears a marked resemblance to the ancient Teutonic burgh and to the early English borough. Each was autonomous and each exercised governmental functions now performed by both county and borough. It has already been pointed out how the shires and the hundreds grew into prominence and gradually took over certain of the powers theretofore enjoyed by the boroughs and how the latter steadfastly struggled to regain them. Especially did they insist that they be on an equality at least with the hundred to which they had been somewhat subordinated. They diligently sought and finally secured exemption from the hundred court and got a court of their own. They were not content to be represented before the king's itinerant justices simply by a reeve and four men but demanded and obtained equal right with the hundred of being represented there by an elected jury of twelve. Gradually boroughs of wealth and importance secured exemption from the jurisdiction of the quarter sessions court of the county and got their own local courts subject only to the king's court for review or correction. In an increasing number of boroughs no inhabitant thereof could be sued in the first instance generally except in his own borough court and not even in the king's court. The boroughs gained the right in 1194 to elect their coroner and many of them even earlier had bought the right to appoint their own sheriff. Thus the boroughs gradually and insistently regained much of their former autonomy and in doing so they developed the "counties of cities" and later the "county boroughs."

The borough of London from the first exhibited a bold independence which even the king could not weaken. It was rich and powerful enough to make its voice heard and respected. Even under the Britons it was visited by traders from the continent and had already become an important port when the Romans came. They called it Londinium and gave to it much of the dignity and the liberties of a Roman *municipium*. Its proud spirit thus instilled and encouraged never has been cowed. Its square mile of area has never been changed. With the growth and development of a great metropolitan district surrounding it the City of London has always stood aloof and independent. Even when, in the early days, Middlesex county was a petty kingdom in which the city sat it did not permit the king to reside within its precincts so that he was compelled to establish himself at adjoining Westminster and was permitted to enter the city "only with ceremony and permission." The election and installation of a Lord Mayor of that great city is second only in pomp and circumstance to that of the coronation of a king of the empire.

Even under the Saxon kings the ancient borough liberty of London was recognized, and it was confirmed by William the Conqueror in the charter of 1066 although in vague terms. Henry I, during his reign, 1100-1135, by royal charter made the city into a county with full right to appoint its own sheriff and made its people exempt from all courts but their own. At that time it had a population of about 100,000 and its wealth and mercantile importance compelled heed to its demands. At the same time the City of York, with a population of about 14,000, was also, by royal charter, made a county. These two cities, then the largest and most important in England, appear to furnish the earliest instance of the creation of a form of consolidated county borough in that kingdom. When King John, in 1215, was compelled to sign the Magna Charta, he therein guaranteed to the City of London "all its old liberties and free customs" and also "those liberties connected with and dependent upon the right to choose its own officers and to regulate its own concerns," and confirmed in its people the right to elect their own mayor and council and to hold their own courts. In the reign of Edward I (1272-1307) the City of London not only got so far as to have elective sheriffs of its own, but they also acted as such for the entire county of Middlesex in which the city was situated, and the city fixed the rates for and collected the taxes from the entire county and paid in lump sum the king's dues,—an extra jurisdictional power not ever exercised by any other borough. It not only elected its sheriff but it had the unusual right of electing its lord lieutenant not enjoyed by any other borough at that time save that of Haverfordwest in Pembrokeshire. London today, while not a true county borough, still appoints its two sheriffs and is governed almost entirely by itself under its ancient charter. It exercises locally larger powers than do the counties of cities or the county boroughs.

In 1373 Bristol was granted its charter as a county itself by Edward III with the right to elect its sheriff. It also had its own assizes and quarter sessions courts. In 1461 the borough of Stamford in Lincolnshire was granted a royal charter under which it asserted that it was exempt from county control, implicitly recognized over two hundred years later in 1663. It boasted, wrote Defoe, "of very great privileges * * * such as being 'freed from the sheriff's jurisdiction, and from being empaneled on juries out of the town; and to have the return of all writs, to be freed from all lords-lieutenant, and from their musters, and for having the militia commanded by its own officers'." Other boroughs, like Lewes in Sussex county, claimed similar immunity. In the reign of Richard III (1482-1485) the

borough of Gloucester was created a county of itself. In
1506 the borough of Chester was created into a county
with the right to elect its own officers. In 1553 Queen
Mary granted a charter to Lichfield stating that it shall
"be from the county of Stafford separate and distinct
and in all things entirely divided and exempted as well
by land as by water," and further that it "be a city of
itself and not parcel of said county," and that it "be forever named, called, reputed, holden and had the County of
the City of Lichfield by itself," and that it shall "forever have one sheriff to be chosen by the bailiffs,
burgesses and citizens of the city." This serves as
an example of these early charters. The tendency toward the consolidated county borough was accentuated
through the purchase by wealthy and influential boroughs of exemption from the jurisdiction of the autocratic county justices and from their court of quarter
sessions. As already noted, many boroughs obtained
their own separate commission of the peace and their
own court of quarter sessions held under an officer called
a recorder, while others simply had a commission of the
peace but no such court. Under the Act of 1882 the area
of any borough having its own court of quarter sessions
was exempted from county rates and was liable only for
payment of the costs of its prosecutions at the county
assizes.

Thus the trend continued toward the separation of
many of the boroughs from their counties, and their creation into geographical counties of themselves. London
had somewhat marked the way. Then came York, Bristol, Haverfordwest, Stamford, Gloucester, Chester and
others, until by 1888 there were nineteen very old boroughs which had become "counties corporate" or boroughs that were "counties in themselves" and were known
as "counties of cities." They were county boroughs of the
"city-county consolidated" American type, with one set
of officers performing both borough and county functions, freed from any control over them by the county

in which they were situate. This came about gradually.
The beginning reached back to the Middle Ages. These
very old boroughs which were thus "counties of cities,"
or "counties of themselves," were: Bristol, Canterbury,
Chester, Coventry, Exeter, Gloucester, Kingston-upon-
Hull, Lichfield, Lincoln, London, Newcastle-upon-Tyne,
Norwich, Nottingham, Poole, Southampton, Worcester
and York in England, Carmarthen and Haverfordwest
in Wales. All selected their own officers, appointed their
own sheriffs, coroners and their police, and performed
all county and borough functions.

During the fifty years next succeeding the enactment by Parliament of the Acts of 1832 and 1835, which
had made much needed and drastic reforms in borough
government and had given for the first time representation in Parliament to those boroughs then grown to
great importance as manufacturing and industrial centers, there was an increasing agitation for an Act which
would reform the counties and free them from the autocratic domination of the quarter sessions court of the
county. In connection with the demand for county reform there was a strong insistence from the large urban
areas that they be given the right to conduct their local
affairs separate and apart from the surrounding rural
territory, and freed from county interference, since their
interests and requirements were not common. However,
the Tories and the wealthy landowners who had so long
dominated county affairs were loath to lose their power
and sought to stem the reform movement by advocating
that the county be made the intermediate body between
the central authority on the one hand and the boroughs
on the other. This would have left the county as an over-
lord in control of the boroughs. But the Whigs and the
people of the boroughs would have none of this scheme
and fought to retain, strengthen and extend the autonomy which they then enjoyed. In this struggle the latter
came out victorious with the Local Government Act of
1888 which dethroned the judicial oligarchy of the court

of quarter sessions in the county, created an elective
council to take the place of the county court as to administrative functions, and restored to the counties their
just rights.

Attention was also given to the demand that the
number of cities then exercising both city and county
functions be increased. Lord North reported to the
Royal Commission that the government could not but be
aware of the existence of certain large cities which by
reason of their vast commercial interests and general
importance were entitled to claim absolute antonomy
in local administration. Then existing were the above
named very old boroughs which were ''counties of themselves,'' separate and distinct from the counties of which
they had once formed a part. However, the bill as introduced included but five of them as county boroughs, viz.:
Bristol, Bradford, Kingston-upon-Hull, Newcastle-upon-
Tyne and Nottingham, and added the great industrial cities
of Birmingham, Leeds, Liverpool, Manchester, and Sheffield as newly created county boroughs empowered to
exercise both city and county functions free from any
control by the county of which they were a geographical
part, but not separated therefrom as were the ''cities
of counties'' above named. Such vigorous objection
was made, however, by Canterbury, Chester, Coventry,
Exeter, Gloucester, Lincoln, Norwich, Southampton,
Worcester and York that the bill was amended so as
to include them. London, fearful of losing some of
its liberties then enjoyed by it under its ancient charter of 1215 reaching back to the days of King John,
refused to have any part under the bill and so it was not
created into and is not now a county borough. However,
in 1888 Parliament created the new County of London out
of a part of old Middlesex, Surrey and Kent counties.
That city, thus included in the new county, retained and
still retains its unique position, entirely governed by
itself under its ancient charter, save that in a few matters
such as education and public assistance it is within the

jurisdiction of the London County Council. At the same
time Parliament created locally elective county councils
for the several county organizations in England.

The limitation to ten county boroughs first proposed
was based upon the claim that each should have a population of at least 145,000, and that no new county borough
should be created until it had attained a population of
at least 150,000. Especially was this limitation insisted
upon by the rural population of the counties since the
creation of county boroughs within their borders with-
drew their area from payment of county taxes. However, an overwhelming sentiment manifested itself, especially in the boroughs having a population of 50,000 or
more, for their separation from the counties in which
they were situated, or for their creation into county boroughs free from any county control or supervision. It
was pointed out that this would afford the best system
for densely populated urban areas, with simplification
of government, a more efficient administration and at a
lessened cost. According to Finer, ''English Local Government,'' (pp. 76-77), the boroughs argued that they
paid more than their just share to the county council
for road purposes; that there were conflicting jurisdic-
tions and lack of collaboration among semi-autonomous
authorities, jealous of their limited independence; that it
was not possible to manage a joint scheme with the same
dispatch and vigour as a single authority could; that a
local government could best be exercised where a single
area, represented by a single council, co-ordinated all
services and the finance of such services. So insistent
was this demand that the bill as introduced was first
amended so as to reduce the required minimum population to 100,000 for the creation of a borough into a county
borough. But that was found not to be satisfactory to
a great number of citizens who were clamoring for relief,
so that the required population was finally reduced to
not less than 50,000. As a result enough boroughs were
created into new county boroughs, in addition to those

counties of cities already existing, to make a total of
sixty-one, made separate and distinct from their counties
as above noted. Provision was made in the bill for the
extension of the boundaries of the county boroughs from
time to time, and for their consolidation if they wished it.
Two such consolidations have occurred, and from 1889
to 1925 some 109 extensions of county borough boundaries had been made and a dozen or more have been
made since then.

The Act of 1888 provided that additional boroughs,
as they reached the minimum population requirement,
might be created into county boroughs by the Ministry
of Health upon a petition being filed therefor by boroughs so qualified. By this method twenty-two new
county boroughs have been created since 1888, making
a total now of eighty consolidated county boroughs in
England and three in Wales, as follows: Barnsley, Bar-
row-in-Furness, Bath, Birkenhead, Birmingham, Black-
burn, Blackpool, Bolton, Bootle, Bournemouth, Bradford,
Brighton, Bristol, Burnley, Burton-upon-Trent, Bury,
Canterbury, Carlisle, Chester, Coventry, Croydon,
Darlington, Derby, Dewsbury, Doncaster, Dudley, East-
bourne, East Ham, Exeter, Gateshead, Gloucester, Great
Yarmouth, Grimsby, Halifax, Hastings, Huddersfield,
Ipswich, Kingston-upon-Hull, Leeds, Leicester, Lincoln,
Liverpool, Manchester, Middlesbrough, Newcastle-upon-
Tyne, Newport, Northampton, Norwich, Nottingham,
Oldham, Oxford, Plymouth, Portsmouth, Preston, Read-
ing, Rochdale, Rotherham, Saint Helens, Salforn,
Sheffield, Smethwick, Southampton, Southend-on-Sea,
Southport, South Shields, Stockport, Stoke-on-Trent,
Sunderland, Tynemouth, Wakefield, Wallasey, Walsall,
Warrington, West Bromwich, West Ham, West Hartle-
pool, Wigan, Wolverhampton, Worcester and York in
England, and Cardiff, Merthyr Tydfil and Swansea in
Wales. Finer gives the population of these county bor-
oughs in 1933 as being: one over 1,000,000; three from
500,000 to 1,000,000; eight from 250,000 to 500,000;

thirty from 100,000 to 250,000; thirty-eight from 50,000 to 100,000; three from 20,000 to 50,000. All the nineteen "ancient counties of cities" are now county boroughs, except Carmarthen, Haverfordwest, Lichfield, London and Poole but which are still counties of themselves. All nineteen are geographical counties and select their own sheriffs, and in most cases their courts and police. Thus there are eighty-eight cities in England and Wales of the city-county consolidated type.

Careful provision was made for the equitable adjustment of assets and liabilities between any newly created county borough and the remainder of the county, and for proper distribution of the proceeds from local taxation licenses and probate duty grants, and respecting all other financial relations, by agreement to be made between their respective councils, and, in case of disagreement, then such adjustment was provided to be made by a commission to be appointed under the terms of the Act. In order to meet the objection raised by the counties that they would be prejudicially affected by the creation of new county boroughs, or by the extensions of county borough boundaries, the effect of which would be to deprive the counties of rateable area, the Act provided that due regard must be taken not only of the existing property, debts and liabilities connected with the financial relations of the county borough and the county but that neither the one nor the other shall be placed in any worse financial position by reason of a borough being constituted into a county borough or by having its boundaries extended. It is further provided that all differences between the county and the county borough shall be settled by arbitration. After thirty-five years of experience under the operation of the Act a strong sentiment developed that the minimum population of 50,000 was too low for the creation of new county boroughs. As a result a Royal Commission was appointed which reported in 1925 that this minimum should be increased to 75,000, and this was done by the Local Government

Act of 1926, whose provisions were re-enacted in 1933. Today a borough can attain the rank of a county borough only through a Private Act of Parliament. The extension of the area of a county borough may be made upon permission granted by the Ministry of Health with the approval of Parliament upon application therefor by boroughs so qualified and a hearing on notice to all county councils and county district councils affected, or it may be made by Private Act of Parliament without such permission.

There must be kept in mind the distinction between the old counties of cities and these later created county boroughs. The former are geographical counties in themselves. Not so as to the county boroughs: they are situated within existing geographical counties, yet they stand apart from them as to all administrative purposes. Finer, in his "English Local Government," says: "The powers of county boroughs are, roughly speaking, the sum of all the functions, compulsory and permissive, of the county councils, and all other local government authorities. The powers are, therefore, very comprehensive. (p. 56). * * * As reorganized by the Act of 1888 it (the county) ceased to have any jurisdiction whatever over the county boroughs. The county boroughs are equal in status to the counties and are independent of their jurisdiction. The powers of the county council stretch all over the county, but are entirely stopped at the county borough. They (the county boroughs) possess all the full range of functions of borough and county, and are independent of county and other authorities." (p. 33.) Woodrow Wilson, in his "The State," says: "The boroughs stand apart from the counties in which they lie, for all purposes of local government, as completely as the several counties stand apart from each other. Except in the single matter of the management of their police force, they may not even arrange with the county authorities for merging borough with county affairs. Their councils may be said, in general terms, to have, within the limits of the borough, all the powers once belonging to the county justices except those strictly judicial in their nature, all the sanitary powers of urban sanitary authorities, and powers of school administration,—all regulative and administrative functions except those of poor law Unions into which all parishes are still grouped. In the case of these 'county boroughs' all powers conferred upon counties are powers conferred upon them also.'' (1918 ed. p. 242.)

Thus it is clear that county boroughs, like the city-county consolidated in America, are separate political entities, divorced from the county in the manner above described. They have sole control of their own police force. However, in a few instances, under agreement with the county the police force of the latter serves a county borough. Generally speaking the officers of the county borough perform all county functions within its borders. Its inhabitants are not liable to contribute to salaries of county officers who render no service to them, but they must contribute their share of the expense of the superior courts of the county, and, of course, are subject to taxation for the support of the central government at Westminster. Most of them have their own quarter sessions court.

The organization of the old borough council was not changed but was retained by the county borough. In addition to the powers and duties formerly imposed upon it as a borough the county borough council also performs the duties and functions which had formerly been performed within its boundaries by the county council. Although by the Act of 1888 county boroughs were thus freed from the jurisdiction of the county councils and had practical local autonomy, yet there were at that time two other classes of elected local authorities administering certain duties within their borders, namely, the School Board as regards education, and the Board of Guardians as regards the poor law. However, in 1902, the functions of the School Board were transferred to

the council of the county borough, and in 1929 the functions of the Board of Guardians were likewise transferred. As a result, the councils of the county boroughs
now constitute the only authority having local governmental jurisdiction within their borders.

The Harts, in their "Introduction to Local Government Law and Administration," say: "The council of
a county borough is, within the area of its jurisdiction,
at once a borough council, an urban sanitary authority
and a county council. This exclusion from the administrative county did not, however, affect the position of
county boroughs in respect to other matters, such as the
administration of justice, for which purposes they are
still reckoned as within the geographical county. These
modern county boroughs are not to be confused with the
older county boroughs of cities, though many of the latter have attained to county borough rank. A borough
which is in itself a county of a city or town is outside the
geographical county for all purposes except the administration of modern local governmental services; and
whether it is also outside the jurisdiction of the county
council in administrative matters depends solely on
whether it has been in modern times a county borough."
(pp. 54-55.)

In every county borough, just as in the ordinary
borough, the burghers have the practically unrestricted
right of suffrage. The council of the county borough
consists of the mayor, aldermen and the councillors, sitting together. Each councillor is elected by ballot in his
respective ward for a three-year term, and may be either
resident or non-resident. He must be a local government
elector of the borough, or own a freehold or leasehold
within the borough, or during the twelve months preceding the day of his election he must have resided in the
borough. These qualifications are alternative. Generally there are three councillors for each of the wards
and one of them retires annually by rotation where wards
are provided for. The aldermen, in number equal to one

third of the councillors, are elected for six-year terms by the councillors either from their own number or of persons qualified for election as councillors. The terms of the aldermen are staggered so that one-half retire every three years in rotation. The mayor is elected annually by the councillors and the aldermen, from the council or from persons qualified for election as councillors, for a one-year term. He is the chairman of the council, is the chief magistrate for his year of office, and for the succeeding year is *ex officio* a justice of the peace. The clerk is appointed by the council and is the most important officer in the county borough. He is generally a solicitor or a barrister, with duties and powers like those of the clerk of the ordinary borough council. The treasurer is also appointed by the council, as are also the various committees which perform many of the functions of the county borough.

It is thus seen that the form of government in the county borough is very simple and centralized, with a short ballot, with responsibility fixed in a single elective body in the first instance, with conflicting interests eliminated that formerly created friction between the county and the borough, and with a resultant lowering of cost to the rate payers. In England it is generally conceded that the best form of local government for densely populated areas is administration by the county borough councils; that the inhabitants of such areas can be better served by a single governing body than by a multiplicity of such bodies and that a more qualified staff is thus secured; that a greater interest is taken in local affairs so managed, and that the members of a county borough council are able to keep in closer touch with their constituents and to exercise more personal supervision over the work of the council's officers than could the members of the old county council.

This form of government has given general satisfaction. Sir Harry G. Pritchard, of Westminster, England, Secretary of the Association of Municipal Corpo-

rations, recently wrote the author that: "In my opinion
the simplified form of government in the county borough,
where there is only one authority to perform all functions, works exceedingly well in practice, and I do not
think that this opinion will be denied." Robson, in his
"The Development of Local Government," says: "It
would obviously be both impracticable and undesirable
to ask any town which at present enjoys county borough
status to give up its independent position. While the
counties fight against the creation or enlargement of the
county boroughs, thus permitting escape from them of
tax revenue, we have seen with unmistakable clarity that
the cities can make out an overwhelming case for the acquisition of county borough status and for the expansion
of their boundaries."

While there are eighty-eight counties of cities and
county boroughs in England and Wales, a much more
liberal use of this form of government has occurred in
Scotland where there are one hundred and eighty-four
"Royal and Parliamentary Burghs" corresponding to
the county boroughs to the south. Robson further says:
"In Scotland the Royal and Parliamentary Burghs are
municipal units separate from the county, and those possessing police forces, together with counties of cities
such as Edinburg, Glasgow, Aberdeen and Dundee, corresponding in most essentials with the county boroughs
of England. The independent Royal and Parliamentary
Burghs are not subject to an arbitrary population minimum. There are sixty-four of them with populations of
less than 20,000, fifty-six with less than 10,000, forty-two
with less than 5,000, and twenty-two with under 2,000.
Several of these independent Royal and Parliamentary
Burghs which maintain their own police forces have a
population of less than 20,000, and one has only 7,500.
The Scottish office were scarcely overstating the position
when they dryly remarked that 'on the whole, it would
seem that independent powers have been more freely en-

trusted to small communities in Scotland than in England.' " (pp. 172-173.)

These two hundred and seventy-two cities in Great Britain of the city-county consolidated type furnish an impressive example of progress in municipal government. Their creation was an evolution made necessary by the desire of their people to exercise freely their liberty of self-government coming down to them from the time of its crude beginning in the early Anglo-Saxon burgh. Just as in the burgh so in the English borough the inhabitants felt the urge and the necessity of attending to their own affairs in their own way and under their own officers. That was hindered so long as they were tied politically and governmentally with a rural population. Their governmental requirements could not be harmonized. The cities required great expenditures for public works, for paved boulevards, for recreational parks and playgrounds, for water and lighting utilities, and the like, while the rural territory had comparatively little need for them. The large cities with the complexity of their manufacturing, merchandising and financial interests needed a judiciary and courts whose cost bore heavily upon the ratepayers of the rural territory against which they objected. Attempts were made to arrive at a just distribution of this burden but always there was dissatisfaction as must be the case under such circumstances. Gradually both populations recognized the objections and difficulties that existed under such conditions and came to a common agreement that it would be better for the city to separate at least governmentally if not geographically from its county. We have seen how that has been done. Its advantages are clearly apparent. The remaining part of the county is left free to operate under a much simpler form of government at less cost in consonance with its requirements. The severed city is made free to conduct its business and its government in order to meet the demands and necessities of a teeming population. This change was not brought about in a day. It was a matter of slow evolutionary growth. Because it was well grounded its stability has been assured. These cities of the city-county consolidated type have gradually increased in numbers. Once established as free cities they have not gone back to the old system which they had discarded. Not only have their numbers increased but their former boundaries have been extended to accommodate an increasing urban population. So that injustice might not result through unjustly depriving the remainder of the county of its taxable property adjustment is provided for to take care of that situation. The provision that a city must have at least a population of seventy-five thousand before it can become a county borough safeguards against its creation before it is financially able to carry on.

Along the same line has come the development of the city-county in America from the colonial period to the present day, with one set of officers to perform both city and county functions, enjoying simplified administration at a lessened cost, to which has been added, in many cases, the power of home rule.

CHAPTER IV.

FREEDOM IN AMERICA

When English colonization of America began, England had degenerated into a sordid autocracy, under a slobbering, licentious, bigoted king who blasphemously proclaimed that he had been chosen by God to rule that nation, made the courts his pliant tools, usurped the powers of Parliament, destroyed many of the rightful liberties of the cities and left his people but little of their original powers of self-government. In addition, he had joined forces with the rulers of the Anglican Church in a relentless persecution of all who dissented from its doctrines or who refused to worship according to its ritual under bishops and a clergy lending themselves subserviently to this destruction of free government.

Bancroft, in his "History of the United States," speaking of the charter granted by this James I to the Virginia Company in 1601, says: "The first charter for colonizing the great central territory of the North American continent, which was to be the chosen abode of liberty, gave to the mercantile company nothing but a desert territory, with the right of peopling and defending it. By an extension of the prerogative, which was in itself illegal, the monarch assumed absolute legislative as well as executive power. The emigrants were subjected to the ordinances of a commercial corporation, of which they could not be members; to the dominion of a domestic council, in appointing which they had no choice; to the control of a superior council in England; and finally to the arbitrary legislation of the sovereign.'' (pp. 86-87.)

Under these deplorable conditions what could be hoped for from the straggling little settlements, fringed along the Atlantic coastline and separated from each other by vast stretches of wilderness? What outlook could there be for free speech, religious liberty, a free press, or of self-government? Henry L. Stoddard, in ''It Costs to be President,'' says: ''Those pioneers had in their keeping Democracy's first trial on the scale of a continent. Where was to be found guidance away from the traditions of monarchy and tyranny that were the world's only history and example—guidance to a national life such as statesmanship had never known or sought. Sovereignty by the people was as pathless in government as was our wilderness then resounding to the first ring of the clearing ax.'' (p. 13.)

While that author evidently overlooked the history of the origin and exercise of self-government that had gone before but seemingly had then been forgotten, yet his language compels attention. Trails had to be blazed by hazardous toil on the part of the pioneers in that wilderness, and also through the tangled mazes of intolerance that blocked liberty of conscience and the exercise of political freedom. It was a long, hard road to travel, both in England and in America, before the shackles of religious bigotry could be broken, before the oppressive suffrage restrictions could be lifted, before the right of free speech and a free press could be exercised. And that road had to be traveled before cities and counties were made free to conduct their own business in their own way under a ''City-County Consolidated'' form of government with all its advantages and benefits.

However, the struggle along that road served to strengthen the moral as well as the physical fiber of the colonists. The great expanse of the new world, its wonderful rivers and forests, breathed the very spirit of freedom. The colonists were not slow to feel this influence. While the Virginia charter of 1606 left but little right in the settlers, yet it did contain a clause that they should "have and enjoy all liberties, franchises, and immunities, within any of our other dominions, to all intents and purposes, as if they had been abiding and born, within this our Realm of England." Because of it the settlers insisted upon the right of electing a General Assembly which they were permitted to do in 1619. In 1621 the Virginia Company confirmed the right of the colonists to elect their General Assembly at regular intervals and at its session in 1623 it promptly enacted a law that "no tax or imposition should be laid upon the colony, their lands or commodities, other way than by its authority."

The Pilgrim Fathers as they neared the shores of Massachusetts in 1620 entered into the Mayflower Compact which contained the first germ of a constitution for a free people. The charter granted to the Massachusetts Bay Company in 1628 provided that its members should create a General Court or legislature. In 1630 its first members were elected and held their first session and took to themselves the powers of government. The Maryland charter granted in 1632 provided that laws could be made only "with the advice, assent and approbation of the freemen or the greater part of them or their representatives."

In 1639 the little towns in Connecticut, not having any charter from the king, chose representatives who held a General Court at Hartford and adopted a written constitution "which stands unique in history as the first written constitution of a self-governing people. In it the people were recognized as sovereign, and the authority and even the existence of the king was ignored." The charter granted to it in 1662 recognized this constitution framed by the settlers twenty-three years before, and by it all power was given to the freemen of the towns to choose the governor, his deputies and assistants, and to elect the members of the General Court (legislature) to make the laws. It served the people of Connecticut so well that they retained it as their constitution until 1818.

In 1643, under Roger Williams, the little plantations in Rhode Island set up a form of government the most liberal of its kind, which was recognized by the charter granted in 1663 and for two hundred years served as its constitution until 1843, with powers very like those of the Connecticut charter.

The charter granted to the Carolinas in 1663 directed that the proprietors should govern "by and with the advice, consent and approbation of the freemen ot said territory, or their deputies or delegates." The Pennsylvania charter granted to William Penn in 1681 provided that laws should be framed "subject to the consent of the freemen."

Thus the inborn spirit of freedom brought by the settlers with them from England, nourished by their very surroundings in the New World, and given opportunity for its exercise by these charter provisions requiring their consent to all laws, made this country from the very beginning the cradle of liberty and of self-government. It must be noted that this power given to the General Assemblies to make the laws included the exercise of the power of taxation. This was a powerful weapon which the colonists did not hesitate to use effectively. The colonial governor who held his commission from England was dependent for his salary on the votes of the colonial assemblies, and, as Benjamin Franklin said, "he has two masters; one who gives him his commission, and one who gives him his pay." Through that power the colonists wrested from the proprietary and the crown governors the selection of officers through whom the exercise of the right of self-government grew apace.

The same kind of political barnacles which had fastened themselves on the ship of state in England, brought to America by the colonial governors, had to be scraped off. They consisted, principally, of religious intolerance, of a limitation upon the right of suffrage, and the continuance of the power of the aristocracy under the

laws of entail and primogeniture. Rhode Island led the
way, under Roger Williams, to combat the first. Judge
Story, in a noted address, said: "In her code of laws we
find for the first time since Christianity ascended the
throne of the Caesars that conscience should be free, and
that men should not be punished for worshipping God
as they were persuaded." William Penn enforced religious freedom in Pennsylvania. It took a little time to
overcome the spirit of intolerance which had reared its
hateful head of bigotry and persecution in many of the
colonies. But by the close of the American Revolution
this had been accomplished. In 1789 Jefferson and Madison had put through the Virginia Assembly a law divorc-
ing church and state from each other. In that same year
came the adoption of the Bill of Rights as a part of the
Constitution of the United States in which it was declared that "Congress shall make no law respecting an
establishment of religion, or prohibiting the free exercise
thereof."

In the same year in which the Declaration of Independence had been adopted, Jefferson caused the General
Assembly of Virginia to repeal the laws concerning primogeniture and entail which militated against equality
among the people by fostering and perpetuating an aristocratic class. The right of suffrage was continuously
extended until today all citizens, women as well as men,
with slight exception, enjoy the full right to vote. Freed
from English rule the colonists took to themselves the
right to elect all their public officers, with few exceptions,
from president down to constable.

This forward movement gained strength rapidly
throughout all the colonies. It was not limited to any
one section. The urban and the rural sections alike par-
took of its benefits. Freedom in the exericse of self
government became fundamental. When the new state
constitutions were framed, beginning in 1777, this spirit
stood out prominently. They were drafted by the people's own representatives. It was carefully provided

that they should not go into effect until they had first received approval by popular vote. The people retained the right to initiate amendments thereto and for their reference to a like vote. In these constitutions free speech, a free press, religious freedom and the right of assembly were carefully safeguarded. Mindful of their bitter controversies with the colonial governors appointed by the proprietors or by the crown, and of the fact that their colonial legislatures had been their only protection, the people at first vested in the elective members of those bodies large powers. As a safeguard they made elective, almost from the first, their state, county and municipal officers. As time went on it was found that legislatures were not always honest, that other public officials were derelict, and so the people provided methods by which to protect their rights as against their faithless servants. Always there was in evidence in the people that spirit which we have seen has so strongly dominated the Teutonic burgh and the Anglo-Saxon borough in their determined insistence on the right of self-government. And that spirit has been a strong factor in moulding the governments of our cities and our counties.

CHAPTER V.

CITIES AND COUNTIES IN AMERICA

During the colonial period, and until 1777 when the first state constitutions were adopted, the creation and establishment of cities and counties was a slow process. As a matter of mutual defense against the Indians, and in order to be near the common supply warehouse, the first colonists settled in small communities which were then neither cities nor counties but were generally called plantations in the South. However, in New England the settlements were much larger from the very beginning and were called towns. They were and still are the local governmental units. Counties have never been important there except in the nature of judicial districts. It was twenty-seven years after the settlement at Jamestown before any counties were created in any colony, and then, at first, they were established for judicial purposes in order that the holding of court might be brought nearer to the inhabitants who had been compelled to travel great distances which made the administration of justice difficult and expensive and in many cases prohibitive. In 1634 eight such districts were established in Virginia as shires, and later their names were changed to counties. In 1636 four judicial districts were created in Massachusetts and in 1643 they were changed into shires or counties. In 1638 the three lower counties of the Delaware were established. In 1650 Maryland was divided into three counties. In 1682 counties were established in Pennsylvania and in New

Jersey. In 1683 New York was divided into twelve counties. In 1729, when the Carolinas were divided into North Carolina and South Carolina, they consisted of but three counties. It was not until 1769 that the first counties were established in New Hampshire. While the counties at first were of a judicial character almost entirely, yet they soon became a part of the local governmental administrative structure of the colony in which they were.

Naturally, the colonists from England at first followed the forms of county government then in vogue in the mother country, with much of the exercise of local self-government intermixed somewhat with that overlordship which still existed there. Just as in England each county had its lord lieutenant in charge of the king's military forces, appointed by the crown, so each new colonial county had its county lieutenant in charge of the militia, appointed by the colonial governor, but with no administrative powers. When the new counties were created, just as is the case of new counties created today, the first officers were appointed by the governor or by the general assembly. In some instances their successors were likewise appointed but this did not become the rule. This departure from the practice in England under which the counties selected their own officers was due to the primitive state of things in the colonies and to the purpose of the colonial proprietors to keep themselves in control, but, as we have seen, that did not last long. During a few years the justices of the peace were appointed by the governor, but even so they never constituted the judicial oligarchy of the court of quarter sessions then existing in the English counties and which largely continued to exist there until 1888. As early as 1639 justices of the peace were made elective in Massachusetts. Quickly this became the rule in the colonies, and along with it came in due time the election of *nisi prius* judges. Today justices of the peace are elected locally in forty-six of the forty-eight states of the Union, and in forty-five of the forty-eight states the *nisi prius* judges are elected by the voters. In 1654 the people of Massachusetts began electing their county treasurers. By 1700 the people of New York, Pennsylvania and New Jersey elected their county boards to conduct all the fiscal and administrative functions of the counties. In 1704 prosecuting attorneys were made locally elective in Connecticut. It has already been noted how insistent the counties were in England in ridding themselves of a sheriff appointed by the crown, and in securing the right to name him locally. In 1705 the people of the counties in Pennsylvania took to themselves the right of electing their sheriff, and today that right is exercised unchallenged in every state of the Union. When the new states of Ohio, Indiana and Illinois were carved out of the Northwest Territory and were given statehood, their first constitutions provided for the local election of three county commissioners, a sheriff, and a coroner, in each county, and soon justices of the peace, county judges, county attorneys and clerks of the circuit court were made elective locally. Today the right of the people to elect all their county officers, and the free exercise of that right, is well-nigh universal. The exceptions are few, viz.: in New Hampshire the coroner of each county is appointed by the governor in council; in Maryland the governor names a board of post-mortem examiners which appoints assistant examiners (coroners) for each county; and in Vermont the members of the elected county court select the county treasurer in each county. With this small exception of the coroners in two states and the county treasurers in one state, all the county officers in the United States are elected by the voters locally. And even in Vermont they are named by a locally elected body, and not appointed by any state officer.

The courts have had much to say about the sovereign power of the state in the matter of appointing from the capital persons to serve as local officers. As has been shown the exercise of that power, if it rightfully exists at all, is so sparingly employed that it is practically *nil*. It is clearly inconsistent with our long established principles of self-government. It is undisputed that the legislature, subject to certain constitutional limitations, may create counties, change their boundaries, prescribe rules and regulations governing the conduct of the county business, provide what officers the county may have, and how taxes must be levied and collected, how the laws shall be enforced, and justice be administered. But that is as far as the state may legitimately go. And that is as far as it practically now goes. To extend the exercise of the sovereign power of the state beyond these limits is to revive that hated autocracy from which the counties in England as well as in this country have freed themselves after years of struggle. It would spell the doom of our democratic institutions.

A county is an involuntary quasi-public corporation created by the legislature and imposed by it upon a subdivision of the state for the primary purpose of enforcing locally its will. If excuse ever existed for the appointment of officers by the governor it would seem to apply to county officers. For they are required and empowered to enforce the state laws which affect generally the entire people of the state. Roughly speaking the sovereign power of the state concerning the functions to be, performed by county officers falls into four classes.

1. *The sovereign power of taxation.* The exercise of this power in the counties is vested in a board of county commissioners, county assessors, tax collectors and treasurers. With one slight deviation in but one state, all are elected by the voters of the county.

2. *The sovereign power of the preservation of the public health.* This is exercised locally by county boards of health appointed or elected in the county.

3. *The sovereign power of the protection of life and property.* The exercise of this power is vested in county sheriffs and constables, — all elected by the voters locally.

4. *The sovereign power of the administration of justice.* This is exercised by prosecuting attorneys, *nisi prius* courts and justices of the peace. With slight exception, already noted, all are locally elected. While in England the judiciary is named by the central government, in America all prosecuting attorneys are elected by the people, and save in three states all *nisi prius* judges, and except in two states all justices of the peace, are locally elected.

This overwhelming rule, of election of their county officers by the people clearly evidences their interpretation of the limitations that must be recognized as existing upon the exercise of the sovereignty of the state. They have been firmly and fundamentally ingrained in our American institutions without which our democratic system would perish. The exceptions are but the bedraggled remnants of a regime long ago discarded by a free people. The successful government in the counties under their own locally elected officers for so many years has exploded the baseless claim that the sovereignty of the state must be, or can best be, exercised by county officers appointed by the governor of the state. That sovereignty is fully maintained by these locally elected officers who obey and enforce the state laws, and sovereignty never rightfully asks more. It is only when we come to the cities that we shall see how these principles have been flagrantly disregarded.

Generally the officers of a county are the commissioners or supervisors (sometimes called the county court), a sheriff, coroner, clerk, recorder, surveyor, assessor, treasurer, a county or probate judge, and sometimes a tax collector. Politically the county, generally speaking, is a sort of nondescript or hybrid organization. It has no executive head. Its board of commissioners or supervisors perform both executive and legislative functions. It enacts the county ordinances and then proceeds to their enforcement in a way. This militates against proper conduct and administration of the public business.

However, many counties in this country have been given the right to frame home rule charters for their own government, in which they may provide for the number and character of their officers, and in some of them they have provided for an administrative officer generally called a "County Manager." This is along the line pursued by cities in which the office of "City Manager" has been created. It was intended that these managers should conduct the public affairs on a business basis independent of political influence or control. But the method of their appointment has often nullified that intention. Experience has demonstrated that when they are appointed either by a city council or by a board of supervisors the result has been more or less a failure. Leonard D. White, professor of political science at the University of Chicago, in his "The City Manager," says: "The failure of the city council is one of the most startling weaknesses of the council-manager plan. * * * The first council selected under the new regime is likely to be satisfactory; but before many years have passed an insidious process of decline sets in. The old crowd regains its courage and persistently prepares to elect one of its representatives to the council, then two, finally a majority. * * * The council-manager plan will not show a clearcut superiority as long as it is forced to labor under this handicap. * * * It ought to be possible in this country to separate politics from administration. Sound administration can develop and continue only if this separation is achieved." (pp. 299, 300, 301.) This applies as well to counties.

The fundamental defect in the manager plan is the method used in the appointment of the manager. The city council or the board of county supervisors generally appoint him, with power not only to hire but also to fire him. He thereby becomes a mere political hireling to carry out the will of his bosses, instead of being permitted to conduct his office independently in the public interest. The most flagrant example of this was recently furnished in Kansas City where the Tom Pendergast corrupt political gang dictated the appointment of the city manager. He was a mere tool of the machine. Pendergast was sent to a Federal prison for crookedness and his city manager died under the cloud of a criminal indictment hanging over his head. Many like failures, perhaps in lesser degree, have occurred, not only in cities but also in counties as well.

To remedy this evil it has been suggested that such managers be selected by a civil service commission. However, such commission in cities is generally selected by the mayor or by the city council or by both acting jointly, and in counties it is generally selected by the board of supervisors. Thus the political control of the manager is but one step removed from the council or the supervisors; it still remains to handicap his effectiveness. To escape that control the charter of the City and County of Denver provides that its civil service commission be appointed by the judges of its district court. In Cincinnati the three members of the civil service commission are appointed, one by the board of directors of the University of Cincinnati, one by the board of education of that city, and one by its mayor. In 1935 a like procedure was provided in a proposed amendment to the charter of the county of Los Angeles by a joint sub-committee composed of members from a committee selected by the county board of supervisors and of members from a committee selected by the mayor of the city of Los Angeles (of the latter committee the author was vice-chairman), consisting in all of fifty-five prominent citizens. They agreed that there should be a county manager to conduct the county business free from political domination. Careful study was made as to how that could be brought about. It was early agreed that this could not be done by leaving the appointment of a manager in the hands of the board of county supervisors, nor could it be done by placing such appointment in the hands of the county civil service commission whose members are appointed by the board of supervisors and so are subject to its control. A supreme court decision had held that judges in California may not appoint members of a civil service commission as is done in Denver. The thought then was to follow the example set by Cincinnati, but to improve upon it. It was agreed that the presidents of the seven largest universities and colleges in the county of Los Angeles should constitute a certification board, and that this board should present to the board of supervisors the names of five persons from which it must select three to become the civil service commission. It was believed that a certification board thus constituted would name five persons of such high class that the board of supervisors could not go far wrong in selecting the three members of the commission. It was then provided that the civil service commission, thus selected, should make a nation wide survey of the best available material for a county manager and should then certify to the board of supervisors the names of three persons from whom the board should select a manager. (Appendix—32.) Again it was felt that the board of supervisors could not go far wrong. Then came the problem of how the proposed charter amendment could be submitted to the electors of the county. One way was to submit it upon an initiative petition which would have required two hundred and twenty-five thousand signers; the other way was by a simple resolution of the board of supervisors. That board, at first, had declared in favor of a county manager to be appointed by it. But when its members learned that the manager was to be a free agent and not simply their dispenser of political patronage they balked. Of the five members of the board four were present at the meeting to consider the submission of the proposed amendment to a vote of the people. Of the two Republicans there present one voted to submit the proposed amendment to the electors of the county and the other voted against it, while the two Democrats who were elected as progressives and as boasted "friends of the people" voted against permitting the people of the county an opportunity of saying by their votes what should be in their own charter. This is an interesting example of the double dealing so often indulged in by so-called public servants, and will help the reader to realize the difficulties to be met with in attempting to better local government.

Outside of the changes caused in England by the creation of county boroughs no material alteration of county boundaries have been made there since the Norman conquest. However, in America new counties have been created or boundaries of old ones changed from the beginning to meet the requirements of a constantly increasing and shifting population. For many years the state legislatures exercised unbridled control over the creation of counties, fixing and changing their boundaries, consolidating two or more into one or carving new counties out of one or more then existing, and fixing and changing the location of county seats. In many instances this power was flagrantly abused. New counties were created or their boundaries were shifted at the behest of designing politicians. County seats were removed to a rival town to reward it for its support of the ticket of the political party then in power in the legislature, and many times this was done to afford rich pickings for real estate speculators in the town thus made the new county seat. The result was that the people of the abandoned county seat saw their property values depreciated and themselves impoverished. This led to civil strife in many cases. The people were aroused by these evil conditions so that amendments were adopted to the constitutions of most of the states forbidding the legislature from changing the boundaries of any county or of the location of its county seat, except upon a vote of the people affected, and providing that

no new county be created having an area of less than a
specified number of square miles or having less than a
prescribed number of inhabitants, and that the remaining portion of the county must have left to it at least a
like area and population. As will be seen in Chapter
IX, some of these restrictions then deemed necessary,
especially as to area and population, were later found
to prevent the creation of a city into a city-county consolidated in several of the states. Subject to those restrictions the legislature is still supreme over county
boundaries and in prescribing county functions, except
in those states where their constitutions have been
amended providing for county home rule.

Of course, before counties were organized small
municipalities had sprung up. Naturally the colonists
first settled in small communities which gradually grew
into villages and towns, and some of them into cities.
This was a matter of slow growth in the Southern colonies, which were mostly of an agricultural character
with large plantations taking the place of villages and
towns elsewhere. On the plantations lived the planter
and his overseers and his skilled workmen with their
families, and also many slaves, thus constituting a sort
of village governed in the early period solely by the
planter who also acted in a judicial capacity as did the
early patroons in New York. In Virginia the first settlements at Jamestown, Henrico, New Bermuda, Charles
City and Elizabeth City were so small that they were
not worthy the name of city. Settlements originally intended for towns did not grow into such, but spread into
disconnected plantations and became counties, such as
James City county and Charles City county in Virginia.
It was not until 1722 that Williamsburg was the first
city to receive a charter after it had been made the
colonial capital. At the time of the American Revolution there were but two cities of any importance in all
the South, — Charleston in South Carolina which was
then the third seaport in size in America, and Annapolis

in Maryland which was then a considerable trading center. Richmond and Norfolk were of small importance and Baltimore had not yet been founded.

On the other hand, in the North where trading, manufacturing, commerce, lumbering, shipbuilding and fishing industries flourished, many towns sprang up and quickly grew into important cities. North of Virginia the first city of importance was Philadelphia which soon gained a commanding position as one of the three largest cities in the colonies. Further north was New York whose strategic position in the world of trade and commerce quickly made it one of the three, while to the northeast Boston with its fine harbor and its progressive citizens made the third. By 1775 they had populations of from 23,000 to 28,000 each and so were considered in the metropolitan class. They prided themselves on their wealth and their political importance.

Outside of New England the cities and towns were of a diversified character. When they graduated from small unincorporated settlements they were called towns or boroughs. The first borough was that of New York chartered by the English governor of that province in 1653. Because of unsettled conditions in the new colony the governor appointed the mayor and many of the borough officers, but the charter of 1686 provided that six councilmen and six assistants be elected annually by the voters in the six wards of the city and that they, together with the mayor and the recorder appointed by the governor, should sit together as the common council with power to make "laws, ordinances and constitutions" for the borough not repugnant to the laws of England, and with power to appoint all other officers. In 1821 the recorder was made elective by popular vote, the mayor was made elective by the common council and in 1834 by popular vote. When William Penn established Philadelphia in 1682 it began at once with a considerable population, under the close corporation form of government then quite prevalent in England under

the autocratic rule of Charles II, with a charter granted
to the city by Penn which named the officers consisting
of a mayor, a recorder, eight aldermen and twelve councilmen. All but the mayor were given life terms with
power in the council to fill all vacancies and to select
annually the mayor. In 1789 Philadelphia had all its
officers made elective by popular vote. Other charters
granted by the colonial governors were as follows: Albany, N. Y., 1688; Annapolis, Md., 1696; Charleston,
S. C., 1704; Perth Amboy, N. J., 1718; Williamsburg,
Va., 1722; Norfolk, Va., 1736; Richmond, Va., 1742; and
Trenton, N. J., 1746. Portsmouth, N. H., had received
its charter in 1653 as an act of incorporation passed by
its colonial General Assembly. In 1754 Baltimore was
governed by a board of town commissioners appointed
by the General Assembly but in 1797 it was granted a
charter under which its people elected a bicameral council consisting of an upper house of one member, and a
lower house of two members, from each ward. In Chapter XI is set forth the history of the Virginia cities
which shows that from the beginning they were of the
city-county consolidated type and largely exercised the
right of self-government. Under the charters of nearly
all the colonial cities the members of the common council
were made elective, with a mayor selected by it, and they
sat together in administering the municipal affairs.

In New England, however, an entirely different system prevailed from the beginning. The Pilgrims, and
only a little later the Puritans, brought with them a
fixed fundamental concept of self-government. They
settled in towns where they put democracy into active
operation. They had no town charters and they had no
mayors for two hundred years. They governed themselves as the Anglo-Saxons formerly did. At least once
annually they gathered together in town meeting and
elected a moderator to preside. The freeholders there
assembled passed upon the public business, mapped out
policies to be pursued during the ensuing year, and

elected the town officers generally consisting of the selectmen who corresponded to members of the city council elsewhere, a constable, town clerk, treasurer, assessor, collector, and an overseer of the poor. The selectmen performed all executive and administrative functions. It was not until 1822 that Boston, with a then population of 40,000, forsook its town meeting as being too cumbersome, and accepted incorporation with the right of electing its mayor and aldermen locally.

The student of the history of this country must be forcibly impressed by the evident intent of our people to preserve their democratic institutions, modified by stress of circumstances to a representative form of government but losing none of the fundamental democratic principles. The sturdy pioneers had come across the sea to escape tyranny and in search of liberty. It is unthinkable that they ever intended to forsake what they thus sought and to attain which they had bravely fought. That spirit kept alive has made America great. Those who would strike it down or even impair it are not worthy the name of Americans. They should recall a glorious past and seek to keep it unsullied. Unfortunately there are those who would lend themselves, wittingly or unwittingly, sometimes foolishly or corruptly, to the destruction of those high ideals upon which our institutions must rest if they are to be maintained. Of such the truth must be spoken unflinchingly. Their subversive doctrines must be exposed and destroyed. That is a patriotic duty which every self-respecting citizen owes to his country. Especially is it incumbent upon the author to discuss a situation which has done much harm to the proper functioning of the city-county consolidated.

Long before the English yoke had been thrown off, and, as we have seen, even during the colonial years of privation and brave struggle, there had been gradually but firmly fixed in the minds of the people the American tradition of liberty in the nation, the state, the counties,

and in the cities, with the priceless right of self-government. Early in the nineteenth century every county and
every city in this country, almost without exception, had
obtained and were enjoying the right of selecting all
their own officers. They rejoiced when England in 1835
enacted the Municipal Corporations Act which made its
cities free. However, after having gallantly gained their
full democratic freedom and having exercised it unchallenged for so many years, our people were rudely
shocked by suddenly finding themselves made subject to
the same kind of political and judicial jugglery which
had been inflicted upon the English counties by the justices of the peace in quarter sessions and by the king's
pliant tools on the bench in decreeing forfeiture of borough charters upon trumped up charges in order to foist
minions of the crown upon the boroughs.

CHAPTER VI.

POLITICAL AND JUDICIAL JUGGLERY

The backsliding from established liberty unrestrictedly enjoyed by the people of all the cities in America came about not through their wishes nor by their request but against their will. It was conceived in minds inflamed by the passions of oncoming war, brought forth by politicians lustful for power aided by subservient legislatures, and given blessing by courts unmindful and even defiant of American traditions and seemingly bent upon serving their masters.

With the rapid growth of cities their control was sought by great combinations of private capital intent on securing valuable gas, electric and transportation franchises from complaisant or corrupt city councils. It was found that boards of police, fire, public works and elections, appointed by the governor and vested with great power and patronage, could be used to swing the election of councilmen and mayors who would be easy to deal with. Members of the state legislature were subject to like influences, so they supinely enacted laws creating these boards and vesting in the governor the power to foist his minions on the cities. And shameful political courts lent their aid!

Under these circumstances, beginning three years before the Civil War and running through the twenty-five years after its close, during those Dark Ages when centralization of power grew in this country to formidable proportions under the domination of predatory interests, these courts in some of the states began announcing doctrines violative of the fundamental principles of self-government in our cities and especially inimical to the creation and development of the "city-county consolidated." This demands particular attention in the treatment of the subject of this book. In preceding pages it has been made clear that in England the boroughs had sprung into being through the efforts of their own people, that never had they been created by the sovereign except for a short time and only in a few illegitimate cases when he usurped power not his by right, that they had never been destroyed by him, and that now for years boroughs have exercised exclusively the prerogative of selecting their own officers. It has also been shown that during colonial days in America, almost from the beginning, that same freedom had been enjoyed by our cities, self-created and self-governed. But these courts, without historic basis and hand in glove with subversive elements, evolved the spurious doctrine that the state at will may create and destroy municipalities and deduced therefrom the illegitimate claim of right to send in its appointees as their officers.

The state of New York led the way in this movement in 1857. The new Republican party had just elected the governor, and controlled the legislature and the court of appeals, — the highest court. Tammany was then in powerful control of New York City under Fernando Wood as mayor and "Boss" Tweed as president of the board of supervisors. The police department, the fire department, and the health department of that city caught the covetous eye of the members of the legislature who decided to take over the juicy patronage and political power incident thereto. But the state constitution of 1846 contained a direct mandate that "all city, town and village officers, whose election or appointment is now provided by the constitution, *shall * * * be appointed by such authorities thereof,* as the legislature may designate for that purpose."

The people of the state had prided themselves on this constitutional provision as an inviolable safeguard for the "home rule" of their cities, towns and villages and of their continued right to name their own officers just as they had been accustomed to do. For many years, and almost from the very time of their early settlement, the City of New York and the City of Brooklyn and the cities in their neighboring counties of Westchester and Richmond had appointed the officers of their respective police, fire and health departments. When the constitution of 1846 was adopted these offices were then in existence occupied by officers thus appointed. The legislature was confronted by this constitutional mandate. But a politician once said: "What is the constitution among friends?"

So, the legislature cooked up a scheme to circumvent the constitution. It recognized that if it created the City of New York, or the City of Brooklyn, alone, into a metropolitan police district the officers thereof would have to be appointed locally. This would not serve the ulterior purpose of the legislature. It, therefore, took the county of New York occupied entirely by the City of New York, the county of Kings in which was the City of Brooklyn, and the counties of Westchester and Richmond with their cities, towns and villages, and lumped them together into the "Metropolitan Police District of the State of New York" under a police board to be appointed by the governor. This was plain legislative jugglery.

In *People v. Draper,* 15 N. Y. 532, decided in 1857, the court in passing upon this law specifically stated that if the legislature had created a single board for each of the cities in the four counties separately to be appointed by the governor it would have violated the constitution. The court said that "if the provisions of the statute had been limited territorially to the City of New York, it would have been in conflict with the section above referred to," and further said that "if the offices are city or county offices it *belongs exclusively to the local power to fill the*

offices, either by election or appointment, as the legislature may direct." The fact was that the officers of the
police department of that city had been selected locally
at least ever since 1776. This the court did not deny. But
the court side-stepped the constitution by holding that by
bunching several home rule cities into a metropolitan
police district a new kind of police officer was created
different from those already there existing and thus this
law was sustained. It was a clear case of judicial jugglery.

Indeed, that court in the later case of *People v.
Albertson,* 55 N. Y. 50, branded the law and that decision
as plain jugglery when it said: "The constitution cannot
be evaded by a change in the name of an office, nor can an
office be divided and the duties assigned to two or more
officers under different names." Furthermore, Judge
Brown, with Judge Comstock concurring, wrote a dissenting opinion in the *Draper* case so logical and convincing
and so firmly based upon the underlying principles of our
American institutions that the same court in the *Albertson* case wholly discredited and practically overruled the
former by saying that "it is to be hoped in the interests
of constitutional government by the people that the occa-
sion to reaffirm its doctrines may never arrive." The
writer of that later opinion further said: "To my mind
the dissenting opinion of Judge Brown, concurred in by
Judge Comstock, presents unanswerable arguments why
the opinion should have been different." In the *Albertson*
case the court held unconstitutional a law enacted by the
legislature in 1873 creating the "Rensselaer Police District" out of the City of Troy and fragments of territory
outside the city limits, under a police board to be appointed by the governor, as being in violation of the
"right of self-government which lies at the foundation
of our institutions." And this has been repeatedly reaffirmed by that court in 150 N. Y. 459, 174 N. Y. 417,
and as late as 1912 in 206 N. Y. 405, in principle.

Yet strange as it may seem, that *Draper* case thus

branded as a black sheep by the very court which gave it illegitimate birth has been followed as a judicial bell-wether by a flock of courts seemingly intent upon judicially clothing as a white sheep a quite visible hungry wolf. Following up this successful assault upon the liberties of these cities the Republican legislature of 1865 created New York City and Brooklyn into the "Metropolitan Fire District of the State of New York," under a board to be appointed by the governor, notwithstanding the fact that from 1798 the former had maintained and had manned its own fire department with officers named by its city council up to the very time the law was enacted. It has been seen that the court in the *Draper* case had specifically stated that if such a law applied to but one city it would be an unconstitutional invasion of its right of local self-government. The fact is that while this law of 1865 ostensibly covered the two cities of New York and Brooklyn, yet it actually limited this board to the exercise of functions and duties in the City of New York alone and left the local fire department of Brooklyn intact. However, the court sustained the law in spite of and paradoxically upon the purported authority of the discredited *Draper* case. That legislature of 1865 also created the "Capitol Police District of the State of New York," under a board to be appointed by the governor. That district covered the City of Schenectady and four miles of territory within the lines of the New York Central Railroad reaching out into the county. This inclusion of this narrow strip of non-municipal territory was a subterfuge so as to creep in under the protection of the *Draper* case. That legislature of 1865 also created the "Metropolitan Sanitary District of the State of New York" out of the counties of New York, Kings, Westchester and Richmond, under a board to be appointed by the governor, in spite of the fact that the cities, towns and villages therein had locally appointed their own health officers from the very beginning of their existence. Upon the doctrine of the *Draper* case that law was sustained as being constitutional in *Board v. Heister,* 37 N. Y. 661, decided in 1868, by a narrow squeak, as four of the nine judges dissented. The court had begun to turn against the doctrines of the *Draper* case which met its Waterloo five years later in the *Albertson* case.

This wholesale assault of the Republicans against local self-government in the City of New York and in the City of Brooklyn vesting in the governor the appointment of the boards having in charge the police, fire and health functions of those important municipalities, and the police functions of the cities of Schenectady and Troy, was carried out with the blessing of the courts in order to gain political control for ulterior purposes.

In Maryland it was the Democrats who invaded the right of self-government so long enjoyed by its cities. In 1860 they elected the governor and controlled the legislature. Partisan and sectional passion flamed to white heat at the outbreak of the Civil War. Baltimore had always had its own constabulary as its police force. But that city was suspected of leaning toward the Union cause, while the up-state with its many slave owners favored the Confederacy. The state constitution provided that the legislature should fix the number of justices of the peace and constables for each ward in the City of Baltimore, *but gave it no power to appoint them.* It further stated that "the mayor and city council may provide, by ordinance, from time to time, for the creation and government of such temporary police, as they may deem necessary to preserve the peace." Clearly a police force, of a temporary character, to supplement the force of locally elected constables in the wards, was authorized by the constitution when required by an emergency. There was no other reasonable need for it. However, the Democrats in the legislature were intent not only that the patronage incident to a police department in that important city should be secured to its followers but also that its martial support should not go to the despised Republicans. So a law was enacted creating a "Board of

Police of the City of Baltimore" to be appointed by the governor, and to make assurance doubly sure it further provided that "no Black Republican" should ever be appointed to any office under that board. The constitution of Maryland limited the appointive power of the governor to "civil officers of the state, whose election or appointment is not herein provided for." As will be pointed out later, policemen are not civil officers of the state. The constitution specifically vested in the mayor and the city council of Baltimore the power to appoint such police officers as they might deem necessary. In the face of this clear provision of the constitution, the court in *Mayor v. State,* 15 Md. 376, decided in 1860, while it expressed hesitancy in doing so yet it sustained the law which foisted upon that city a police force under the domination of the governor. And this was done on the specious theory that this authorization of the mayor and the city council to appoint temporary police, to supplement the force of constables when needed, left open the door to the legislature to empower the governor to appoint a "permanent police force" whether needed or not, for the purpose of supplanting the already existing municipal constabulary authorized by the constitution. This smacks much of legislative and judicial jugglery indulged in at a time of tense passion which swayed the people and the courts away from those fundamental principles which cannot safely be abandoned even for a time. Certainly this decision is not one to serve as a legitimate precedent to be followed in working destruction of the long established right of our cities in making their own selection of their officers. The discredited *Draper* case here sired its first offspring since it is cited as authority by the Maryland court. The progeny was tainted with the same disease that afflicted the parent stock. Notwithstanding that fact both of these cases have been seized upon by courts, too indolent to learn the historical truth or too prone to pull political chestnuts out of the fire, as we shall see, in order to clothe with seeming dignity decisions that strike at the very fundamentals of our form of government.

Again it was the Democrats in Missouri who invaded the right of the people of St. Louis to select their own officers. In 1860 that party had elected the governor and it controlled the legislature and the supreme court. St. Louis was strongly for the Union, while the outside counties favored the Confederacy. In that year the legislature, in order to get control of the city for partisan purposes as well as for political patronage, enacted a law creating a "Metropolitan Police Force" for the City of St. Louis. It empowered the police board, not only to control the police of that city but, in extraordinary emergencies to be determined by it, to require the sheriff to act under its control and to summon a *posse comitatus* and to employ the same at the board's direction. It also authorized the board to call to its aid any military force lawfully organized in the city. It further made it compulsory that the city council levy taxes to meet this cost and that they be spread over the entire county, to furnish all funds required by the police board, without any right in the people to question the necessity for, or the amount of, such expenditure. This was autocratic government by the central authority with a strong arm. In *State v. St. Louis,* 34 Mo. 546, decided in 1864, this law was sustained. No case was cited in support of the decision. The only question argued or passed on was the right to tax property outside of the city to support the metropolitan police force. The question of the right of the city to select its own police officers was not even argued or presented to the court. And yet that case is cited by other courts in later decisions in purported support of the doctrine that the state is sovereign and may do as it pleases with municipal corporations even to the extent of depriving them of the right of selecting their own officers.

Next came the Republicans in Michigan who cast longing eyes upon the patronage and political power in-

cident to the control of the police department of the City
of Detroit. In 1865 that party had the governor, the
legislature and the supreme court. Prior thereto the
city had its own police department locally manned and
maintained. In that year the legislature enacted a law
creating the "Board of Metropolitan Police" for the City
of Detroit, to be appointed by the governor. In *People
v. Mahaney,* 13 Mich. 481, decided in 1865, the constitutionality of that law was sustained. However, only two
questions were argued or passed upon. The first objection
was that the law embraced two subjects which could not
properly be joined in the same bill, and this appears to
have been correctly denied. The second objection was
that the people of the city, without having a voice in the
matter, were required to furnish funds demanded by the
board, and that this was taxation without representation.
Although that objection was denied, as it has also been
denied by the courts of Missouri, on the ground that the
members of the legislature from the city there represented it, such doctrine has been vigorously denounced
by other courts. In *Rathbone v. Wirth,* 6 Hun. (N. Y.)
277, the court said: "But it may be said that the legislature is composed of the representatives of the people,
and that therefore, their acts are presumed to be the acts
of a majority of the people, and that while this act deprived a majority of the people in one locality of their
power, still it is in accordance with the will of the majority of the people of the whole state, and that thereby
the principle of majority government is recognized. There
would be force in this suggestion but for another principle
in our constitution—the principle of local self-government. * * * Local self-government is the school which fits
the people for self-government. Local self-government
is the result and also the most efficient preserver of civil
liberty. * * * The principle is one that runs through our
entire system of government, from the road and school
district to the Federal government." And, in *State v.
Denny,* 118 Ind. 382, the court by Chief Justice Elliott

said: "The municipal corporation, as a local government, is not represented by the general assembly, and to permit that body to designate the officers who shall govern local affairs would be to tax the citizens of the corporation without representation. * * * It is no answer to say, as it is sometimes said, that the municipal corporation has representatives in the general assembly, for as a municipal corporation it is not, as to its local affairs, represented by that body, for that body represents the state and legislates in state affairs and only incidentally as to local affairs."

Furthermore, in the *Mahaney* case the Michigan court cited not a single case in support of its decision. As will be seen later, had the question of this invasion of the right of the people of that city to select their own officers been properly or at all presented to the court, its decision would probably have been to the contrary. Chief Justice McGrath of that court commented on this situation in a later case as follows: "Section 14 of article 15 of the constitution (as to home rule) was not referred to in the brief of counsel (in the *Mahaney* case), nor was it alluded to in the opinion. Counsel did not claim that this section had been violated, and the court expressly refrained from discussing a provision of the constitution not pointed out or relied upon." (105 Mich. at page 137.) So that, the question of the right of the city to select its own police officers was neither argued nor presented and was not decided. Yet the *Mahaney* case has been added to the discredited *Draper* case (15 N. Y.) and to the *Mayor* case (15 Md.) and to the *St. Louis* case (34 Mo.), all equally ill-considered, which we shall see have been herded together and frequently cited by certain courts as purported authority for striking down the right of cities to select their own officers.

In 1868 the Kentucky legislature enacted a law which provided for "The Police Commission of the City of Louisville and Jefferson County" to consist of three commissioners elective by the voters of the entire county.

The governor had nothing to do with their appointment. They were elected. Prior thereto the cities of Kentucky had exercised full control over their own police force. This new law provided for two sets of police officers: one for the city to be paid for by the city, appointive by this new county commission, and the other for the county outside the city to be selected by the county court (board of county commissioners) to be paid for by the county, although there was no requirement that the county court ever make such selection of county police. The practical result was that this county commission was thus placed in power only over the police of the City of Louisville displacing the force theretofore selected by the city. In *Police Commissioners v. City of Louisville,* 66 Ky. (3 Bush) 597, the court held that these commissioner picked policemen were a kind of policemen *different* from those theretofore selected by the city, followed the example of twisting tactics set in the *Draper* case (15 N. Y.), later fully discredited, and sustained the law. This was but another instance of political and judicial jugglery, just as was its progenitor. And yet they are joined together by other courts as a basis and excuse for depriving cities of their right to select their own officers.

In 1868 the Republican "carpetbaggers" were in control of the state of Louisiana. The constitution of 1864 had provided that cities should select all their officers. But in 1868 under this regime a new constitution was adopted which omitted that provision safeguarding this right in the cities, undoubtedly for the ulterior purpose of paving the way for the later passage that year of a law creating a "Board of Police Commissioners" for the City of New Orleans to be appointed by the governor. In *Diamond v. Cain,* 21 La. Ann. 319, decided that year by a partisan court, that law was sustained without the citation of a single case in support. Commenting thereon the supreme court of Nebraska in the *Moores* case (55 Neb. at p. 518) said: "In *Diamond v. Cain,* 21 La. Ann. 309, the right of self-government was not discussed or adjudicated." Yet this Louisiana case is another of those cited in alleged support of the doctrine that the state may deprive cities of their lawful right to select their own officers.

Prior to 1876 cities in Ohio had exercised full power in the selection of all their officers. However, in that year the legislature enacted a law creating a "Board of Police Commissioners" to be appointed by the governor, for all cities having a population of 200,000 or more. Cincinnati, whose police department offered large political patronage to those who might control it, was the only city covered by the act. In *State v. Covington*, 29 O. St. 102, decided in 1876, that law was sustained on the cited authority of the foregoing cases in 15 N. Y., 15 Md., 3 Bush, 21 La. Ann., 34 Mo., and 13 Mich., hereinbefore shown to be entitled to little, if any, weight. In 1880, just four years later, evidently the legislature had heard the voice of the people in protest, for it enacted a law which provided that "all police powers and duties connected with and incident to the appointment, regulation and government of a police force in cities of the first class shall be vested in the mayor." However, six years later the politicians, eager to control the patronage incident to the Cincinnati police department, caused the legislature to re-enact the law giving the governor the power to appoint a police board for that city and it was sustained in *State v. Smith*, 44 O. St. 348, decided in 1886, on the cited authority of the same old stalking horses, —15 N. Y., and its fellow travelers. There was no justification or excuse for that court to cite in support of its decision those discredited cases which rested on no legitimate constitutional grant to the legislature empowering it to vest in the governor the making of such appointments. For the constitution of Ohio specifically provided that as to all officers not made elective or appointive locally, appointments thereof "shall be made in such manner as may be prescribed by law." Since the police force was not made elective or appointive locally by the constitution the legislature was therein given specific power to act. There is nothing here to support the doctrine that the legislature may do so in the *absence* of such constitutional grant. The citing of these Ohio cases by certain courts in support of that doctrine seems to be wholly unwarranted.

Prior to 1887 the cities of Nebraska had exercised the untrammeled right of selecting all their officers including police and members of the fire department. In that year the legislature enacted a law creating a "Board of Fire and Police Commissioners" for cities of the metropolitan class, to be appointed by the governor. This applied to the city of Omaha. In *State v. Seavey,* 22 Neb. 454, decided in 1887, the act was sustained. But the question of the legal right of the governor, in the absence of constitutional authorization, to appoint this Fire and Police Board was not even raised, and so it was neither argued nor passed upon. In 1897 a similar law was enacted by the legislature under which the governor appointed a "Board of Fire and Police Commissioners" for the City of Omaha, which was held to be unconstitutional in *State v. Moores,* 55 Neb. 480, decided in 1898, in which the court said: "It is evident that the constitution was framed upon the theory of local self-government,—the right of the people to determine for themselves who shall be their officers." The same question was again raised in *State v. Kennedy,* 60 Neb. 300, decided in 1900, in which the court reaffirmed its decision in the *Moores* case in an opinion by Judge Sullivan who stated that the question involved was governed by the rule of *res adjudicata* and that "once ascertained and determined it is forever concluded." However, the very next year the political powers intent on gaining control of the fire and police department of Omaha brought the question for the third time before the court and Judge Sullivan promptly forgot the rule he had just announced in the *Kennedy* case, "settling the question forever," and joined in making a majority of that court

(63 Neb. 219) in overruling the two former cases. And to support this decision the majority opinion cited the discredited cases in 15 N. Y., 15 Md., 13 Mich., 34 Mo., and 21 La. Ann., already discussed.

In 1885 Boston had become Democratic while the rest of the state was Republican. In that year the legislature, in the absence of constitutional authorization, enacted a law by which the governor was empowered to appoint police commissioners to have charge of the police of that city. In *Commonwealth v. Plaisted,* 148 Mass. 375, decided in 1889, that law was sustained in what appears to have been a "friendly suit." The supreme court of Nebraska in commenting on it in the *Moores* case, *supra,* discredited it as follows: "The court, in the opinion, concede that the question of invalidity of the law, on the ground that it deprived the city of the power of self-government in matters of internal police, was but little relied upon in the argument, and the question was disposed of by the court without much consideration and without the citation of a single authority in support of the conclusion reached." And yet this *Plaisted* case is cited by other courts as a beacon light illuminating the doctrine that the state may deprive its cities of that very right.

Prior to 1887 cities in Kansas had exercised the right of selecting all their own officers. However, some of its cities had come into almost open rebellion against the state in their flagrant violation of the prohibitory liquor laws. Leavenworth was a hot-bed of bootleggers and lawless saloon-keepers, so the legislature in 1887 enacted a law empowering the executive council to appoint a "Board of Police Commissioners" for that city especially directed to enforce the prohibitory laws, but with the proviso that when the executive council should no longer deem it necessary then such board was to be dispensed with and appointment of the police force was to be restored to the mayor and the city council. This does not properly fall within those cases where a

permanent police board had been created, but rather it
comes under the right of the state temporarily to send
in its own officers to supplant for the time being those
local officers who fail or refuse to enforce the state laws
in the municipality. It cannot justly be cited in support of the deprivation of cities of their right of self-
government. That law was sustained in *State v. Hunter,*
38 Kan. 578, decided in 1888, on the cited authority of
the foregoing cases in 15 N. Y., 15 Md., 13 Mich., 3 Bush
and 21 La. Ann. In 1903 the law was repealed.

In 1883 the Indiana legislature had begun tinkering with the local government of its cities. In 1889 it
enacted a law creating a ''Metropolitan Police and Fire
Board'' for cities having a population of 29,000 or more,
the first members of which were named by the legislature in the act itself and thereafter were to be appointed
by the mayor. In *Evansville v. State,* 118 Ind. 426,
decided in that year, this act was held to be unconstitutional on the ground that the legislature itself had no
power to name any officers for any city. At the same
time the legislature enacted a law creating a board of
public works for certain cities to be appointed by the
governor, but it was also held to be unconstitutional in
State v. Denny, 118 Ind. 382, on the ground that it
was an invasion of the municipal right of self-government. In 1891 the legislature enacted a law under which
the governor, secretary of state, auditor and treasurer
appointed a board of police commissioners for Terre
Haute, and in *State v. Koslem,* 130 Ind. 434, decided that
year, the law was sustained on the alleged authority of
15 N. Y., 15 Md., 13 Mich., 3 Bush, 29 O. St., 22 Neb.,
and 38 Kans., weak reeds upon which to rely, as has been
shown. Not only did the court dignify these cases as
authorities for striking down the right of cities to name
their own officers but in a burst of unbridled enthusiasm
coupled with an evidence of lack of ordinary research it
declared that: ''The power of the legislature to provide
for the appointment of members of a municipal board

of police has been affirmed in every instance in which it
has been so challenged and presented as to require the
judgment of courts.'' Strangely that court cited the
Evansville case in purported support of its decision in
the face of the fact that in that case a law was held
unconstitutional under which a metropolitan police and
fire board was attempted to be foisted upon the two
largest cities in the state, and in which that court then
said: ''If the act related alone to the police department,
and the state was proposing to take *upon itself the burden of maintaining the department* as well as its management, or if it were made to appear that the city had
failed to furnish a police force, or one that was *insufficient* for the protection of persons and property, then a
very different question would be presented for consideration. *Except so far as an efficient* police department
goes, which is for the protection of the public at large,
the people of the state are not interested in any of the
matters to which said act of the legislature relates, but
the citizens of Evansville and Indianapolis, the two cities
to which the act relates, *are alone interested.* It, therefore, becomes a question whether or not the legislature
may take from the people of these two cities the right
of self-government, the right to manage and control their
own purely local affairs in their own way, and place the
management of all local affairs under state control. We
do not believe that the legislature has any such power.
Before written constitutions, the people possessed the
full power of local self-government, * * * they still
possess such of that power *as has not been delegated.*
All the power which the people have delegated is what
has passed from them by the constitution.'' Why were
these salutary principles ignored in the *Koslem* case
and how could the court there say that no challenge had
ever been made of such outside appointment? And
why did that court bolster its decision by citing the
Draper case (15 N. Y.) in support when it must have
known that in 1873, eighteen years before, it had been

discredited and practically overruled in the *Albertson* case? And finally, the law of 1891 was undoubtedly unconstitutional under the later decision in *Campbell v. City*, 155 Ind. 186, on the ground that it was special legislation. However, in *State v. Fox,* 158 Ind. 126, decided in 1901, a board of public safety appointed by the governor to take charge of the fire and police departments in Ft. Wayne was held to be unconstitutional. The court said that "municipalities have the same right to select their own officers, as the state has, without outside interference by the state or by the United States. * * * If the governor may appoint fire commissioners for Ft. Wayne without its consent, he may be empowered to appoint every officer, except judicial, in every city and town. To thus deprive the people of a locality of the right to choose their own immediate local officers is to rob them of their freedom, and to defeat one of the great ends for which government was established."

In some of the Indiana cases and in the decision of the courts in some of the other states legislative acts were upheld as to police boards yet acts were strongly condemned which vested in the governor the power of appointing members of fire, health, public works and other like boards. The distinction attempted to be made between them and police boards does not seem well grounded. The only excuse for appointment of the latter by the governor is that the state in its sovereign capacity is interested in protecting the life and property of its people. Certainly a health department is necessary for the protection of their lives, and it is clear that a fire department is quite necessary for the protection of their property. They are just as necessary for these purposes as is a police force. To hold that appointment by the governor of the latter is a proper exercise of state sovereignty and in the same breath to hold that his appointment of the former is an assault on the right of self-government and is destructive of our democratic institutions simply does not make sense. The naked truth is that there is no lawful or logical basis for any legislature to empower a governor to make any of such appointments, and that such authorizations are political subterfuges.

Prior to 1887, cities of Colorado had selected all their own officers. The constitution of that state provided that "the general assembly shall not delegate to any special commission * * * any power to make, supervise or interfere with any municipal improvement, money, property or effects * * * or perform any municipal function whatever." In that year the legislature, generally called "The Robber Seventh" because its members carted off home with them much state personal property, disregarded this constitutional provision by enacting a law which created a "Board of Public Works" for Denver with power to make, supervise and interfere with all public improvements to be made in that city, and to control the money, property and effects of the city used in connection therewith. *In Re Senate Bill,* 12 Colo. 188, decided in that year, this law was sustained on the specious plea that a board of public works specially created was not a "special commission," and that the state had the sovereign power to provide how city offices should be filled either by election or by appointment of the governor. This case cited none of the old standby cases heretofore discussed.

Prior to 1889 the cities of Georgia had exercised the right of selecting their own officers. In that year the legislature enacted a law under which the governor appointed a police board for the city of Americus. It was sustained in *Mayor v. Perry,* 114 Ga. 871, decided in 1902, on the authority of 15 Md., 21 La. Ann., 29 O. St., and 38 Kans. But in that same year the people, evidently in revolt, elected a legislature which amended the law so as to restore to the mayor and four members of a board to be elected by the voters full powers over the police of that city.

In 1900 the legislature of New Hampshire enacted

a law authorizing the governor to appoint police commissioners for the town of Exeter. In *Gooch v. Exeter,*
70 N. H. 413, decided in that year, the court sustained
the law and bottomed its decision on the cases in 15 Md.,
34 Mo., 38 Kans., 29 O. St., 148 Mass., and 3 Bush, which
have already been sufficiently discussed. That court
also espoused the doctrine of the Missouri court that
police officers are state officers which, as we shall see,
has been denounced quite generally by the courts and
the people of other states.

The latest example of an attempt to yoke cities to
the state chariot was in 1900 in Rhode Island when its
legislature enacted a law creating a "Board of Police
Commissioners of the City of Newport," to be appointed
by the governor by and with the advice and consent of
the senate. This law was sustained in *City v. Horton,*
22 R. I. 196. But public protest compelled its repeal
in 1906.

We have just seen that the *Police Commissioners*
case in Kentucky (3 Bush) did not involve the appointment by the governor of officers for a city, since they were
made elective locally. Eliminating, then, that state there
remain but thirteen of the forty-eight states where, at
some time or another, their courts have listened to the
fallacious doctrine that the state may intrude its appointees into the offices of its cities in derogation of the
right of their people to select them. It has been pointed
out that the bell wether of the flock was the case of
People v. Draper, 15 N. Y. 532, where the court warped
the constitution in order to place political favorites in
control of the patronage of the large cities of that state,
denounced by later decisions of that court, and that it
was joined by the case of *Mayor v. State,* 15 Md. 376, in
which the constitution of that state was likewise twisted
in order to place partisans of the Confederacy in control
of the City of Baltimore.

It has also been pointed out that in *State v. St. Louis*
(34 Mo.), *People v. Mahaney* (13 Mich.) and in *Diamond*

v. Cain (21 La. Ann.), not a single case was cited in support of the theory that the state could authorize its
governor to usurp the rightful powers of cities to name
their own officers, while as to *Commonwealth v. Plaisted,*
148 Mass. 375, the supreme court of Nebraska (55 Neb.
480, 518) said: " . . . the question was disposed of by
the court without much consideration and without the
citation of a single authority in support of the conclusion reached." It seems strange that these cases from
New York, Maryland, Missouri, Michigan, Louisiana and
Massachusetts should, under these circumstances, have
been dignified in some decisions of the courts of Ohio,
Nebraska, Kansas, Indiana, Rhode Island, New Hampshire and Georgia, as affording reputable support of acts
of the legislature authorizing the governor to appoint
permanent officers of their cities.

It has been noted that the *Draper* case in New York
and the *Mayor* case in Maryland were grounded upon
the false assumption that their state constitutions affirm-
atively empowered the legislature to authorize the governor to appoint police boards for their cities. By gradual steps the few courts which fell in their wake, despite
the historical evidences in this country and in England
to the contrary, began to enunciate the doctrine that the
state may appoint all their officers if it so decrees. In
the next chapter this doctrine will be discussed and will
be shown not to be the law, and that its practice has been
discarded in practically every state.

The courts in some half dozen states have expanded
that doctrine so as to embrace the claim, probably best
enunciated in *State v. Mason,* 153 Mo. 23, that "the protection of life, property, liberty and the preservation of
the public peace and order in every part, division and
subdivision of the state, is a governmental duty. * * *
From this duty existing in the nature of the state flows
the corresponding power to impose upon municipalities
of its creation a police force of its own creation, and to
compel its support from the municipal funds." When

the supreme court of Missouri announced so bald a doctrine of unrestricted autocratic rule certainly James I and Charles I and James II must have stood up in their graves and applauded. Fortunately there are now but three states which follow that treacherous path,— Maryland, Missouri and Massachusetts.

This un-American doctrine has been vigorously condemned by the courts of the country, none more pointedly than in the *Albertson* case (55 N. Y. 50) in which the court said: "Carried to its logical and legal results, it would permit every city and village of the state to be governed by a police force appointed by a power located at the capitol of the state and emanating from the central head of the state government, to the entire disfranchisement, to this extent, of the local electors." Judge Cooley, in the *Hurlbut* case (24 Mich. 44) aptly said that if the legislature may appoint municipal officers it may send them in from abroad, with power to expend money freed from any control by the inhabitants who must bear the burden, and thus the control of the cities "might be taken over by the party for the time being in power, and municipal government might easily and naturally become the spoils of party." Clearly no court should ever approve a principle of government under which our institutions may be destroyed and our people placed under the rule of an oligarchy.

Of course there is no question that it is the duty of the government to protect the life, liberty and property of its people and to preserve the public peace and order. But it is a *non sequitur* to deduce therefrom that the state, in order to perform that duty, may send down its governor appointed minions into cities and counties to work their will and to have themselves and their appointees paid out of the local treasury such sums as they may demand. Why is this sacred duty of the state performed only in the large cities which afford opportunities for swollen patronage and fat profits for the political bosses and their hangers-on? Is not that sacred duty just as binding upon the state as to its counties? However, in each county is a sheriff, constables, and a prosecuting attorney, whose duties are to see that the laws of the state are enforced. Yet in every county in this country they are elected by the voters. In no instance does the governor appoint them. Is it because they have such comparatively small patronage that they do not tempt the cupidity of the politicians? Or is it because the state has no legitimate power of appointment at all? The county assessor, treasurer, tax collector and controller represent the sovereign power of the state in county fiscal matters, but our history shows with what vigorous determination the people wrested from the colonial governors the appointment of these officers and took over the control of the public purse by making them locally elective. The local judiciary which represents the sovereignty of the state in the administration of justice in the enforcement of the laws of the state is practically all 'elective.

Counties are involuntary corporations created by the state to carry out locally state functions. If any excuse could exist for state appointment of local officers certainly it would be as to the counties. This is not done. But when it comes to cities, which are voluntary corporations, organized by their inhabitants for carrying on their own business, with their own police, fire, health and public works officers, we find a few of the states claiming that they must inject their governor appointees into their cities in order to "safeguard the life, liberty and property of their inhabitants and preserve the public peace and order." The truth, which everyone knows, is that this is done solely in order to build up great political machines in the interest of the party in power in the state. The better reasoned decisions by the great majority of the courts hold that the state is interested only that public functions shall be performed locally and not as to what persons shall perform them so long as they are faithfully performed.

The sovereign power of the state is thus properly exercised and the people are thus fully protected in their persons and in their property.

The supreme court of Missouri and some other courts in its wake have made the bald assertion that a city policeman is a state officer and that therefore he is subject to state appointment. That statement will come as a surprise to the average citizen and has been condemned by courts of the highest standing. Judge Brown in his dissenting opinion in the *Draper* case (15 N. Y.), which dissent we have seen was later adopted as the opinion of that court in the *Albertson* case (55 N. Y.), said: "It cannot be denied, I think, that the police, whose single duty it is to preserve the peace and execute criminal process, by whatever name it may be called, is a local force and its members local officers." In *People v. Coler,* 173 N. Y. 103, that court held that a police commissioner is a city officer. That same court in 1912 in the *Prendergast* case (206 N. Y.) said: "The police department and the departments of education and health in any city are engaged in the discharge of duties which very vitally affect the general public, and yet it would be opposed to widespread and well settled opinion to hold that the members of such departments are state officials in the sense of being engaged in its service." In 1899 the supreme court of California (123 Cal. 456) held that the fixing of salaries of the police and fire departments is a city affair, and in 1907 the court of appeals of that state (6 Cal. App. 217) held that the removal of a chief of police is also a municipal matter.

These decisions conform, as we have seen, to the well established rule in England long in force before she established her colonies in America, and to the practice during all the colonial period in this country and for many years thereafter.

Some of our courts have sought to justify their decisions sustaining the control of police by the state on the claim that it is a part of the state constabulary.

But that is far fetched. The state constabulary is an organization separate and apart from that of the local police. They are as distinct from each other as is the state militia from the precinct constables. The state constabulary enforces laws state-wide in their operation while the police enforce local municipal ordinances and regulations. The jurisdiction of the former reaches throughout the state; that of the latter is limited to a locality. The state constabulary is paid by the state; the police is paid by the city. To confound them is to destroy common sense.

Dr. Munro in his "Municipal Administration" clearly analyzes this situation and points out that the chief argument in favor of state control of municipal police is the claim that thus it is kept out of the control of local politicians who sometimes make use of it corruptly; that the exercise of local police power is an element of state sovereignty for the preservation of the public peace and safety, although it be an affront to the principle of municipal home rule; that while in some cases state control over city police may have resulted beneficially, for a time, yet, on the other hand, governors and other high state officials have used it as a means of promoting their own political interest; that the policy of state interference in municipal administration is always resented by the taxpayers who have to pay the bill and have no say as to what they shall pay, imposed by authorities who have no strong incentive to keep the expenditures down; that while the courts have differed as to whether city policemen are state officers, yet the average citizen does not look upon them in that light, since they get their pay checks at the city hall, ordinarily have no jurisdiction outside the city limits, their badge is that of the city and not of the state, and that "it is hard to convince him that state police control is not a ruthless invasion of his right to municipal home rule." (pp. 314-315.)

After this chapter had been set up in type word

came from St. Louis that its people are finally taking steps to free themselves from governor domination. Under an ordinance adopted by its city council Mayor Dickmann appointed the "Mayor's Advisory Committee" and, on February 20, 1941, it made its report laying emphasis on how that city is scourged by a governor-appointed police board, bolstered up by the courts. That report, among other things, says: "Some of the powers conferred upon this board go unbelievably far in infringing upon and restricting the powers of local goverment of the city as a municipal corporation. For example, the city authorities are required to allow the board the use of property * * * owned by the city * * * thus deprived of the use and control of its own property. The legislative body of the city is peremptorily required to set apart and appropriate whatever amount the board of police commissioners may specify as needed, without recourse or power of review of the estimates as to policy or need, no matter how extravagant the estimates may be in relation to the financial condition of the city and the measures of economy that might have to be applied to other city activities, or what new policies they might provide committing the city to future heavy expense beyond its ability to finance without serious detriment to other important functions. Irrespective of any such appropriations, the city must audit and pay all claims passed by the board and certified as entitled to payment, up to the total of the estimates. The city is forbidden to provide, or to pay for, any other police force, * * * and in the event of failure of the board to provide adequate police service the city can do nothing to assure peace and order within its own limits."

The report continues: "These provisions were made on the pretext that the policing of the larger municipalities is a state function. But the making and enforcing of police regulations, in the broader sense, ordinarily are accepted as the very heart and essence of local government and the management and control of local affairs. Police administration has very close interrelationships with many, if not most, other matters of local government, calling for close coordination with other activities in many important respects. It cannot be taken out of the scheme of local government without leaving a void. As a matter of fact, the steps taken toward making the police force in any city covered by such legislation a state agency in any real sense, fall so far short of being complete, that the pretext that local policing is a state function is revealed as a very flimsy one."

The report aptly says: "The laws under discussion apply to cities of 200,000 or more population. The question naturally arises why the essential *character* of police administration, as state or local, should vary with the size of the city. If the ground of the assumption of the powers by the state is alleged to be poor local police administration in the larger cities, then the whole groundwork of justification for 'home rule' in municipal government in the state, and the effect of constitutional provisions therefor, begin to crumble."

Finally the report lays squarely at the door of the courts blame for this condition: "The courts have done their bit toward nullifying the effects of 'home rule' and 'city-county consolidation' provisions of the constitution, and their expressions of state policy in such matters, and toward making a patchwork affair of the organization of local government in the city." (Further on this point see Chapter XVII.)

CHAPTER VII.

A RETURN TO LAW AND REASON

The preceding Chapter presents a sorry picture of political and judicial jugglery. Legislatures and courts alike had flouted the constitution and had ruthlessly trampled upon the rights of the people. Legislatures generally ran true to form in their avid quest for partisan advantage. Several of the courts were as fickle in their decisions as are the shifting winds. Hardly was the ink dry on a decision when they reversed themselves upon the entry of a new judge elected by the reactionaries. Some courts espoused the doctrine that the existence of municipalities and their right to select their own officers rested upon the capricious and precarious will of the legislature. Some of them had even gone so far in boosting partisan control of our cities as to elevate a city policeman to the dignity of a state officer. The constitution was twisted into a mere rag by both the legislatures and the courts. Chief Justice Charles Evans Hughes once said: "We are under the constitution, but the constitution is what the courts say it is."

The courts further, by a species of legerdemain, created a legal pyramid which they stood on its apex as its unstable base. For a while they bolstered it up by the legalistic fetish of "precedent" which meant more to many of them than did justice and common sense. Take for instance the *Draper* case (15 N. Y.) which that court later said *was not the law*. But it was used as a precedent and the basis upon which the *Mayor* case (15

Md.) was made the second story of this legalistic pyramid. Then a third story was added in the *Police Commissioners* case (3 Bush) based on the two former cases
as precedents. A fourth story was then added in the
Covington case (29 O. St.) and a fifth story was further
added in the Smith case (44 O. St.) based upon the former four cases as precedents. A sixth story was also
added by the *Redell* case (63 Neb.) based upon the
former five cases as precedents. A seventh story was
added by the *Hunter* case (38 Kans.) based upon the
former six precedents. An eighth story was added by
the *Koslem* case (130 Ind.) based upon the former seven
precedents. A ninth story was added by the *Perry* case
(114 Ga. 871) based upon the former eight precedents.
A tenth story was added by the *Gooch* case (70 N. H.)
based upon the former nine precedents. By this time
this legalistic pyramid with its towering height, resting
on its apex at its base *upon an overruled case* used as an
illegitimate forbear for all these later cases piled upon
each other as precedents, became very top-heavy and
finally it fell under decisions of the courts themselves or
under laws forced from legislatures by an outraged public or by constitutional amendments adopted by the people under their sovereign power. The legalistic idol was
toppled from its throne.

Fortunately, under our system of government, courts
and legislatures are quite uniformly dependent upon the
will of the people expressed at the ballot box. The voters
were not slow in retiring faithless judges and in replacing
them with those who could be trusted. The people,
aroused to action, elected legislators who repealed reactionary laws which had trenched upon the liberties of the
cities. In many of the states the people amended their
constitutions so as to make doubly sure that neither the
courts nor the legislatures could ever again trifle with
the right of the municipalities to manage their own affairs under officers of their own choosing. Thus was
brought about a return to law and reason.

Some of the courts had gone so far as to announce the pernicious doctrine, dignified by several law text writers, that the state may create and destroy municipalities at will and had deduced therefrom the power in the state to appoint officers for its municipalities. There is no sound basis for any such holding. Municipalities are voluntary corporations created upon the request or consent of their inhabitants to serve their own local needs under officers locally selected. Any deviation is isolated and without factual historic basis. At best such exception is a mere legalistic theory fondly embraced by some courts. Chief Justice Marshall in the famous *Dartmouth College* case stated that while it is the theory of the British constitution that Parliament is omnipotent over corporate charters yet to put that theory into practice "might give a shock to public opinion which that government has chosen to avoid." Judge Cooley in his work on "Municipal Corporations" says that while a legislature might create a municipality against the will of its inhabitants, yet to do so "is antagonistic to the republican spirit and repugnant to the principles of democracy." (p. 38.)

In America, just as in England, the general practice has been that a municipal corporation is created only upon the direct request or by the free consent of its own people. As laid down in 43 *Corpus Juris,* p. 84, "the creation of a municipality with the consent of the inhabitants is in keeping with the Anglo-Saxon spirit and American institutions, especially the principle of home rule in self-government," although the contrary has been held by a few courts. Chief Justice Green in *City v. Society* (24 N. J. Law) clearly stated the prevailing rule as follows: "Under the British constitution charters are usually granted by the crown, in the exercise of its prerogative. It is essential to their validity that they be accepted by the corporation. * * * In regard to public or municipal corporations, sound principle requires that they should not be forced upon the corporators without

their consent. Such is the well settled principle in
England in regard to all municipal corporations created
by the crown. Though the king has the power to create
corporations, he cannot impose them upon his subjects
without their consent. Whether it be an original act of
incorporation, or a charter by which the franchises of
a pre-existing corporation is altered, it must be accepted
by a majority of those to whom it is granted. It is not
denied that a municipal corporation may be, either by
the legislature or by the British parliament by virtue of
the plenitude of its powers, imposed upon the corporators
without their consent. It doubtless may be done. But it
would be alike against the genius of our government and
the spirit of the British constitution. It would be, in the
nervous language of Lord Thurlow, an atrocious violation of principle, which would cut every Englishman to
the bone. Almost invariably in practice municipal charters have been granted or altered by our legislature, in
accordance with the expressed will of the corporators.
The exceptions are very rare. They have occurred in
seasons of high excitement; they cannot be reconciled to
sound principle. They are to be regarded as beacons to
be shunned, not as precedents to be followed." The supreme court of Ohio in *Hamilton Co. v. Mighels* (7 O. St.
109), quoted with approval in *Kahn v. Sutro,* (114 Cal.),
thus stated the rule: "Municipal corporations proper are
called into existence through the direct solicitation or by
the free consent of the people who compose them." Already noted is Finer's statement concerning the English
boroughs that "they were not created by the central authority" but that they simply "came to be regulated and
given legal form by it."

Regardless of any legalistic theory to the contrary,
the actual practice is so universal that a municipal corporation may rightfully be created by the state only upon
the request or consent of its inhabitants that it must
logically follow that a municipality may not be destroyed
except upon its request or consent. Indeed, many of the

state constitutions or statutes now provide that even the consolidation of cities, or their annexation, or the extension of their boundaries, may not be made except upon the vote of the people directly affected.

In Chapter II mention has been made of the judicial oligarchy which, for many years, dominated the officers of the parish and the county in England, and of the corrupt forfeiture by the king's bench of the charter of London and of other boroughs. In time this evil control by the courts over county, parish and borough, was ended by the English people. While kings had sporadically usurped the power of creating illegitimate boroughs for selfish ends, yet it must be noted that none of them had ever claimed or exercised the power of destroying them save through the corrupt medium of their complaisant courts. At the most neither king nor Parliament directly did more than to consolidate boroughs in the public interest and for the mutual welfare of their inhabitants, generally with their consent or at their request.

Therefore, the broad statement made by some courts and text writers that the state may create and destroy municipal corporations at will is not legally sound in practice. Outside the power to consolidate them, and the prevailing rule now is that this may be done only upon the consent of the inhabitants affected, the power of the state is limited (1) to prescribing their corporate form, (2) to designating their functions and powers, and (3) to specifying what officers the people may locally select to exercise those functions and powers except as controlled by specific constitutional provision. Beyond that the legislature may not rightfully go. For centuries this rule has been followed as to the English boroughs. For nearly two hundred years this rule had been followed in America until it was ruthlessly overturned for a time by some courts under the trumped up doctrine that the state may create and destroy municipalities at will and under that spurious cloak may steal away their liberties. The state has neither moral nor legal right to take from a municipality its right to select its own officers, so long as they faithfully perform the duties and functions required of them, and certainly it has no right to displace them by appointees of the governor under the plea that they are state officers. To justify this latter practice a few courts invented the theory that a city policeman holds the dignified position of an officer of the state but the prevailing rule is that he is but a local officer walking flat-footedly on his limited beat.

It will be recalled that the ill-starred *Draper* case (15 N. Y.) was the first to depart from the path of judicial rectitude on this point, leading a herd of deluded followers along the wrong trail. However, in that case Judge Brown in a dissenting opinion concurred in by Judge Comstock, which soon was made the prevailing rule of that court in the *Albertson* case (55 N. Y.), forcefully warned the court that it was blindly forgetful of the lessons of history. He said: "We learn from Blackstone and the elementary writers, that the civil administration of England, its counties, hundreds, tithings, or towns, date as far back as the times of the great Alfred. In all the changes of policy, of dynasty, of feuds and internal war, and even of conquest, which that country has undergone since the day these organizations were created, they have never been abated or abandoned. They are substantially at this time what they were before the Norman invasion. Wherever the Anglo-Saxon race have gone, wherever they have carried their language and their laws, these communities, each with a local administration of its own has gone with them. * * * Here have been the seats of modern civilization, the nurseries of public spirit, and the centers of constitutional liberty. They are the opposites of those systems which collect all power at a common centre, to be wielded by a common will, and to effect a common purpose; which absorb all political authority, exercise all its functions, distribute all its patronage, repress the public activity, stifle the public voice and crush out the public liberty."

Some courts, in order to bolster up the invasion by
the legislature of the right of our cities to select their
own officers, have announced the doctrine that when the
states adopted their first constitutions their people surrendered to the state the right of their municipalities to
manage their own affairs under officers of their own
choosing. But that theory runs counter to historical
fact. Municipalities had existed long before these constitutions were framed, and they had freely exercised the
power of selecting their own officers. It is unthinkable
that their people ever intended to surrender home rule
rights for which they had battled so courageously and
to which they had clung so tenaciously through the years.
The constitutions did not say that these rights should be
lost to them.

Since the New York court, as has been seen, started
the trend of decisions in the wrong direction it is well to
note how it later rectified its wrong. Judge Brown in
his dissenting opinion in the *Draper* case, later made the
rule of that court, said that the legislature "may enlarge
or circumscribe their (the municipalities') territorial limits, increase or decrease their numbers, separate them
into parts and annex some of their parts to parts of
others, but they must assume the form and be known and
governed only as counties, cities and towns, because their
distinctive character and attributes cannot be changed or
destroyed without confounding the entire scheme of civil
government provided in the instrument (the constitution). * * * These considerations lead me to the conclusion that it was designed to place these civil divisions
and the powers of appointment, election and local administration which the people then exercised, beyond
the reach of legislative abrogation." Even Judge Denio,
who wrote the majority opinion in the *Draper* case, said
that "we must keep in mind that the constitution was not
framed for a people entering into a political society for
the first time, but for a community already organized
and furnished with legal and political institutions

adapted to all or nearly all the purposes of civil government, and that it was not intended to abolish these institutions, *except so far as they were repugnant to the constitution* thus framed.''

In the *Albertson* case (55 N. Y.) the court said: ''The theory of the constitution is that the several counties, cities and villages are, *of right,* entitled to choose whom they will have to rule over them, and that this right cannot be taken from them and the electors and inhabitants disfranchised by any act of the legislature, or of any or all the departments of the state government combined. This right of self-government lies at the foundation of our institutions and cannot be disturbed or interfered with, even in respect to the smallest of the divisions into which the state is divided for governmental purposes, without weakening the entire foundation, and hence it is a right not only to be carefully guarded by every department of the government, but every infraction or evasion of it to be promptly met and condemned, especially by the courts, when such acts become the subject of judicial inquiry.''

In the later case of *Rathbone v. Wirth,* (150 N. Y.), the court said: ''The right of local self-government, — a right which *inheres* in a republican form of government, *and with reference to which our constitution was framed,* — is something which we took over, or rather continued, from the English system of government, and, as Judge Cooley has remarked with reference to the constitutions of the states 'if not expressly recognized, it is still to be understood that all these instruments are framed with its present existence and anticipated continuance in view.' (Cooley, Const. Lim. 35.) The principle is one which it takes but little reflection to convince the mind of being fundamental in our governmental system as constituting strength to the national life, in its educational and formative effect upon the citizen. It means that in the local, or political, subdivisions of the state, the people of the locality shall administer their own local affairs, to the extent that that right is not restricted by some constitutional provision."

This last sentence merits especial attention, since it sets forth the rule that municipal corporations, under the history of the development of our system of self-government, have the right to administer their own affairs *"to the extent that the right is not restricted by some constitutional provision."* It is true that the broad statement is made by courts that the Federal constitution is a grant of powers and must be strictly construed but that state constitutions are a limitation upon the powers to be exercised by legislatures and in the absence of such limitations they are supreme. But it must be remembered that the people themselves are the state; that legislatures are but their servants or agents; that it is unthinkable that the people would blindly surrender their right of local self-government into the keeping of untried agents who have all too often proven to be faithless. Repeatedly in this chapter statements of the courts are quoted that the right of self-government in the cities and villages of this country *existed and was fully exercised before any constitutions were framed, and that the people, in framing and adopting them, never itended to abandon their dearly prized right of selecting all their own officers.* Disagreement with this judicial point of view by some courts has brought much woe to some of our cities.

In *People v. Tax Commission* (174 N. Y.) the court said: "Even prior to the Magna Charta some cities, boroughs and towns had various customs and liberties which had been granted by the crown, or had subsisted through long user, and among them was the right to elect certain local officers from their own citizens, with some restrictions, to manage their own purely local affairs. These customs and liberties, with other rights, had been so often trampled upon by the king as to arouse deep hatred of centralization of power, and we find among the many grants of the Great Charter that 'the city of London shall have all its ancient liberties and free customs as well by land as by water. Furthermore, we will and grant that all other cities and burghs and towns * * * shall have all these liberties and free customs.' * * * The rights thus secured after a long struggle and by great pressure, although at times denied and violated by the ruling monarch, were never lost, but were brought over by the colonists the same as they brought the right to breathe, and they would have parted with the one as soon as the other. The liberties and customs of localities reappear on a novel and wider basis in the town meetings of New England and the various colonies, including the colony of New York. The right of the inhabitants of townships and manors to meet at stated times in public town meeting, elect town officers and transact town business, was well established while we were a colony and was recognized by different statutes enacted by the governor's council and by the general assembly. * * * *The powers and duties* of these officers were regulated by statute, but *the right to select them* resided in the people of the locality and was stubbornly insisted upon as inviolable. * * * The constitution of 1777 recognized local self-government. * * * Thus our earliest *constitution did not create* the right to elect the administrative officers of towns, *but continued* it as it had existed during the history of the colony while it was under the dominion of the English crown.''

It has been noted how the Kentucky court fell into the wake of the *Draper* case which was later overruled. In the *Police Commissioners* case (3 Bush) it had sustained a law taking from Louisville its long used right of selecting its police officers. Evidently that case was overruled in the later *Carrithers* case (126 Ky.) where that court said: ''As this country was settled by Englishmen, who brought over the customs and laws of the mother country, it was to be expected that substantially the same system of town government was instituted here. After the Revolution the sovereignty of the king and

Parliament was lodged in the state. Thereafter it granted
charters to towns, *not as privileges* conferred by favor
and for price, but as a part of a system conserving the
principles of liberty as found in self-government.'' In
the earlier *Thompson* case (113 Ky.) that court said:
''There were cities and towns before the constitution was
adopted. At the date of its adoption they were managing their own little affairs. They were employing and
paying members of their fire departments, as in times
gone by they had managed their own voluntary fire department.'' The same was also true of the police departments and the public works departments of the cities of
that state and of those in every other state when they
adopted their first constitutions.

It has also been noted that the Michigan court in the
Mahaney case (13 Mich.) had sustained a law authorizing
the governor to appoint police officers for Detroit. But
in that case the question of the home rule right of that
city to appoint its own officers was not raised. In the
later *Hurlbut* case (24 Mich.) that court clearly indicated
that its decision would have been different had it been
raised. Chief Justice Christiancy, and Judges Campbell
and Cooley, each wrote opinions in the *Hurlbut* case
which have merited and have received high approbation.
The chief justice pointed to the history of our country,
the nature of our institutions, the vital importance given
to local self-government in all the states, as well as the
general hostility to every thing in the nature of interference therewith by the state, which made it improbable
that the framers of the state constitution, and the people
in adopting it, intended to vest in the legislature the appointment of local officers or to deprive towns and villages of the right of selecting them. Judge Campbell,
in speaking of that constitution, said: ''We must not
forget, in studying its terms, that most of them had a
settled meaning before its adoption. *Instead of it being
the source of our laws and liberties, it is, in the main, no
more than a mere recognition and re-enactment of an*

accepted system. The rights reserved are ancient rights, and the municipal bodies recognized in it, and required to be perpetuated, were *already existing,* with known elements and functions. They were not towns or counties or cities and villages, in the abstract—or municipalities which had lost all their old liberties by central usurpation — but A m e r i c a n and Michigan municipalities of common-law origin, and having no less than common-law franchises. * * * Incorporated cities and boroughs have always, both in England and in America, been self-governing communities within such scope of jurisdiction as their charters vest in the corporate body. * * * Our constitution cannot be understood or carried out at all, except on the theory of self-government; and the intention to preserve it is quite apparent. In every case where provision is made by the constitution for local officers, they are selected by local action. All counties, towns and school districts are made to depend upon it. All elections are required to be in local divisions where the electors reside. * * * It certainly cannot be that the state can control these bodies by sending its own agents there. * * * A city has no constitutional safeguards for its people, or it has the right to have all its officers appointed at home.'' Judge Cooley said: ''The legislature has created this board, and it has appointed its members; and both the one and the other have been done under a claim of right which, unless I wholly misunderstand it, would justify that body in taking to itself the entire and exclusive government of the city, and the appointment of all its officers, excepting only the judicial, for which, by the constitution, other provision is expressly made. And the question, broadly and nakedly stated, can be nothing short of this: Whether local self-government in this state is or is not a mere privilege, conceded by the legislature in its discretion, and which may be withdrawn at any time at pleasure?'' He exhaustively reviewed the sources of government in this country, and then said: ''The historical fact is that local governments universally

in this country were either simultaneously with, or pre-
ceded, the more central authority." He pointed out that
in Massachusetts, originally a democracy, this was true,
and that in Connecticut the several settlements originated
their own governments, while in Rhode Island the local
organization with its self-government was first, and that
always the power of choosing officers was exercised locally. He also pointed out that if the legislature may
appoint municipal officers it may send them in from
abroad, with power to expend money freed from any
control by the inhabitants who must bear the burden, and
thus the control of the cities "might be taken over by
the party for the time being in power, and municipal
government might easily and naturally become the spoils
of party, as state and national offices unfortunately now
are. * * * When the state reaches out and draws to itself
and appropriates the powers which from time immemo-
rial have been legally possessed and exercised, and in-
troduces into its legislation the centralizing ideas of con-
tinental Europe, under which despotism, whether of the
monarch or commune, alone has flourished, we seem
forced back upon and compelled to take up and defend
the plainest and most primary axioms of free government, as if even in Anglican liberty, which has been
gained step by step, through extorted charters and bills
of rights, the punishment of kings and the overthrow of
dynasties, nothing was settled and nothing established."

To show how inconceivably wrong was the decision
in the *Horton* case (22 R. I.) which sustained a law vesting in the governor the power of appointing a board of
police commissioners for Newport it is only necessary to
recall the pure democracy enjoyed by all the New England towns during two hundred years from the time the
first was founded and how Roger Williams had braved
a wilderness to establish a free community at Providence.
In each of these towns the people selected all their officers. When Rhode Island became a charter colony in
1647 it was formed by the union of the four independent

settlements of Providence, Newport, Portsmouth and Warwick. They reserved the right to manage their own affairs. Thus local government became a vested right. After having enjoyed this right for 180 years, to 1843 when the first constitution was adopted, it is unthinkable that the people ever intended to surrender their most prized possession by approving that instrument.

The Indiana court in the *Koslem* case (130 Ind.) had sustained a law authorizing the governor and other state officers to appoint a board of police commissioners for Terra Haute. The doctrine of that case was evidently overruled in the later *Fox* case (158 Ind.) where the court held unconstitutional a law authorizing the governor to appoint a board of public safety for Fort Wayne, and said: "It is an historical fact that the first settlers of this country were induced to hazard the unknown in the hope that they might escape the oppressions of a government concentrated in a single man, and find a country where all civil power should reside in the people, and be exercised by the people alone in determining their modes of government. It was the right to participate * * * in the selection of ruling officers * * *. The first comers' love of freedom, which had been intensified by their hatred of tyranny, found expression in the simplest forms of local self-government, in the towns and villages of New England. Self-government is free government. * * * It was taught in the schools, the churches and town meetings. Incorporated communities practiced it without restriction or question, and, as population increased, cities, boroughs, counties and states sprang up, the right was carefully protected, fostered and observed, until today it may be said that for two hundred years before the adoption of our constitution the right of local self-government had been the heart, the soul, the life of our political system." That court, in the *Evansville* case, (118 Ind.), had already said that "before written constitutions, the people possessed the full power of local self-government. * * * *They still possess such of that* *power as has not been delegated.* All the power which the people have delegated is what has passed from them by the constitution."

The Ohio court in the *Covington* case (29 O. St.) had sustained a law vesting in the governor the power to appoint a board of police commissioners for Cincinnati. The doctrine of that case was evidently overruled in the later *Commissioners* case (54 O. St.) where the court said: "The system of self-government existed under general laws at the adoption of the present constitution, and there is nothing in it, nor in any of its provisions, from which a design can be inferred to in any way impair it; on the contrary every provision of that instrument, in any way related to the subject, manifests a purpose to preserve it unimpaired to the people. * * * Commenting on the general features of a written constitution, Judge Cooley observes: 'Local self-government having always been a part of the English and American systems, we shall look for its recognition in any such instrument. And if not expressly recognized, it is still to be understood that all these instruments are framed with its *present existence and anticipated continuance* in view.' Constitutional Limitations, 45."

Thus it is seen that practically all the courts that went wrong under the leadership of the discredited *Draper* case (15 N. Y.) rectified their error and announced that prior to the adoption of state constitutions the right rested in the people of municipalities to select all their officers, — that this right was not lost by the adoption of the constitutions but that it remained unimpaired. In addition, where courts or legislatures had interfered with that right, the people had been quick to elect legislators who enacted laws to rectify the situation, or constitutional amendments have been adopted by the people so as to prevent any attempt to interfere with its exercise.

Also in 1873 the New York legislature elected by an outraged public repealed the laws which had been enacted depriving New York City, Brooklyn, Schenec-

tady, Troy and other cities of the state of their right to
select the officers of their police, fire and health departments, and for sixty-eight years there has been no interference with that right. In 1877 the Louisiana legislature revested in New Orleans the right to select the
officers of its police department which the "carpetbaggers" had taken from them nine years before, and for
sixty-four years the exercise of that right has not been
disturbed. In 1892 the people of California by constitutional amendment restored to San Francisco the right
to name all its officers which had been interfered with
by a court decision in 1878, and for forty-nine years that
right has not been disturbed. In 1896 the Michigan legislature confirmed in the cities of that state the right of
selecting their own officers which had been assailed in
1865, and for forty-five years this has not been changed.
In 1898 the Kansas Legislature restored to Leavenworth
the right to name its police officers which had been taken
from it temporarily in 1887, and for forty-three years
that right has not been molested. In 1902 the Georgia
legislature restored to Americus the right to select its
police officers of which it had been deprived in 1889, and
for thirty-nine years that right has not been disturbed.
In 1902 the Legislature of Ohio revested in its cities the
right to select its police officers which had been interfered with intermittently since 1866, and for thirty-nine
years that right has not been interfered with. In 1902
the people of Colorado by constitutional amendment restored to Denver full power over all its officers with which
the legislature had interfered in 1887, and for thirty-nine
years, with a slight interim, that right has not been molested. In 1905 the Indiana legislature revested in the
cities of that state the right to select their officers, and for
thirty-six years no change has been made. In 1906 the
legislature of Rhode Island, only six years after it had
taken from Newport its age-old right to select its police
officers, restored it and for thirty-six years that right
has not been disturbed. In 1909 the Nebraska legislature

revested in the cities of that state full power to select all their officers which had been interfered with in 1887, and for thirty-two years that right has not been interfered with.

Thus the people of this country have overwhelmingly repudiated the spurious doctrine that the state may interfere with the right of municipalities to select their own officers. Judge Cooley, in the *Hurlbut* case (24 Mich.) clearly defined the legitimate power of the state over its cities as follows: *"The state may mould local institutions* according to its views of policy and expediency: but local government is matter of absolute right; and the state cannot take it way. It would be *the boldest mockery* to speak of the city as possessing municipal liberty where *the state not only shaped* its government, *but at discretion sent in its own agents to administer it."* And again attention is called to Finer's statement concerning English boroughs that "they were not created by central authority" but that they simply "came to be *regulated and given legal form by it."* Maltbie, in his article on "Municipal Government" in *The Americana* (encyclopedia), in speaking upon this point, says: "There should be central *administrative supervision instead of legislative interference.* * * * The state should control, *but not administer,* and the extent of this control should vary with the state's interest. *In no case is it pardonable for the state to appoint local officers.* If the function is a local function and if the expense is borne locally, the state should not interfere, except possibly to remove an officer who has been guilty of malfeasance, or to appoint when a locality refuses to perform the duties imposed by the state." Judge Cooley, in the *Hurlbut* case, further said: "The right in the state is a right, *not to run and operate the machinery* of local government, *but to provide for and put it in operation."*

In the absence of constitutional restrictions the legislature may define the powers and duties of officers of cities and prescribe the manner in which they may be exercised. Thus does the state "mould local institutions," and thus is the government of cities and counties "shaped." Beyond that the state may not legitimately go. To go further is to violate every principle of liberty and to destroy the right of self-government.

Indeed, an analysis of the cases broadly stating that cities are the creatures of the legislature and derive their powers and existence therefrom, will disclose that in most of them the question there passed upon was not whether the state could send its appointed agents into the county or into the city to supplant officers that had been locally selected, but was limited to the question of what *powers* the city or the county could exercise in the conduct of its affairs. Thus it has been held in such cases that, without authorization from the legislature, a city may not impose an occupational tax (316 Ill. 519; 124 Ark. 346; 314 Ill. 316; 313 Ill. 98; 220 Ill. 319; 87 W. Va. 191; 106 Kan. 363, but to the contrary see 143 Cal. 553); nor prevent a telephone company from constructing its lines in the street (226 Fed. 82); nor enact an ordinance as to fire hazards (39 Ia. 447); nor fixing opening and closing hours for businesses (87 W. Va. 127; 131 N. C. 814); nor authorize the issuance of a subpoena for the production of private records (184 N. Y. Supp 518); nor as to the issuance of liquor licenses (150 N .C. 799); nor as to regulating hours of labor (21 Okla. Crim. 168). It is evident that cases, such as these, lend no support to the claim that the state may interfere with the rightful power of cities to select all their officers.

Outside of the little town of Exeter in New Hampshire, there remain but three states which retain laws empowering the governor to control the police force in their four largest cities, — Baltimore, Boston, St. Louis and Kansas City. The latter city was driven into the group only last year by the corrupt use of its police department under the notorious Pendergast political machine, now fortunately driven from power. It was a case, however, of the people jumping from the frying pan into the fire. The people of Boston have repeatedly tried to free themselves from the appointment of its police commissioner by the governor but have been thwarted by the up-state politicians intent on retaining the patronage and power enjoyed by them thereunder. Baltimore, however, is evidently content, since in 1920 its people voted 87,111 to 73,510, under a referendum authorized by law, against transferring from the governor to the mayor the appointment of its police commission. For eighty years the people of St. Louis have been somnolently content to have a governor appoint their police board with power to write its own ticket for expenditures which must be paid by the taxpayers without right of protest or objection either as to reasonableness or necessity, and likewise have seemed content that a governor appoint a board to run their elections. However, we have seen on page 117 that the city is now finally rousing itself. The town of Exeter in New Hampshire is the only one in that state where the governor appoints its police board and its people seem to be doing nothing about regaining their former liberties.

In that connection it is well to note what this overlordship of the governor as to the police in these cities costs their taxpayers. Eliminating Exeter since it is a small town, and also Kansas City which has only recently gone under governor domination, we find that the police departments of Baltimore, Boston and St. Louis during the last fiscal year cost their people an average of $6.42 per capita. In comparison then note that the police departments of the City and County of San Francisco, the City and County of Denver, the City and County of Honolulu, and the cities of Cincinnati, Rochester, Houston, Seattle, Cleveland and Washington, during the last fiscal year under local appointment and control, cost their people an average of but $3.94 per capita or only 61% of the cost in the cities of Baltimore, Boston and St. Louis under governor domination. In Houston the cost per capita was but $2.18, in Honolulu $1.88 and in Denver $2.97. In the nine last named cities the combined population is 4,304,379 as against only 2,445,958 in Baltimore, Boston and St. Louis, yet the total police cost is almost as much in the three as it is in the nine. The police department in Kansas City even under the corrupt Pendergast regime cost $1,149,602 in the fiscal year ending April 30, 1939. On July 12, 1939, the board of police commissioners appointed by the governor took office under the new law and up to April 30, 1940, had expended $1,024,033 or at the rate of $1,280,665 per year, or $131,063 more than the local administration had expended, an increase of 11.4 per cent just as a starter. It costs to have governor appointed boards run municipal affairs!

These conditions would seem to justify emphasizing the words of the supreme court of Michigan (58 Mich. 212) in its stirring declaration that "the form of our state government presupposes that the people of each locality, each municipal district or political unit, are intelligent and virtuous enough to be fully capable of self-government, and the idea that the further removed the election officers are from the people the less we encourage fraud and the more nearly we attain virtue at the ballot box, is not in harmony with the theory and spirit of our institutions." The same might be said as to a police force, a board of public works, a health or a fire department. The supreme court of California (51 Cal. 15) said: "If there is danger in a city that the indifference of the more honest and efficient may suffer the corrupt to seize and abuse the local authority, this risk equally exists with reference to the state and national government. To a certain extent the danger that the people may neglect their public duties exists everywhere, and can only be guarded against by greater diligence; it is an incident to our form of government—the price we pay for our inestimable freedom." To shirk this duty by supinely permitting the state to send in its appointed agents to perform functions within a city constitutes an indictment

against its people not easily defended against. In New
York (6 Hun 277) the court said: "Local self-government is the school which fits the people for self-government. Local self-government is the result and also the
most efficient preserver of liberty," and again its highest
court (150 N. Y. 459) declared that the right of self-
government is a cardinal principle of our form of republican government and is one "which takes but little reflection to convince the mind of being fundamental in our
general system as contributing strength to the national
life, in its educational and formative effect upon the
citizen."

After wandering in the wilderness for a time and
having indulged in the worship of false gods set up by
designing legislatures and faithless courts the people in
practically every state have returned to the faith and
practice of their fathers upon which must securely rest
the permanent structure of local government. Any departure leads to its autocratic control, and that means
disintegration of individual and political liberty. The
slightest infraction of that liberty and of its free exercise in the government of our cities corrupts the administration of public affairs and inculcates in the minds of
their citizens a disregard of law.

Fortunate it is that the people through amendment
of their state constitutions or by their control over their
laws through the initiative and the referendum have
brought back into a living force the logical and wise
definition of Judge Cooley, worthy of repetition, as to the
legitimate power of the state over cities as follows: "The
state may *mould* local institutions according to its views
of policy and expediency; but local government is matter
of absolute right; and the state cannot take it away. It
would be the *boldest mockery* to speak of a city as possessing municipal liberty where the state not only *shaped*
its government, *but at its discretion sent in its own agents
to administer it.*"

To the extent that the state violates this fundamental principle it destroys local government, debases the stamina and character of the people of our municipalities, and makes them the helpless prey of designing and cheap demagogues appointed by some governor more anxious to take care of his political gang than to serve his state. In succeeding chapters will be found many notorious examples of this faithless performance of a public trust.

CHAPTER VIII.

SELF-GOVERNMENT IN CITIES AND COUNTIES

The invasion by courts and legislatures of the free exercise of the right of self-government and of choosing their own officers aroused the people to action and this greatly influenced courts in reversing their pernicious decisions and legislatures in repealing destructive laws. The people decided, however, that these evils should not be repeated and took steps to stop them. Fortunately, the initial weapon was at hand. It had been forged in the constitutions of the various states and in the constitution of the United States wherein had been provided the referendum and the initiative. When Massachusetts framed its first constitution in 1778 it was submitted to a referendum vote of the people for adoption or rejection. This method of adopting a constitution was followed by all the original thirteen states, later by all the new states, and when the Federal constitution was adopted in 1787 it was by referendum vote of the several states. In these constitutions provision was made that they could be amended only by submitting the amendment proposal to a vote of the people or their representatives, and Congress and the states were given the right to initiate such proposals. Thus was firmly embedded in the organic law of the nation and of the states the principle of the initiative and the referendum. When evils threatened destruction of self-government the exercise of this power was extended so as to vest in the people the right to initiate and to have referred to their vote not only constitutional amendments but also state laws and city ordinances. As to the latter Missouri led the way when, in 1875, it adopted an amendment to its constitution vesting in St. Louis the power of the initiative and the referendum and in 1879 California by constitutional amendment vested in San Francisco like power. The state of Washington, in 1889, extended this power so as to cover state laws. In less than a generation this great movement to place the people in control of their constitutions and of their laws had spread into the great majority of the states reaching from Minnesota to Louisiana and from Maine to California.

But with all these safeguards thrown around the nomination and election of public officers, and with the initiative and the referendum giving the people power over their constitutions and their laws, there was found to be one thing wanting. And that was the lack of power to get rid of a faithless, or an incompetent or even a corrupt, public officer except through the tedious and cumbersome method of impeachment. It is worthy of note that the early settlers felt this lack. The first mention of it is when the hardy pioneers in western North Carolina (now Tennessee) met in Watauga in 1772, drew up a temporary form of government under the title "Articles of the Watauga Association" and provided therein for the "recall of unsatisfactory judges." Even at that early day judges were evidently sometimes faithless to their trust. During the generation when most of the states were placing in their constitutions or in their laws the power of the initiative and the referendum they were also placing therein the power to recall public officers. The new state of Washington led the way in 1889 by adopting a section in its constitution that all state officers could be recalled and that specified city officers could be recalled. This was followed by many of the states and several have provided for the recall of judges.

These great movements helped restore to the people their rights which, at times, had been filched from them by the courts and by the legislatures, and threw safeguards around them from further assault. In order further to protect the cities there arose a strong movement for "Home Rule." As tersely stated by the supreme court of California in 1875 in the *Lynch* case (51 Cal. 15) : "The advantages of having home work done at home commends itself to every mind." This feeling was accentuated by the constant tinkering with city charters by the legislature, often against the best interests of the people affected. The supreme court of Ohio, in the *Ridgeway* case (108 O. St. 245) described the situation in that state as follows: "Municipalities of the state, especially the larger ones, were continuously at the door of Ohio's General Assembly asking for additional power or modifications in some form of previous delegations of such power. * * * Municipalities were, therefore, largely a political football for each succeeding legislature, and there was no stability of law touching municipal power, nor sufficient elasticity of law to meet changed or changing municipal conditions." The Missouri constitutional convention of 1875 in presenting to the people the constitution framed by it in which "Home Rule" was provided for all cities of 100,000 or more in that state, said: "The evils of local or special legislation have become enormous. We need but look to our session acts to be satisfied that this species of legislation occupies the larger portion of the time of our General Assemblies to the neglect and prejudice of public interests" and that resulting "combinations by which private interests have been advanced and dangerous monopolies created, are well known."

We have just seen how the evil control of the legislature by crooked politicians intent on feathering their nests or of furthering the schemes of predatory wealth led to that great uprising of the people which resulted in placing in their hands the direct power of the initiative, the referendum and the recall. During almost that same period in which these great reforms swept the country, the demand for home rule in cities achieved like importance. The people were aroused to militant action because the legislature misused its power. Frequent legislative changes were made both in city charters and in the general laws making the administration of local affairs unsettled and uncertain. Old offices were abolished so as to curtail the power and patronage of the opposition political party. New offices were created in order to make place for the favorites of the political party in power in the state legislature. The cities became a pawn on the political chess-board of each political party and each used that power without regard to the best interests of the people of the cities. The legislatures went further. They created special boards having charge of great administrative functions in the city and empowered the governor to name the members of those boards. The most notable of such boards was one having charge and control of the fire, police and excise, another having charge of public works, and another having control of the registration of electors, the holding of elections and of appointing judges and clerks thereof. The vast patronage resulting from the creation of these alien boards, the horde of employees placed under them, and the control of the elections and of liquor licenses, brought into being a political machine with resultant graft that practically destroyed that self-government which the cities had originally possessed and exercised.

The first step taken in any state to rectify this condition of affairs was by Missouri in 1875 when it adopted a new constitution which provided not only for the separation of the City of St. Louis from its county and its creation into a city-county consolidated, but also that its people might elect a board of thirteen freeholders to prepare a home rule charter to become the "organic law of the city and county," subject to the constitution and the general laws, to go into effect when a certified copy thereof had been deposited in the office of the secretary of state, without requiring any approval by the legislature. The lawmaking authorities of the city were vested

with power to submit charter amendments to its qualified
electors to become effective if approved by a three-fifths
vote of the latter voting thereon. (Appendix—6.) Every
city of over 100,000 population was given the same home
rule power. The people of these cities fondly believed
that they had achieved freedom from interference by the
legislature in their municipal affairs. But they were
doomed to be disillusioned by repeated decisions of their
supreme court which have whittled down their intended
constitutional powers, as has already been noted in Chapter VI and will further be noted in Chapter XVII.

The second state is California, whose people were
compelled to amend their constitution eleven times before
getting real home rule freed from interference by the
legislature and by the courts, as will more fully appear in
Chapter XVI. In 1879 its people adopted a new constitution by which any city, or consolidated city and county,
of more than 100,000 inhabitants, was empowered to elect
a board of fifteen freeholders to frame a charter which
"shall become the organic law thereof, and supersede
any existing charter and all amendments thereof, and all
special laws inconsistent with such charter" and that it
"may be amended at intervals of not less than two years,
by proposals therefor submitted by the legislative authority of the city, to the qualified electors at a general or
special election, * * * and ratified by at least three-
fifths of the qualified voters voting thereat," and also
that "in submitting such charter, or amendment thereto, any alternative article or proposition may be presented for the choice of the voters, and may be voted
on separately without prejudice to others." (Appendix—9.) It was further provided that before such charter or amendments should become effective the same
must receive the approval of the legislature. Passing
upon this provision the supreme court in *Fragley v.
Phelan,* 126 Cal. 383, decided in 1890, said: "As the legislature alone has the power to approve a charter, it
inherently, in the absence of constitutional prohibition,

must have the power to prescribe the terms, conditions and mode upon which it will give its approval. * * * Notwithstanding all the people of the municipality with a single voice may ask for a new charter, yet the state, by or through its legislature, may deny that request.'' The legislature has not exercised that power of veto, or at least so sparingly that the people have not been stirred to amend their constitution in that respect. The legislature has no power to make any alteration or amendment of a city charter, but its sole power is to ratify or reject it. (36 Cal. App. 133.) Section 7 of this article provides that ''city and county governments may be merged and consolidated into one municipal government'' (Appendix —8) and section 9 speaks of the ''consolidated city and county.'' In 1887 the constitution was amended so as to extend this home rule power to ''any city, or consolidated city and county, containing a population of 10,000.'' (Appendix —11.) The growth in sentiment in favor of home rule is evidenced by the fact that only five years later the constitution was again amended so as to extend that power to municipalities over 3,500. (Appendix—12.) Of paramount importance is a provision contained therein that not only should the charter be the ''organic law'' of the municipality, but also that it shall ''supersede *all laws* inconsistent with such charter.'' This is the first instance in which the charter of a municipality was made to supersede the general laws of the state, thus, it was hoped, emancipating it from interference by the legislature as to the selection of its officers. In 1896, by a constitutional amendment, this exemption from the general laws was limited to ''municipal affairs.'' (Appendix—14.) In Chapter XVI will be found a discussion of this situation. The constitution of 1879 gave these municipalities the right to frame a charter but did not specifically include the right to frame a new one. The supreme court of Missouri (186 Mo. 675) held that the right to frame a charter was a continuing one, but the supreme court of California in 1900, in *Blanchard v. Hartwell,* 131 Cal.

263, held to the contrary and said that once a charter had been adopted the right was exhausted and that the only power left was that of amendment. Accordingly, in 1906, the California constitution was again amended so as to authorize the framing of succeeding charters. (Appendix —16.) In 1902 the constitution was amended so that when fifteen per cent of the qualified voters of any city shall petition the council thereof to submit any proposed amendment or amendments to its charter the same must be submitted. (Appendix—15.) In 1911 a constitutional amendment was adopted which set out more fully the charter powers of a consolidated city and county as to all its officers and employees, as to their election or appointment, for their recall or removal, and confirming charters theretofore adopted. (Appendix—17.) At the same time a constitutional amendment was adopted which provided that a board of freeholders to frame a charter may be elected at a general or a special election in pursuance of an ordinance adopted by a vote of two-thirds of the council, or other legislative body of such city, that such election shall be held if a fifteen per cent petition of qualified electors is filed requesting the same, that the charter may be amended by proposals therefor submitted by the legislative body of the city, and that it may provide for the borough system. (Appendix—18.) Also, at the same time a constitutional amendment was adopted giving to *any county* the power to frame its own charter in the same manner and with like broad powers, and that amendments thereto may be proposed by a ten per cent petition of the qualified voters. (Appendix-19.) In 1914 a constitutional amendment was adopted which provided that cities and towns may amend their charters so as to become empowered to make and enforce all laws and regulations "in respect to municipal affairs," subject only to the restrictions and limitations provided in their several charters, "and in respect to all other matters they shall be subject to and controlled by general laws." (Appendix-20.) This might seem to limit the home rule powers of cities, were it not that at the same time a constitutional amendment was adopted which reiterated that their charters "shall become the organic law of such city or city and county, and supersede * * * *all laws* inconsistent therewith." (Appendix—21.) Another amendment was adopted that same year which provided that"it shall be competent in any * * * city or consolidated city and county, and *plenary power* is hereby granted * * * to provide therein or by amendment thereto, the manner in which, the method by which, the times at which, and the terms for which the several county and municipal officers and employees whose compensation is paid by such city or city and county, except judges of the superior court, shall be elected or appointed, and for their recall or removal, and for their compensation, and for the number of deputies, clerks and other employees that each shall have, and for the compensation, method of appointment, qualifications, tenure of office and removal of such deputies, clerks and other employees. All provisions of any charter of any such city or consolidated city and county, heretofore adopted and amendments thereto, which are in accordance herewith, are hereby confirmed and declared valid." (Appendix—22.) These provisions were reiterated in a constitutional amendment adopted in 1922, in which it was further provided that petitions for charter amendments must be filed with the legislative body of the city not less than sixty days prior to the general election next preceding the regular session of the legislature, and also that in any city its charter may be amended "by proposals submitted by the legislative body of the city on its own motion, or on petition signed by fifteen per cent of the registered electors, or both," to be voted on by the registered electors. (Appendix-23.) In *Simpson v. Payne*, 79 Cal. App. 780, decided in 1926, it was held that legislation by a county on a subject authorized by the constitution "is exclusive and supersedes all acts of the legislature relative to the same subject matter and inconsistent therewith."

Especially must it be noted that in the California constitutional amendment of 1914 it was further provided that "it shall be competent in any charter or amendment thereof * * * framed * * * by any city having a population in excess of fifty thousand * * * to provide for *the separation of any city from the county* of which it has theretofore been a part and the formation of said city into a consolidated city and county, to be governed by such charter, and to have *the combined powers of a city and county,* as provided in this constitution for consolidated city and county government." This provision was repeated in a constitutional amendment adopted in 1918 which is still in full force. Provision was also made as to what territory might be included in the consolidated city and county and for adjustment of debts and liabilities and property interests therein, and that separation of a city from its county could be made only on a majority vote of all the qualified electors of the county voting on that question. (Appendix—22.) In no other state have the people given such loyal support to the principle of home rule, evidenced by their unfaltering and constant amendment of their constitution in order that their cities might ultimately be free.

In 1889 the people of the state of Washington amended its constitution so as to empower any city of 20,000 inhabitants or more to adopt a charter for its own government framed by an elective board of freeholders, to become its organic law subject to the constitution and the laws of the state, with power in its electors on a fifteen per cent petition to amend the same, and with power in the legislative authority of the city to submit charter amendments proposed by it. In 1925 it was provided that a twenty-five per cent petition of the qualified electors would compel the election of a charter convention.

In 1896 and in 1898 the people of Minnesota amended its constitution so as to provide that any city or village may adopt its own charter, in harmony with and subject to the constitution and laws of the state, to be framed by

a board of freeholders to be appointed by the district
court of the judicial district in which such city or village
may be situated, to go into effect when approved by a
vote of three-fourths of its electors, and that amendments
thereof might likewise be made. Five per cent of the legal
voters may petition for a charter amendment and alternative propositions may be submitted. In *Grant v. Berris-
ford,* 94 Minn. 45, decided in 1904, the court, in passing
on the provision that a charter "shall always be in harmony with and subject to the constitution and laws of
the state," said that "this does not require the charter
to be similar to and contain all the general laws upon
the subject. * * * This limitation forbids the adoption
of any charter contrary to the general policy of the state,
as declared by general laws, or to its penal code—for
example, provisions providing for the licensing of prize-
fighting or gambling or prostitution, or those which are
subversive of the declared policy of the state as to
the sale of intoxicating liquor. But it does not forbid
the adoption of charter provisions as to any subject
appropriate to the orderly conduct of municipal affairs,
although they may differ in details from those of existing general laws. This is necessarily so, for otherwise
effect could not be given to the constitutional amendment which fairly implies that the charter adopted by
the citizens of a city may embrace all appropriate subjects of municipal legislation, and constitute an effective
municipal code of equal force as a charter granted by
act of the legislature." This rule was again announced
in 106 Minn. 94, and in 153 Minn. 122. Upon this same
point a discussion will be found in Chapter XVII.

In 1902 the people of Colorado, by constitutional
amendment, created the consolidated City and County
of Denver, and vested in its people the exclusive power
of making, altering, revising and amending their charter,
with the right to select all officers. It provided that no
charter amendment or measure adopted or defeated
should be repealed or revived except upon petition of its

people and upon their vote. All cities having a population over 2,000 were likewise empowered. Appendix—26 and Appendix—27, and Chapter XVIII.)

In 1906 the people of Oregon amended their constitution so as to empower any city then or thereafter having a population of 3,500 or more to adopt a charter, subject to the constitution and the criminal laws of the state, to be framed by a board of fourteen freeholders and approved by vote of its people and by the governor, and provided that charter amendments may be proposed and be submitted by the council, or upon a petition of twenty-five per cent of the electors.

In 1908 the people of Oklahoma amended their constitution so as to provide that any city with a population over 2,000 may adopt a charter consistent with and subject to the constitution and the laws of the state, to be framed by a board of freeholders elected two from each ward, to be approved by vote of its people and by the governor, and provided that charter amendments may be proposed and submitted by the city council, or upon a petition of twenty-five per cent of the total vote cast at the then next preceding election.

Arizona, in its first constitution adopted in 1910, provided that any city containing then or thereafter a population of 3,500 may frame a charter for its own government, consistent with and subject to the constitution and laws of the state, to be framed by a board of fourteen elective freeholders and approved by the electors of the city and by the governor, and that amendments may be proposed and submitted by the city council or upon a petition of twenty-five per cent of the electors.

Michigan, in 1908 and in 1912, amended its constitution so as to provide that under general laws the electors of each city and village shall have the power and authority to frame, adopt and amend its charter, and to amend existing charters, and to pass all ordinances relating to municipal concerns, subject to the constitution and the general laws of the state. In 1909 the

legislature provided that the city or village legislative
body, by a three-fifths vote, may, and upon a fifteen per
cent petition of the voters must, submit to the electors
the question of a charter revision and for the election
of members of a charter commission, and that charter
amendments may be proposed by like vote of the legislative body or by like petition of the voters and be submitted to the governor; if he disapproves then the legislative body initiating the amendment may overrule the
disapproval of the governor and submit it to vote of the
electors; but if such amendment be initiated by such petition it shall be submitted to such vote notwithstanding
an objection by the governor.

Nebraska, in 1912, amended its constitution so as
to empower any city having a population of over five
thousand inhabitants to frame its charter, and provided
that the city council, or the electors by filing a five per
cent petition, may submit amendments thereto. The
supreme court of that state held that such charter, as
to matters of local concern, is independent of state legislation and takes priority over general laws concerning
the same (115 Neb. 861).

Ohio amended its constitution in 1912 empowering
any municipality to frame and adopt a charter under
which it may exercise all powers of local self-government, and may adopt and enforce within its limits such
local police, sanitary and other similar regulations as
are not in conflict with general laws. Under the latter
clause the legislature has not interfered with local control of police, fire and public works departments. The
supreme court (88 O. St. 339) held that cities were
authorized to determine what officers shall administer
their affairs, elected or appointed as they may choose,
and sustained a provision in the Cleveland charter which
provided for the preferential ballot and said that as to
municipal affairs the charter is "as much a law as a
statute passed by the general assembly." The constitutional amendment also provided that the legislative

authority of the city or village by a two-thirds vote of its
members may, or upon a petition of ten per cent of the
electors must, provide by ordinance for the election of
commissioners to frame a charter, and that amendments
thereto may be submitted to the voters by a two-thirds
vote of such legislative authority or must be submitted
on petition of ten per cent of the electors. In 1933 the
constitution was further amended so as to provide that
any county may frame and amend its charter determining its form of government and what officers are to be
elected and for the manner of their election, and that
the legislative authority of the county, upon its own
motion may, or upon a petition of ten per cent of the
electors must, submit the question of the election of a
charter commission, and that charter amendments may
be submitted in like manner.

Wisconsin amended its constitution in 1912 empowering its cities and villages to determine their local
affairs and government, subject only to the constitution
and such legislative acts as are of state-wide concern.
In 1929 a law was enacted by which the city council, by
a two-thirds vote, may enact, amend or repeal the whole
or any part of a charter, or call a charter convention,
subject to a referendum to the voters, and that a seven
per cent petition of the electors could force the passage
of such ordinance.

Virginia amended its constitution in 1912 so as to
provide that the old charters of its cities should be continued, except that the legislature might amend them
so as to conform to the constitution. Thus charters were
preserved which reached back to the time when they
were granted by the crown which, together with others
later granted, now govern in all the twenty-four cities
of that state having a city-county consolidated form of
government. (Chapter XI.) Under authorization of that
constitutional amendment the legislature enacted a law
in 1916 which provides that when any city has a population of more than 60,000 a petition of twenty-five per

cent of its electors requires the election of a charter commission of seven,—the charter framed by it and approved by the voters then to be approved by the governor.

The legislature of South Carolina, in 1912 and again in 1922, enacted a law by which any city may frame and amend its charter to be consistent with the constitution and the laws to go into effect when approved by the governor and filed with the secretary of state, and that a petition signed by a majority of the electors of the city will compel the submission by the council to the voters of any proposed amendment.

Maryland amended its constitution in 1915 so as to provide that on demand of the mayor and the city council of Baltimore, or upon the petition of twenty per cent of the voters of that city or of any county, the board of election supervisors thereof were required to provide for the election of a charter board of eleven members to be voted on at the next ensuing election, and that nominations of such members may be made by the mayor or by the city council of said city, or by the county commissioners of such county, or by the petition of not less than five per cent of the registered voters, but in any case 2,000 signers to be sufficient. It was provided that the charter so framed shall be subject only to the constitution and any public laws inconsistent with it.

The legislature of Nevada, in 1915, enacted a law by which cities under the commission form of government were empowered to elect a charter commission of fifteen to prepare a charter not in conflict with the constitution and the laws of the state, and that amendments thereto may be proposed by the city commissioners or by a petition signed by ten per cent of the electors. In 1924 a constitutional amendment provided that the legislature may, by general laws, permit and authorize the electors of any city or town to frame, adopt and amend a charter for its own government, or to amend any existing charter of such city or town. In 1929 the legislature enacted a law requiring a sixty per cent petition of electors for an amendment to charters.

North Carolina amended its constitution in 1917 so as to provide that within the limitations prescribed by the constitution and the general laws any municipality may amend or repeal its charter or any part thereof or adopt a new charter. An amendment may be proposed by the governing body of the municipality or by petition of twenty-five per cent of the electors.

Pennsylvania, in 1922, amended its constitution so as to provide that cities may be chartered whenever a majority of the electors of any town or borough having a population of at least 10,000 shall vote at any general or special election in favor of the same; that cities, or cities of any particular class, may be given the right and power of framing and adopting their own charters, subject to such restrictions, limitations and regulations as may be imposed by the legislature. This did not give much home rule.

New York amended its constitution in 1923 so as to provide that every city shall have the power to adopt and amend local laws not inconsistent with the constitution and laws of the state, relating to the powers, duties, qualifications, number, mode of selection and removal, terms of office and compensation, of all officers and employees of the city, and the manner of transacting all business, and that the legislature at its next session should provide by general law for carrying out these provisions. Accordingly the legislature in 1924 enacted a law, amended in 1929, by which it is provided that in any city its legislative body may submit to its electors a proposal for the election of a commission to draft a charter not inconsistent with the constitution and laws of the state. The charter thus framed is submitted to the qualified electors for approval or rejection. It was provided that cities having a commission form of government may frame their charters which may be amended upon proposals submitted by a fifteen per cent petition of the voters. The courts of that state have ruled that a charter is a local law and that any city may amend the same.

Utah amended its constitution in 1932 so as to provide that the legislative authority of any city may, by a two-thirds vote, and upon a fifteen per cent petition of its electors it must, submit to the voters a proposal for the election of a charter commission of fifteen members. The charter thus framed is to be the organic law and shall supersede any existing charter and all laws affecting the organization and the government of such city when it shall have been filed in the office of the secretary of state and in the office of the city recorder.

Thus nineteen of the states have placed safely in their constitutions provisions which have provided, in whole or in part, for the emancipation of their cities from the political overlordship of the legislature. In several other states, without amendment of their constitutions, their legislatures have enacted laws along the same lines. In 1913 the Texas legislature enacted a law which provided that cities having a population over 5,000 may, by a majority vote of its electors, adopt and amend their charters, subject to such limitations as may be prescribed by the legislature, such charters not to be inconsistent with the constitution or the general laws of the state; that the governing body of any such city may, on its own motion, or on a ten per cent petition must, submit at an election the question of electing a charter commission, and that such governing body, on its own motion may, or on like petition must, submit charter amendments to the voters. In 1937 the West Virginia legislature enacted a law by which the voters of any city may frame, adopt and amend its charter, and that the governing body by a two-thirds vote may on its own motion, or on a fifteen per cent petition must, provide for the election of a charter commission to frame a charter or charter amendments.

No longer in these states which have adopted the

initiative, the referendum and the recall, are their people helpless against the insidious practices of powerful interests which seduce public servants from the path of duty. The people simply took to themselves their rightful power of dismissing from their service, by the recall, any incompetent or corrupt public servant, and, through the referendum, of repealing bad laws and ordinances which their faithless official servants had been induced to enact, and, through the initiative, of enacting any law or ordinance desired by the people but which a recalcitrant or corrupt legislature or city council had failed or refused to enact. By the adoption of "Home Rule," where its proper exercise has not been hampered by legislatures and courts, cities have been confirmed in the right of self-government to which they were always lawfully entitled from the beginning.

Perhaps no greater advance in self-government has taken place in any generation in the history of the world than during the quarter-century in which these reforms were achieved in this country. It was not easily done. It was opposed by all the entrenched interests whose usurpations of power were thus being assailed. The struggle was a fierce one and many times the result seemed in doubt. But the people would not be denied. They were determined to get back into their own hands their rightful powers of self-government which had been filched from them, and they succeeded. Sometimes these powers have been abused by unscrupulous politicians or designing demagogues. In California, especially, where a great influx of neer-do-wells and communists has furnished a fertile field for hare-brained agitators, there has been forced upon the taxpayers the tremendous cost of recurring elections on measures that had been defeated at a preceding election just held. In some states this evil is met by the provision that a measure once defeated by vote of the people cannot be submitted until a fixed interval has expired. On the whole, however, the initiative, the referendum and the recall have been used wisely and beneficially for the public good. After all, like the hickory switch kept handy for correction purposes during our youthful days, it is not so much the use of it as it is the knowledge that it is available for use if needed. Wherever real "Home Rule" is in practice in our cities the results have been uniformly beneficial. Especially has that been the case where that right has been embedded in the constitution.

Wherever constitutions have not been amended and the legislature alone has acted the door has been left open to it to play politics with the cities to their detriment. Indeed, it will be noted in subsequent pages that even constitutional provisions adopted by the people have been flouted by the courts, especially in the case of the home rule cities of New York, Baltimore, St. Louis, City and County of San Francisco and City and County of Denver, which fall within the class of the city-county consolidated.

CHAPTER IX.

OBSTACLES TO CITY-COUNTY CONSOLIDATED

There are two ways by which a city-county consolidated may be created. One is by an act of the legislature and the other is by a provision in the constitution. Concerning the latter method there is no question as to the power of the people in their constitution to separate a city from its county and to create such city into a city-county consolidated. Examples of this method are found in the City of St. Louis and in the City and County of Denver.

Examples of the creation of a city-county consolidated by the legislature are numerous. The five counties of New York, The Bronx, Kings, Queens and Richmond were consolidated by the legislature into the City of New York. The twenty-four cities of Virginia having a city-county consolidated form of government were created by the legislature and made separate from their respective counties. The California legislature carved the City of San Francisco from its county and created it into the consolidated City and County of San Francisco. The Maryland legislature separated from its county the City of Baltimore and gave it a city-county consolidated form of government. The Pennsylvania legislature consolidated the City of Philadelphia with its county. The Louisiana legislature consolidated the City of New Orleans with the parish of Orleans. The territorial legislature of Hawaii created the City and County of Honolulu out of the county of Oahu and its cities. All this

was done under the general rule that, except as restrained
by the constitution, the legislature may change boundaries of counties, consolidate two or more into one, and
create new counties out of the territory of one or more
existing ones.

However, if a city-county consolidated is a "county," as to which there is considerable conflict of authority, then it will be found that the constitutions of several
states contain restrictions that present obstacles to the
creation of a city-county consolidated form of government therein. It is necessary to consider this situation.

One method of creating a city-county consolidated
would be to create a city into a county and then to consolidate city and county functions under one set of officers. But this is questioned by the requirement in some
constitutions that a new county must have at least a
certain area and, in several cases, that there must be left
in the old county a certain area. For instance, in North
Dakota and in South Dakota the area required for a new
county must not be less than twenty-four congressional
townships and that like area must be left in the old
county. Of course that makes it impossible for the legislature to create a county out of any city with so wide
an expanse of territory. In Louisiana a new parish
(county) must have an area of not less than 625 square
miles and the constitution requires that similar area must
be left in the old parish. Since New Orleans is already a
city-county consolidated there is no other city in that
state large enough to justify making it into a county. In
Arkansas the area of a new county must not be less than
600 square miles and like area must be left in the old
county. In Alabama there is the same requirement as to
area of a new county but the area to be left in the old
county is not to be less than 500 square miles. In Kansas
432 square miles is required for a new county but there is
no requirement as to what area must be left in the old
county. In Iowa the same area is required for a new
county and the same must be left in the old county. In

South Carolina a new county must have not less than 400 square miles and the remainder to be left in the old county must not be less than 500 square miles. In Idaho, Illinois, Indiana, Kentucky, Maryland, Nebraska, Ohio, Pennsylvania and West Virginia a new county must have not less than 400 square miles and the same area must be left in the old county. In Tennessee a new county must have an area of not less than 275 square miles and the old county must be left at least 500 square miles.

If these limitations and requirements apply to the creation of a city into a city-county consolidated then the legislatures of these eighteen states cannot adopt that method since they have no cities large enough to justify doing so, except in Illinois where Cook county has an area of 933 square miles and if Chicago were created into a new county comprising 400 square miles there would still be left an area of 533 square miles in the old county, and also in Tennessee where Shelby county has an area of 801 square miles and if Memphis were created into a new county with an area of 275 square miles there would still be left an area of 526 square miles in the old county, so their constitutions would be complied with. Since Hamilton county in which Cincinnati is located has an area of only 407 square miles, and Cuyahoga county in which Cleveland is located has an area of but 463 square miles, and Marion county in which Indianapolis is located has an area of only 397 square miles, it is evident that the creation of any of these cities into a new county would not leave the area required to be left in the old county. In Ohio, however, its constitution provides that any county having a population exceeding 100,000 may be divided by the legislature whenever a majority of the qualified electors residing in each of the proposed divisions, voting on the question, shall approve such division. This would seem to obviate the area requirements as to Hamilton and Cuyahoga counties and leave a means by which Cincinnati and Cleveland might be separated from their respective counties and be created into a city-county consolidated.

In a few states modification of the requirement as to area has been made in their constitutions. In Alabama and in Tennessee the legislature, by a two-thirds vote of each house, may make that requirement inoperative. In the latter state the legislature, by a majority vote, may also create new counties out of certain old ones but none of them have any city large enough to warrant its creation into a city-county consolidated. In 1936 an amendment to the Alabama constitution was proposed which would have authorized the legislature, from time to time, by general or local law, to change, merge, alter, consolidate or abolish, county offices in Jefferson county, in which the important city of Birmingham lies (excepting the offices of probate judge and sheriff), with power to change, modify or transfer their duties, except as to those conferred by the constitution, and to create new and different offices whose occupants were to perform the duties therefore fulfilled by such changed, merged, consolidated or abolished offices. Had this amendment been adopted the county of Jefferson and the city of Birmingham might have been created by the legislature into a city-county consolidated. But it was defeated.

The Kentucky legislature in 1936 proposed a constitutional amendment by which it would be authorized to consolidate a county and its included municipalities. Assistant Attorney General Herdman of that state wrote the author in 1938, that "the object of this was to economize in the conduct of county and municipal governments, and it was especially desirable in Louisville which is in Jefferson County to have fiscal officers such as assessors and collectors for the whole county including the city, and thereby save these separate expenses of office which could be discharged by one officer." But the proposed constitutional amendment was defeated, undoubtedly because the cities in the county generally did not favor relinquishing their home rule powers and thus surrender

their affairs into the hands of the county officers. Had
the proposal been simply to carve Louisville out from its
county and create it into a city-county consolidated with
one set of officers the result might have been different.
Three years ago there was a movement for consolidation
of city and county offices but nothing came of it.

Especial note must be made, however, that most of
the constitutions of the states now under consideration
do not limit the legislature simply to the creation of new
counties. But in addition it is left with the power, under
certain limitations, to change county lines and to alter
county boundaries by cutting off a part of a county and
adding it to one or more adjoining counties. In that way
a city may be carved out from its county by shifting the
county lines so as to leave the city alone and by attaching
the remainder of the old county to neighboring counties.
This requires but a majority vote of the legislature and
a vote of the inhabitants affected. In Arkansas, Idaho,
Maryland, Washington and Wyoming a majority of the
electors voting on the severance is required in the territory proposed to be cut off from the county. In Colorado
and in Kentucky the vote is taken in the old county before
such severance may be made. In Missouri, North Dakota,
Ohio and South Dakota the vote is required in the old
county and also in the county to which the severed territory is to be attached. In Utah the vote is required in
the old county and also in the part to be severed under
such restrictions as the legislature may prescribe. In
Illinois the vote is required in the county to which the
severed territory is to be attached and when a majority
of the voters living in such territory petition for severance. In Washington such severance may be made under
general laws upon petition of a majority of the voters
living in the territory proposed to be severed. In Oklahoma such severance may be made upon a sixty per cent
vote of the electors voting on the question and residing
in the territory proposed to be severed and also of a
majority vote of the old county. In Louisiana all laws

changing parish lines, before the same may become effective, must be submitted to the electors of the parishes to be affected thereby, at a special election, and be approved by a two-thirds vote cast thereat.

As a matter of law, where a constitution is silent as to placing a limitation upon the power of the legislature concerning the matter of altering the boundaries of a county, it may do so without hindrance. Thus, since the constitutions of North Carolina, Texas and West Virginia contain no such limitation, it would seem clear that their legislatures may take from a county a part of its territory and add it to another county without any vote or voice of those affected thereby except as their representatives in the legislature may be heard. In that connection it will be noted that the supreme court of Maryland (69 Md. 460 and 133 Md. 247) held that the legislature had power to extend the boundaries of the City of Baltimore into adjoining counties and thus alter their boundary lines, even though the constitution of that state provided that the lines of a county could not be changed without the consent of the legal voters residing within the district, which, under the proposed change, would be taken from its county, and the court held that such consent was required only as to the creation of a *new* county. Under that rule all the requirements for a local vote for altering county lines, above noted, would seem to apply only to the organization of a *new* county. Thus the legislature is left free to carve a city out of its county, just as was done in the creation of Baltimore and in enlarging its boundaries, and then to create such severed city into a city-county consolidated and attach the remainder of the old county to adjoining counties.

The requirement in some constitutions concerning population does not seem to hinder the creation of a new county nor to altering county lines since in Arkansas it is but 5,000, in Louisiana 7,000, in Maryland 10,000, in North Dakota 1,000, in Ohio 100,000, in Oregon 1,200, in South Carolina 15,000, in Tennessee 700, in Washington

2,000, in West Virginia 6,000 and in Wyoming 1,500 for the new county, and a like population to be left to the old county. Nor does the taxable property required for a new county and for the remainder of the old county furnish any obstacle. In Idaho the amount thereof must be at least $6,000,000. In South Carolina the amount thereof in a new county must be at least $1,500,000 and there must be left in the old county at least $2,000,000. In Wyoming the amount thereof in a new county must be at least $2,000,000 and there must be left in the old county at least $3,000,000.

There is also the question of how close a changed county line may run to the county seat or the court house of an adjoining county. In Alabama it must not run closer to the court house of the old county than seven miles, in Tennessee eleven miles, while in Colorado, Illinois, Kentucky and Pennsylvania it must not run within ten miles of the county seat of the old county. In California the line of a new county must not pass within five miles of the city or town in which the county seat of any county proposed to be divided is situated. Evidently such provisions cannot reasonably be applied to the case of a city-county consolidated. In every instance where a city has been created into that new form of government, as in Baltimore, San Francisco, St. Louis and Denver, the city thus separated from its county was a county seat. In every instance where a city is large enough to justify its creation into a city-county it is a county seat. It is clear that these constitutional limitations were meant to apply to the creation of a new county outside of the territory occupied by the county seat, and not to apply to the creation of the county seat itself into a new county. For its boundaries would be its own limits and could not possibly be miles outside thereof. Any other construction would reduce these constitutional limitations to an apparent absurdity and must be rejected. (See p. 164.)

Furthermore, these constitutional provisions con-

cerning counties and their lines may well be said not to
apply to the city-county consolidated at all. For it is not
a city alone, nor is it a county alone. Fundamentally they
are entirely different from each other. A city is a voluntary association of its people generally initiated by
them, while a county is an involuntary organization created by the state. When they are joined together they
lose their individual characters. The city-county consolidated is a *new* political entity, *sui generis,* and is not
a county in its generally accepted sense. It is a municipal
corporation whose officers must perform county functions
imposed upon them in addition to their duties as city
officers. The most perfect example is the consolidated
City and County of Denver. The constitutional amendment creating it tersely provides that "every charter
shall designate the officers who shall, respectively, perform the acts and duties required of county officers to be
done by the Constitution or by the general law, as far as
applicable." For a short time the supreme court of
Colorado held that the consolidated City and County of
Denver is a county and must have a set of county officers
in addition to a set of city officers. But in the later
Cassiday case (50 Colo. 503) the former case was overruled and the court said: "In the City and County of
Denver * * * there are no county officers and there can
be no such officers, purely as such." Under this holding
that there can be no county officers as such in a city-
county consolidated it must follow that this political
entity does not fall within the generally accepted definition of a county. Judge Temple in his dissent joined by
Chief Justice Beatty in the *Sutro* case, (114 Cal. 316),
well said that when the City and County of San Francisco was created all its officers were officers of the new
municipal corporation; that in no sense could it be said
that some of them were county officers and that some
were city officers; that the City and County of San Francisco is not a mere county, but is recognized in the constitution itself, again and again, *as constituting a class*

apart.'' The supreme court of Missouri (69 Mo. 514 and
408) said that the general purpose of the framers of the
constitution, so far as the political status of the City of
St. Louis is concerned, will be found to divest it of all
county government, and that the language of the constitution ''is totally inconsistent with the idea that the
City of St. Louis is one of the counties of the state.'' In
California the courts wobbled so that the people repeatedly amended their constitution so as to conform to the
statement of Judge Temple (Chapter XVI), but the
Missouri courts are still on unsteady legs as will appear
in Chapter XVII. In this connection it must be noted
that when the legislature of Maryland in 1851 severed the
City of Baltimore from its county it was not then nor has
it since been created into a county. (Chapter XIV.)
And finally, under the California constitution which provides that there shall be a ''uniform system of county
and township government throughout the state,'' the
supreme court in the *Martin* case (126 Cal. 404) said:
''It is too obvious for question or argument that the general law establishing a uniform system of county government does not apply to the City and County of San
Francisco.'' These instances seem decisive that a city-
county consolidated is not a county within the meaning
of the constitutional requirements here under discussion.

And that would seem also to dispose of the provision
in the constitutions of Georgia, Kansas, Utah, Washington and Wyoming that the legislature shall establish a
system of county government which shall be uniform
throughout the state, since it is not applicable to a city-
county consolidated form of government in that it does
not have a form of county government. Likewise the
provisions in the constitutions of several of the states
that certain county officers must be elected in each county
and that the legislature by general and uniform laws
must provide for the election of such officers do not
apply to the city-county consolidated for the same rea-

son. Even if they did, such officers may be elected therein and have imposed upon them the performance of such city functions as may be provided by the charter and thus real consolidation may be effected.

Furthermore, while a city-county consolidated performs the functions of a city and also those of a county, it has additional attributes and it would seem to be proper to place it in a separate system or classification. Law writers indicate that this would be legal. The general rule laid down is: "Statutes concerning municipal government are valid as general laws whenever based on classifications reasonably germane to the subject embraced therein, and if so the legislative classification is conclusive on the courts, although only one of a class may exist when the act goes into effect." (36 Cyc. 1003; 59 Corpus Juris, 759.) Such classification made on the basis of population is sustained, and a classification made on the basis of form of government in a city-county consolidated should be sustained, just as a classification made on the commission form, or city manager form, of government has been sustained.

One of the clearest enunciations of this rule is that made by the highest court of New Jersey. In 1875 the constitution of that state had been amended so as to provide that the legislature shall pass general laws regulating the affairs of towns and counties. In 1878 the supreme court of that state, concerning that provision, said: "All legislation is based, of necessity, on a classification of subjects, and when such classification is fairly made, and the legislation founded upon it is appropriate to such classification, such legislation is as legitimate now as it would have been prior to the recent amendments to the constitution." (40 N. J. Law 1, 8). And that court in 1901 thus again expressed the rule: "If the only limitation contained in a law is a legislative classification of its objects it is a general law. Hence if the objects of a law have characteristics so distinct as reasonably to form, for the purpose legislated upon, a class by itself, it is general notwithstanding it operates upon a single object only.'' (66 N. J. Law, 133, 135-6).

While as to some of the states above discussed it seems improbable that a city-county consolidated form of government may be established therein until they have amended their constitutions, yet in many of them it would seem quite possible that this may be done.

But few cases have been decided by the courts concerning the application of the constitutional requirements above discussed, and none of them upon the points mentioned. If it be held that the requirements as to area needed for the creation of a new county applies to that of a consolidated city-county then in many cases the constitution must be amended. But if the courts hold, as they should, that the city-county does not fall within the definition of a county as the term is used in the provisions as to area, then such requirements would be held to apply only as to the remainder of the former county from which the new city-county is separated and the constitution would not need to be amended so long as such area remained. Wherever the courts are composed of judges actuated by a desire to forward the interests of municipal government they will decide that a new city-county does not fall within the area requirements. But where the courts are composed of judges of reactionary tendencies or who are under the control of politicians intent upon manhandling the cities they will decide to the contrary. This may seem a hard thing to say of our courts but throughout the pages of this book are many illustrations of its sad truth. Therefore, in each case the judicial horizon must first be scanned carefully before the road to follow can be determined upon. Instead of amending constitutions it is better at times to revamp recalcitrant courts. But that should never be done by packing the court with "yes men" as was recently attempted in order to gain control of the United States supreme court. Left to the exercise of their rightful powers the people in the states at the polling places generally make selection of judges who will respect their oath of office, especially in times when a question has arisen over faithlessness in their judiciary concerning the right of self-government. While courts should never be used to overturn the plain provisions of a constitution yet they should not be permitted to so construe them as to destroy their true meaning. When they do the latter they have usually been taken in hand by the electorate in no uncertain way.

CHAPTER X.

CONSTITUTIONS AUTHORIZE CITY-COUNTY CONSOLIDATED

Many of the states have no provisions in their constitutions limiting the power of the legislature over their cities and their counties as to their form. Thus they are free to create a county and its included municipalities into a city-county consolidated, or to separate a city from its county and create such city into a city-county consolidated, with one set of officers. This appears to be true in the states of Arizona, Connecticut, Delaware, Maine, Massachusetts, New Hampshire, New Mexico, Rhode Island and Vermont. Attorney General Green of Delaware wrote the author, in 1938: "I feel that you are correct in your conclusion that there is nothing in the constitution of this state limiting the power of the legislature to create a county into a consolidated city-county with one set of officials or to separate a city from its county and create it into a consolidated city county." Assistant Attorney General Fernandez of New Mexico wrote the author, in 1938: "In my opinion, there is no reason why cities could not be consolidated into counties with one form of government. A new county can, no doubt, be created co-extensive with the limits of a city, and by general legislation the city could, no doubt, consolidate itself with the county and the same government could be provided for the consolidated city and county."

The constitution of Vermont provides that its legislature "may constitute towns, boroughs, cities and counties," without any limitation on the exercise of such power. It is clear that the legislature there has full power to create a city into a city-county consolidated with one set of officers to perform both city functions and county functions.

The constitution of Maine does not limit its legislature in its powers over cities and counties, the only provision being that "the legislature, from time to time, shall provide, *as far as practicable,* by general laws, for all matters usually appertaining to special or private legislation." At the close of the preceding chapter it was pointed out that this does not prevent the legislature from creating a county with its included municipalities into a city-county consolidated, nor does it prevent the legislature from creating a city into such city-county, with one set of officers to perform both city and county functions.

The constitution of New Jersey vests in its legislature absolute power over cities and counties, their organization and powers, provided only that the legislature shall not enact any private, local or special law regulating the internal affairs of towns and counties. However we have just seen that its highest court has held that the legislature may classify cities on the basis of population. From this it seems clear that the legislature may place its largest cities in a class and further provide for the separation of any of them from its county and for its creation into a city-county consolidated with one set of officers.

In the constitution of Connecticut there is no limitation on the power of its legislature over cities or counties, except that in each county there shall be an elected sheriff. Therefore, the legislature may create a county with its included municipalities into a city-county consolidated with one set of officers, or it may detach a city from its county and create it into such city-county with a sheriff who may be made *ex officio* chief of police or commissioner of safety if so desired.

The constitution of New Hampshire contains no limitation upon the power of its legislature concerning cities and counties, except that certain officers shall be elected in each county. Therefore, the legislature may create a county into a city-county, or it may separate a city from its county and create it into a city-county and provide that such county officers shall, *ex officio,* perform city functions and thus eliminate a dual set of officers.

However, we have just seen that these requirements in constitutions concerning officers for counties do not apply to the city-county consolidated and, therefore, they are free to consolidate offices and functions if authorized so to do by the legislature.

Under the constitution of Massachusetts the legislature has full power to create cities and counties and to provide for their powers. For two hundred years Boston kept its town meeting, and it was not until 1822 that it became incorporated as the Town of Boston when it abandoned the town meeting at which eight thousand were entitled to attend, as it was found impracticable under those conditions. At that time Suffolk county contained that town and the little town of Chelsea and a small rural territory. The legislature might well have consolidated the small county and these two municipalities into a City and County of Boston, but instead of doing so it saddled on the taxpayers of Boston the total expense of the county jail and of the courts, leaving the outside part of the county free from this burden. Corporation Counsel Parkman of that city, in 1939, wrote: "The original arrangement for the payment of Suffolk county expenses by the City of Boston was entered into when those expenses were extremely small and in return for their assumption by the city the title to certain property was vested in the city. This arrangement has been confirmed by legislative action and when conditions changed it has proved impossible to change it, not because the people of Boston submitted to it or because of their failure to exercise their great voting power, but because Boston's representatives in the legislature have always been in the minority and they simply have not had the voting strength to make a change. Constant attempts have been made by representatives of the city to obtain such legislation but without success.''

Various attempts have been made to find a remedy for this condition. Bills were introduced in the legislature to provide that the other towns of the county, — Chelsea, Revere and Winthrop, — pay their just share of this cost, but without avail. The excuse offered was that because of their small population adequate representation could not be given them on any joint board of management. In 1896 a plan was proposed by the Metropolitan District Commission appointed by the legislature to combine all the municipalities into a so-called metropolitan area, comprising all of Suffolk county and portions of four other counties with their included municipalities, into a single metropolitan district to exercise ordinary county functions and also the more important municipal functions but leaving to the included cities a limited control over certain of their local affairs somewhat like that now existing in the five boroughs of New York City. Naturally the four adjoining counties objected to having portions of their territory cut off and thus losing the revenue from valuable taxable areas, and the included municipalities objected to what practically amounted to losing their political lives, and so the proposition was defeated. In 1911 a committee of the Boston chamber of commerce reported in favor of a similar plan, but nothing came of it. Indeed, for the reasons just stated, nothing can ever come of such a plan. In 1919 Mayor Peters of the City of Boston in his annual message appealed for the creation of a ''Greater City of Boston,'' but he was not heeded. This search for bigness is an *ignis fatuus* that leads to the morass of despair and defeat. Cities, instead of consolidating their functions, simplifying their form of government, decreasing the number of their tax-eaters and thus lessening the load on their taxpayers, make a mistake in reaching out for territory which is not urban in character and not assimilable, in a boastful striving for an increased waist-line.

The Massachusetts legislature has full power to consolidate the county of Suffolk and its included municipalities into a city-county consolidated, or it may carve the City of Boston out from its county and make of the city alone a city-county consolidated. Already some functional consolidation has been effected. The Boston city council performs all the duties of the former board of county commissioners of Suffolk county. The city treasurer and the city auditor now perform all the duties formerly performed by the county treasurer and the county auditor. Other small consolidations have also been made, and Boston, with its historic past filled with progressive achievement, certainly will not hesitate much longer to make consolidation complete.

In the Illinois constitutional convention of 1870 a provision was agreed to authorizing any city having a population over 200,000 to organize itself into a separate county, but it was later stricken out. In 1892 Mayor Washburne of Chicago in his annual message to the city council advocated the union of that city with Cook county in which it is located. He said: "With our city and county limits so nearly identical it is the opinion of many that the abolishment of county and city lines and the union of both under one form of municipal government would result in great benefit to the community." And in his 1893 message he said: "Our hydra-headed system of county, city and town governments, which in effect cover but one population, are matters which need to be considered and to be altered." In 1899 a bill introduced in the legislature for doing this was defeated. In 1901 a proposal authorizing the formation of a County of Chicago, subject to a referendum of the inhabitants affected, was defeated in the legislature. In 1903 a bill to consolidate the city of Chicago with that part of Cook county within the city limits under one government, and to create two new counties out of the remainder of Cook county, was defeated in the legislature. Since that county has an area of 933 square miles and the constitution requires that each new county must have an area of only 400 square miles it is apparent that this requirement as to area need not stand in the way of creating the City of Chicago, by simple legislative act, into a city-county consolidated, since it might well occupy an area of 400 square miles thus leaving to the old county an area of 543 square miles, and the voting power of the city is so overwhelming in the county that the Chicago voters could control a vote on separation of the city from its county.

The constitution of Washington empowers its legislature to create a new county to have at least 2,000 inhabitants and leaving at least 4,000 inhabitants in the remainder of the old county, upon a majority petition only of the electors in the proposed new county. Since Seattle has the population required for its creation by the legislature into a city-county consolidated, and since that would leave the required area and number of inhabitants in the remainder of the old county and only the vote of the electors of that city would be required, it would seem entirely feasible that this be done. While its people have been quite progressive in matters of government they have been slow to grasp the opportunities for simplified municipal government at less expense. Mayor Langlie of that city wrote the author in 1938 that "there has been very little agitation for consolidation of city and county governments, although there are those who feel that such action would be a distinct advantage to the taxpayer. No plan of any kind, however, has been offered."

The constitution of Pennsylvania provides that no new county may be created which will reduce any existing county to an area of less than 400 square miles or with a population of less than 50,000. But that constitution also provides that the legislature may classify counties and cities and that laws concerning the same shall be deemed to be general legislation. Under that power the legislature, in 1854, consolidated the City of Philadelphia with its county and it likewise has the power to consolidate the City of Pittsburgh with its county into a city-county consolidated. Indeed, in 1906 the legislature enacted a law by which that city absorbed Allegheny City, and the supreme court sustained it. By the same rule the City of Pittsburgh may be authorized to absorb the entire county. In 1916 the demand for this consolidation had grown to great strength. In 1923 a commission appointed by Governor Pinchot recommended consolidation but nothing came of it. The politicians were against this plan because it would interfere with giving jobs to their henchmen. To quiet the public they caused the legislature, in 1928, to submit a proposed constitutional amendment purporting to permit consolidation but they cunningly slipped in at the last moment a clause which required a two-thirds majority in the affirmative in each municipality within the county. It was simply a hocus-pocus. To carry it on they caused the legislature to enact a law, in 1929, which provided for an election under this impracticable constitutional amendment upon the question of entire consolidation in Allegheny county but it was foredoomed to defeat and it was defeated at the hands of a minority of the whole. In 1935 a consolidation bill was introduced in the legislature but it died in committee. Agitation along this line has waned although still alive. If the City of Pittsburgh is to separate from its county and be created into a city-county consolidated the constitution must be amended on account of the area requirement. Without it the legislature may consolidate the entire county into a city-county consolidated at this time.

In Wisconsin the legislature is given full power to create new counties, subject only to a majority vote of the old county from which the part is to be stricken off. Therefore, it would seem that the legislature, subject to such local vote, may separate a city from its county and create it into a city-county consolidated with one set of officers. Mayor Hoan of Milwaukee wrote the author, in 1938, that he has been advocating consolidation of city and county governments in Milwaukee county for the past twenty years, but that he doubts the advisability of detachment of the city from the county and creating it into a city-county consolidated form of government because when such consolidated city outgrows its boundaries annexation becomes more difficult and the same condition is likely to develop that caused consolidation in the first place. But that objection does not seem to be well taken. In the first place the advantages to be gained by the City of Milwaukee are too great to forego them from fear that a condition may arise requiring something additional be done in the uncertain future. In the second place the boundaries of the new city-county consolidated may be made extensive enough in the beginning so that no subsequent enlargement would be required within any reasonable period of time. Attorney General Rentz of the state of Wisconsin wrote the author in 1939, "that from time to time plans have been submitted to the legislature providing for a consolidated county-city form of government for Milwaukee County which is the largest city in the state." The latest bill to be proposed to the legislature for that plan seems to have been offered at the 1934 session of that body and the then attorney general rendered an opinion that relief could not be had in that way, on the ground that it would violate the provision of the constitution that there be but one system of town and county government. But it must be noted that while the constitution of Wisconsin says that "the legislature shall establish but one system of town and county government," yet immediately following that language is the qualifying phrase that such system shall only be "as nearly uniform as practicable." That qualification clearly leaves the door open, as we have seen, for the creation by the legislature of a city-county consolidated form of government with one set of officers for the City of Milwaukee and in such other cities as the legislature may deem fit to place in the same class. For it must be apparent that it is not "practicable" to include a city-county consolidated form of government in any system of ordinary town and county government, and so a different classification may be made of the former under that authorization given.

The constitution of Nevada gives its legislature full power over its cities and counties, and provides that it "shall have power to increase, diminish, consolidate, or abolish the following county officers: county clerks, county recorders, auditors, sheriffs, district attorneys, county surveyors, public administrators and superintendents of schools. While the constitution provides that the system of county government shall be uniform throughout the state, yet these specific provisions of the constitution as to abolishing county officers, coupled with what has been said in the preceding chapter about the uniformity clause, apparently leaves with the legislature full power to create a city-county consolidated in that state.

Next to be considered are those states whose constitutions have been framed or amended so as to give direct authorization by which a city-county consolidated may be created by the legislature but where it has thus far failed to act under its granted power, or if it has acted nothing has resulted.

The constitution of North Carolina provides that "the general assembly shall have full power by statute to modify, change or abrogate any and all of the provisions of this article (concerning counties and municipal corporations) and substitute others in their place, except sections seven (concerning indebtedness) and nine (requiring uniform taxation) and thirteeen (forbidding assumption of debts or interest contracted in aid or support of rebellion)." In 1933 a movement was inaugurated in the city of Durham by its chamber of commerce to secure an act of the legislature authorizing it to become a city-county consolidated, but nothing came of it.

Michigan, in 1850, was the first state to place in its constitution a provision directly authorizing the legislature to organize any city into a separate county, when it has attained a population of 20,000, provided a majority of the electors of such city and of the remainder of the county vote approval. (Appendix—2.) In 1908 this provision was amended raising to 100,000 the population required. (Appendix—3.) This power has not been exercised by the legislature, although there has been agitation for it in Detroit.

Minnesota placed in its constitution of 1858 a provision identical with that in the 1850 constitution of Michigan. (Appendix—4.) Deputy Attorney General Erickson of that state wrote the author, in 1938: ''We know of no reason why the legislature may not enact a law to create St. Paul into a separate county.'' The constitution of that state further provides that the legislature may provide for performance by county officers of city functions when a majority of the electors of the city may so determine. Under these broad and specific constitutional powers the people of the City of St. Paul have made but little progress toward consolidating their local government, notwithstanding the fact that the city has approximately ninety-six per cent of the population of Ramsey county in which it is situated. Former Mayor Nelson of that city read a paper in 1923 before the National League of Municipalities in which he pointed out the wasteful duplication of offices and the excess burden to the taxpayers under the existing dual city and county system. He started a movement to create St. Paul into a city-county consolidated with one set of officers but it failed.

However, some consolidation has occurred there. The mayor of that city is *ex officio* the permanent chairman of the board of county commissioners of Ramsey county;

there is a joint city hall and court house commission of six members of whom three are members of the city council and three are appointed by the board of county commissioners. The mayor acts as chairman of the commission. This commission manages the one building in which most of the county and city offices are housed, the cost being paid equally by the city and the county. A joint city and county committee, two of its members elected by the board of county commissioners and one by the city council, supervises the city hospital, the county home, and the city and county outdoor relief, two-thirds of the cost thereof being paid by the county and one-third by the city.

The Missouri constitution of 1875 authorized the people of the City of St. Louis to separate from its county and to frame and amend their charter for their local government. This was done and is more fully discussed in Chapter XVII. That constitution further provides that in all other counties having a city therein containing a population of over 100,000 inhabitants the city and the county governments thereof may be consolidated in such manner as may be provided by law, but nothing has been done thereunder. (Appendix—5 and Appendix—6.)

In 1902 Colorado amended its constitution creating the consolidated City and County of Denver with one set of officers. This amendment is set forth in Appendix 26 and is very fully discussed in Chapter XVIII.

By a constitutional amendment adopted by California in 1914, and repeated in a constitutional amendment in 1918, it is provided that "it shall be competent in any charter or amendment thereof, which shall hereafter be framed * * * by any city having a population in excess of fifty thousand * * * to provide for the separation of said city from the county of which it has theretofore been a part and the formation of said city into a consolidated city and county to be governed by said charter, and to have the combined powers of a city and county, as provided in this constitution for consolidated city and county government, and further to prescribe the date for the beginning of the official existence of said consolidated city and county.'' If no additional territory is proposed to be added, then if the electors of the city voting thereon vote to ratify such charter and it is approved by the legislature, and if the majority of the electors of the entire county voting thereon vote their consent to such separation, the city thereupon becomes a consolidated city and county. If additional territory is proposed to be added then the consent of its voters must be had in like manner, and at the same time the terms of the assumption of any indebtedness shall be voted upon. (Appendix—22.) It confirmed the City and County of San Francisco created by the legislature in 1856. In the amendment of 1914 and also in that of 1918 provision was made for a borough system if desired. No city has separated from its county under these provisions. In Alameda county an attempt was made in 1921 to consolidate the entire county under the borough system but it failed on a vote of its electors, because of the local jealousies in the various districts affected.

For nearly fifty years there have been sporadic movements in Los Angeles county looking toward consolidation of governmental functions. The first official notice made of it was by Mayor Hazard of the City of Los Angeles in his message to the city council in 1891. From 1916 to 1921 three reports were made on city-county consolidation. In 1917 the Taxpayers Association of California had reported that ''local communities waste taxpayers' money on account of needless duplication.'' Mayor Cryer, in his message to the city council in 1928 said: ''Whether considered from the standpoint of economy, efficiency, harmony of operation, or of ability to accomplish the purposes of local government, a consolidated city and county would be an improvement'' and later he said: ''Why should there be a city treasurer and a county treasurer, a sheriff and a chief of police, a city health officer and a county health officer, a city librarian and a county librarian, a city motor squad and a county motor squad, a county surveyor and a city engineer, a city planning commission and a county planning commission, a city playground commission and a county playground commission? Why should there be a board of supervisors and a city council?'' Every mayor since then, including the present incumbent, has voiced similar sentiments. In 1932 the Bureau of Budget and Efficiency of the City of Los Angeles, after having made an exhaustive survey, reported that: ''For the present fiscal year it is estimated that in excess of nine millions of dollars might have been saved taxpayers of the City of Los Angeles by the functioning of a combined city and county government, rather than supporting a separate city government and helping to support a separate county government.'' Some examples of this wasteful duplication in 1940 are as follows: the city expended nearly $723,000 on its health department while the county health department cost $1,030,770 and performed no services whatever within the city whose taxpayers paid fifty-three per cent of its cost; the city expended nearly $2,360,000 on its engineering department while the county surveyor and engineer expended nearly $671,000, no part of it within the city whose taxpayers paid said percentage thereof; the city expended nearly $6,711,000 on its police department while the county sheriff's office expended nearly $1,250,000 for services none of which were performed for the benefit of the city whose taxpayers must have paid said percentage thereof. Other wasteful duplications are mentioned in the foregoing statement of Mayor Cryer. Much controversy has arisen between the city and the county over the division of the gasoline tax, the tax on motor busses and trucks, and the motor vehicle license fees. All these are collected by the state in the first instance and then a certain portion thereof is allocated and paid over to each county, with the purpose that it be equitably distributed throughout the county by the board of county supervisors. The City of Los Angeles insists, and with seeming reason, that it is unfairly treated by the county in the matter of such distribution. The allocation and payment to the counties by the state of the gasoline tax and the tax on motor busses and trucks is based upon the number of motor vehicles registered in the respective counties. Sixty per cent of the motor vehicles registered in Los Angeles county are in the City of Los Angeles, and it insists that it should receive sixty per cent of the allocations and payments made to the county by the state from those sources. The allocation and payment of the motor vehicle license fees is based upon population. Since the City of Los Angeles has fifty-six per cent of the population of the entire county, it insists that it should receive that share of those fees allocated and paid to the county by the state. The total that has been paid by the state to the county on account of gasoline taxes and taxes on motor busses and trucks is $70,774,188, and sixty per cent thereof is $42,-464,513, which the City of Los Angeles would have received direct from the state had it been a city-county consolidated. The total that has been paid by the state to the county on account of motor vehicle license fees is $26,830,036, and fifty-six per cent thereof is $15,024,820, which the city would have received direct from the state had it been a city-county consolidated. This makes a total of $57,489,333 which it would thus have received had it been the consolidated City and County of Los Angeles. But the county paid over to the city only the sum of $23,955,417. So that the city has lost, on that account alone, $33,533,916 during the period ending on January 1, 1941. Two methods have been suggested for ending this folly: one is to create the entire county into a city-county consolidated, but there are forty-five municipalities included within its boundaries whose affirmative vote, separately, must first be had as required under the constitution, and local civic pride and a deepseated love for home rule make that method impracticable; the other is to separate the City of Los Angeles from the county and create it into the City and County of Los Angeles, with a simplified form of government and a resultant reduction of the burden on its taxpayers, — but comes pride of being part of a county whose agricultural and horticultural products make it the richest rural section of its kind in this country, and if there is any one thing upon which the average Californian prides himself it is in being bigger and better than anyone else. So its people of Los Angeles continue to feed the fires of boastfulness that consume much of its taxes which might well be used for better purposes. The physical facts evidence quite clearly that the City of Los Angeles has sufficient territory, population and wealth to justify its creation into a city-county consolidated, separated from the rest of the county. The city stretches from the Santa Susana mountains on the north to the Los Angeles Harbor on the south, and from Pasadena on the east to the Pacific Ocean on the west. It has an area of 450.631 square miles and thus it is apparent that it has plenty of vacant space in which to grow. The remainder of the county has many times that area. The United States census for 1940 gives the city a population of 1,504,277 and the remainder of the county a population of 1,281,366. The assessed valuation of the city for tax purposes is approximately $1,-300,000,000 while that of the remainder of the county is approximately $1,200,000,000. In population, in territory and in wealth each is large enough to be a separate county. There is a growing sentiment that this be done.

However, there is a partial consolidation of city and county functions performed by county officers. The annual valuation of property made by the county assessor is used as the basis by nearly all the cities in making their levy for city taxes. The city and the county taxes are collected by the county tax collector who reports his collections of city taxes to each such city and makes regular remittance thereof. For that service each city pays the county an agreed sum. The county also performs health services for thirty-eight of the cities, but on a very inequitable basis. At first such cities paid the county for that service. But politics crept in and last year they paid only a cent and a half per capita while the service cost the county $1.35 per capita. Los Angeles, Long Beach, Pasadena, South Pasadena, Beverly Hills and Vernon have their own health departments. Their taxpayers, through payment of county taxes, were compelled to pay over $300,000 of the loss occasioned by this practically free service to the other cities authorized by the county board of supervisors. Its own committee characterized this as being on the basis of "bargaining, 'horse trading,' wire-pulling and politics" in its report. Request was made that the board submit to the voters an amendment to the county charter compelling these cities to pay the actual cost of such service, but the board denied it.

Dr. Clarence A. Dykstra, President of the University of Wisconsin, formerly of Los Angeles, wrote the author: "I know of no spot in the United States where a consolidation of local government would do more for economy and effective administration than in the great county of Los Angeles. Such a reorganization, plus the appointment of a strong and farseeing manager, would save the community millions of dollars."

The Wyoming constitution of 1889 provides that the legislature may consolidate offices in the state, county and municipalities, respectively, and when so consolidated the duties of such consolidated office shall be performed under an *ex officio title*. (Appendix—24.) But nothing has been done under that authority.

In 1922 the constitution of Montana was amended so as to provide that the legislature may, by general or special law, provide any plan, kind, manner or form of municipal government for counties, or counties and cities and towns, or cities and towns, and whenever deemed necessary or advisable may abolish city or town government and unite, consolidate or merge cities and towns and county under one municipal government, regardless of any existing limitations in the constitution; provided, however, that no form of government so permitted shall be adopted or discontinued until after its submission to the qualified electors of the territory affected and they vote their approval. (Appendix—25.) In 1923 the legislature passed a special act authorizing the consolidation of the City of Butte and its county, and the other cities and towns included therein, into one municipality to be known as the City and County of Butte. This act was sustained by the supreme court (70 Mont. 355), but the people of Silver Bow county defeated the consolidation proposal at an election held in 1924. In 1931 another attempt was made to bring about this consolidation but it failed. In 1923 the legislature passed a like act for the consolidation of the county of Ravalli and all the cities and towns therein into one municipal government under the name of the City and County of Ravalli, but a proposal to apply the law was defeated by vote of the people of the county in 1932.

In 1924 Georgia amended its constitution so as to authorize its legislature to consolidate and combine all governmental functions and powers vested in and exercised by cities and municipalities having a population of more than 52,900 according to the Federal census of 1920, with the governmental functions and powers vested in and exercised by the authorities of the county in which such cities or municipalities are situated; to abolish all municipal offices and to create new offices, all without regard to the uniformity clause of the constitution. (Appendix—28.) In 1933 the legislature enacted a law which provided that the City of Macon and the County of Bibb might merge if approved by a majority vote of the electors of the city and also of the county electors outside the city. In that year a merger proposal was defeated by such vote. There is some agitation for consolidation of Atlanta with Fulton county, Macon with Bibb county and Brunswick with Glynn county but nothing yet has resulted.

It has already been pointed out in Chapter VIII

that in 1912 Ohio amended its constitution so as to give its cities the home rule power of making and amending their charters. In 1917 a proposal for a constitutional amendment was introduced in the legislature to permit counties having within their borders a city of over 100,000 inhabitants to reorganize and consolidate the local governments within the county or any part of it. That proposal passed the senate but did not receive the required three-fifths vote in the house. In 1919 the Civic League of Cleveland presented to the legislature the question of authorizing any county having a population of over 200,000 inhabitants to provide by a charter for the abolition of any or all existing governments within such county, and in place thereof to provide for a municipal government over the entire county, with districts for administrative and self-governing purposes or for assessment and taxation purposes of a local character. But nothing came of it. However, in 1933, the people decided to take the matter into their own hands and no longer beg the legislature to do something. Through an initiative petition they amended their constitution that year so as to provide that any county may frame and amend a charter determining its form of government, and what officers are to be elected, the manner of their election, and that the legislative authority of the county may, upon its own motion, or must upon a petition signed by ten per cent of the electors, submit the question of the election of a charter commission, and that charter amendments are to be submitted in like manner. At the same time the people, through an initiative petition, amended their constitution so as to empower any county to frame and adopt a charter, and to amend the same, providing for the concurrent or exclusive exercise by the county, in all or in part of its area, of all or of any of the designated powers vested by the constitution or laws of the state in municipalities, and to provide for the succession by the county to the rights, properties and obligations of the municipalities and townships therein incident to the municipal power so vested in the county, and for the division of the county into districts for the purposes of administration or of taxation or both. It was further provided that such charter or amendment vesting any municipal powers in the county should not become effective unless it shall have been approved by a majority of those voting thereon (1) in the entire county, (2) in its largest municipality, (3) in that part of the county outside of such municipality, and (4) in each of a majority of the combined total of the municipalities and townships in the county excluding therefrom that part of the area of any township lying within a municipality. (Appendix —29.) Acting under the provisions of that constitutional amendment the people of Cuyahoga county, in which the City of Cleveland is situated, by a vote of almost two to one, elected the Cuyahoga County Charter Commission. In 1935 it submitted a proposed charter for that county which provided that the county should exercise not only all county powers vested in it by the constitution and laws of the state, but also all powers which might be vested in it by contract with or by transfer from municipalities or townships therein, and that such powers should be exercised by, through and under the direction of a county council to consist of a president and eight councilmen to be elected at large. That charter received a good majority of the votes in the entire county, but forty-eight of the sixty municipalities and townships returned majorities against it, and, if the charter vested any municipal powers in the county, then that vote defeated it; otherwise it was adopted. The supreme court in *State v. Krause*, 130 O. St. 455, decided in 1936, held that the charter was unconstitutional. Among other things the charter provided that the county council might enact ordinances instead of using the usual term ''resolutions,'' and the court held that this trenched upon municipal powers. In California and in most of the other states the formal acts of every board of county commissioners are called ordinances. This objection by the court

seems to be trivial. The charter provided for a director
of public safety to perform the duties of sheriff and used
the term "police" for deputy sheriffs, and that they
should perform all duties in the enforcement of the laws
of the state and of the ordinances of cities and villages
within the county, but the court held that this was unconstitutional as trenching on municipal powers, notwithstanding that for years the statutes of the state had
provided that a sheriff or a deputy sheriff "shall arrest
and detain a person violating an ordinance of a city or
village until a warrant can be obtained." (Page's New
Annotated Ohio General Code, sec. 13492.) The court further held that the constitution did not vest in counties
the power to create a civil service commission nor to
authorize the exercise of the initiative and the referendum, for which the charter made provision, and held this
to be bad although not citing any authorities in support.
But this objection need not have been used to destroy
the other parts of the charter. Much criticism has been
made of this decision. Dr. Earl L. Shoup, professor of
political science at the Western Reserve University,
scathingly condemned it in his university lecture series in
1936. Cincinnati framed a county charter under the
constitutional amendment but it was defeated when submitted to the voters. It is unfortunate that when the
people of Ohio initiated the constitutional amendment
they failed to follow the examples afforded by the constitutions of California and Colorado which had stood
the test of the courts.

Florida amended its constitution in 1934 by a vote
of nearly two to one authorizing its legislature to establish, alter or abolish, a municipal corporation to be known
as the City of Jacksonville, extending territorially
throughout the present limits of Duval County, subject to
the approval of a majority of the qualified electors participating in an election to be held in said county. (Appendix—30.) In 1935 the legislature enacted a law carrying
into effect all that was thus authorized, and provided

that the City of Jacksonville should exercise all the powers and perform all of the duties conferred on Duval County, the City of Jacksonville, the City of Jacksonville Beach, the towns of Atlantic Beach, Neptune and Baldwin, and those conferred on the county and its cities and upon the officers and boards thereof. A city council of eleven was provided for of which five were to be elected by wards and six were to be elected at large, with power to elect its own president. The mayor, with five other commissioners, were to exercise all the powers and duties of a board of county commissioners, except that the city council should act as the equalization board. One set of officers was provided for performing both city and county functions. In July, 1935, an election was held in the county on the question of approving or rejecting the law and it was rejected. In 1936 Florida amended its constitution by a vote of more than five to one authorizing its legislature to create the City of Key West out of Monroe County and all its included municipalities, in the same language as that contained in the constitutional amendment concerning the City of Jacksonville. But the legislature has passed no act thereunder.

The constitution of New York empowers the legislature to create corporations for municipal purposes by special act. There are no constitutional provisions to prevent the legislature from creating a city-county consolidated. Indeed the constitutional amendment of 1936 appears to give the legislature that power, since it provides that it may abolish any county office, except judicial offices, and may provide for the exercise by the board of supervisors, *or other elective body,* of powers of legislation and administration, the transfer of any and all functions and duties of the county, and of the cities, towns, villages and districts and other units of government in the county, to each other or to the state, and for the abolition of offices, departments, agencies or units of government when all their functions are so transferred. It is further provided that such law before going into effect must be referred to the voters and must be approved by each city having over twenty-five per cent of the population of the county, and also by that part of the county outside of such cities. Except in New York City but little seems to have been done toward consolidation. Corporation Counsel Diamond of Buffalo wrote the author, in 1938: ''There has been, from time to time, some agitation in favor of separating the City of Buffalo from the County of Erie and creating a new county, the boundaries of which would be those of the City of Buffalo. This agitation, however, has never been carried out in a systematic way, and I would hazard a guess that there is no possibility in the immediate future of anything coming from it.'' In the City of New York much has been done in the way of completing its creation into a city-county consolidated, as will appear in Chapter XII. (See also Appendix—31.)

Washington, D. C., is a city-county consolidated, created by Act of Congress. It resembles somewhat the ancient city-state. It has an unique form of government, almost oligarchic in character. Its people have no part in its government. The President of the United States appoints three commissioners, with the advice and consent of the Senate, to administer its affairs, one member from each of the two dominant political parties and a third from the corps of the army. All subordinate officers, including an auditor, assessor, collector of taxes, corporation counsel and purchasing agent, are appointed by the commissioners. The laws of Congress, corresponding to state laws, and the regulations enacted by the commissioners, corresponding to ordinances, govern. The expenses of government are paid, one-half from the revenues of the district and one-half from the treasury of the United States. Congress determines on all public improvements; nothing can be done without its authority; the commissioners have no power to appropriate money; every cent is appropriated specifically by Act of Congress. Generally the city is well administered.

CHAPTER XI.

CITY-COUNTY CONSOLIDATED IN VIRGINIA
(1708)

Virginia was the first permanent English colony established in America, and it has the distinction of starting, in 1708, the first movement in this country for the establishment of its cities on the model of the existing "counties of cities" in England already described in Chapter III. Today there are twenty-four of these cities in Virginia of the consolidated city-county type, created by the legislature.

This development of the city-county consolidated in the Virginia cities is not historically clear, although it appears that it had its beginnings in the early colonial days. Mr. Wilmer L. Hall, Librarian of the Virginia State Library, wrote the author that: "Strangely enough there is little information in regard to the governmental independence of Virginia cities. It appears that when Williamsburg was incorporated as a city, it was planned like English cities and was made a separate corporation without reference to a county. When Norfolk was incorporated, the same procedure was followed and this precedent has prevailed in Virginia ever since." Williamsburg was incorporated as a city in 1722 and Norfolk was incorporated as a town in 1736. Mr. Morton L. Wallerstein, Executive Secretary of the League of Virginia Municipalities, wrote the author as follows: "I would advise that the separate autonomy existing as to our cities, that is those over five thousand population,

has existed so long that, despite our efforts to find out
how this happened, all any of us know is that it has always been that way, and that there seem to be no sections
(in the statutes or the constitution) on it whatsoever,
but just a tradition which goes back a couple of hundred
years. We have endeavored on previous occasions to
ascertain as to how this situation arose. All of our
twenty-four cities exist under this situation, except the
city of Hampton which has a joint city-county arrangement.'' Since that letter was written Hampton has
joined the ranks of the other twenty-three cities that
perform county functions. Mr. Rowland Egger, Director
of the Budget, Commonwealth of Virginia, wrote the
author as follows: ''There is nowhere in the constitution
or laws of Virginia a statement containing the term 'independent city' nor specific provision for city-county consolidated government. The reason is that we did not
proceed from the customary form in which city property
also pays county rates to a unified plan, but our system
is a derivative of the English system of county boroughs
only we call them cities. These ideas were brought over
by the colonists, because county boroughs existed in
England by virtue of special legislation and for certain
boroughs by the Municipal Corporations Act of 1835 long
before the county-borough system was formally organized in the Local Government Act of 1888.''

This lack of historical records kept during the first
century of Virginia's colonial existence is explained by
the fact that the first printing press was not set up in
America until 1639 at Cambridge, Massachusetts, that
in 1719 there was not a single printing press in all the
South, including Virginia, and that it was not until 1728
that the first one was set up in the capital at Williamsburg in that province. With no printing facilities at
hand many matters of public importance were not made
of permanent record and many times such records as
existed became scattered only to be collected many years
later from private individuals into whose hands they had

come. Fortunately, in 1808 the Virginia General Assembly authorized William Waller Henning to collect and have printed the various colonial charters, the acts and resolutions of the General Assembly that had been passed and were yet obtainable, and a record of its proceedings to that date. This he did and in 1819-23 he published his work in thirteen volumes entitled "Henning's Statutes at Large, a Collection of all the Laws of Virginia from the First Session of the Legislature in 1619." It sheds considerable light upon the situation but not as fully as might be wished.

In Chapter III of this book is a description of how, beginning in the Middle Ages, certain boroughs in England, because of their wealth and importance, began to exercise county functions in addition to borough functions, so that by 1708 there were several very old boroughs which had become "counties corporate" or boroughs that were "counties in themselves." They had the right of muster of their own military forces, of having their own sheriff and coroner, of holding their own courts, and of selecting their own officers who performed both borough and county functions. It will be found that these examples existing in England were followed by the colonial settlements in Virginia as they grew into cities.

However, during the first hundred years after the settlement at Jamestown in 1607 the establishment of cities in Virginia was slow. Naturally they were first made along the principal rivers such as the James, the York and the Rappahannock, and on the shores of Chesapeake Bay, for they afforded access by shipping which was then the only means of transportation. In 1611 venturesome settlers moved up the James River a few miles and established new settlements at Henrico and at New Bermuda now known as Bermuda Hundred, seventy years before Norfolk was settled and a hundred and twenty-six years before Richmond was laid out, while down the river near Chesapeake Bay they had established a settlement called Elizabeth City and another called

Charles City. These early settlements were mere stock-
ades protected by palisades against attacks from the Indians and none of them could properly be called cities at
that early period. In 1619 only two of them seem to have
been of enough importance to be entitled to send burgesses to the first General Assembly held that year. The
other burgesses were sent up from the plantations and
landings where little settlements had been established for
agricultural or port purposes. The General Assembly
of 1623 provided that courts be kept once each month in
the "corporations of Charles City and Elizabeth City"
and of course at Jamestown, the capital of the province,
where the governor and his council sat as the highest
court. So that these so-called cities then had a recognized legal status as such.

However, the settlers, after the first gold fever had
subsided, gave their attention almost exclusively to the
cultivation of tobacco which brought them the best shipping returns. As a result large plantations were developed with their own river landings from which they made
shipment of their produce and at which they received
consignments of goods from England. Among these
settlements was one called the "Middle Plantation"
situated midway between the James and the York rivers
in the county of James City. The colonial capital was
destroyed by fire in 1676 and again some twenty years
later so that in 1699 the General Assembly authorized a
new capital to be built in the Middle Plantation at a
settlement called Williamsburg, and this law was re-
enacted in 1705. About that time the English merchants
interested in development of the colonial trade inaugurated a movement looking toward the development of
towns which had been almost entirely neglected. Especially was it desired that ports be established to which
imports and exports of goods would be limited, not only
that business be stabilized and the collection of duties be
made more certain but also that smuggling be curtailed.
So, in 1705 Queen Anne issued instructions to the Vir-

ginia authorities to bring about the establishment of such ports, and the colonial governor recommended to the General Assembly that this be done. However, when the General Assembly took action in 1708 in this matter it did not stop at the creation of sixteen ports, naming among them Hampton, Norfolk, Nansemond and York-town, but it further provided that "a township or burgh be established at each of the places appointed by this act for ports," and to encourage settlement of these burghs it was also provided that the inhabitants thereof should "be acquit for three-fourths of the duties that all other persons shall be obliged to pay" and that they "be free and acquit from all levies that shall be laid on the poll in tobacco for the space of fifteen years" next after the passage of the law, except for support of the parish, and that no inhabitant thereof "should be obliged to muster without land whereof he shall be an inhabitant," and not be forced to march therefrom except in case of actual war and then not further than fifty miles. This latter provision as to muster reminds one of the claim of Stamford and of Lewes in England made as early as 1461 of exemption from county control over the local militia. It was further provided that "as soon as and whenever a court of Hustings shall be established in any of the burghs to be constituted by virtue of this act, no inhabitant of such burghs shall be held to plead or go to court for any summons of law business without the burgh, except in local actions where the cause shall arise without the jurisdiction of such town, or where the value of the thing in demand shall exceed thirty pounds sterling, or in the general court or to bear evidence in some court as the laws of this country direct, neither shall they be forced to serve on a jury in any court without such burgh, except in the general court." This was an exemption from the jurisdiction of the courts of the county like those enjoyed by the boroughs in England which had gained their freedom from the oligarchic court of quarter sessions. It was further provided that all fines and mulcts be paid to the town for its own use and benefit and for no other purpose.

It must be noted in this connection that as early as 1623, only six years after the first colonists had landed, provision was made by the General Assembly "that there be courts held once each month in the corporations of Charles City and Elizabeth City for the deciding of suits and controversies not exceeding the value of one hundred pounds of tobacco and punishing petty offenses." (Henning, Vol. 1, p. 125.) This precedent was thereafter followed as to all the cities when incorporated and ripened logically into their independence judicially from the counties in which they were situated.

Under that law of 1708 each town was constituted and established a "free burgh," with the right when there were thirty families resident in the town it should elect eight of its principal inhabitants to be called benchers of the guild hall "for the better rule and governance of the town and for managing the public affairs thereof." These benchers were then to choose a director, and sitting together they constituted a court of record of the town with "all causes of meum and tuum, bargain, traffique and trade within their town, and harbour thereto belonging, or wherein any inhabitant of the town is or shall be concerned, not exceeding the value of thirty pounds sterling, and all penal statutes of the county, as also of everything relating to the town lands, saving and reserving always a liberty to any party not content with their judgment to have an appeal to the general court; provided that all causes of greater value than thirty pounds sterling arising within the jurisdiction of any burgh may be tried, heard and determined by the respective county courts wherein the said burghs lay in the same manner as might have been done before the making of this act." This town court was given jurisdiction over misdemeanors like that generally exercised by justices of the peace with power to bind criminals in a greater degree to the general court. The judges were required to hold court once a week, called hustings, with power to choose a clerk, a bailiff, a cryer and a constable, with jurisdiction especially concerning the maintenance of peace and good order in the town.

This law of 1708 enacted at the very beginning of towns in Virginia evidences the purpose of its people to adopt the county borough system then in vogue in many of the English boroughs which enjoyed both governmental and judicial freedom from their respective counties. However this law provided that it should not go into effect for three years and in the meantime selfish interests brought pressure for its repeal. The big planters fought it because they felt that the creation of towns would interfere with their business of raising tobacco. The textile manufacturers in England fought it because they feared towns might foster local manufacturing and thus decrease their sales to the colony. Between them such pressure was brought on Queen Anne, in 1710, that she caused the Virginia colonial governor to repeal the law of 1708.

However, that Act set a precedent that was followed in charters granted to the burghs and later to the cities of that Commonwealth, in making them independent of the counties in which they were situate. The first of these were Williamsburg and Norfolk. A small settlement was planted in the Middle Plantation in 1632 at the site of Williamsburg. In 1693 the college of William and Mary was established there. In 1705 the town was made the new capitol of the province. In 1722 it was granted its charter as a city. Norfolk was first settled in 1680, incorporated as a town in 1736, and chartered as a city in 1845. Both of these cities, the oldest in Virginia, were granted quite full independence from their counties patterned on the Act of 1708. They not only had a mayor, aldermen and members of the common council, but they had their own local hustings court and were granted the right of local muster of their militia. In 1738 a colonial law was enacted that no inhabitant of Williamsburg or of

Norfolk could be compelled to make appearance at any muster of militia outside the borough or go outside thereof on any military service without the order of the governor, or, in case of invasion or insurrection, without express order of the lieutenant of the county. This marks a decided independence of these boroughs from their counties. In 1736 a colonial law had been enacted creating a court of hustings in Williamsburg to have the same jurisdiction as any county court, and it was provided that the mayor, recorder and aldermen should be justices of the peace in the borough. In that same year Norfolk was created a body corporate with a mayor, recorder, eight aldermen and sixteen members of the common council, all of whom were empowered to act as justices of the peace in the town. The local court of hustings in Williamsburg and in Norfolk was empowered to grant licenses to keepers of ordinaries and the justices of the peace comprising that court were given jurisdiction to regulate and suppress these places the same as the justices of any county court might do. In 1736 Norfolk was empowered to hold a court of hustings once each month which should appoint its own clerks and other officers, and with jurisdiction "in trespass and ejectment, and of all writs of dower for lands and tenements within the borough, and of all other actions, personal and mixed, within the same, so as the demand did not exceed twenty pounds of current money or four hundred pounds of tobacco, and, as a court of record, to give judgment and issue judgment thereon." In 1765 the jurisdiction of that hustings court was extended to suits in chancery and to attachments and to all breaches of the peace the same as county courts. In 1782 the General Assembly provided that "the court of hustings in said borough (Norfolk) shall have jurisdiction of all criminal cases arising within said borough, in as full and ample manner as the county court." (Henning, v. 2, p. 158.) In that year it was provided that Williamsburg have a city sergeant to exercise the powers of a sheriff, and Richmond was incorporated with the right to elect its mayor, recorder, four aldermen and six members of the common council, and that the mayor, recorder and aldermen, or any four of them should hold a court of hustings. In 1784 the General Assembly provided that the freeholders of the town of Petersburg, which had been incorporated in 1748, should elect their mayor, recorder, four who were made justices of the peace, aldermen and six members of its common council, and that the mayor, recorder and aldermen, or any four of them, were empowered to hold a court of hustings on the first Wednesday in every month, which was made a court of record with power to try criminal cases, to license tavern keepers, to receive probate of wills and deeds and grant administrations "in as full and ample manner as the county courts by law can or may do." In that same Act the General Assembly provided that "the courts of hustings in the city of Williamsburg and the borough of Norfolk * * * may receive probate of wills and deeds, and grant administrations, in the same manner and under like restrictions as the court of hustings of the town of Petersburg can or may do." (Henning, v. 2, p. 386.)

These Acts of the General Assembly, beginning in the early colonial period, show the judicial separation of the cities from their respective counties, and this has continued to this day. Many of them have their own circuit court which corresponds to the circuit courts of the counties, each having like jurisdiction but separate from each other. Others have their own corporation court which also corresponds to the circuit court of the county with like jurisdiction but separately exercised. In a few cases a city may lack one of these courts and litigation which would fall there if they existed is cared for by the appropriate court in the county and the proper share of the cost thereof is borne by the city. But practically all the cities are independent judicially from the county. Their inhabitants may be sued only in their own courts up to a certain demand, unless the cause of action accrued outside the city.

A like administration and political separation of the cities from their counties also occurred. From their very inception the towns and cities were made independent of the county, which appears more from implication than by direct enactment, as, for instance, in 1705 the General Assembly provided that the officers of the county should have no jurisdiction within any incorporated town or city. On the other hand these officers of the town or city had jurisdiction in civil matters only within their boundaries, but in criminal matters their jurisdiction extended one mile outside the city limits for police purposes. As a result of this separation of the cities from their counties the voters in the cities, except in rare instances, have not been and are not now permitted to vote for county officers, such as a county treasurer, a county commonwealth's attorney, a county sheriff, a county clerk or a county commissioner of revenue. The state constitution of 1869, following the general rule which had theretofore prevailed, provided that in all cities having a population over five thousand there be an elective clerk of its corporation court to act as clerk of their circuit court to be appointed locally except in cities over thirty thousand where such clerk should be locally elected, and that each such city have an elective commonwealth's attorney, a city sergeant who usually performs the duties of sheriff, a city treasurer whose duties are similar to those of the county treasurer, a commissioner of revenue, a mayor and a common council. Similar provisions were contained in the constitution of 1902. Several of the cities now have the mayor-council form of government but the majority of them have the commission form of government. Generally the peace duties of sheriff are now performed by the chief of police while attendance on the courts and the service of writs is by the city sergeant or by the high constable. Where a city has a hustings court the city sergeant acts, but where it has a magistrates court the high constable acts.   Further marking the separation of the city from its county is the fact that the former constitutes an independent school district.

Each of these cities was thus made and still is a city-county consolidated.   Each is practically as separate from its county as the several counties are separate from each other.   Generally the city was carved out of one county.   But it is interesting to note that the town of Petersburg was carved out of three counties, — Chesterfield, Dinwiddie and Prince George.   It thus became a city-county in itself in 1748 separate from any of these counties.   Already the city of Williamsburg, when it received its charter in 1722, was separated from its county of James City, and Norfolk was separated from its county in 1736, so far as judicial and administrative fuctions were concerned as above outlined.   Richmond was laid out by Col. William Evelyn Byrd in 1737 and was incorporated as a city in 1742.   It was first carved out of Henrico county and was thus separated from its county.   Later the city of Manchester, lying across the James river in Chesterfield county and already separated from its county, was annexed to Richmond.   Together they constitute a city-county consolidated separate from any county.   In 1779 Richmond became the capital of the new state and in 1782 it received its charter as a city. In Virginia, as soon as a city was incorporated it practically ceased to be a part of any county.

Mr. Egger writes: ''The practice of incorporating cities in a manner which rendered them independent of the counties in which they were located grew up during the days when municipal charters were separately granted to each municipality by the General Assembly. Although in general these 'independent city' charters were not granted except to municipalities of considerable populations or of considerable promise, some exceptions did occur, so that we now have, as a result of ancient charters, Williamsburg (population 3,778) and Buena

Vista (population 4,002) (1930 census) with status to which they are not entitled by reason of population."

In 1906 a formal legislative classification of municipalities was made by the General Assembly under which it was provided that all cities thereafter attaining a population of ten thousand should be of the first class and automatically become city-county cities, and that those with a population between five thousand and ten thousand be cities of the second class. However, it is left somewhat optional with the second class cities themselves to determine when they shall become cities of the first class since their change of class is made only upon their request made to the court having jurisdiction to declare such status. This classification did not at all affect the charters then existing as to those "independent cities" which had theretofore been incorporated as such.

Today there are twenty-four cities in Virginia which are city-county consolidated, with their 1940 respective populations, as follows: Alexandria 33,523; Bristol 9,768; Buena Vista 4,335; Charlottesville 19,400; Clifton Forge 6,461; Danville 32,749; Fredericksburg 10,066; Hampton 5,898; Harrisonburg 8,768; Hopewell 8,679; Lynchburg 44,541; Martinsville 10,080; Newport News 37,067; Norfolk 144,332; Petersburg 30,631; Portsmouth 50,745; Radford 6,990; Richmond 193,042; Roanoke 69,287; South Norfolk 8,038; Staunton 13,337; Suffolk 11,343; Williamsburg 3,942; Winchester 12,095. It is to be noted that these cities are classified in the 1940 United States census report under the heading of "independent cities."

Hampton did not join the class of city-county consolidated municipalities in Virginia until 1940. It is situated in Elizabeth City county and formerly it operated as one of the three magisterial districts of that county whose affairs were run by a board of supervisors of three, — one from Hampton and one from each of the other two districts. The two members in the county continued to outvote the member from Hampton and increased the tax already levied on that city to run the county. Thereupon the people of Hampton called an election under the law of 1936 and voted to divorce that city from the county, just as the other cities are divorced from their several counties.

The government of these cities is as separate from the county as the government of one county is from another. They have their own officers and they assess and collect their own taxes. They have their own police under their sole control. As early as 1632 the General Assembly provided that "there shall be a watch kept by night when need requires," following the age-old English custom which placed the police under local control in their cities. Virginia has never succumbed to the siren song of the crafty politician that the state in the exercise of its sovereignty should appoint police commissioners for its cities. It is abhorrent to the principles of democracy espoused and advocated by Jefferson, — an honored son of the "Old Dominion." These independent cities are city-counties with all the duties and responsibilities of a county devolved upon them. They are rid of the expense of a dual system of government. The cost of their government is less per capita than that in cities not having a city-county consolidated form of government. Their police cost is an average of but $3.59 per capita while that cost in the seventeen largest cities in this country, not having that form of government, is $4.80 per capita, or 33.7 per cent higher.

Two hundred and thirty-two years ago the cities of Virginia, at their very inception, were thus given the form of the city-county consolidated, which has resulted in elimination of jurisdictional conflicts between them and their counties and in economy of administration. During all that time not one city has gone back to the outmoded dual system of a city and a county imposed upon its people with a needless burden of increased taxation. Just recently Dr. Raymond B. Pinchbeck, of the University of Richmond and Chairman of the Virginia Commission on County Government wrote the author that: "We feel that this separation is a desirable feature for the simplification of county and city government," and in the July, 1940, issue of the National Municipal Review he further wrote: "In the main the complete independence of the Virginia city has proved to be a wise political policy during the past two hundred and twenty-eight years of experience. Certainly it has obviated the controversy which continues in other states where this complete separation does not prevail. It eliminates duplicated offices, services, and equipment, and completely avoids overlapping of political authority. * * * It has placed responsibility for the efficient administration of Virginia city government squarely on the city officials who cannot allege county official interference in municipal affairs or costs."

The "Old Dominion" has well led the way and is justly proud of its fine record.

CHAPTER XII.

THE CITY OF NEW YORK
(1730)

In 1730 this city furnished the first example in America of *a city and an entire county* with coterminous boundaries, which was later followed by New Orleans (1807), Philadelphia (1854), and the City and County of Honolulu (1907). Even as early as 1683 this consolidation in New York had become so nearly complete that the city and county were generally referred to as "The City and County of New York," although not its legal title. The other instances in this country of the city-county consolidated are where a city has been carved out of its county and created into a separate governmental entity performing both city and county functions.

From its earliest beginning the history of New York City has been of fascinating interest. When Henry Hudson sailed into New York Bay in 1609, it was after he had vainly sought the Northwest Passage in the frigid north where he had been blocked by gigantic icebergs and by impassable seas of frozen ice in his quest of a way to India. Thence he had sailed south past Cape Cod and on to Chesapeake Bay there to learn that the English had been in possession of Virginia for two years, and then, turning again to the north, he had the good fortune to reach one of the greatest harbors of the world. There the Dutch East India Company immediately planted a trading post for traffic in furs, where it held sway, with slight interruption, until 1674 when England took final possession. Under the Dutch occupation the city was under the rule of a director-general appointed by that company. Peter Minuit, as director-general, drove a sharp bargain with the Indians in 1626 when he bought for the company all of Manhattan Island, comprising 22,000 acres, for $24.00 paid in beads and trinkets. Each side to the bargain was so highly satisfied that all celebrated with a grand carousal in commemoration of which the Indians named the place "Manahectanienks," a reveling name importing "the place where they all got drunk," out of which was evolved the name "Manhattan." When the English took possession they changed the name of the town from New Amsterdam to New York in honor of the Duke of York who later became Charles I. He and his successors appointed the governors of the province. These governors, in turn, for many years appointed the mayor of the city and some of its officers.

In 1652 the States General of the Dutch Republic had incorporated the City of New Amsterdam. It was granted its first charter by that government in 1657. In 1664 the city was taken over by the English and in 1665 Governor Nicolls granted it its first English charter. Eight years thereafter it was reoccupied by the Dutch who renamed it New Orange, but in 1674 it passed permanently to the English and it retook the name of the City of New York. The Nicolls charter declared that: "The inhabitants of New York, New Harlem, and all other of his Majesty's subjects, inhabitants upon this Island, commonly called and known by the name of Manhattan Island, are and shall be forever accounted, nominated and established, as one body politic and corporate, under the government of a Mayor, Aldermen and Sheriff." These officers were named in the charter. Thus the whole of Manhattan Island was constituted the City of New York. At that time there were no counties in the province of New York.

In 1683 the first general assembly of the province divided the colony into twelve counties and provided in quaint spelling that: "The Citty and County of New York, to containe all the Island commonly called Manhatans Island, Mannings Island, and the two Barne Islands, the Citty to bee called as itt is, New York, and the Islands above specyfyed the County thereof." From this it would appear that the "city as it is" referred to its boundaries as being those of Manhattan Island theretofore described in the Nicolls charter, and that the city and Mannings Island (now Welfare Island) and the two Barne Islands (now Ward's Island and Randall's Island) together constituted the county of New York. These three islands were comparatively small and for all practical purposes the boundaries of city and county were coterminous. It will be noted that thus early they were jointly called "The City and County of New York."

In 1691 the colonial general assembly provided that: "The City and County of New York (shall) contain all the island commonly called Manhattans Island, Manning's Island the two Barne Islands and the three Oyster Islands, Manhattan's Island to be called the City of New York and the rest of the islands the county." Again it will be noted that while the city and the county retained separate identities yet the boundaries of the city and of the county were practically coterminous and together were called "The City and County of New York." Unfortunately there appears to be no map showing the delineated boundaries of either the city or the county for that period.

However, in 1730, colonial Governor Montgomerie granted a new charter to the city in which he stated that it "shall be and remain a free city of itself" and therein described its boundaries as follows: "To begin at the river, creek or run of water called Spytden Duyvel, over which King's bridge is built, where the said river or creek empties itself into the North River, on Westchester side thereof, at low water mark, and so to run along the said river, creek or run, on Westchester side, at low water mark, into the East River or sound, and from thence to cross over to Nassau Island, to low water mark there, including Great Barn Island, Little Barn Island and Manning's Island, and from thence all along Nassau Island shore, at low water mark, unto the south side of the Red Hook; and from thence to run a line across the North River so as to include Nutten Island, Bedlow's Island, Bucking Island and the Oyster Island, to low water mark on the west side of the North River, or so far as the limits of our said province extends there, and so to run up along the west side of the said river at low water mark, or along the limits of our said province, until it comes directly opposite to first mentioned river or creek, and thence to the place where the said boundaries first began." In that connection it will be noted that the names of most of these islands have been changed as follows: Nassau Island is Long Island; Great Barn Island is Ward's Island; Little Barn Island is Randall's Island; Manning's Island is Welfare Island formerly Blackwell's Island; Nutten Island is Governor's Island, and Bucking Island is Ellis Island.

Clearly this description includes all the territory of the county as set forth in the foregoing County Acts of 1683 and 1691, and thus the boundaries of the city and the county were made coterminous beyond question in 1730. Because thereof the city and the county were generally referred to during this period as "The City and County of New York." (Ill. Const. Convention Bulletin No. 11, 1920.) In McKinney's Laws of N. Y. (v. 11, p. 9) it is said: "It has already been shown that the city and county of New York were, at the granting of the Montgomerie charter, coterminous, and that they remained so until the title of the territory known as the city and county of New York was changed (in 1897) to the borough of New York (Manhattan) by the Greater New York Charter." Here was the beginning in this country, in 1730, of a "City-County Consolidated" by making *an existing city and an existing county into one geographical unit.*

Further light is thrown upon this situation by a report made in 1774 by Governor Tryon to the English government in which he stated that of the representatives to the provincial general assembly "the City of New York sends four. * * * *All the other counties* * * * send two. * * * The province is at present divided into fourteen counties, viz.: The City and County of New York * * * the County of Albany * * *." (Lincoln's Const. History of New York (v. 1, pp. 38, 42). Thus it appears that the city was, in certain respects, treated as a county early in its history. In the first state constitution of 1777 it was provided that the "city and county of New York" should constitute one senatorial district and nine representative districts, and like provision, with increased representation, was made in the constitution of 1846. It is to be noted that when the legislature of 1874 enacted a law to "consolidate the *government* of the city and county of New York" it thereby recognized their territorial identity. In 1882 the legislature enacted a law which extended these boundaries by providing that "the city and county of New York shall contain the islands and also the towns of Morrisania, West Farms and Kingsbridge in Westchester county," and further declared that "the city of New York contains all that part of the state comprehended within the bounds of the county of New York as consolidated by the Act of 1874." As has been noted, the Act of 1874 was for the consolidation of "government" and not of territory but it inferentially confirmed the territorial consolidation which had its beginning in 1730.

In addition to the Act of 1882 the legislature extended the boundaries of the coterminous city and county of New York by taking parts of Westchester county lying to the north of the Harlem river. In 1912 this annexed portion was created into the county of The Bronx, but it still remained a part of the city. In the meantime a strong movement had gained headway for the consolidation of the cities of New York, Brooklyn and of adjacent

towns into the "Greater City of New York." In 1890
the legislature created a commission to inquire into the
expediency and method of such consolidation. In 1894 a
bill was introduced in the legislature which provided for
submission to a vote of the people of the affected municipalities the question of consolidation under a single
administration. In 1896, after the voters of New York,
Brooklyn and several other contiguous towns had voted
their approval, the legislature enacted a law consolidating the local governments of the territory within the city
and county of New York, the counties of Kings and
Richmond, and Long Island City and the towns of New-
ton, Flushing and Jamaica and part of the town of Hemp-
stead in the county of Queens. This law was subject to
veto by any mayor of the included cities. The mayors of
New York City and Brooklyn vetoed it, but the legislature repassed it over their veto and it became a law on
May 11, 1896. Thereupon the governor appointed a commission which drafted a charter for the new consolidated
city and in 1897 the legislature approved it by a law entitled "An act to unite into one municipality under the
corporate name of The City of New York, the various
communities lying in and about New York harbor, including the city and county of New York, the city of
Brooklyn and the county of Kings, the county of Richmond and part of the county of Queens, and to provide
for the government thereof." This charter was vetoed
by the mayor of New York but the legislature repassed it
over his veto. It provided that the boundaries, jurisdiction and powers of the City of New York for all purposes
of local administration and government were to be co-
extensive with the territory above described. That part
of Queens county not specifically included under the
charter remained outside the city. Subsequently, by the
Act of 1898, it was formed into the new county of Nassau. Since then the entire counties of New York, Kings,
Queens and Richmond, and later The Bronx, have been
and are now included within the outer boundaries of The

City of New York. The total area is 319.92 square miles. The United States census of 1940 gives the population of the five counties as follows: New York, 1,971,414; The Bronx, 1,385,777; Kings, 2,660,419; Queens, 1,291,314; Richmond, 171,215.

While this consolidation of territorial area was going on there was also taking place a consolidation therein of property rights and interests and of political functions. In 1874 the legislature enacted a law which provided that all the rights, property, interests, claims and demands of the county and of the supervisors or board of supervisors of the county were thereby vested in the city. In 1898 when the five counties were consolidated into the Greater City of New York the law vested in the city the ownership of all property theretofore owned by the several counties, and all their debts were assumed by the city. While the counties, as such, were not consolidated with the city so as to lose their political identity, yet as said by the court of appeals of that state (219 N. Y.) "all of the property of every character and description, whether of a public or private nature, owned by the counties became vested in the City of New York and divested out of said counties."

With this territorial and property consolidation into the greater city, almost from the beginning and increasing as time went on, there had been a marked and gradual consolidation of governmental functions. Under the colonial charters the common council of the City of New York appointed the treasurer who acted as such not only for the city but also for the county of New York. In 1784 an act of the legislature provided that the supervisors of the counties should apportion the share of one hundred thousand pounds sterling to be raised but as to "the City and County of New York the proceedings for the levy and collection of the tax were delegated to the mayor, recorder and aldermen," and in the same year an act was passed extending the power of the city auditor over the entire county. The Acts of 1801 and 1813 provided that "the mayor, recorder and aldermen of the City of New York shall be the supervisors of the City and County of New York." In the Act of 1874, confirming the territorial consolidation of the city and county, it was provided that "for all purposes of local administration and government of the city and county all the powers and duties that now are or hereafter may be conferred or charged upon the board of supervisors of said city and county shall be exercised and performed by the board of aldermen of said city as such." Gradually all the fiscal functions of the county were transferred to and vested in the officers of the city. Under the Greater New York Charter (1897), as revised in 1901, a board of estimate and apportionment for the city was created to consist of the mayor, the comptroller and the president of the board of aldermen, each with three votes, the presidents of the boroughs of Manhattan and Brooklyn, each with two votes, and the presidents of the boroughs of The Bronx, Queens and Richmond, each with one vote. The work of financial administration both of city and county, was largely consolidated under that board. The several functions of the former treasurers, comptrollers, and departments of taxes and assessments, of each of the five counties and of the included municipalities, except as hereinafter noted, were transferred to and vested in that city board. Nearly all the fiscal affairs of the five counties and of the five boroughs were thus centered in it. And so it remains today. The city treasurer is the treasurer for all five counties. The comptroller of the city audits all expenditures of the five counties. Under the 1897 charter he was authorized to consolidate the bureau for the collection of revenue, the bureau for the collection of taxes, and the bureau for the collection of assessments and arrears, into one bureau to be known as the bureau of city collections. This consolidation was effected in 1928. Under the new charter of 1938 this bureau became a part of the office of the treasurer of the city. The board of estimate and apportionment, now called the board of

estimate, together with the board of aldermen, now the
city council, make all tax levies for both city and county
purposes, and determine the salaries not only of all city
officers but also of all county officers so far as not fixed
by state law.   Powers once exercised by the county
board of supervisors are now vested in the council of the
greater city.   The actual management of property used
for the few county purposes remaining is exercised by
various city departments under the general administrative control of the mayor.   All local charities are in
charge of the city departments.   The schools, penal and
correctional institutions, fire and police stations in the
five counties are under the control of the city.   The fire
and police department of the city serves all five counties.
The city controls all main sewers and all parks and recreation grounds.   It utilizes the boroughs as administrative districts for some of the centralized city departments, such as the parks, but under the control of those
departments.

The charter of 1897 provided for the borough system.   The county of New York was divided into two boroughs: that part south of the Harlem river was made
the borough of Manhattan and the remainder was made
the borough of The Bronx; the county of Kings was
made the borough of Brooklyn; the county of Queens,
after having been shorn of that part taken for Nassau
county, was made the borough of Queens, and the county
of Richmond was made the borough of that name.   In
1912 the borough of the Bronx was separated from the
county of New York and was created into the county of
The Bronx.   Thus each of the five counties became and
still is a borough.   The charter of 1936 continued the
borough system.   Its framers carefully considered the
plea that the city is one city, not five, that the boroughs
should in effect be abolished as administrative units and
that the city should operate only through city-wide departments, but they came to the conclusion that local
authorities could best look after the smaller affairs of a

community and that it is a very natural and just demand that strictly local improvements, which are paid for by local assessments, be initiated and directed by local officers readily accessible and directly responsible to the people to whom the cost is to be charged. Under this system each borough elects a president who is, *ex-officio*, a member of and presides over the several improvement districts within his borough with the right to vote. He may be removed by the governor upon charges filed and a hearing had thereon. He may appoint and may remove a commissioner of public works who may take his place in certain contingencies. The borough president has control of the highways, sidewalks, public use facilities, local sewer and drainage systems but not the main intercepting trunk lines which are under control of the city, and of bridges and tunnels except those which cross navigable streams, and of constructing, improving and repairing those in his charge.

The city is divided into twenty-four improvement districts whose boundaries may be altered from time to time by the council, governed by a board consisting of the borough president of the borough in which such district is located, any councilman elected at large for such borough and the councilmen representing each councilmanic district any part of which is embraced within such local improvement district. The members serve without compensation. Such board, upon petition of property owners affected or upon a statement of the borough president that the public interest requires that an improvement be made, shall have power to initiate proceedings for creating an assessable improvement district. If it is made to appear that such improvement will not cost to exceed ten thousand dollars and not more than one-half the value of the property benefitted and to be assessed, and that such improvement conforms to the master plan of the city, the board may order the improvement after a hearing of those affected thereby; but if the cost exceeds said sum it must first be approved by the board of estimate.

In 1923 the state constitution was amended so as to provide that every city shall have the power to adopt and amend local laws not inconsistent with the constitution and laws of the state, and commanded the legislature at its next session to provide by general law for carrying into effect the provisions of the section. At the same time the constitution was amended so as to provide that: "The legislature shall not pass any law relating to the property, affairs or government of cities which shall be special or local either in its terms or in its effect, but shall act in relation to the property, affairs or government of any city *only by general laws* which shall in terms and in effect apply to *all* cities except upon message from the governor declaring that an emergency exists and the concurrent action of two-thirds of the members of each house of the legislature."

Undoubtedly the people believed when they adopted that amendment to their constitution that they were safeguarding home rule in their cities from being tampered with by the legislature, just as we have seen they had believed the constitution of 1846 had protected that right but, for a time, the legislature and the courts had stepped in to disappoint them. The same influences, now for a time at least, have again blighted that hope. The constitution of 1894 had provided that "laws relating to the property, affairs and government of cities * * * are divided into general and special city laws; general city laws are those which relate to all the cities of one or more classes, special laws to those which relate to a single city or to less than all the cities of a class." In 1912 the "Rapid Transit Act" placed under state control the local transportation business in the City of New York, notwithstanding the fact that the city owned a large part thereof, and this law was sustained (206 N. Y. 110) on the specious theory that this local transportation business concerned the people of the entire state and, therefore, that the law concerning it was a general law. Every one knows, and even judges should know, that in 1912 courts lent a very attentive ear to the seductive pleas of the public utility corporations that their grip on the street-car business should not be interfered with, and decisions rendered under that subversive influence should not be countenanced. However, in 1929, the legislature enacted the "Tenement House Act" and made it applicable only to cities having a population of 800,000 or more, of which the City of New York was the only one. It has been noted that in 1923 the constitution had been amended by striking out the provision that "general city laws are those which relate to all the cities of one or more classes" and in place thereof provided that the legislature should not pass any law relating to the property, affairs or government of *any* city "which shall be special or local in its terms or in its effect." It took from the legislature the power to classify cities and to enact special or local laws for a class, save only upon message from the governor declaring that an emergency exists and the concurrent action of two thirds of the members of each house of the legislature." In 1929 the Tenement House Act, which prescribed, among other things, the height of tenements, the dimensions of their rooms, their sanitary facilities, and other building requirements concerning them, limited in its application to the City of New York, came before the court in *Adler v. Deegan,* 251 N. Y. 467, and it was sustained as being constitutional. Two of the judges dissented upon the ground that the legislature was without power to enact the law except upon a message from the governor declaring that an emergency existed and then only upon the concurrent action of two thirds of the members of each branch of the legislature. This requirement had not been complied with. However, the majority of the court held that the regulation of the height limit of tenements and their arrangements and facilities in the City of New York did not relate to "the property, affairs or government" of that city; that while the colloquial significance of those words naturally indicated to the minds of the voters when they adopted that constitutional amendment that anything touching or appertaining to the affairs or government of the city or of the people there was within the scope of its intent, yet, under the Rapid Transit case, the words "property, affairs and government of cities have become words of art * * * and we would be unfair to the people of this state if we now changed their meaning." It might well be asked: What could be more unfair than to destroy the admitted intent of the people when they amended their own constitution? And what could have been fairer to them than to uphold what they honestly meant when they placed words in their constitution clearly limiting the powers of their legislature? The court talked about "art." The only art apparent was the hocus pocus used to fool the people in their hope for real home rule.

Furthermore, the court in the *Adler* case predicated its decision on the theory that the meaning of the words, "property, affairs and government of cities," is limited to those matters in which the city is *exclusively* interested and not to those in which the state as well as the city is generally interested. What municipal activity is there which does not affect, in some degree, the people of the state of which the city is a part? Where is the line of demarcation? Who is to draw that line? If by the courts, it will be as wobbly as the election returns. However, the most disturbing thing about this situation is that the new constitution of 1938, in the sections on home rule for cities, makes use of the words, "property, affairs and government," in at least three places, and so the decision in the *Adler* case may rise up like the ghost in Hamlet. For, if the legislature may enact laws concerning tenement houses in cities, what is to prevent it from enacting laws concerning every other building or improvement in the city? Again, the constitution of 1938 contains many weasel worded provisions. In one breath it purports to give the right of home rule to all cities under the power to frame and amend their charters, but in the next breath it provides that these charters shall not be inconsistent with the laws of the state. It purports to give cities exclusive power over their property, affairs and government, except upon an emergency message from the governor and the concurrent action of two-thirds of the legislature, and then it provides that nothing shall be deemed to restrict the power of the legislature to enact laws relating to matters other than the property, affairs and government of cities. Here is an opening as wide as a barn door under the decision in the *Adler* case, which may cause legislative and judicial jugglery such as has been noted in Chapter VI.

In 1934 the legislature enacted a law empowering the mayor to appoint a charter revision committee of nine. Pursuant thereto mayor La Guardia in that year appointed such committee which filed its report in 1935, together with a proposed charter. In 1936 it was approved by the legislature, and also by the electors of the city by a vote of 952,916 for to 603,072 against, and is now in force with slight amendments since made. It is a model of brevity and clearness. Attention has already been called to its provisions concerning the boroughs and the public improvement districts. It provides for the merit system under a bi-partisan civil service commission appointed by the mayor, no member or employee of which may hold office or serve as a member of any committee in any political club or association or serve as a delegate to any political convention. City elections are held in odd numbered years so as to keep them as far removed as possible from state and national politics.

The charter provides for the "strong-mayor" or federal plan, with slight modification, and also provides for probably the shortest ballot in any city of this country. The mayor, comptroller and the president of the council are the only officers elected at large, and have four year terms. The members of the council are elected by boroughs for a two year term by proportional representation with the right of the voter to indicate his first, second and third choice as to candidates. Prior to the charter of 1936 there were sixty-five aldermen, but then there was substituted in their place a council whose members are elected from each of the boroughs on the basis of one for every seventy-five thousand votes cast at the councilmanic election, and with an additional councilman for a remainder of fifty thousand votes or more, but no borough to have less than one. At this time there are twenty-one members of the council, as follows: five from the borough of Manhattan, four from the borough of The Bronx, seven from the borough of Brooklyn, four from the borough of Queens and one from the borough of Richmond. The enactments of the council are called laws instead of ordinances. The mayor and the president of the council may be removed from office by the governor upon charges and after service of a copy thereof and an opportunity to be heard in defense.

In addition to the officers thus elected, the mayor appoints the corporation counsel, a treasurer, and a commissioner for each of the following departments: police, fire, parks, health, hospitals, welfare, correction, housing and buildings, standards and appeals, public works, docks, water supply, gas and electricity, sanitation, licenses, purchase, investigation, markets, a supervisor of the City Record and a chief medical examiner. He also makes other minor appointments. He may appoint an assistant mayor to take over some of the burdens of his office. The mayor also appoints the president and six members of the tax commission which names assessors to value property for purposes of taxation subject to revision and correction by the commission; the council fixes the tax rate thereon. Already has been noted the board of estimate with very broad powers. Subject to the provisions of the charter and of the general law, it shall exercise all the powers vested in the city.

A very important provision of the charter is for a

capital budget. The director of the budget is appointed by the mayor. Annually he reports to the mayor his recommendation as to the maximum amount and nature of debt which in his opinion the city may soundly incur for capital projects during each of the six succeeding calendar years, the probable effect of such expenditures upon the expense budgets for each of such years, with his comments and recommendations. The mayor then sends the same to the planning commission with his recommendations as to capital projects to be included in the capital budget as to the maximum amount of debt which in his opinion the city may soundly incur as to capital projects during the ensuing calendar year. After hearings thereon the city planning commission submits to the board of estimate, to the council, to the director of the budget and to the comptroller, a budget and program detailing the items of capital expenditure that may be incurred during the succeeding five calendar years and for what purposes. After hearings thereon modifications may be made and then it must be passed upon by the board of estimate and by the council. This method systematizes capital expenditures, checks wasteful appropriations, and compels uniformity and continuity in the making of public improvements to be paid for out of public funds.

Perhaps the most important of all is the city planning commission consisting of the chief engineer of the board of estimate and six members appointed by the mayor. Its primary duty is to prepare, and from time to time modify, a master plan of the city which shall show desirable streets, roads, highways and the grades thereof, bridges, viaducts and tunnels, parks, public places and sites of public buildings, zoning districts, docks, wharves, routes of railroads, omnibuses and ferries, locations of drainage systems, sewers and sewage treatment plants, water conduits and other public utilities privately or publicly owned. The plan is intended to co-ordinate such facilities as will provide for the city the most convenient

means of travel between centers of residence and of work
and recreation, and to take into consideration the distribution of population, its comfort, health and the beauty
of the surroundings in which it lives. It is intended that
thus parks, playgrounds and schools shall be placed
where the future needs will be greatest and in relation to
means of transportation in order that they may be con-
veniently accessible to the population they are intended
to serve, and the same also as to public buildings, courts,
fire houses, police stations, public health stations and
hospitals. This commission has charge of zoning and
prepares and is to keep up to date a land use map on a
grand scale projected over a period extending of necessity many years to come, and thus to control and direct
the proper growth and development of the city. Under
the lead of Mr. Rexford G. Tugwell such a map has just
now been presented officially for the first time.

The importance of a planning commission of this
type is at once apparent to the student of municipal government. In many cities no control is exercised over
subdividers who lay out streets that do not conform to
those already existing in abutting tracts. This results
in bottle-necks that impede traffic. Worse still are those
subdividers, greedy for profits, who lay out narrow streets
so as to have more area left for sale. When the city
grows, as cities do, these bottle-necks must be removed
and these narrow streets must be widened, with resultant tremendous burdens placed upon the general body
of the taxpayers in order to pay the cost. A planning
commission vested with proper powers will prevent this.
Furthermore, some subdividers install poor paving, curbs
and sidewalks or insufficient sewers which soon require
replacement at the cost of the city or of the property
owners, which a planning commission should be empowered to prevent. The control by the New York commission over the location of public buildings, schools,
parks and recreation grounds and of the facilities afford-

ed the public for reaching them is most important. Especially valuable is its zoning powers by which systematic development of the city may be compelled instead of the haphazard growth which too often destroys good residential districts by the intrusion of apartments, business and manufacturing structures, that destroy values and make unsightly and undesirable an entire neighborhood. Now that tremendous sums are being expended by public authorities under the name of slum-clearance, it behooves the taxpayer to demand planning control so that slums may not be created or tolerated, either by preventing them in the first place or by compelling owners of property to keep their premises in sanitary condition and in liveable repair or to close them.

Under the Act of 1924, as amended, a new charter may be framed by the local legislative body or by a charter commission to be submitted to vote of the people. Amendments may be made by local law or may be initiated by a petition of not less than fifty thousand qualified voters to be submitted to the vote of the electors. Such amendments are limited in scope to the manner of voting for elective officers, abolishing any elective office or creating a new office, including transfer of powers to the newly created office or the disposition of any office so abolished. This affords opportunity for a partial further consolidation of offices already well on the way to completion.

With the marked tendency throughout the years toward a consolidated city and county form of government in the City of New York it is strange that it still tolerates and retains parts of a useless hulk of the old county form of government in the five counties with its double expense. Each of them retains the administration of justice as in counties generally throughout the state. Each of them has a district attorney, a sheriff, a public administrator, a county clerk, and a register (except in Richmond). To consolidate the courts and to reduce the district attorneys and the county clerks to one, the constitution must be amended. Most of the other county offices are sinecures filled with local political leaders at unconscionable salaries who place on the public payroll a horde of district leaders, election district captains and all around handy men for the political machines. The office of sheriff is outstanding. It pays a salary of fifteen thousand dollars in each of the counties of New York, The Bronx and Kings, with practically nothing to do since their important functions have been taken over by the city police, department of corrections and other city agencies. Hon. Alfred E. Smith, former sheriff of New York county, in an attempt to divest the counties of their sheriffs, said: "Why leave the sheriff? So far as the City of New York is concerned the office of sheriff is all finished. I was sheriff myself and I was busy looking for something to do." As governor, in 1932, he presented a plan to the Hofstadter Committee for the elimination of the five county governments, except that they remain as judicial districts. In 1935 the constitution was amended so as to vest in the city council the power to abolish the office of any county officer, other than judges, clerks of courts and district attorneys, and to assign the duties thereof to city offices or departments. (Appendix—31.) Unfortunately, up to this time, the council has failed to act, and the conditions preventing action are forcibly described by Hon. Newbold Morris, president of the council, as follows:

"The so-called 'County Reform Amendment' to the New York constitution invested the local representative body of the City of New York with power to consolidate certain of the five county offices, their powers and duties. That power can be exercised by local law only. These offices are under control of organization Democrats. The city government consists of a fusion of Republicans, Independent Democrats and groups of civic-minded citizens. The organization Democrats have been in control of the local legislative body before and since 1935, and their disposition is not to do anything about abolishing,

merging or transferring powers to city officers. They
seem to be quite willing to transfer powers and duties of
the out-moded county offices to the courts which are pre-
dominantly Democratic. By transferring the powers,
duties and functions to the courts or officers under court
control, the city would lose control over the budgets of
the county offices which are striking illustrations of un-
scientific budgeting and political favoritism. It is, therefore, no surprise that exactly nothing concrete has been
done by the local legislative body to reform county offices
which are unpleasant reminders of a past made notorious
by such political 'bosses' as Tweed. The counties within
New York City continue an independent, albeit, in most
instances, a wanton and wasteful existence. All that we
are permitted to do about these offices is to pay the expenses which they incur under state laws. The county
offices of the five counties within the territorial limits of
the city are about as obsolete as the street gas light of
the 1850's. The legal duties of such offices duplicate each
other and similar duties performed by city officers. Those
duties could be more efficiently and economically performed by city officers. The money saving resulting
from the abolition of the county offices and the transfer of
their duties to city or court offices has been variously
estimated from $450,000 to $2,400,000 a year. The economy is not so important, however, as the resultant improvement in efficiency and morale in the civil service.
These offices are filled with the men who man the polling
places for Tammany on election day. It is the last
refuge of the clubhouse loafer under an enlightened administration led by Mayor La Guardia. We have been
driving this type of payroll parasite from the city service
since 1934. They still infest the county offices over which
we have had no control as yet. The city service is now
composed almost 100% of competitive civil service employees; *the county service is nearly 100% exempt from
the requirement that employees be appointed and pro-
moted as a result of competitive examination."*

That last clause lays bare the root of the opposition to a real consolidation of city and county offices. The politicians do not propose to let the county offices fall under the competitive civil service and thus put an end to the practice of placing political camp-followers on the public payroll. (The author wrote two letters, enclosing self-addressed stamped envelopes for reply, to Mr. Edward F. Flynn of The Bronx, national chairman of the Democratic party, asking for his statement concerning the foregoing situation so that a fair presentation of the facts be made, but he did not reply. Therefore it seems admitted that what is said above is true. Corroboration thereof has come from other New York sources which say that Mr. Morris' statement is very mild to what it should be.) It will be seen, especially in Chapters XV and XVII, how, in the cities of Philadelphia and St. Louis, these reactionary influences have obstructed the betterment of municipal government and the saving of tremendous sums to the taxpayers. In an editorial in the *Saturday Evening Post* of January 27, 1940, commenting on the election held in 1937 in an effort to correct this situation it said: "When the final returns were in, Tamanny had elected enough councilmen to block Mayor La Guardia's No. 1 reform project, the elimination of useless jobs costing the New York taxpayers $2,400,000 a year." The council thus elected and controlled continued its refusal to pass a law (ordinance) making the consolidations which it is authorized by the constitution to make. In order to take the question directly to the people a measure was initiated providing for consolidation to be voted on at the election in November, 1940, but the court of appeals in one of those four to three decisions, which generally indicates politics, invalidated the petitions on the ground of alleged defects in the signatures.

However, the day must inevitably come when an aroused public will compel the consolidation authorized by the constitution. Thus will be eliminated the present overlapping of jurisdiction and of functions with attendant conflict of authority. It will extend the merit system under civil service to all public servants. It will separate from the public crib a horde of political parasites. It will better the city government and at the same time lessen the burden of taxation. The City of New York has made a splendid record of municipal progress. Its future continuance along that line cannot be doubted.

CHAPTER XIII.

THE CITY OF NEW ORLEANS
(1805)

The City of New Orleans furnishes the second example in this country of the complete territorial consolidation of a city and a county. We have just seen that the City of New York was the first. Governor Montgomerie made the boundaries of that city and its county coterminous in the charter granted by him in 1730. The City of New Orleans and its county were given identical boundaries by the first session of the legislative council of the Territory of Orleans in 1805.

For nearly two centuries after the first English settlements were made along the Atlantic coast, the great Mississippi valley received but scant attention. Earlier, from the then Territory of Florida had come the Spanish conquistadores in their unsuccessful quest for gold. In 1528 Narvaez had discovered the mouth of the Mississippi. In 1539 de Soto and his companions had marched laboriously from Florida and had been the first white men to cross that great river. Over a hundred years later the French voyageurs, bent on trade and fired by religious zeal, had braved the trackless wilderness on their way from Canada to the headwaters of the Mississippi river and thence to the south. After them came Fathers Marquette and Joliet and, in 1683, La Salle had gone down that river in his canoe past the present site of New Orleans and on to the Gulf of Mexico.

The first white settlement on the Mississippi river

was made at the present site of the City of New Orleans, originally occupied by an Indian village. In 1699 it was first visited by a French expedition under Bienville, who, in 1718, obtained the consent of his government to establish a trading post there. He laid out a village and named it New Orleans in honor of the Duc D'Orleans. The vast territory claimed by the French had been given the name of "Louisiana" by La Salle but in 1718 it was given the name of the Territory of Orleans which was later changed to the Territory of Louisiana. In 1726 the village of New Orleans was made the territorial capital. Later the territory fell into the hands of John Law, one of the greatest gamblers the world has ever known, with his "Mississippi Bubble" scheme, but he surrendered it to Louis XV in 1732. In 1762 it was ceded by France to Spain. In 1800 Spain ceded it back to France. In 1803 it was purchased by the United States under the administration of President Jefferson.

Under the French and Spanish regimes New Orleans was an unincorporated town. The territorial governor appointed its mayor, recorder and others of its few officials. The first session of the legislative council of the Territory of Orleans, on February 7, 1805, approved an act incorporating "The City of New Orleans," with boundaries lying on both the right and the left bank of the Mississippi river, including the present parishes of Saint Charles and Saint John. On April 10, 1805, the legislative council approved an act dividing the territory into twelve counties. One was named the county of Orleans and its boundaries were made identical with those of the City of New Orleans. In 1807 the term county was dropped, except for purposes of taxation and representation, and the territory was then divided into nineteen parishes and so the county of Orleans became the parish of Orleans and has so remained. In creating the new parishes the former county of Orleans was divided into three parts: Orleans parish and two new parishes, Saint Bernard and Plaquemines.

In 1812 the first constitution divided the new state of Louisiana into fourteen senatorial districts, and the City of New Orleans and its parish were designated as one. In 1825 the parish of Jefferson was created out of a part of Orleans parish. Later some of that territory was returned.

With the Louisiana purchase, and even before, there was an ever increasing influx of American settlers. They had been attracted there by the river transportation afforded their produce on the Ohio and Tennessee rivers and the other tributaries that flowed into the Mississippi river and thence down to the port of New Orleans and its markets, in the days when water transportation was the only practicable method available. These American settlers were of the aggressive frontier type and frequent quarrels arose between them and the other inhabitants and also between the French and Spanish residents. These quarrels and racial jealousies led to the division of the city into three separate municipalities in 1836, each having a council, a recorder and other municipal officers of its own, but over them was a common mayor and a general council of the City of New Orleans for all three. This unusual situation resulted in so much confusion that they were reconsolidated in 1852. In that year the town of Lafayette came back from the parish of Jefferson to become a part of the city. In 1870 the towns of Algiers and Jefferson, and in 1874 the town of Carrollton, also came back from the parish of Jefferson to become a part of the city. These annexed towns automatically became a part of the parish of Orleans. So that, while the boundaries of the city and of its parish underwent these changes, and there was a short interim of divided municipal authority, the territorial consolidation of city and parish continued from the beginning. All these changes were made by the legislature which had framed and amended the various charters under which the city had been governed. The habitable area of the city is now forty-nine square miles and its population as given by the United States census of 1940 is 494,537. It is the metropolis of the deep South.

At the same time that this territorial consolidation of city and parish took place there was a very marked vesting in the city of those governmental functions which were ordinarily exercised by the officers of a parish. For instance, the administrative and legislative powers of each parish in Louisiana, other than of the parish of Orleans, were vested in bodies known as police juries, commonly designated elsewhere as boards of county commissioners or supervisors. But as early as 1813 the legislature provided that "the authority of the police jury of the parish of Orleans shall not extend to the City of New Orleans within its present limits." Since the boundaries of the city and of the parish have always been the same it follows that all the usual powers of the police jury have been and now are vested in the city authorities. Except as to taxation, almost all matters of a fiscal nature of both city and parish are in charge of the city department of finance under its treasurer and auditor. As to taxation, however, seven assessors are elected at the city election, one from each of the seven municipal districts of the city, whose valuations are subject to change by the seven assessors sitting as a board and to review by a parochial board which may recommend increases or decreases to the state tax commission. Its valuation and classification thus fixed are used as the basis for city tax purposes, but the commission council of the city may adopt a different percentage of such valuation not less than twenty-five per cent of that fixed by the state tax commission. All officers, both city and parochial, are elected at the municipal election held quadrennially in April. The functions of many parochial and city officers have been united under one head as, for instance, the parish physician is the city physician. While it makes but little difference in many respects whether an officer is called a parochial officer or

a city officer, since he is elected by the voters of the city
who are also the electors of the parish, yet there is a
material difference as to matters of coordination. The
nisi prius judges, two sheriffs (one for civil and the
other for criminal business), a district attorney, coroner,
recorder of mortgages and a register of conveyances
are elected by the voters of the city. But they are separate and distinct from, and have no part in, the administration of city affairs, nor has the city any power or
control over them. Thus, there is no possibility of consolidation of these offices or their functions with those
of the city unless either the constitution or the laws be
amended. It makes not so much difference as to the
nisi prius judges or their clerks or as to the district
attorney since consolidation of their offices or functions
with that of officers of the city is not practicable and is
not done in the city-county consolidated elsewhere.
However, the offices of sheriff and of superintendent or
chief of police may be consolidated in the office of a commissioner of safety, and the offices of recorder of mortgages and of register of conveyances may likewise be
consolidated in the office of a commissioner of records.

The provision of the constitution of Louisiana is an
anomalous one. It reads: ''The electors of the City of
New Orleans and of any political corporation which may
have been established within the territory now, or which
may hereafter be embraced within the corporate limits
of said city, shall have the right to choose their officers.
This section shall not prohibit the election of any officer
by the Commission Council or appointment by the
Mayor, nor the filling of vacancies for the unexpired
term as now or hereafter provided by law; nor shall
it apply to the Board of Liquidation, City Debt, or to
any Board of Civil Service Commissioners or Examiners; nor as prohibiting the Legislature from appointing
or authorizing the appointment of any board or commission with full authority in the City of New Orleans
other than that of controlling the ordinary governmental

functions of municipal government.'' In one breath the
constitution started out by vesting in the electors of the
city the right to choose their officers, and then in the
next breath it provided that the legislature might take
from the city its right to choose three boards, all
municipal in character and functions, and also gave the
legislature full power to appoint and authorize the
appointment in the city of as many boards as it pleased,
with the inocuous limitation that they exercise powers
''other than that of controlling the ordinary governmental functions of municipal government.'' Thus the
door was thrown wide open to that political and judicial
jugglery spoken of in Chapter VI.

The political jugglery has now begun. In 1940 the
legislature of a so-called ''reform administration'' enacted a law under the foregoing section of the constitution striking down the provision of the present charter
that the mayor and two of his appointees shall constitute
the civil service board of the city, and in lieu thereof
provided that, beginning on July 1, 1942, there be a new
civil service commission to be composed of one member
to be appointed by the commission council of the city
and two members to be appointed by the state civil service commission. This latter commission is appointed by
the governor and thus the public service of the city is
placed in the hands of the politicians in control of the
state.

Under the foregoing section of the constitution giving the legislature power to appoint or provide for the
appointment of boards in the city it is overrun by them.
Some of them are doing good work but many of them
might well be dispensed with. Each of these boards has
its set of officers and several of them employ a force of
attorneys to the exclusion of the city attorney's staff
and this results in wasteful duplication and conflict in
authority. Many of them are empowered to determine
what they will expend and the public is compelled to foot
the bill. In a fiscal and administrative survey of the

city made in 1933 it was reported that this appointment of these more or less agencies independent of the city has resulted in detriment to a co-ordination of the functions of municipal government. Assistant City Attorney Boizelle writes: "For every major function of our government there seems to have been created a board, some of which have no relation to the commission council of the City of New Orleans and some of which have some relations with it. We even have two separate boards handling the administrative affairs of two of our large city parks, the Audubon Park Commission and the City Park Improvement Association. This last association is a privately incorporated association which has been vested with the management of the city park. These boards fix the amounts that must be included in the city budget for the upkeep of these parks."

There are fifteen city commissions or boards whose members are appointed by the mayor, five commissions or boards have members appointed by joint action of the mayor and unofficial private agencies, while there are ten other commissions or boards whose members are selected largely by private organizations. In a few cases such appointments are made subject to the approval of the commission council. It is to be noted that one of these commissions is worth while. It is called the Vieux Carre Commission which has charge of preserving, as far as possible, the old part of the original town, about a mile square, filled with structures of historic or ancient architectural interest. In addition, there are eleven so-called state agencies or boards in the city in the appointment of whose members the governor has a hand and exercises control. Many of them have large powers and considerable patronage. It will be seen that the city is over-blessed with boards to the detriment of a proper administration of the public business.

The legislature, if it would, can remedy these evils. It has full power to enact laws taking from the governor the power of making these appointments and placing that power in the people of the city or their own officers. There is where it belongs under our democratic system of local self-government. With these boards thus placed under municipal control many of them might be consolidated and some might be eliminated altogether; they would be compelled to budget their expenses just as the other city departments are required to budget theirs and thus the council commission would be able to systematize the proper allocation and expenditure of public funds upon a planned budgetary basis. Unfortunately, as shown by past experience, the legislature does not intend doing any such thing. Unless the people of the city, with their large voting power, rise up in their might and change the membership control of the legislature and it still fails to afford relief, then the only remedy left will be to amend the constitution.

New charters were framed by the legislature in 1892, in 1896, and in 1912 for the city. The present charter, as amended in 1936, provides for a highly centralized commission form of government, consisting of a mayor and four commission councilmen elected at large for four year terms. This is probably the simplest set up for any municipal government in this country. This commission exercises all administrative and legislative powers for both the city and the parish. Three members constitute a quorum with power to transact business. The mayor presides and has a vote in addition to having the power of veto. It takes a four-fifths vote to override his veto.

The branches of the government are grouped into five subdivisions. The mayor is the head of the department of affairs and appoints the city attorney, clerks of the recorder's courts, auditor of public accounts, chief engineer of the fire department, superintendent of police, superintendent of public health, city engineer, city chemist, and makes all other appointments not otherwise provided for in the charter. The four commissioner councilmen are each assigned to a department by a majority vote of the mayor and themselves, and with like vote may make changes whenever they deem that the public service will be benefited thereby. One is the head of the department of public finance and has under him the receipt and expenditure and accounts of public money and coordination of the public service. One is the head of the department of public safety and has under him fire prevention, police, health, and charity and relief. One is the head of the department of public utilities and has under him public service and utility corporations and franchises. One is the head of the department of public property and has under him streets and alleys, parks and playgrounds, public buildings, public baths, all other public property, and markets.

The board of civil service commissioners now consists of the mayor and two citizens of the city appointed by him. Formerly the police board was selected in a very unusual manner, viz., one member from each of the following organizations in the city: the Young Men's Business Club of New Orleans, the New Orleans Athletic Club, the New Orleans Association of Commerce, the faculty of Tulane University of Louisiana, the Property Owners Association of the city, and the Central Labor Council, with staggered terms of seven years each. However, in 1936 the charter was amended so that now the police board consists of the mayor (who is chairman), the commissioner of the department of public safety, and three other members to be appointed by the mayor.

In the main, there is a real consolidated city-county form of government in the City of New Orleans, although it is far from being complete. Its government has been greatly simplified over the dual system prevailing in many other cities. Its ballot has been shortened so that there are but five officers to be elected each four years. It is easier for the voter to make proper selection among the few candidates thus presented than where so great a number of officers are to be elected that the voter is confused and cannot ascertain who are best fitted for the office. For the city and the parish there is but one clerk, one treasurer, one auditor, and one legislative and administrative body. The coroner and the city physician are one. Many other consolidations have been made. It is worthy of note that the people of New Orleans are gratified over the advance thus made and that under no circumstances would they consent to surrender the advantages now enjoyed by them. Former Mayor Walmsley wrote the author as follows:

"As a former President of the United States Conference of Mayors and after consulting with Mayors of all of the largest cities, you can quote me as saying that it is the opinion of the Mayors of the United States that there should be more consolidation of Government in the municipalities and wherever possible a complete absorption of county duties by the municipalities, as the work can be done more efficiently at considerable less cost without duplication of effort. If anyone feels that the people of New Orleans would like to divide up the form of government and revert to the old dual system he does not know the facts as they exist here. The real movement at the present time is more towards the concentration and consolidation of our government. Any statement that the City of New Orleans can operate more economically by the dual system of government than the consolidated form is positively ridiculous and childish and can not be borne out by any statement of fact or figures of present day governmental costs of the City of New Orleans."

The most recent expression of opinion concerning this situation is that voiced in an article in the National Municipal Review of November, 1940, by S. S. Sheppard and L. L. Mock in which they say: "From the standpoint of parish-city consolidation, the union has been so natural that separation would be unnatural. The city is not plagued by duplication, rivalry and waste many metropolitan cities face in this respect."

CHAPTER XIV.

THE CITY OF BALTIMORE
(1851)

The City of Baltimore, following the example set by the Virginia cities, is a city *separated from its county by legislative act* and created into a practically complete city-county consolidated form of government. Its history is interesting and its transformation from the old dual system into the new is instructive.

It was in 1632, twenty-five years after the first English settlement at Jamestown, that a proprietary charter was granted by Charles I to Lord Baltimore, who thus became the first Lord Proprietary of the Province of Maryland. Really this grant conflicted with that made by James I to the proprietors of the Virginia colony, but neither the words nor the grants of kings have ever been of much worth.

Captain John Smith, of Pocahontas fame and of adventurous spirit, believing that all the territory bordering on Chesapeake Bay was a part of Virginia, made two extensive sailing voyages along its shores and inlets in 1608, and made a very good map of his exploration and discovery. Undoubtedly he entered the Petapsco river at its outlet into that bay and probably viewed the future site of the City of Baltimore.

The settlement of Maryland was deferred because of the quarrel with Virginia, so that it was not until 1649 that St. Mary's, or the first capital, was founded in St. Mary's county adjoining the county of Baltimore. The

first house erected on the present site of the City of
Baltimore was built in 1662 and, of course, it was a lonely
one-roomed log cabin with a water front to the east and
the wilderness to the west. During the ensuing seventeen years other hardy pioneers came so that in 1729
Baltimore Town was laid out under an Act of the General Assembly of that year. In 1732 another town was
laid out called Jones Town (now the "Old Town" of
Baltimore, the original Baltimore Town being the "New
Town"). In 1745 these two towns were consolidated as
"Baltimore" and, in 1747, it was made the county seat
of Baltimore county. In 1796 an adjoining settlement
was annexed to it and, in 1797, it received a charter from
the General Assembly as "The City of Baltimore." Prior
to that time the town had been governed by commissioners
appointed from Annapolis. However, the Act of 1797
provided for a mayor and a bicameral council. The
members of the first branch were elected by the residents
of the eight wards respectively, into which the city was
then divided, and at the same time the voters of each
ward, by *viva voce* vote, chose one person to be known
as an elector. The electors thus selected then met in the
court house and elected by ballot a mayor and eight members of the second branch to serve for two years. This
method of choosing the mayor continued until 1832 when
he was made elective by vote of the citizens.

The City of Baltimore soon grew to be the chief city
of the southern colonies and it is still the largest city in
the South, with a present population of 858,100 according
to the 1940 United States census. With its development
in colonial days and in the early half of the nineteenth
century into a thriving business and shipping center its
interests naturally became different from those of the
rural part of the county. The relationship between them
gradually widened and friction developed. Just as in San
Francisco where sharp controversy over wanton expenses of the city government caused its separation from
its county in 1856, and in St. Louis in 1875 and in Denver

in 1902 where dissatisfaction over the disproportion-
ate share of the county expense placed upon them con-
tributed to their separation from their respective counties, so the separation of Baltimore from its county seems
to have been caused largely over dissatisfaction concerning what was felt to be an unfair distribution of the burdens of taxation. This was especially true as to the expense of the courts. As the city grew in population the
legal business had likewise grown, and it required and
demanded a more expensive judiciary to handle that
business. On the other hand the rural population of the
county had comparatively little litigation and wanted
a simple judicial system at relatively small cost. Like
difficulties arose over taxation to build and maintain expensive public buildings all of which were located in the
city and somewhat inaccessible to those who lived in the
remote parts of the county. Both the city and the county
were dissatisfied with the fact that they were compelled
to share the services of certain officers. The county of
Baltimore was joined with the county of Harford in one
judicial district and this was unsatisfactory to the people of the City of Baltimore who wanted a judicial district of their own. And this ambitious plan was opposed
by the other part of the county because of the added cost
which would thus be created. This situation was further
aggravated by the apportionment of members of the General Assembly as between the city and the outside territory. The city felt that the representation given to the
outside territory was unfairly large.

As the result of this growing dissatisfaction over
tax burdens, the demands for and the objections to
greater expenditures in the administration of justice, the
complaint of unfair apportionment of members of the
legislature, there gradually grew up a common desire on
both sides of the controversy that the city be separated
from the county which culminated in a harmonious agreement that the new constitution of 1851 should pave the
way for doing so. That constitution made no specific

provision for the separation of the City of Baltimore from its county, yet its language impliedly recognized that this was to be done. It must be noted that the city was not created into nor was it even designated as being a county of the state by anything said in that constitution. In all its provisions concerning counties it provided no county officers as such for the city but simply stated that the City of Baltimore should constitute a separate judicial district, and that the city should have an elective sheriff, a state's attorney, a clerk of the court, and a surveyor, whereas prior to that time the city did not have a separate court, or a sheriff, or a state's attorney, for itself.

In that same year the General Assembly enacted laws by which the territory outside the city was created into the County of Baltimore with its county seat at Towsontown, and the city was given the corporate name of the "Mayor and City Council of Baltimore. Its legal name is now "The City of Baltimore." By the act creating this city-county consolidated the county commissioners were superseded by the mayor and the city council, the county treasurer was superseded by the city register, the city comptroller took over the duties of the county auditor, the city surveyor superseded the county surveyor, and all the principal county and city offices were consolidated. Naturally this resulted in a simplification of the city government and in a saving of expense of its administration.

Common sense prevailed in making this separation. The disposition of the property held jointly by the city and the county was determined by negotiation. The city bought the interest of the outside part of the county in the court house, the county jail, the record office, and the other county property within the city. It was further arranged that the outside county territory should have the use of these buildings for three years from January 1, 1855, upon payment of its proportionate share of maintenance expense. By the United States census of

1850 the population of the City of Baltimore was 169,054, and the population of the outside territory was 41,592.

In 1888 the legislature passed an act extending the boundaries of the city by annexing to it three parcels of unincorporated territory in Baltimore County. The matter was submitted to vote of the electors. Two of the parcels voted for annexation and one against it. In the case of *Daly v. Morgan,* 69 Md. 460, decided in 1888, it was held that "the legislature had the power to extend the boundaries of Baltimore City by including therein parts of Baltimore County with or without the consent of the voters residing within the districts annexed."

In 1918 the legislature passed an act further extending the boundaries of the city by including therein additional unincorporated territory in Baltimore County and also some unincorporated territory in the adjoining county of Anne Arundel. This was not submitted to vote. In the case of *McGraw vs. Merryman,* 133 Md. 247, decided in 1918, it was pointed out that the constitution of Maryland specifically provided that "the lines of a county could not be changed without the consent of the legal voters residing within the district, which, under the proposed change, would form a part of the county different from that to which it belonged prior to said change." But the court held that this provision applied only to the organization of *new* counties, and said: "The framers of the constitution well knew that the time would come when the extension of the limits of a great city like Baltimore would be absolutely necessary to its proper growth and development, and that, if they meant to deny the exercise of this power by the legislature, and to say that its limits as then defined by the charter should for all time remain the same, they would have said so." Thus the court held that the legislature had full power to annex to the City of Baltimore any adjoining unincorporated area in whatever county it might be situate, without any vote being had by the people affected.

Here was an early example of a court construing the

constitution liberally so as to keep step with the progress of the times. As the result of these annexations the City of Baltimore now has an area of 91.93 square miles. The extension of its boundaries has not been hindered as will be seen to be the case as to the City and County of San Francisco and as to the City of St. Louis. The remaining portion of the former county has an area of 607 square miles.

It is interesting to note that, under the annexation acts of the legislature, there were prescribed different rates of assessment and taxation for city purposes, as between property within the districts annexed and property within the former limits of the city, so that the included farming lands and vacant properties would enjoy a qualified exemption for a limited period from the heavy burdens of city taxation. The courts held that this, in effect, created the annexed territory into a separate taxing district and the provisions were sustained. However, in some instances, they were used by cunning tax evaders to escape paying a just share of the public burden. At this time the tax rate is uniform throughout the entire city.

After having been accustomed through centuries to the existence of counties as a part of the governmental machinery, it is not strange that the political, and indeed the judicial, mind was unable to visualize a form of government without a county. Here was the City of Baltimore created without any mention of it being a county. Thus was created a form of government, *sui generis,* and, as such, it should have been treated as a new governmental entity without having any old tags attached to it. Of course the city was a part of the state and it was its duty to see to it that the sovereignty of the state was respected and its governmental powers were enforced. All this could have been done, as was attempted to be done in the City of Philadelphia and later was completely done in the City and County of Denver, by simply providing that the city should designate those of its officers who were to perform the acts and duties required of county officers to be done, by the constitution or by the general laws. This is all that the state is entitled to.

Instead of doing this the question was left unsettled. In the case of *Mayor vs. State*, 15 Md. 376, decided in 1859, the status of the City of Baltimore was adverted to. There the court pointed out that the city had been recognized as one of the territorial divisions of the state. occupying, politically, the rank and position of a county, subordinate to the powers of the state, having the legal status of a county, although it is not so officially named. This judicial obfuscation of the real point decided nothing. The court did not mention the fact that the Act of Separation of 1851 did not provide for county officers but specifically stated that those who formerly had been county officers were to be city officers to perform county functions and designated them as being city officers and to this day they are designated as city officers. It failed to sense the real situation. As a result the city, while it has gained much in the consolidation of offices by the elimination of the former offices of county attorney, county treasurer, county surveyor, county commissioners, and several others, it still is burdened with so-called county officers whose duties might well be devolved upon city officers, thus more fully simplifying government and greatly lessening expense. However, it must be noted with satisfaction that the city government performs all of the administrative and most of the fiscal functions of a city and of a county, so that it is, in a large measure, a true city-county consolidated.

Before and after its separation from the county, and until 1918, the City of Baltimore had been governed by a charter framed by the legislature. However, in 1915, a constitutional amendment was adopted which authorized any of the counties, and also the City of Baltimore, through the election of a charter board, to propose to the voters for their approval a charter, or form of government, for any county, or for the City of Baltimore.

Acting under that authority a charter board was elected by the voters in the City of Baltimore in 1918 and framed a charter which was ratified by the voters. It was not required that it be submitted to the legislature.

The right of the legislature to amend the charter thus framed by the city is limited to increasing or diminishing certain powers to be exercised by the city. Within those minor limitations the city may amend its charter without reference to the legislature. For example, in 1923 an amendment was made to the charter by petition, in accordance with the home rule amendment, which provided for a unicameral city council instead of the bi-cameral system which had theretofore been in use. Charter amendments have also been made by the city, consolidating some of the city departments, such as the department of public works. The City of Baltimore has taken a marked forward step in securing for itself the right of local self-government.

While the constitution of 1851 tacitly provided that the City of Baltimore should be a city-county yet, until its amendment in 1915 establishing home rule for cities and counties, the legislature was supreme in respect to the manner in which both city and county functions should be performed within its boundaries. In large measure the city officers were vested with all powers over local governmental affairs. Prior to the Civil War, among its other powers, the city was in control of its police department. However, in 1860 a police board was created consisting of the governor and three of his appointees. (Chapter VI.) Its functions were suspended by the United States government 1861-62. Until the end of the war and during reconstruction days the police department fell into the hands of politicians who started a vicious circle by which the police force elected the mayor and he then helped perpetuate the board. This "scratch-my-back" system caused so much evil that the new constitution of 1867 vested in the General Assembly the power of appointment of the board which it exercised directly until 1900 when it was vested in the governor. In 1920 the voters of the city were given the right to place that power in the hands of their mayor but they voted against it.

Under the present charter the voters of the city elect the mayor, comptroller, surveyor and president of the city council at large, and eighteen members of the city council by districts. The mayor appoints the city solicitor, auditor, chief engineer, collector of city and state taxes, a civil service commission of three members, and members of the department of safety consisting of the commissioner of health, the buildings engineer, the engineer of street cleaning and the board of fire commissioners with three members, all subject to confirmation by a majority vote of all the members elected to the city council. The city register is elected by the city council. He is really the treasurer. The commissioners of finance are the mayor, comptroller, register, and two appointees of the mayor. The very important board of estimates consists of the mayor, comptroller, president of the city council, city solicitor and the chief engineer. The board of awards consists of the mayor, comptroller, register, city solicitor and the president of the city council. The board of public improvements consists of the chief engineer, highways engineer, water engineer, harbor engineer and building engineer. The department of legislative reference consists of the mayor, city solicitor, president of Johns Hopkins University, president of the Baltimore Association of Commerce, and the president of the Municipal Art Society. Assessment of property for taxation purposes, and levy, collection and disbursement of taxes, for both city and county purposes, is made by city officers. Appropriations of funds for both city and county purposes are made by the city council. A constable for each city ward is now appointed by the city people's court. The clerk of the superior court is also the recorder of instruments. There still remain vestiges of the old county since, at the general state election, clerks of courts, a state's attorney, sheriff, surveyor and register of wills are elected. While the city departments are under civil service yet these so-called county departments are not, largely due to political influences, and thus a more complete consolidation of offices and functions is prevented. For instance, the office of the sheriff and the department of police might well be consolidated into a department of safety.

However, there has been an almost complete consolidation of city and county in the City of Baltimore. That city is entitled to the creditable distinction of having taken a great forward step among the cities of this country in divesting itself of nearly all the useless county officers and of the useless, wasteful and overlapping dual system of former years. The friction that had once existed between the city and the rural territory has been entirely eliminated. The form of city government has been much simplified. The ballot has been shortened. The cost of administration has been decreased. A homogeneous community has been enabled to conduct its own business in its own way and in the interest of its own people.

Recently Dr. Horace E. Flack, Director of the Department of Legislative Reference in the City of Baltimore, wrote to the author as follows: "I believe that the people of Baltimore, as well as the people of Baltimore county, are pleased with the present arrangement, since the city does not have to deal with any problems of county government, nor does the county have to deal with any municipal problems. There has never been the least discussion of having Baltimore City restored as a part of the county, and I doubt very much if Baltimore County would like to have the city within its boundaries. Certainly Baltimore City does not wish to be burdened with a county government in addition to its present government."

CHAPTER XV.

THE CITY OF PHILADELPHIA
(1854)

The City of Philadelphia is the third example in this country of the complete territorial consolidation of an entire county with a city. This was done by *an act of the legislature* in 1854.

That splendid city bears the indelible stamp of William Penn, whose name appears in that of the Commonwealth. His father, one of the great English admirals of his day, grew wealthy in the service, first under Cromwell and later under Charles II. To that impecunious king he loaned a total of sixteen thousand pounds sterling which, of course, was unpaid when the admiral died. In 1680 William Penn, who had become an ardent Quaker while attending at Oxford and who wished a haven for his persecuted brethren, asked repayment of that loan in lands in America. The king was glad thus to relieve a troublesome debt by transfer of something to which he had no rightful title. On March 4, 1681, he deeded to Penn the province of Pennsylvania as its sole proprietor and named him as its governor.

In 1682 Penn came to America and then designated a site for the future City of Philadelphia at the junction of the Schuylkill and Delaware rivers, happily selected on account of its excellent facilities for water transportation. In planning the city he unfortunately used as a model the semi-feudal city government of Bristol, England, established a body corporate under the name of

"The Mayor, Council and Freemen of Liberties of Philadelphia," and empowered it to govern the area later incorporated as a city. At that time there were already some 360 Swedes and Dutch and over 800 English immigrants in and about the vicinity of the city. The community grew rapidly. The first charter incorporating Philadelphia was granted by Penn in 1701, under the name of the "Mayor and Commonalty of the City of Philadelphia." In it he named the first officers of the city, consisting of a mayor, recorder, eight aldermen and twelve councilmen. The mayor was elected annually thereafter from the aldermen by vote of the common council. The recorder, aldermen and councilmen held office for life. The number of councilmen could be increased from time to time as might be desired by them. Any alderman or councilman might be removed for misconduct by vote of the mayor, recorder, and nine of the entire number of aldermen and councilmen. Vacancies in the aldermen and in the council were filled, respectively, by them. It was a close corporation much like some of the boroughs that once existed in England.

This situation continued until 1776, when the American Revolution put an end to all proprietary charters. From 1776 to 1789 the city government was in a state of suspended animation. Municipal affairs were conducted in a way by commissioners under the skeleton of the wreck of the old corporation. In 1789, thirteen years after the adoption of the first state constitution, the General Assembly granted a new charter to the city under the name of "The Mayor, Aldermen and Citizens of Philadelphia." It created a city government of the people in place of the medieval character of the old proprietary charter. Fifteen aldermen were made elective sextenially by the freeholders, and thirty councilmen triennially by the freemen. The mayor was to be elected by the aldermen from their own number. The recorder was to be selected by the mayor and the aldermen jointly from the freemen of the city.

In 1796 the charter was amended by legislative act which provided that the qualified voters were to elect twenty members of the common council for a term of one year, and twelve members of a select council for a term of three years, thus constituting a bi-cameral elective house for legislative purposes. The recorder and aldermen were divested of legislative powers theretofore exercised by them and their duties were largely limited to judicial functions. They were appointed by the governor to serve during life or good behavior. The mayor, with few exceptions, had the power of appointment of all officers created by ordinance of councils. The treasurer was elected by the councils. It was not until 1839 that the charter was amended so as to make the mayor elective by the people of the city.

From the first, law enforcement was generally feeble. This came about largely from the underlying character of the settlers. William Penn was a broad minded liberal and a staunch defender of religious liberty. He had spent many years in various prisons in Europe for his outspoken opinions. He invited immigrants of all nationalities and religious faiths to make their homes in the new colony. But, as was too often the case, these settlers lacked the tolerant broadmindedness of their patron. They had fled from the persecution of the old world to become, in turn, bigots in the new. The English, German, French (Huguenots), Swedish and Dutch inhabitants quarrelled racially, religiously, politically and socially. In these, and other quarrels, the police force was singularly inefficient. This was strikingly shown in the Negro riots of 1835. In 1838 a mob attacked and burned Pennsylvania Hall at Sixth and Haines streets, while the police stood idly by. A similar situation arose in the labor riots of 1843. In 1844 occurred what was known as the Native American riots, where the police did nothing and even the militia at first refused to respond to the call of the governor.

As a result of this deplorable condition of affairs a

movement was begun in 1836 toward ultimate consolidation of the outlying part of the county with the City of Philadelphia. In that year the legislature enacted a law permitting the annexation of Moyamensing and Passyunk to the city should they agree thereto, but nothing came of it. In 1845 an attempt was made to force annexation by legislation but it was defeated. Steadily the sentiment grew for consolidation of the entire county with the city into one governmental unit with one set of officers clothed with strong law enforcement powers. There was also a demand for divorcement of executive and legislative powers. Step by step the executive powers of the mayor had been largely taken away from him until he remained a mere figurehead, and they had been vested in the council. All branches of executive supervision and control were scattered among a dozen committees whose personnel was changed from year to year; there was no fixed policy and the usual disastrous results followed with an unnecessary increase of cost. Accentuating the burden of taxes was the fact that in the county the taxpayers were compelled to support not only the city government of Philadelphia, but also the cost of government in thirteen townships, six boroughs and nine incorporated districts, besides the unincorporated territory. The situation became so bad that the business interests and the better element banded together in a strong organization and procured from the legislature the "Act of Consolidation," approved February 2, 1854, by which the then City of Philadelphia and all of the outlying part of the county comprising the aforesaid townships, boroughs, incorporated districts, and unincorporated territory, were consolidated into one government under the name of the "City of Philadelphia." At that time the city had a population of 127,376 and the remainder of the county had a population of 391,424. In 1916 the legislature annexed to the city a portion of Cheltenham township in Montgomery county. There have been no subsequent annexations. The city now has an area of 128 square

miles, with a population of 1,931,334 as shown by the
1940 United States census.

By the Consolidation Act of 1854 not only were the
boundaries of the city made coterminous with those of
the county but the title to all county property was vested
in the city which, in turn, assumed all public debts of its
included parts. In addition to this territorial and property consolidation there was a consolidation of offices and
functions. The offices of the included six boroughs, nine
incorporated districts and the thirteen townships, and
also the board of police of the district, were abolished.
The Act transferred the policy-determining, taxing,
spending and borrowing powers of the county commissioners to the "city councils of said city and the officers
thereof." It further provided that "the commissioners
of the county of Philadelphia, the treasurer and auditors
thereof, the county board, the commissioners of the sinking fund and the supervisors of the townships, shall
cease and terminate, except so much thereof as may be
necessary to enable the City of Philadelphia as established by this Act to collect the outstanding debts and
make a full and complete settlement of the affairs
thereof: Provided, that all treasurers, police and other
officers of the aforesaid corporations, county and townships, shall continue to discharge the duties of their respective offices *until superseded or dismissed by the authority of the City of Philadelphia.*" Clearly the city was
thus authorized to supersede and dismiss all of said officers and to fill their places with city officers. The Act
further provided that many of the administrative duties
formerly performed by the county commissioners were
thereafter to be performed by a board of three elective
city commissioners whose duties were to be carried on
"under the direction and control of the councils." This
board of city commissioners administered the election
machinery, except such duties as fell to the registration
commission appointed by the governor. The Act specifically provided that duties and functions theretofore de-

volved on officers of the county should be exercised by officers of the city. The functions of the county treasurer and of the county auditor were devolved upon the city treasurer and the city controller, respectively, of the new City of Philadelphia. After imposing certain duties on the city controller the Act declared that "he shall perform all the duties now enjoined by law on the county auditors." The city treasurer took over the duties then enjoined by law on county treasurers. To assist him the office of "city receiver of taxes" was created and he was empowered to "collect and receive all taxes and public assessments payable and receivable within the limits of said city," and daily to pay the same to the city treasurer who was required to pay "into the treasury of the state the amount of the state tax assessed within the limits of said city." It is to be noted that these three important officers, performing both city and county functions, were made elective at the city elections to be held in May thereafter.

As was aptly said in *Philadelphia vs. Commonwealth,* 52 Pa. St. 451, at 455, decided in 1866: "By the Consolidation Act of 1854 the City of Philadelphia was expanded so as to embrace the whole territory of the county of Philadelphia—and the powers of the city, as enlarged and modified by the Act, were to be exercised and have effect within the whole county and over all the inhabitants thereof. Taxation in all its forms and departments, for imposition, collection and payment over, was committed to the city, and appropriate officers were provided to supervise this important subject, and the functions of county officers in this regard were suspended."

While the Consolidation Act provided that the county of Philadelphia should be one of the counties of the state and that officers not superseded by its terms, such as the sheriff, district attorney, the judges of the *nisi prius* courts and their clerk (prothonotary) should be retained, yet *they were denominated as officers of the city.* For a short time they were made elective at a time different from that when the other city officers were elected, but in 1861 the legislature enacted a law which provided that all be elected at the same time. Every Act of the legislature designated all officers as those of the City of Philadelphia, and not otherwise, and that is still the rule and practice. The city officers performed and still perform a very great part of the duties in that city required to be performed by county officers elsewhere. This was along the line later adopted in the constitution of Colorado by which the City and County of Denver was created and which provided that every charter "shall designate the officers who shall, respectively, perform the acts and duties required of county officers to be done by the constitution or by the general law, as far as practicable." (Appendix-26 and also Chapter XVII.)

The result of this consolidation gave general satisfaction to the people of the City of Philadelphia. No longer were the lawless elements in the community winked at or encouraged by the police force. The head of that force was made elective by the councils, — later by the Act of 1856 made appointive by the mayor. The number of patrolmen was immediately reduced from 850 to 650 and this reduction was maintained for ten years despite the growth in population of the expanded city and it was more efficient than had been the aggregate police forces of the former city, the six boroughs, thirteen townships and nine incorporated districts. From this, as well as from the consolidation of offices, there resulted a great saving to the people. The cost of maintaining one set of public officers was materially less than many sets had required. Instead of jurisdictional friction there was harmony. On every account the benefits of consolidation were clearly apparent.

For twenty years this system of city-county consolidation prevailed. Then came the constitutional convention of 1874. Through oversight, or for political ends, proper consideration was not had or provision made to safeguard this situation. That constitution contained a clause that "county officers shall consist of sheriffs, coroners, prothonotaries, registers of wills, recorders of deeds, commissioners, treasurers, surveyors, auditors or controllers, clerks of courts, district attorneys, and such others as from time to time may be established by law."

Since it was well known that, for twenty years, there had been no county officers as such in the City of Philadelphia, it must be evident that the members of that constitutional convention were thinking of and providing for county officers only in the remainder of the state and had no intention of disturbing the then existing situation in the City of Philadelphia. It is true that in 1876 an Act was passed which provided that in all cases where a city containing over 300,000 inhabitants is coterminous with the county (applying alone to the City of Philadelphia) "all of the officers shall be regarded as county officers." But clearly that Act was only for fixing fees to be charged in the performance of county functions by the city officials performing them. It is self-evident that the legislature never intended any other meaning to the broad language that "all of the officers shall be regarded as county officers." For that would have made every city officer a county officer. And all the acts of the legislature negative any such construction.

However, in 1883, Robert E. Pattison, who was then ending two terms as "city treasurer" was elected governor. A dispute arose as to whether the governor or the mayor should fill the vacancy thus created in that office. The court in *Taggart v. Commonwealth,* 102 Pa. St. 354, decided in that year, held that the "city treasurer" was a "county officer" and that the governor should fill the vacancy. It is unfortunate that the court did not adopt the sensible rule laid down by the Maryland court in the *McGraw* case (133 Md. 247), where the legislature was given credit for common sense and where the court kept step with the progress and requirements of the times. It is to be noted, however, that while the court in the *Taggart* case held that there must be a county auditor yet it said that "whether all these duties and obligations (of the city controller) are lawfully imposed on the (county) controller, as well as to what extent a county officer may be subjected to the authority of the city councils, are not questions before us and we express no opinion thereon."

In 1891 a vacancy occurred in the office of the "city controller," and the court in *Commonwealth v. Oellers*, 140 Pa. St. 457, decided in 1891, held that the "city controller" was a "county officer" and that the governor should fill the vacancy. However that was a 4 to 3 decision and, had it not been for the legal fetish of "stare decisis" that has too often shackled the bench and the bar from doing the just and proper thing, it is quite evident from what was said therein that the *Taggart* case would have been overruled.

In the *Oellers* case, Mr. Justice Mitchell, in his dissenting opinion, pertinently said: "No person has been elected to an office styled 'county treasurer' in the City of Philadelphia for nearly forty years. A person has been elected and commissioned as city treasurer during all that time. * * * The change (under the 1874 Constitution) in no manner affected the practical substance of the office or the officer, and so clear has this been to all eyes, that no change has been made even in his title. He is still, under the Constitution as under the Act of 1854, legally known as the city treasurer, and under that title, county officer though he be, that act prescribes the scope of his office, its powers, duties and liabilities."

However, these decisions have fortunately not altered the governmental structure of the City of Philadelphia. All its officers are still designated as officials of "The City of Philadelphia," and are not designated as county officials. They simply perform in great measure, as such city officials, those functions required of county officers to be done in the other counties. Only in case of vacancies in the so-called county offices the persons to fill them are to be appointed by the governor instead of by the mayor. Otherwise all officers are elected by the voters of the city and at the time of the city election.

While the governmental structure has not thus been altered, yet these decisions of the court have resulted in depriving the people of the city of the exercise of their just powers over their own local government. In the first place they cannot consolidate offices and simplify their government as they might do if those decisions had not been made. In the second place, by placing officers in the category of "county officers" the legislature exercises control over them. It fixes their compensation, powers and duties, and the number and salaries of their employees. The tax payers of the city are left helpless to say anything about it. All they can do is to pay. The officers, both constitutional and legislative, falling under this control are the three county (city) commissioners, the city treasurer, city controller, board of revision of taxes, register of wills, district attorney, sheriff, coroner, recorder of deeds, judges of the court of common pleas and its clerk, judges of the municipal court and of the orphans court, and twenty-eight magistrates most of whom are elected. In addition the court of common pleas appoints a board of prison inspectors, a board of education, and the commissioners of Fairmount Park.

Aggravating that situation and increasing the burden of tax thus imposed is the fact that the three county (city) commissioners, recorder of deeds, sheriff, register of wills, board of education, registration commission, and commissioners of Fairmount Park, each have a solicitor separate from the city solicitor, at additional and unwarranted expense to the taxpayers of the city. The result of this situation is much increased patronage over which the city has no control as to expenditures. In addition, the state house crowd has taken good care to keep in its hands control over elections held in the city. The legislature created an election commission whose members are appointed by the governor. This increases the patronage to be distributed to the faithful and insures much control over the results of elections. Furthermore, while all city appointees and employees are under civil service, the legislature has failed to place under civil service of any kind any of the so-called county appointees or employees or of any of the commissions and boards created by it. That condition fosters and perpetuates a tremendous voting power under political domination which has been used as we shall presently see to prevent real consolidation in the City of Philadelphia just as we have seen it has been used in the City of New York.

If the legislature were not controlled by designing politicians intent on retaining their wasteful and pernicious patronage and power in the city it would provide for civil service in all departments in the city under whatever name. It may easily do so since it is supreme in its power over city charters. While the constitution of Pennsylvania provides that "the General Assembly shall not pass any local or special law regulating the affairs of counties or cities, nor changing the charters of cities, or creating offices in counties and cities," yet, in 1901, it enacted the notorious "Ripper Bills" which placed Pittsburg, Allegheny and Scranton in a class apart, deposed their mayors and empowered the governor to appoint a recorder in each to perform the former duties and powers of the mayor. In *Commonwealth v. Moir,* 199 Pa. St. 534, decided in that year, this Act was held constitutional. The court announced that the legislature has full power to classify cities according to population, that such legislation is thus made general and not special, and that this matter is wholly legislative in character over which the courts may not exercise any supervision or control. The constitution also provides that the legislature may classify counties on the basis of population. Under that power the county of Philadelphia has been designated as the only county of the first class. Under the decision in the *Moir* case, clearly the legislature may not only provide for universal civil service in the City of Philadelphia but it may also provide for consolidation of offices and functions. But it has done nothing along this line and past experience evidences its intent to do nothing.

However, for many years there has been an articulate sentiment in the City of Philadelphia in favor of abolishing the so-called "county offices," so that instead of the present hybrid city-county government there be a real consolidated city-county with the resultant elimination of a useless duplication of officers, a simplification and unification of its government, and a lessening of expense. In 1931 the Bureau of Municipal Research of Philadelphia framed a constitutional amendment which provided that "all functions of county government and of county officers in Philadelphia be performed by the city officers." It left to the legislature the power to designate what city officers should perform county functions. But nothing came of it. Not deterred by this defeat, the forward looking citizens of that city kept at work. As a result the legislature adopted a joint resolution in 1935 for an amendment to the constitution which provided that "the County of Philadelphia as distinct from the City of Philadelphia be abolished, and that all county functions be devolved upon the officers of the city." Pursuant to the requirement of the constitution that such resolution must be adopted by two successive sessions of the legislature before a constitutional amendment may be submitted to a vote of the people that resolution was again adopted by the legislature in 1937. It was voted on in the state in 1938. In the meantime a new administration had come into control of the City of Philadelphia, and the political crowd formerly in power frowned on this constitutional amendment which would lessen its grip on its remaining patronage there in the county offices. While the city chairman of the Republican organization in the city announced his support of the amendment yet a majority of his party members there joined with the Republican county officers and their appointees who were opposed to being placed under civil service or of chancing the loss of their jobs. The Republican national committeeman for the state opposed the amendment and he carried the up-state vote with him. The vote in the city was 184,720 for and 121,938 against the amendment, or a favorable majority there of 62,782, while the up-state vote was 565,494 for and 754,239 against. So that the total vote was 750,214 for and 875,168 against, and thus the amendment was defeated.

The voters of Pennsylvania worked a rank disservice to the people of their largest city in blocking this attempt to better its form of government. City Solicitor Joseph Sharfsin wrote the author in 1939: "There is no doubt but that a thorough unification in lieu of a dual form of government is bound to accomplish a great deal in reducing operating expenditures through the elimination of duplicated functions. Such a simplification of Philadelphia's structure of government should prove particularly advantageous because our city enjoys the same boundaries as the county within which it is located. The dual form of government divides the jurisdiction over the so-called 'purse strings' between the legislature, which has control of the county offices, and the council in charge of the city departments and employees. It is obvious that this restriction upon local officials prevents the adoption of a strict pay-as-you-go policy in the administration of the city affairs because they have no voice in the expenditures of the county offices. A mayor may find it necessary to reduce the municipality's annual expenditures so that they will be within the estimated annual receipts and so make his recommendations to the City Council. This body which may or may not be 100%, in accord with the chief executive's views, under the dual form of government is prevented by the legislature from exercising any control over that important portion of the budget which covers the county offices. And so, irrespective of the sincerity that these officials may evince, their limited power over these expenditures actually is a barrier to any plans of governmental economy. It seems reasonable, then, that the control over the 'purse strings' should be with the officials in whose hands lie the power to tax and to make appropriations from the revenue received therefrom.''

That statement by the city solicitor of the largest city in the state is a stinging indictment of domination by the legislature over its local government. Pennsylvania is generally looked upon as one of the worst boss ridden states in the Union. Already have been noted the notorious ''Ripper Bills'' enacted by the legislature at the behest of the politicians, and also the defeat by them of the constitutional amendment which would have given Philadelphia one set of officers to conduct its business economically and systematically. While the people of other states have armed themselves with the weapons of democracy, the initiative, the referendum and the recall, in Pennsylvania they are left undefended from attack by subversive interests.

The cities of Pennsylvania have practically no home rule powers. The legislature makes and amends their charters. Sometimes heed is paid to the wishes and needs of the city but too often the voice of the scheming politician is the more potent. In 1921 a small bit of home rule power was given by the legislature to the cities by empowering their electors by vote to vest in the city council the control of the city finances, the right to fix the tax rate, to prescribe the salaries of city officers, and to fix the number and compensation of their employees and attaches. The four statutes which have constituted the important charters of the City of Philadelphia are: the Act of 1789, the Consolidation Act of 1854, the Act of 1885 known as the Bullitt Bill, and the Act of 1919 generally known as the City Charter Act, which, among other things, provides for a small unicameral council. Under the latter Act, which is the present charter, the number of executive departments of the city are fourteen: mayor, public safety, public works, public health, public welfare, wharves, docks and ferries, city transit, city solicitor, city treasurer, city controller, civil service, sup-

plies and purchases, and city architecture. The department of city receiver of taxes was created by separate
legislation.

While the city council is forbidden by the charter
framed by the legislature to create departments in addition to those above named, yet it has, from time to time,
created various bureaus or boards as adjuncts to the
named departments but having no part in the performance of county functions. If the city had "Home Rule"
under which it could frame and adopt its own charter
and designate those of its officers who should perform
the acts and duties of county officers as well as those of
the city the way would be clear for a proper consolidation
of officers, thus eliminating useless waste and conflicts.

The mayor, by and with the advice and consent of
the city council, appoints the head of each department.
He and the city treasurer, the city receiver of taxes and
the city controller, are elected at large by the voters of
the city. The members of the civil service commission
are elected by a majority vote of the elective members of
the city council. The city treasurer is the custodian of
all city and county funds and remits state taxes to the
state treasurer. The city controller is the fiscal and accounting officer of the city-county. The city receiver of
taxes collects all taxes and other revenues and turns the
same over to the city treasurer, except that school taxes
are paid over to the school board. Twenty-two members
of the city council are elected in the various state senatorial districts of the city in proportion to the population
thereof, as determined by the then last United States
census. The ratio for the election of councilmen is determined by dividing the whole population of all the senatorial districts in the city by twenty-two. One councilman shall be elected for each such ratio and an additional
councilman shall be elected for any fractional portion of
such ratio in excess of fifty per cent thereof. The fifteen
members of the board of education are appointed by the
board of judges of the court of common pleas. In addi-

tion, the following so-called "county officers" are elected
at large: sheriff, coroner, recorder of deeds, register of
wills, district attorney, clerk of quarter sessions court,
judges of the municipal court, and also magistrates of
whom two thirds are elected by the majority political
party and one third is elected by the second largest political party, provided that where there are three candidates a voter may vote for but two.

The City of Philadelphia has taken a creditable place
among the cities that have made material progress toward real city-county consolidation. While its people
have been temporarily blocked in their recent attempt to
make that consolidation complete yet, undoubtedly, the
spirit that ruled in Independence Hall and still inspires
the citizens of that great metropolis will lead them on to
ultimate victory.

CHAPTER XVI.

THE CITY AND COUNTY OF SAN FRANCISCO
(1856)

San Francisco is one of the outstanding examples in this country of complete consolidation of city and county, after long travail, *with one set of officers performing both city and county functions.* It was created in 1856 by an *act of the legislature separating it from its county.*

The history of that city, especially in its earlier days, is filled with romantic interest. In 1542 Cabrillo sailed along the coast of what was then thought to be an island known as California. In 1579 Sir Francis Drake in his ship, the "Golden Hind," sailed past the Golden Gate and touched land at a creek a few miles north of that entrance to a great harbor, ignorant of its existence. In 1602 Vizcaino explored the coast as far as the northern line of the present state of California. In 1769 Gaspar de Portola was appointed by King Carlos III of Spain as the governor of the new country called California. When he took possession at San Diego with his Spanish followers there came with him Fra Junipero Serra whose abiding faith in his God and his love for all men gave his statue a place in the rotunda of our national capitol. At once Portola set out from San Diego in search of Monterey Bay which he reached without recognizing it and then continued north where one of his scouts, Francisco de Ortega, looked down from the hills for the first view by a white man on San Francisco Bay.

It was not until 1775, the year of the battles of Lexington, Concord and Bunker Hill, that Juan Manuel de Ayala sailed through the Golden Gate into that beautiful harbor. The next year Lieutenant Jose Joaquin Moraga, with sixteen Spanish soldiers and seven colonists with their families and their herds, accompanied by two Franciscan friars, after an overland journey from Monterey, planted a settlement on the present site of San Francisco and named it Yerba Buena. By that name it was known until the American occupation in 1847 when it was changed to San Francisco to correspond to the name of the bay. The year after the American occupation, a common council of six persons was elected, and the alcalde assumed some of the functions of a mayor, presided at the meetings of the council, cast a vote in case of a tie, but could take no part in the proceedings. The police force consisted of two constables.

The discovery of gold in 1848, about one hundred miles northeast of San Francisco, quickly and completely changed the picture. It brought in a flood of newcomers from all parts of the world in their mad quest for riches. At first, San Francisco was almost depopulated by the rush of its inhabitants to the new placer mines. Its two weekly newspapers were suspended, the banks were closed, at one time there was but a single officer clothed with civil authority. However, in 1848 an election was held and the town government was reconstituted. In 1850 California was admitted as a state, and by Act of April 15, 1850, passed by the first legislature, the City of San Francisco was incorporated under a special charter.

The city started out under very bad auspices after the first municipal election held on May 1, 1850. The council at its first meeting promptly proceeded to plunder the city treasury by fixing the mayor's salary at $10,000 a year and the salaries of the recorder, marshal, and city attorney, at from $4,000 to $6,000 a year. Expenditures absorbed all available resources and necessitated the issuance of scrip. In nineteen months public expenditures had risen to more than two million dollars.

This was out of all reason in a time of financial panic for a city most of whose citizens had joined the mad procession to the gold fields. Those who were left belonged largely to the criminal class. To those who returned disillusioned from a vain search for gold was added a motley crowd of criminals from all quarters of the globe attracted by the opportunity of fleecing the miners who, with their pouches of gold dust and nuggets, had come to the city intent on hours of relaxation. San Francisco became a wide-open town filled with lawlessness. It was placed at the mercy of Tammany trained leaders from New York and others of like breed from Philadelphia and Baltimore. They packed city conventions, stuffed ballot boxes, and held back election returns for days so as to manipulate the results. One of the leaders was a cold-blooded murderer. One of the city officials so elected had been an inmate of Sing Sing prison in New York. Finally the law abiding citizens organized the famous "Vigilance Committee" in 1851 which proceeded to hold some salutary hangings of the ringleaders. Conditions were better for a time but by 1856 crime and corruption in the city again became intolerable, the city treasury was brazenly looted, the expenditures for both city and county in 1855 had reached the swollen sum of $2,646,000 notwithstanding the fact that the city was in the throes of another financial panic.

This situation which had been the result of years of fraud, corruption and mismanagement on the part of the city officers aroused public sentiment so that a movement was started in that year for a consolidated city-county government. In contrast with the inefficiency, extravagance and flagrant corruption of the city government, the county government was being run in an economical and efficient manner. A committee of the better citizens decided upon separation of the city from the county, but to retain the county officers as the officers of the new city-county. It will be noted that this was the reverse of what had occurred in New York, New Orleans,

Baltimore and Philadelphia, where the city officers were retained to perform the powers and functions theretofore exercised by the county officers. Here the county officers were to be retained to conduct the city functions. Accordingly, that committee petitioned the legislature in 1856 for relief from the excessive weight of taxes and debt piled up by the city gang which, it was stated, "supported an army of officers and dependents of little practical use either in preserving order or keeping the streets in repair; that the whole police force was a useless expense whose duties could well be discharged by the sheriff and ordinary constables; that no utility was seen in having a city government separate from that of the county, as county officers could well discharge all the duties of city government."

Finally, on April 19, 1856, the legislature passed an act extending the limits of the city, separated the city as thus enlarged from the county and created it into the City and County of San Francisco. It was the second governmental entity in this country designated as a "City and County." The legislature passed another act creating the remainder of the old county into the new county of San Mateo and such it still remains. There was no vote of the people required or taken. Objection was raised that the act creating the City and County of San Francisco violated the requirement of the constitution that "the legislature shall establish a system of county and town governments, which shall be as nearly uniform as practicable throughout the state." But in *People v. Hill*, 7 Cal. 97, decided in 1857, the constitutionality of the act was sustained. The United States census of 1860 gave the population of the City and County of San Francisco as being 56,802, and that of San Mateo county, the part of the old county which had been stricken off, as being 3,088. The area of the City and County is now and from its creation has been 46.5 square miles. The area of the remaining part of the former county, now the county of San Mateo, is 447 square miles. The population of the

City and County of San Francisco as given by the United States census of 1940 is 634,536.

The Act of 1856 provided that all public buildings, lands, rights of property and rights of action, and all moneys and revenues including collections from taxes then delinquent, should become the property of the new city and county. All officers were required to be elected at the times and in the manner prescribed by law for the election of state and county officers. It was provided that all the existing laws defining the powers and duties of county officers (excepting those relating to supervisors and boards of supervisors), so far as the same were applicable and not repealed by the separation act, were to be considered applicable to the officers of the new city and county. In harmony with the desire of the citizens of San Francisco, it was provided that the then county auditor, assessor, recorder, and attorney, should become, respectively, such officers of the new consolidated city and county; that the county supervisors should supersede the city council, and that the county marshal should supersede the chief of police. Besides these, there were also retained the other county officers, viz.: judges, clerks of courts, district attorney, sheriff, coroner, public administrator, and surveyor.

The Act of 1856 further provided that at the then next general election, as the officers of the city-county consolidated, there should be elected at large: a president of the board of supervisors, county judge, district attorney, sheriff, recorder, clerk, treasurer, auditor, tax collector, assessor, surveyor, police judge, chief of police, superintendent of schools, superintendent of streets, and two dockmasters for the port of San Francisco; and also that the following officers be elected by districts: supervisors, justices of the peace, constables, school directors, an inspector and two judges of election. The campaign carried on for that election was without precedent for its bitterness. James King, editor of the *San Francsico Bulletin,* led the fight for the ticket of the Reform Party.

Against him were lined up the remnants of the old criminal gang behind the Democratic ticket. The ticket of the Reform Party was elected by a vote of 6,882 to 3,928. A few days later King was shot down on the street by one of the gangsters. Immediately the "Vigilance Committee" reassembled, two murderers were hanged the next day, a horde of criminals fled from the city, much of the political corruption was purged, and the committee then disbanded and was not again required. With the newly elected high-minded officials having in view only the public welfare, the new city-county was finally launched.

This separation from the county and the creation of the city into the City and County of San Francisco, with one set of officials instead of being burdened with the former double set, resulted in immediate benefit to its people. The city, plunged into debt by its former rascally officials, soon saw the debt materially lessened. Hittel in his "History of San Francisco" (p. 263) says: "The new administration was a marvel of economy. The expenses of the city and county had been $2,646,000 in 1855, and in 1857 only $353,000. Much of this saving was due to the consolidation act adopted by the legislature in April, 1856; but a large part of it to the new officials." The government was simplified and official responsibility was fixed. Everyone, except the criminal and corrupt element, was satisfied. Judge Hager, chairman of the committee on municipal corporations in the constitutional convention of 1879, said: "I do not agree that the tendency (in a consolidated city and county) is to multiply offices. The tendency is to reduce offices. Instead of a set of city officers, and a set of county officers, they are consolidated. We have a sheriff who is the sheriff of the city and county. We have a tax collector, and we have an auditor, who acts for both; formerly we had one for each. The tendency of a consolidated government is to reduce the officers from two to one in every sense, and to reduce the expense in every particular." Judge Hager was a delegate from San Francisco to that constitutional convention and spoke from experience after the Separation and Consolidation Act of 1856 had then been in successful operation for twenty-three years.

In 1875 the state of Missouri had adopted a new constitution, containing provisions for the separation of the City of St. Louis from its county and for the creation of the former into a new city-county entity having one set of officials, and also providing for "Home Rule." For several years the sentiment had been growing throughout the country in favor of local self-government instead of government imposed by the legislature. That sentiment had permeated California so that in 1879 when the constitutional convention met in that state it placed in the new constitution a ratification of the legislative creation in 1856 of the consolidated City and County of San Francisco and further provided that its people should have the right of framing their own charter.

The Act of 1856 had provided that "the corporation or body politic known as the City of San Francisco shall remain and continue to be a body politic and corporate, in name and in fact, by the name of the City and County of San Francisco." The courts seem to have been puzzled as to the legal status of the new city and county, as we shall see was also the case in Missouri. They failed to recognize it as an entirely new entity, — neither a city nor a county, — yet endowed with the powers and functions of both. It should have been recognized as being a municipal corporation *sui juris*. And so it should have been treated. As said by Judge Temple in his dissent in the *Sutro* case (114 Cal. 316), "the City and County of San Francisco is not a mere county, but is recognized in the constitution again and again as constituting a class apart." Unfortunately the court did not adopt this clear statement of fact.

In 1857, in the *Hill* case (7 Cal. 97) the court said: "It was evidently the intention of the legislature to repeal the act incorporating the City of San Francisco, and to merge the city and county into one, as a county govern-

ment, and under the direction of county officers." To the
seeming contrary that court in the *Board* case (21 Cal.
668), decided in 1863, said: "The corporation—the City
of San Francisco—is not destroyed, but continued. Its
name only has been changed." In the *Desmond* case
(55 Cal. 242), decided in 1882, the court, in speaking of
the city and county, said: "Politically, it was regarded
in that instrument (the constitution) as a municipal corporation." However, in the latter case the court reached
the conclusion that the provisions of the constitution of
1879 applicable to cities, and also those applicable to
counties, were applicable to the new city and county, and
in the *Sutro* case the court held that the city and county
has the attributes of both a city and a county, and also
attributes as distinguished from either; that politically
it is regarded in the constitution as a municipal corporation and in matters of government is to be regarded as a
city, yet the territory over which that government is
exercised, considered in its political and judicial relations
to the portions of the state, is a county. That was a
rather cumbersome way of saying that it is a corporation
sui juris, with attributes of a city and also of a county,
yet also with attributes distinguished from either. A
still simpler statement would be that it is a municipal
corporation empowered to perform the functions both of
a city and of a county, under one set of officers instead of
having a set of officers for each.

That was made quite clear by the provision in the
constitution of 1879 that "city and county governments
may be merged into one municipal government, with one
set of officers," and that "the provisions of the constitution applicable to cities, and also those applicable to
counties, shall be applicable to such consolidated form of
government." (Appendix—8.) The fact is that this but
restated and confirmed the provisions of the Act of 1856
which created that city and county, since it provided for
but one set of officers empowered to perform both city
and county functions. The constitution made a very im-

portant addition to its powers, as well as to those of each
city containing a population of more than one hundred
thousand, by authorizing them to frame their own charters which "should become the organic law thereof, and
supersede any existing charters and all amendments
thereof, and all special laws inconsistent with such charter." (Appendix—9.) In *People v. Hoge,* 55 Cal. 612,
decided in the next year after the adoption of the constitution, the court said: "It is manifestly the intention
of the constitution to emancipate municipal governments
from the authority and control formerly exercised by the
legislature."

However, there immediately began a struggle between the people on the one hand and the legislature on
the other in which the latter strove to regain its overlordship and in this it was abetted by the courts. In the very
next year after the declaration in the *Hoge* case that the
constitution had emancipated the cities from the authority and control of the legislature the latter enacted a law
that all elective municipal officers of the City and County
of San Francisco should be elected at the time of the state
election in November instead of in April as such elections
had been held formerly, and this interference by the legislature was sustained in *Staude v. Commissioners,* 61
Cal. 313, decided in 1882.

Following that came the adoption by the City of Los
Angeles of a home rule charter, ratified by the legislature,
in which a municipal (police) court was provided for. But
in *People v. Toal,* 85 Cal. 333, decided in 1890, the court
held that this charter provision was unconstitutional,
that such court must be established by general law, and
that ratification of the charter by the legislature did not
suffice. Two judges dissented. To the average mind it
seems clear that a police court is strictly a municipal
affair which properly fell within the charter. Evidently
the people of the state thought so too for at the election
held in 1892 they amended the constitution so as to provide that a home rule charter "shall supersede *all* laws

inconsistent with such charter,'' and in 1896 they further amended the constitution so as to authorize a home rule charter to provide "for the constitution, regulation, government, and jurisdiction of police courts, and for the manner in which, the times at which, and the terms for which the judges of such courts shall be elected or appointed, and for the compensation of said judges and of their clerks and attaches." (Appendix—14.)

However, the people of San Francisco were fated soon to suffer another blow to the right to attend to their own affairs in the manner provided for by their charter. The supreme court in the *Sutro* case (114 Cal. 316) decided in 1896, in seeming disregard of the provision of the constitution of 1879 that "city and county governments may be merged into one municipal government, with one set of officers," held that the City and County of San Francisco must have a separate set of county officers to be elected as such and that the time of their election and their terms of office were determined by the legislature in the County Government Act of 1893. It held the following to be county officers who must be elected at the November state election: district attorney, sheriff, clerk, recorder, coroner, assessor, public administrator and superintendent of public schools, instead of being elected at the municipal election in April.

There was a dissenting opinion by Judge Temple concurred in by Chief Justice Beatty, in which it was said: "The Consolidation Act of 1856 * * * consolidated the government of the city and county. The two governments were merged, and both, as far as rights and liabilities and public functions were concerned, were continued in a *new* corporation then created, — *the consolidated city and county.* All its officers were officers of the municipal corporation. In no sense can it be said that some were county officers and that some were city officers. The sheriff and the county clerk are as much officers of the municipal corporation as the mayor or the police judge. Whatever may be said of their powers and duties

they are part and parcel of the corporation known as
'The City and County of San Francisco.' Any one officer
is no less so than another. The legislature could then
have made the new corporation anything it chose, and it
chose to create a consolidated government upon which it
imposed the duties and to which it granted the powers,
both of a city and of a county. * * * The officers of the
consolidated government, who had the powers and performed the duties elsewhere performed by county officers,
did so as officers of the new consolidated municipality.
These powers and duties were expressly conferred upon
them in the Act of 1856 as officers of the municipality.
* * * We cannot, therefore, select certain officers and say
that they are county officers. * * * The City and County
of San Francisco is not a mere county, but is recognized
in the constitution itself, again and again, as constituting
a class apart.'' Had the majority opinion followed the
clearly logical opinion in this dissent the people of the
state would have been relieved of the necessity of again
amending their constitution. It is interesting to note
that in Colorado its supreme court (50 Colo. 503) made
the doctrine of that dissent the rule there applicable to
the City and County of Denver. (Chapter XVIII.)

So incensed were the people of California by the majority opinion in the *Sutro* case that, in the same year in
which it was rendered, they adopted a constitutional
amendment not only empowering home rule cities to provide in their charters for a police court, as above set
forth, but they also included therein a provision that
''where a city and county government has been merged
and consolidated into one municipality, it shall be competent in any charter * * * to provide for the manner in
which, the times at which, and the terms for which the
several *county officers* shall be elected or appointed, for
their compensation, and for the number of deputies each
shall have, and for the compensation payable to each
such deputies.'' (Appendix—13.)

Following the rebuff thus administered by the peo-

ple of the state in adopting that amendment to their constitution directly on the heels of the decision in the *Sutro*
case it is interesting to note the reaction of the court in
the *Martin* case (126 Cal. 404), decided in 1899, in which
it is apparent that it approved the dissenting opinion in
the former case by saying: "Since the Consolidation Act
the county of San Francisco has ceased to be a body politic or corporate, independently of, and separate from, the
municipal corporation created by that act and known and
designated as 'The City and County of San Francisco.'
One of the contentions of appellants is that, although the
former city and county were consolidated, they were not
'merged' within the meaning of the constitution. * * * It
would seem difficult to more effectually merge two separate bodies into one." The conclusion must be that this
merger created a new political entity. This is further
enforced by denial by the court in that case of the further
contention made by appellants that said constitutional
provision conflicted with the requirement of the constitution that there shall be a uniform system of county and
township government throughout the state. The court
said: "The act establishing a uniform system of county
government does not apply, and never has applied, to the
county of San Francisco in the sense claimed by appellants. * * * The county of San Francisco, as already
shown, since the passage of the Consolidation Act, has
never, as such, owned or possessed any property or performed any of the acts of a corporate body. Further,
the general law provides that each 'county must have a
board of supervisors consisting of five members. The
county of San Francisco has never had such board, or any
board of supervisors since the Consolidation Act. The
general county government act also provides for justices
of the peace and constables in the several townships of
the county, and there are no justices of the peace or constables in the townships of the county of San Francisco.
In fact, it is too obvious for question or argument that
the general law establishing a uniform system of county

government does not apply to the City and County of San Francisco.'' Thus the court quite clearly made the dissenting opinion in the *Sutro* case the rule of law which it should have been in the beginning. In that connection it must be noted that in the *Babcock* case (114 Cal. 559) it was held that the supervisors in the City and County of San Francisco are not county officers but are city officers.

It must be noted, however, that the term ''municipal affairs,'' used in the constitutional amendment of 1896 (Appendix—15) did not help much to clarify the situation. In 1899 the court in the *Fragley* case (126 Cal. 383) was divided as to what it meant, three of them holding one way, three in another, and one still in another. The court said: ''There has been much discussion in our decisions as to what matters are embraced in this term, and it has been said that it is very difficult, if not impossible, to give a general definition clearly defining the term 'municipal affairs' and its scope. In *Helmer v. Superior Court,* 48 Cal. App. 140, the court held that the term is ''not a fixed quantity, but fluctuates with every change in the conditions upon which it is to operate.'' The court might better have said that it depends upon the training, the predilections, the political bias and beliefs of the judges, and sometimes upon the election returns. So unstable is it that the courts of the various states disagree among themselves as to what should or should not be held to be a ''municipal affair.'' There is always uncertainty, unless the question has already been passed upon, as to just what power a chartered city may exercise under home rule. Even now if it properly be a municipal affair, but is not set forth in the charter, the door is left open to the legislature (157 Cal. 416), but if stated in the charter the general laws are thus superseded (29 Cal. App. 24).

In California it has been held that the following are not municipal affairs: prescribing rules governing the making of street improvements and payment of the cost thereof; the procedure for taking private property by

right of eminent domain (contrary to the rule in Missouri) ; the method of changing city boundaries; controlling the use of streets by telephone and telegraph
companies; the matter of construction of viaducts or
subways at intersections of streets and railway tracks;
prohibiting the operation on the streets of vehicles in an
unsafe manner; prescribing the distance of city poles
from railway tracks. It must be noted, however, that the
imposition of a license tax on a business or occupation
(141 Cal. 204 and 143 Cal. 553, decided in 1904) and the
fixing of salaries of the police and fire department of a
city (123 Cal. 456, decided in 1899) and the removal of a
chief of police (6 Cal. App. 217, decided in 1907) are municipal affairs (opposed to the rule in Missouri). In *Ex
Parte Daniels,* 183 Cal. 636, decided in 1920, the court held
that if there is a reasonable doubt as to whether traffic
regulation is a municipal affair, "that doubt must be re-
solved in favor of the legislative authority of the state."
Thus the benefit of a reasonable doubt operates in favor
of the overlordship of the legislature, under this decision
of the court, in making determination as to what falls
within the power of home rule cities. That decision is
quite a questionable one. It would seem that the rule
should be the opposite.

In the face of repeated amendments of the constitution, and despite the decision in the *Martin* case evidently
intended to set home rule cities free as to all their officers
and employees, yet in the *Crowley* case (132 Cal. 440),
decided in 1901, the court held that the civil service provisions of the San Francisco charter did not apply as to
deputies of the sheriff, clerk, recorder, and the other so-
called county officers, thus letting loose the political gang
at the public crib. This was one of those four to three
decisions by which the rights of the people are sometimes
taken from them by a narrow squeak by reactionary
judges. The opinion of the three dissenting judges insisted, as had recently been held in the *Martin* case, that
there were no county officers as such, and, therefore, that

all officers and employees were subject to the charter provisions. They emphasized that public opinion favored the merit system and that courts should adopt a liberal construction and should resolve all doubts in favor of such recognized public policy. But to no avail.

After having repeatedly amended their constitution in order to free their cities from the invasion of their right of home rule thus guaranteed to them, it came as a distinct shock to the people of San Francisco when the *Nicholl* case (157 Cal. 416), decided in 1910, declared that while the City and County of San Francisco has the powers and performs the functions of a city and county yet the constitutional provisions had no application to it except in so far as that subdivision of the state possessed and exercised municipal functions and constituted a city as distinguished from a county; that with respect to the powers and functions of a county exercised there, as in any other county of the state, that constitutional amendment did not apply; that the power of the legislature to enact general laws for the government of counties, as such, including that city and county, remained unaffected and unimpaired by that amendment and did not make its charter paramount to such laws. It would seem that when the court said that "the City and County of San Francisco has the powers and performs the functions of a city and a county," it necessarily followed that when it adopted its charter it acted as a county as well as a city, and had full right to say what officers it should have and which of them should perform county functions under the plain terms of the constitution itself.

It was discouraging and exasperating that the legislature and the courts were so non-cooperative in safeguarding to their people their right of self-government. The people had amended their constitution year after year so as to escape domination by the legislature and keep their cities free. And now they were confronted by the decision in the *Nicholl* case.

But the people of the City and County of San Francisco did not tamely submit. They rallied the people of the state to their aid and in the very next year, 1911, they amended their constitution so as to read that in their charter they should have the power to provide ''for the manner in which, the times at which, and the terms for which the several county and municipal officers and employees whose compensation is paid by such city and county, shall be elected or appointed, and for their recall and removal, and for their compensation, and for the number of deputies, clerks and other employees that each shall have, and for the compensation, method of appointment, qualifications, tenure of office and removal of such deputies, clerks and other employees. All provisions of any charter of any such consolidated city and county heretofore adopted, and amendments thereto, which are in accordance herewith, are hereby confirmed and declared valid.'' (Appendix—17.) These provisions were repeated in the constitutional amendment adopted in 1914. The last sentence of this constitutional amendment must especially be noted in that it ''confirmed and declared valid'' the charter of the City and County of San Francisco, and thus foreclosed the legislature and the courts from further tinkering with it. Since then the courts have not interfered.

As a result of that long and victorious struggle, the people of all the charter cities and counties in the state joyfully learned that their supreme court in more recent decisions had finally recognized and announced the true rule that, under their home rule powers as exercised in their charters, they have full right to devolve the performance of state and county functions upon whomsoever they please and that the state is not concerned as to what person or persons perform such functions so long as they are performed. Since the constitution of 1879 cities in California have had the exclusive right to say in their charters what officers they may have to perform municipal functions. The contest had been as to the right in county charters and in charters in the city-county consolidated to say what officers should perform county functions there. After adoption of the constitutional amendments in 1911 and 1914 the courts finally sustained charters which provided for the discontinuance of certain county offices and vested the performance of their functions in other offices. In the *Crowley* case (132 Cal. 440), decided in 1903, the court said: ''Not only is the state itself interested in county officers as parts of its necessary governmental machinery, but the people of any particular county of the state are interested—and in someme of them are frequently deeply interested—in county officers, such as sheriffs, recorders, clerks, etc., in other counties. The functions of such officers are general, not municipal. And while, in the American system of state governments, the people of the whole state have generally kept in their own hands control over such important public governmental agencies as county officers, still, if they choose to yield up part of that control by adopting a constitutional amendment such as section 8½, there is no apparent reason why they may not do so, unless the amendment be so revolutionary as to be destructive of a republican form of government, as the same is understood in this country. Section 8½ cannot be said to be of that character.'' In that connection it will be noted in Chapter XVIII that the supreme court of Colorado, in *People v. Cassiday,* 50 Colo. 503, decided in 1911, held that the City and County of Denver has no county officers as such but that so long as its charter provides for officers who shall perform county functions this is not destructive of a republican form of government. Under the fundamental rule that the people by their constitution may empower cities and counties to say what officers shall perform county functions, as is the case in California, the 1916 charter of the county of San Bernardino provided that the sheriff should be *ex-officio* the coroner, and this was sustained in *More v. Board,* 31 Cal. App. 388. In 1921 the charter of Tehama county provided that the county clerk should be *ex-officio* the county recorder, and this was sustained in *Jones v.*

De Shields, 187 Cal. 33. In 1934 San Mateo county amended its charter so as to provide that the county engineer should be *ex-officio* the county surveyor, and this was sustained in *Reuter v. Board,* 220 Cal. 314, in which the court said: ''While the state may have a general interest in the roads and highways of the counties, *it is not concerned with the particular individual or official* whose duty it is simply to employ the men and teams and other help necessary to construct such roads and highways.'' Like office consolidation provisions of the charters of Alameda, Butte and Sacramento counties have been sustained. And this, the court in the *Reuter* case said, was under the power granted by the constitution to counties ''to provide for the powers and duties of their county officers.''

Thus the old order finally was changed. Under the system that had theretofore generally prevailed the existence of a county was deemed to be a necessary part of the governmental structure of the state. From long rule and usage it had become fixed in the public mind that the county must exist as a separate entity in order that state functions could be carried on locally. The instrument for carrying out these functions had become the subject of worship instead of giving heed to the purpose. It has been noted above, early in our history, that in every county in this country the officers who were to exercise those functions were made elective in the county. The state takes no part in their election. It does not designate the individuals who shall perform the county functions. That is left to the people of the county. It is clear that the state is concerned only that those functions be exercised by some one, and not as to the person nor as to the official name by which he is designated, so long only as such functions are carried on. Perhaps no provision in any constitution covers this point more clearly and tersely than does Section 2 of Article XX of the constitution of Colorado which provides that as to the City and County of Denver ''every charter shall designate the officers who shall, respectively, perform the acts and duties required by county officers to be done by the constitution or by the general law, as far as applicable.'' (Appendix—28, and Chapter XVIII.)

It is unfortunate that in their struggles through the courts and in their frequent battles to amend their constitution in order to safeguard their right of ''Home Rule'' the people of San Francisco did not include in the amendments a provision at least similar to that contained in the Colorado constitution just mentioned. Instead it seems that they have clung to the false notion that they must have county officers as such, notwithstanding the fact that their courts have decided that all the state is interested in is that county functions be performed and not as to what officer performs them. Section 8½ of Article XI of the constitution grants to any consolidated city and county plenary authority to provide in its charter, or by amendment thereto, ''the manner in which, the method in which, the times at which, and the terms for which the several county and municipal officers and employees whose compensation is paid by such city or city and county, except judges of the superior court, shall be elected or appointed, and for their recall and removal, and for their compensation, and for the number of deputies, clerks and other employees that each shall have, and for the compensation, method of appointment, qualifications, tenure of office and removal of such deputies, clerks and other employees.'' The city and county is thus given the fullest power over all its officers except that some of them must be county officers as such. Section 18 of the charter provides that ''each county officer shall have all the powers conferred and shall discharge all the duties imposed by the general laws upon said officer of a county or a city and county of this state, and shall have such other powers and duties as in this charter specifically provided.'' The ''county officers'' therein referred to are the sheriff, recorder, clerk, coroner, district attorney, public administrator, registrar of voters, tax collector, members of the board of education, and members of the adult and juvenile probation board. It will be noted that such officers, in addition to performing county functions, shall also perform such city functions as the charter specifically provides. In this manner consolidation of functions and resultant reduction of the number of officers may be brought about. As an instance, the district attorney not only prosecutes those charged with violations of state laws but he also prosecutes those charged with violating the city ordinances. Another consolidation that might well be made would be to combine the sheriff's office with the police department under a department of safety with one head who should act as the coroner. The office of tax collector might also be combined with that of treasurer.

After the constitution of 1879 had been adopted the City and County of San Francisco had great difficulty in framing a charter acceptable to its people. In 1880 a charter was framed but was rejected at the polls. Kessling in "San Francisco Charter of 1931" says: "Conflicting interests, and, in many instances, merely an objection to some isolated feature of proposed charters defeated the efforts made in 1883, 1887 and 1896. All these elections indicated a lack of any general interest." It was not until 1898 that the people of the city and county approved a charter which was ratified by the legislature on January 26, 1899. In the meantime the consolidated city and county had been governed under the Consolidation Act of 1856, with certain amendments made from time to time by the legislature.

The charter under which the City and County of San Francisco now operates was adopted by the electors in 1931, with amendments made thereto by vote of its people in 1932, 1933, 1934, 1935, 1937 and 1940. One of its noticeable features is a shortened ballot resulting from a staggered system of electing officers. On the odd-numbered years, the election of the officers of the city and county are held in November. At one of them a mayor, district attorney, sheriff, assessor and six supervisors are elected at large for four-year terms, and six municipal judges are elected at large for six-year terms, or a total of but sixteen offices to be filled at that election. Two years thereafter a city attorney, a treasurer, and five supervisors are elected at large for four-year terms, and six municipal judges are elected at large for six-year terms, or a total of but thirteen offices to be filled at that election. At the general election held on even numbered years the public defender and superior court judges are elected for six-year terms. Of the latter, five are elected at one election, five at the next and eight at the next. All the foregoing officers are elected on a non-partisan ballot.

The mayor appoints the following commissions: fire, police, public utilities, parks, recreation, library, civil service and city planning. The art commission consists of ten members appointed by the mayor and five *ex officio* members consisting of the respective chairmen of the following commissions: public library, park, city planning, de Young Memorial Museum and California Palace of the Legion of Honor. The retirement (pension) board consists of the president of the board of supervisors, the city attorney, a resident official of a life insurance company and an officer of a bank appointed by the mayor, and three members of the city and county employees association. He also appoints the controller, subject to confirmation and approval by the board of supervisors (elsewhere denominated the city council).

In 1931 the charter was amended creating the position of an administrative officer with powers and duties similar to those exercised by the city manager in many of the cities of this country. He is appointed by the mayor and is made responsible to the mayor or to the board of supervisors for the administration of all the affairs of the city and county that are placed in his charge. It is made his duty to exercise supervision and control over all administrative departments which are under his jurisdiction, to appoint the heads of departments under his control, to prescribe general rules and regulations for the administrative service under his control, to have a voice but no vote in the board of supervisors, to propose such measures to the mayor, the board of supervisors or its committees, concerning the affairs of the city and county in his charge as he may deem necessary to coordinate the functioning of the several departments relating to the control of traffic and to provide for the budgeting and control of publicity and advertising and expenditures of the city and county. He is made subject to removal in the same manner as elective officers, and also by vote of not less than two-thirds of the board of supervisors, upon written charges and a hearing.

He appoints, to serve at his pleasure, a director of public works, a director of public health, a city purchaser, a director of finance and records (which department includes as sub-departments the register of voters, public administrator, recorder, county clerk and tax collector). No confirmation is required. Other department heads under the chief administrative officer occupy civil service status acquired under the charter amendment of 1933 by virtue of occupancy, and later, as vacancies have occurred, through civil service examination.

An unusual but commendable feature is that the mayor has a seat but no vote in the board of supervisors and in any board or commission appointed by him, with the right to report on or discuss any matter before such board or commission concerning the departments or affairs in his charge. He is given power to designate a member of the board of supervisors to act as mayor in his absence. The board of supervisors, by ordinance or resolution, exercises all the legislative power, subject to the veto of the mayor, and acts as a board of equalization and fixes the tax rate. Under authority of the constitution the charter provides for the initiation of a charter or of charter amendments, and for the initiation and reference of any ordinance, act or other measure which is within the power conferred upon the board of supervisors to enact, or any legislative act which is within the power conferred upon any other board, commission or officer to adopt.

Painful experience has developed a firm determination in the citizens of the City and County of San Francisco not to permit any interference by the state in its local affairs, and also not to permit any undue interference by the board of supervisors with any other city-county department. The charter provides that "neither the board of supervisors, nor its committees, nor any of its members shall dictate, suggest, or interfere with the appointments, promotions, compensations, disciplinary actions, contracts, requisitions for purchases or other administrative recommendations or actions of the chief administrative officer, or of department heads under the chief administrative officer, or under the respective boards and commissions, and that any dictation, suggestion or interference herein prohibited on the part of any supervisors or member of a board or commission shall constitute official misconduct."

The charter provides that all or any part of the area of the County of San Mateo may be consolidated with the City and County of San Francisco, upon the affirmative vote of each, and for the creation of such added area into a borough with certain local powers in case its people so desire. A few years ago there was some agitation along this line but the people of San Mateo county did not fall in with the plan and so nothing came of it. There is no present need for extension of the city-county boundaries and there is no present movement for it.

For eighty-four years the City and County of San Francisco has now existed with no thought of reverting to the discarded dual system of government with its excess of officers, its conflict of authority, its burdens of useless taxation. After strenuous years of militant fighting it has emerged into the full right to govern itself in the manner it wishes, with the officers it wants, elected at the time, for the term, and in the manner it may choose, and at the salary and having such clerks and employees as it may wish, free from any control or interference by the legislature. It is a record of which any city may be proud.

Mayor Angelo Rossi has been in the public service of the City and County of San Francisco for nearly a quarter of a century, more particularly as recreation commissioner for seven years, a member of the board of supervisors for eight years, and as mayor for eight years, to which office he was re-elected last year. Recently he told the author that in his opinion the people of the City and County of San Francisco are well pleased with the results of a city-county consolidated form of government which they have enjoyed now drawing close to the century mark and that they would not think of going back to the outmoded dual form of government which they once endured. He especially emphasized the simplicity of their form of government and the economy of its operation.

CHAPTER XVII.

THE CITY OF ST. LOUIS
(1876)

The City of St. Louis, correctly Saint-Louis, is the first example in this country of the separation of a city from its county and its creation into a city-county consolidated, *by an amendment of the state constitution.* This was done in 1876 under the new constitution of 1875.

The first settlement at the site of the future city was made in 1764 by a party of Frenchmen under the leadership of Auguste Chouteau, a fourteen year old boy, who was sent up from New Orleans by his stepfather to establish a post there for trading with the Indians. To this day it is the greatest fur mart in this country. The little village was named Saint Louis in honor of king Louis IX of France. Its growth was such that in the next year the settlers elected to govern themselves. The village followed the fate of the Territory of Orleans by cession to Spain, back to France and then to the United States under the Louisiana Purchase in 1803. Immediately thereafter settlers from the United States and soon from Germany flocked in. In 1808 the town of St. Louis was incorporated by special act of the territorial legislature and was thereafter governed by like acts until 1822 when it was granted a charter. It provided for a unicameral council which was changed to a bicameral council by a new charter in 1839, but in 1859 the legislature again amended the charter to provide return to a unicameral council. In 1870 the city of Carondolet was annexed to the City of St. Louis.

As early as 1842 the people of St. Louis had begun an active campaign for the separation of that city from its county. In that year they lodged with the legislature a request for action and in 1843 that body adopted a resolution which provided that at the then next general election in the county a vote be taken on the question of such separation; but it was provided that "no resident citizen of the City of St. Louis shall be allowed to vote upon this question." It was thus foredoomed to defeat at the election held in 1844. However, the agitation in the city for separation continued, and gradually there was coupled with it a demand for "Home Rule."

Already in Chapter VIII has been set forth the struggle to emancipate cities and counties from legislative dictatorship. It was seen that under the earlier constitutions legislatures were given power to enact special laws for the government of cities and that this power was prostituted to ulterior political purposes. City charters were tinkered with by each succeeding legislature to advance individual schemes and to further selfish ambitions. Missouri suffered from this unfortunate condition. St. Louis, as its largest city and offering the richest field for political pickings, was made the target for these assaults. Between 1852 and 1875 its charter was changed at almost every session of the legislature. These changes were not generally for the benefit of the city but were made from political expediency in order to give some advantage to the political party in control of the legislature at the time. Frequently these charter amendments were procured by the city's own representatives to serve their own private ends and for purposes of purely personal or political advantage. These evils were not limited to St. Louis alone. They afflicted every city in the state. A strong sentiment arose throughout the commonwealth against this system, and the people determined to change it.

Not only did the citizens of St. Louis chafe under these conditions affecting their charter, but in addition they resented the dominance of county politics in their city affairs and urged separation of the city from the county. Charges of extravagance on the part of the county officers were freely made. No adequate check was kept upon expenses. Officeholders were prosperous, and embezzlement of county funds was not unknown. There were a great many more officers than were required for the administration of the public business. As pointed out by Studenski in his ''Government of Metropolitan Areas'' and by Loeb in ''Government of the St. Louis Metropolis,'' the citizens of St. Louis felt that their county government was not only incompetent but that it was extravagant, and that it was engaged in plundering the city for the benefit of the outside territory. They were dissatisfied with the two distinct systems of local government to which they were subjected, — one a city government and the other a county government with their dual cost, — with attendant irresponsibility, extravagance, corruption and political rings. The county government levied high taxes on the city property and expended the revenues derived therefrom for the benefit of those residing outside the city limits.

In 1872 a Taxpayers League was organized in the city in advocacy of the separation of the city from the county. From then, until the convention met in 1875 to frame a new state constitution, a vigorous campaign was carried on. An example of the arguments for separation of the city from the county is contained in the *St. Louis Republican* of that time in which it was charged that ''there are two cumbersome and costly governments in the City of St. Louis, — one the regular city government, the other the county government. The county government, in point of fact, has nothing to do with city affairs, it sits within the municipal limits to govern a territory entirely outside these limits. The county court (county commissioners) is a sort of irresponsible body, with power to spend money pretty much as it pleases to. Its largest item of expenditure ($300,000) is for roads and bridges in the rural part of the county. The separation scheme is simply a proposition to get rid of one of these costly governments and the expense of maintaining it— to remit the rural portion of the county to the simple and cheap form of administration suitable to it and leave the city to its unclogged municipal machinery—to allow the city to govern itself and the county to govern itself.''

This deepseated dissatisfaction of the citizens of St. Louis with these conditions against which they rebelled, was coupled with the resentment they felt against the continual tinkering with their charter by the legislature, in which feeling the other cities of the state joined. The widespread cry for relief had much to do with the calling and holding of the convention in 1875 to frame a new state constitution. At that time the City of St. Louis was the largest city in the state and its delegates in that convention wielded great influence. Naturally other delegates from counties in which cities were located, who were also anxious to stop the untrammelled rule of the legislature over their city charters through special acts, joined with the St. Louis delegates in a common cause to obtain ''Home Rule,'' and aided them in their campaign to separate the City of St. Louis from its county.

Article IX of the new constitution, as framed by that convention, was devoted to cities and counties and provided for their government. Section 7, of major importance to those delegates just mentioned, provides that cities and towns must be organized, classified, and their government prescribed, ''by general laws'' instead of by special acts theretofore in vogue. Sections 10 and 11 require a sheriff and a coroner to be elected in each county and provide that a vacancy shall be filled by the county court and that in case of a *new* county the governor appoints them. Then come sections 15 and 16 of especial interest here. Section 15 reads as follows: ''In all counties having a city therein containing over one hundred thousand inhabitants, the city and county government thereof may be consolidated in such manner as may be provided by law" (Appendix—5). Section 16 empowers any city containing over one hundred thousand inhabitants to frame a charter consistent with and subject to the constitution and laws of the state, and that it may be amended by proposals therefor and submitted by the law-making authorities of the city, — such charter to be approved by a four-sevenths vote of the qualified electors and such amendment to be approved by a three-fifths vote thereof. In 1920 this section was amended to provide that alternative sections or articles may be proposed by the law-making authorities of the city or upon a ten per cent petition of the electors.

In framing section 15 of Article IX of the constitution the convention evidently had before it the provisions of the 1850 constitution of Michigan (Appendix—2), and the identical provisions of the 1858 constitution of Minnesota (Appendix—4). Unfortunately, the convention failed to adopt the language therein contained. In each of those constitutions the legislature was authorized to organize any city in the state into a county, — thus to become a city-county consolidated, separated from the county in which it might then be situated. But the Missouri convention went into reverse. It did not authorize the legislature to organize any city containing over one hundred thousand inhabitants into a county, — thus to become a city-county consolidated. On the contrary it authorized only the consolidation of such city and of its entire county. In 1875 the City of St. Louis had a population of approximately 350,000, while the next largest city in the state, Kansas City, had then a population of approximately 35,000. Therefore, when the convention adopted sections 15 and 16 it seemingly had in mind the City of St. Louis alone since it was the only city with the population required. This did not suit the plans of the delegates from that city. They did not want their city and their county to be consolidated. They wanted them to be separated. And they did not propose to await the pleasure of some legislature in the uncertain future to act.

Nor were they content with the limited powers contained in section 16 concerning the framing and amending of a charter. So they worked out a plan to add additional sections to Article IX of the constitution which would provide for immediate and automatic separation of their city from its county, without let or hindrance from the legislature, for enlarging its then boundaries, for the election of a board of thirteen freeholders to prepare a scheme for such separation and a charter for the enlarged city to be submitted to such voters, and that the remainder of the county be created into a new county to retain the name of the county of St. Louis. The legislature was left entirely out of the picture. Mr. Joseph Pulitzer, one of the St. Louis delegates, then on the (St. Louis) *Westliche Post,* later founder of the *Post Dispatch,* was one of the first to urge that this procedure be adopted, but in his plan he left in the legislature the power to amend such charter. However, this power of amendment was eliminated. It was then presented to the convention in practically the same form as it now appears in the constitution. (Appendix—6).

Unfortunately, these provisions were presented to the convention so late in its work that proper coordination was not made between them and the other sections of Article IX, above noted, with the result that much litigation and the whittling down of the intended benefits followed which might have been avoided by proper care. Speaking upon this situation the supreme court of Missouri in the *Walsh* case (69 Mo. 408), decided in 1879, said: "It must be conceded that there are some general and important provisions of the constitution which should be applicable to all the primary political subdivisions of the state, which are not susceptible of easy and perfect adaptation to the political entity created by the special provisions relating to the city of St. Louis. This is doubtless attributable to the fact shown by the records of the convention which framed the Constitution, that the provisions relating to the scheme and charter were added

to the body of that instrument after it was mainly completed, and on the eve of adjournment, and that critical
revision of the language of the entire instrument, which
would have removed all apparent incongruities and presented its parts in complete and perfect harmony, was
never made.''

The new constitution was approved by the voters in
1875. Sections 20, 21, 22 and 23 of Article IX (Appendix
—6) provided that the right of ''Home Rule'' should be
enjoyed by the people of the City of St. Louis, — the
first city in the world to have vested in its electors that
self-governing power through a provision of a constitution. By virtue of sections 16 and 17, above referred to,
Kansas City, in 1889, having attained a population of one
hundred thousand, framed its own charter. This distinction, between the sections applicable to St. Louis and
those applicable to Kansas City, noted in *State v. St.
Louis*, 319 Mo. 497, decided in 1928, must be kept in mind
when reading the decisions affecting the powers of these
two cities. For, while the charter of Kansas City must
be ''consistent with and subject to the constitution and
the laws of the state'' yet it will be shown that the powers
granted to St. Louis are much broader.

Pursuant to the provisions of the new constitution a
board of thirteen freeholders was elected by joint ballot
in the City of St. Louis and in the county of St. Louis. It
framed and proposed a scheme for the separation of the
city from the county, and also a charter for the government of the enlarged city. Their adoption by the people
was fought by the office holders who would lose their
official positions and political patronage and by those
who were looting the public funds through crooked public
improvement contracts. Such frauds were perpetrated
at the election held on August 22, 1876, that, while the
charter was approved by the voters of the city, the
''Scheme of Separation'' was certified by the county
court as having lost by 1416 votes. On appeal the court
(3 Mo. App. 388) eliminated the fraudulent votes and

declared that the scheme of separation had been approved by a majority of 1253 votes.

The board of freeholders was empowered by the constitution, in the framing of such scheme, to extend the city limits so as to embrace the parks then within its boundaries, and other convenient and contiguous territory, as it might decide upon. Under that authority additional county territory, comprising Carondolet, Central and St. Louis townships, was added so as to increase the area of the city by more than 300 per cent. Two-fifths of the new territory thus brought within the extended limits of the city was urban in character, while the other three-fifths consisted of farm lands. Evidently in order to forestall possible opposition of those residing in the included rural area the constitution provided that provision might be made in the new charter for the graduation of the rate of taxation for city purposes, and this was done. That differential tax rate has long since ceased, as that entire area has become urban in character. The population of the City of St. Louis as shown by the United States census of 1870 was 310,864, while that of the remainder of the county was 40,325. The population of the city as shown by the 1940 United States census is 816,048. The area of the enlarged city was and now is sixty-one square miles, and the area of the remainder of the former county is four hundred and eighty-seven square miles. This residue of the old county retained the name of the county of St. Louis with Clayton as its county seat. The constitution provided that the city and the county should be independent of each other, and that the city should be exempted from all county taxation.

The scheme provided that the school districts and parts of districts within the additional territory thus annexed to the city should become a part of the school district of the city and that proper adjustment of property values and indebtedness be made between it and the new county, and that "all the public buildings, institutions, public parks, and property of every character and description heretofore owned and controlled by the County of St. Louis, within the limits as extended, including the Courthouse, the County Jail, the Insane Asylum and the Poor House, are hereby transferred and made over to the City of St. Louis, and all the right, title and interest of the County of St. Louis in said property, and in all public roads and highways within the enlarged limits, is hereby vested in the City of St. Louis and divested out of the County; and in consideration of the city becoming the proprietor of all the county buildings and property within its enlarged limits, the city hereby assumes the whole of the existing county debt and the entire park tax." The municipal assembly was empowered to provide by ordinance for the management of such property and public institutions. Provision was made under which the outside county was permitted to send its paupers and insane to the institutions then existing within the city upon payment of actual cost of maintaining them. This relieved the outside county of the burden of erecting new buildings for that purpose until such time as it wished to do so.

Not only was all county property located within the city vested in it but careful provision was made by which city officers were to be elected who should perform all functions theretofore performed by county officers. The scheme provided that the mayor of the City of St. Louis should order an election at which should be elected *"a Sheriff of the City of St. Louis,* and *a Coroner for said city,* who shall be *commissioned by the Mayor.* A Public Administrator *for said city* shall also be elected at the general election aforesaid. * * * And said officers shall respectively perform within the city limits such duties as are now provided by law in regard to the Sheriff, Coroner and Public Administrator of St. Louis County." It was further provided that "the Marshal of the City of St. Louis, in addition to his other duties, shall assume and discharge all the duties heretofore discharged by the Marshal of St. Louis County, within the limits of the

City of St. Louis.'' It was also provided that "the present State and County Collector shall continue in office until the expiration of his official term, and thereafter his duties shall be discharged *by the City Collector.*"

It must especially be noted that the constitution itself provided that "the city, as enlarged, shall collect the state revenue and perform all other functions in relation to the state in the same manner as if it were a county as in this Constitution defined."

The scheme further provided that at the general election in November, 1876, there be elected members of a bicameral municipal assembly to continue in office until the city election to be held in April 1881; all other offices to become vacant and to be filled at the city election to be held in April, 1877. It was provided that the metropolitan police force of the City of St. Louis under the state law be retained. The justices of the peace and constables for the city were to be elected at the general election in 1876. Their commissions were to be issued *by the mayor.* It was provided that *"the Sheriff of the City of St. Louis* shall, within the limits of said city, exercise the authority now vested by law in the Sheriff of the County of St. Louis, and after this Scheme shall go into operation, all writs and other process which are now by law provided to be executed by the Sheriff of the County of St. Louis, within the city limits, shall be directed to and executed by the Sheriff of the City of St. Louis. The City Marshal, after this Scheme goes into operation, in addition to the duties now required by law to be performed by him, shall, within the city limits, exercise the same power and perform the same duties as are now provided by law in regard to the County Marshal.'' The Municipal Assembly was given the powers theretofore exercised by the county court (the county commissioners) of the county of St. Louis.

It must especially be noted that this scheme was *adopted by the voters under direct authorization of the constitution,* and not under any act of the legislature.

Clearly it became the paramount law since in the constitution it was denominated "the organic law." Its provisions as to procedure and jurisdiction were out of and beyond the power of the legislature to change. No provision was there made, just as none was made in the constitution itself, for the election of a single county officer, as such, for the City of St. Louis, but it was specifically provided that they should solely be officers of that city, and that they "shall be commissioned by the Mayor," and that they "shall respectively perform such duties as are now provided by law" to be performed by county officers. At the same time that the board of freeholders framed the scheme it also prepared a charter for the City of St. Louis which was approved by its electors on August 22, 1876. That charter named every officer who was to perform any functions within its limits *as a city officer* and not otherwise. It provided that a general election of all elective officers required by it be held on the first Tuesday of April, 1877, and every four years thereafter, except as otherwise provided in it or by the scheme. The judges of the courts (except those of the police court), the justices of the peace and the constables, the circuit attorney and the prosecuting attorney were not covered by the charter and were to be elected at the general November election. All other elective officers were to be elected at the city election in April as *city officers.*

The benefits that followed after the first city election under the charter were highly satisfactory. The doing away with county officers in great part, and the devolving of their duties upon city officers, resulted in a great saving in expense of government. As was said in the *Finn* case (8 Mo. App. 341), decided in 1880: "In divesting the city of the burden of a double government through city and county organization certain offices and their functions were necessarily abolished." So great was the retrenchment in outlay, especially by the board of public improvements, that the machine politicians sought to abolish that board or to amend the charter so as to put themselves back at the public crib, but they failed. The tax rate had been $3.42 in the hundred. At once it was reduced to $2.80 in the hundred. The issue of so-called "anticipation" bonds, necessitated because of lack of funds with which to meet the expenses of the government, which had reached the total of $1,550,000 in 1875, was reduced to $350,000 in the biennium of 1879-1880. The management of public institutions and the performance of public service was more efficient while the system of administration of public works was much improved. Responsibility for the conduct of the public business was fixed and consolidation of functions made for efficiency. It seemed that the City of St. Louis was on the high road to good government on a business basis, free from outside political interference.

But, as has already been pointed out, the provisions of the constitution concerning the City of St. Louis had been somewhat poorly drawn and their language had not been made to harmonize with the other provisions of that instrument as nearly as might be. A field day was thereby provided for the courts and the legislature, both of which have done much damage. In order to visualize this unfortunate situation it will be helpful to state the eight basic features of these provisions of the constitution, as follows:

(1) The people of the City of St. Louis were empowered, *without legislative interference,* to frame and adopt their charter, which was not required to be submitted to the legislature but which went into effect upon a certified copy thereof being filed in the office of the secretary of state and in the archives of the city.

(2) Such charter shall *always be in harmony with and subject to the laws and the constitution of the state.*

(3) But such charter shall be "*the organic law* of the city and shall *supersede* the charter and all amendments thereof."

(4) That the City be enlarged and then be separated from its county.

(5) That "the *residue* of the county shall remain a legal county of the state of Missouri, under the name of the County of St. Louis."

(6) That the City of St. Louis *was not created into a county,* and it was specifically provided that "the city shall be *exempted from all county taxation."*

(7) That "the city, as enlarged, *shall* be entitled to the *same representation* in the General Assembly, *collect the state revenue and perform all other functions in relation to the State,* in the same *manner as if it were* a county as in this Constitution defined."

(8) That "notwithstanding the provisions of this article, *the General Assembly shall have the same power* over the city and county of St. Louis that it has over other cities and counties of this State."

A cursory reading of these eight basic features might cause the unthinking mind to conclude that there is a fatal conflict between them. But it is a fundamental rule of construction, binding upon the courts, applicable as well to constitutions as to laws, that every reasonable effort must be made by the judiciary to harmonize and make effective all of the provisions of the constitution under consideration, so as to carry out the intention of its framers and of the people who adopted it by their vote. Unfortunately the courts of Missouri have not always adopted that rule but have seemingly been swayed at times by political exigencies. McBain in his "Law and Practice of Municipal Home Rule" says: "The course of decisions upon the subject is fairly illustrative of the carelessness and disregard for previous utterances which the Missouri court has so frequently shown in interpreting the confusing clauses of the constitution relating to cities." (p. 124.) In the *Police Commissioners* case (184 Mo. 109) the supreme court itself confessed: "It would be futile at this time to tread again the mazes of adjudication, perhaps to become lost in the labyrinth of the ingenious and divergent reasons which pervade the cases in respect to the power of municipalities incorporated under article nine of the constitution.''

Indeed, the supreme court of Missouri often met itself coming around the corner without batting an eye and not even recognizing itself.

It must be remembered that the provisions of the constitution separating the City of St. Louis from its county and the provisions vesting in it the power of home rule are inextricably joined together. It is the first instance in history when this has occurred under a constitution. It seems, therefore, justifiable to devote some time to the consideration of this new situation and of how it has been buffeted by the legislature and by the courts. Twenty years before, the City of San Francisco had been separated from its county and was created into the consolidated City and County of San Francisco. For a long time the courts of California floundered about in trying to determine what sort of political and governmental entity it was. (Chapter XVI.) It must be remembered that courts are composed simply of lawyers given a little brief authority. As lawyers and when they become judges they too often are shackled by precept and steeped in prejudice against change. It seems difficult for them to recognize that this new form of government is an entirely new political entity clothed with power to perform the functions of both a city and a county. To fasten to it the old names, the cumbersome rules, and the requirement that needless officers be retained, seemed necessary to some legal minds, and, unfortunately some of these warped minds got on the bench. They had reactionary tendencies, or were frankly antagonistic to the new idea of home rule, or were unable to visualize a political entity that had no county but which nevertheless performed county functions. The courts of Missouri were no exception. The poorly drafted provisions of the constitution, not properly correlated, furnished some, but not much, excuse for conflicting and sometimes destructive holdings.

It will be noted in the first place that the constitution provides that the city's home rule charter shall be its "organic law." It then provides that such charter "shall supersede the (then existing) charter and all amendments thereof." In the same breath, and paradoxically, it then provides that such charter shall "always be in harmony with and subject to the constitution and the laws of Missouri." Now the existing "charter and the amendments thereof," which the new charter superseded, had been enacted as special laws by the legislature. As special laws, under the rule of statutory construction, they were even more controlling than were the general laws, since they constituted specific legislation on a particular subject and the law is that the specific controls the general. As Professor McBain in his "Law and Practice of Municipal Home Rule" asks: "By what logic is a freeholders' charter made to supersede the state laws which constitute its existing legislative charter, if the legislature may immediately re-enact the law thus repealed?" (p. 125.) It does not make sense that a charter shall be an "organic law," and, as such, shall *supersede* the laws enacted by the legislature, and then in the next breath say that such charter shall be "in harmony with and subject to" the laws of the state. What, then, is meant by these terms?

In the early life of this new City of St. Louis the courts of Missouri, just as was the case with the courts of California when the City and County of San Francisco was vested with the power to frame its own charter as its "organic law," attempted to define its status. In the *Gleason* case (15 Mo. App. 25), decided in 1884, it was held that the charter of the City of St. Louis must be regarded in law as a grant from the state of equal dignity with a municipal charter conferred by an act of the legislature. If they are of equal dignity, then by what rule of law can the charter be interfered with by any act of the legislature? That would destroy the admitted fact of equal dignity. For equal dignity cannot exist in the presence of overlordship.

In the *Western Union* case (149 U.S. 465), decided in 1893, the United States supreme court said: "The City of St. Louis occupies an unique position. It does not, like most cities, derive its powers by grant from the legislature, but framed its own charter under express authority from the people of the state. * * * Its charter is an organic act, so defined by the constitution, and is to be construed as organic acts are construed." In the *Dorr* case (145 Mo. 466), decided in 1898, the court said: " 'Organic law' is a term usually applied to constitutional law only. It certainly implies a high degree of authority." And in the *McGee* case (249 Mo. 266), decided in 1913, the court held that the provisions of a freeholders' charter "are to be regarded as having the same force and effect as if they had been enacted into a statute by the General Assembly of the State."

The Missouri courts have also defined, sometimes with wavering steps, how this "organic law" may be "in harmony with and subject to the laws of the state." In the *Ewing* case (15 Mo. App. 441) in line with the *Grant* case (94 Minn. 45), the court said: "Harmony is not identity. An agreement between two systems in the fundamental principles of their action upon the rights of persons and property and the administration of justice will satisfy the most exacting demand for harmony. The constitutions of all the states are understood to be in harmony with the Federal constitution. And yet no two of them are alike in all details, and not one is a copy of the common superior. There is nothing in this limitation which would subject the city charter to an exact conformity with the legislative designation of a particular officer who is to perform a certain duty. *Harmony with the general laws may require that a particular duty,* as the appointing of judges and clerks of elections, *shall be discharged by some one. But beyond this, all is mere detail in structure and machinery,* which the constitution

wisely left to the framers of the charter. * * * The new
city government, as compared with other constitutional
agencies, is * * * an immediate representative of the
supreme power—the sovereign people of the state. It
no more owes allegiance or duty to the general assembly
than the general assembly owes to the city government.
The two are co-equal partners in the same creative
energy, which has not placed either above the other. Even
the right to change a single provision of the new charter
is expressly given to the qualified voters within the limits
of the municipality, and so the idea of any such control
in the general assembly is conspicuously ignored.'' It is
true that the supreme court in a review of that case (85
Mo. 64) sadly wobbled in order to save the life of a political elections board, but the later *Dorr* and *Walsh* cases,
infra, seemingly brought it back on the right track. Still
later that court in the *Shreeve* case (317 Mo. 736), decided in 1927, said: ''If the legislation is to be construed
to mean that the charter must be consistent with every
provision of the constitution and every law of the state,
then the limitation simply nullifies the grant (of home
rule). * * * The above constitutional limitation was construed * * * in *Kansas City v. Bacon,* 147 Mo. 259: 'Consistent with does not import exact conformity, but means
substantial harmony with the *principles* of the Constitution and the general laws of the State.' '' In the *Oil
Company* case (140 Mo. 458) the court said: ''That the
people of Missouri, in their sovereign capacity and by
their organic law, could delegate to the people of a municipality this power to frame a charter for their own local
government, we have no doubt whatever. Such a right
is in accord with the genius of our institutions, bringing
the regulation and government of local affairs within the
observation of those who are to be affected thereby, and
at the same time prevent officious intermeddling with the
charters of our cities, without the knowledge of those
whose rights are affected. It is to be observed in this
connection that the permission to frame a charter nec-

essarily carries the privilege of providing a system different from that adopted for the state at large, provided
it shall not override or collide with the constitutional
guarantees and restrictions and shall not be out of harmony with the general laws of the State. It must be
borne in mind that the grant of the right to frame a charter of its own would have been utterly without force and
meaningless, if the convention which framed the Constitution and the people who adopted it meant that such a
charter should be in all respects exactly like the general
charters framed by the general statutes for the class to
which it would have belonged but for that privilege. We
are forbidden by the rules of fair construction to ascribe
such a restricted meaning to the words in so important
a document as the Constitution of the State. As was
said in *State v. Field,* 99 Mo. 352: 'Charters thus adopted
will of necessity be more or less at variance and that they
will be unlike in many respects, is within the contempla-
tion of the Constitution.' "

A thus rather full presentation of these decisions of
the Missouri court seems justifiable in view of its contra-
dictory views referred to later on herein. Enough is said
to make it clear that the charter, as the "organic law,"
need not be "in harmony with and subject to" the laws
of the state in the ordinary sense of those terms, and, in
fact, in only a very limited sense.

Controversy arose over the term "city and county of
St. Louis," as used in the constitution. At first blush
the use of that term might indicate an intention that the
City of St. Louis was to be a county. But it must be remembered that both the city and the new outside county
were being considered. The one was the City of St.
Louis and the other was the outside territory which retained the name of "the county of St. Louis." When
the constitution spoke of the "city and county of St.
Louis" it was with reference to these two separate political entities. In the *Walsh* case (69 Mo. 408) the court
in commenting on section 23 of article IX of the consti-

tution which provides that "the city and county of St. Louis shall be independent of each other," said: "The word 'city' is undoubtedly used in contradistinction to the word 'county.' The 'city' and 'county' are to be independent of each other." As has been pointed out, there is not a word in the constitution, nor in the scheme, nor in the charter, which even intimates that the City of St. Louis shall be a county. What is said is to the contrary."

However, upon this point we find a false start made by the court. As has been pointed out the returns of the election of August 22, 1876, on the question of the adoption of the scheme of separation, showed its defeat. Therefore, county officers for the old county were voted for at the regular November election in 1876. The candidate returned as having been elected sheriff of the old county claimed the office, but in the meantime the court had decided that the vote for separation had carried and that the old county had ceased to exist. The office of sheriff of the City of St. Louis was thereupon claimed by an appointee of the governor. The only ground upon which appointment by the governor could be justified was that the City of St. Louis was *a county, newly created,* and that under section 10 of Article IX the governor is empowered to appoint a sheriff for a *new* county. In the *Finn* case (4 Mo. App. 347), the court said that the City of St. Louis "is not a *normal* county of the State." So, in order to preserve the political patronage of the governor, it had to resort to the subterfuge that it must be some other sort of a county. The court had to do something which neither the constitution, nor the scheme, nor the charter had done. None of them had created the City of St. Louis into a county. So, the court usurped a sovereign power which it did not lawfully possess and by its judicial fiat it declared that the City of St. Louis is a county. As a basis for doing so it invoked section 1 of article IX of the constitution which reads: "The several counties of the state, as they now exist, are hereby

recognized as legal subdivisions of this State.'' The
court declared that this is the nearest approach to a definition of a county which the constitution affords. In
order to use it as a definition to fit the case at bar it had
to twist that definition around so as to read: "Legal
subdivisions of the state shall be recognized as counties.''
But the constitution said no such thing. To have said that,
the constitution would thereby have made every township, city, town and school district in the state, into a
county. For they are all "legal subdivisions of the
state.'' However, that decision gave to the governor
the political plum of naming a sheriff instead of leaving
to the City of St. Louis its rightful power of naming him,
just as we have seen was done to the City of Philadelphia
by the supreme court of Pennsylvania in the *Taggart*
case (102 Pa. St. 354) and in the *Oellers* case (140 Pa. St.
457), (Chapter XV.)

In the same year in which the *Finn* case was decided
a controversy arose as to what officer should perform the
functions theretofore performed by the county marshal
within the city. For the reason stated in that case that
no county sheriff had been elected at the general election
in 1876 the court in the *Mason* case (4 Mo. App. 377) held
also that no county marshal had then been elected. But,
strangely enough, that same court held that the charter
of the City of St. Louis had the sole power of designating
those city officers who should perform the duties and
functions theretofore performed by county officers within
the boundaries of the city, and so the court held that the
city marshal provided for in the charter should perform
the functions theretofore performed by the county marshal in the city. These two decisions of that court seem
to be in flat contradiction with each other in principle.
The only possible basis for the decision in the *Finn* case
was the abortive court creation of the City of St. Louis
into a county, which was specifically disowned by the
supreme court in two later decisions.

Indeed, in the very next year the supreme court in

the *Walsh* case (69 Mo. 408) said: ''The general purpose
of its framers (of the constitution), however, so far as
the political status of the city of St. Louis is concerned,
will, on a careful examination of these clauses bearing
directly upon the separation of the city from the county,
be found to be to *divest the city of all county government,*
and to withdraw it from the operation of many acts of
the General Assembly in force in the county of St. Louis.
Of course the general law of the State *relating to persons
and property and regulating the administration of justice*
remained in force after the separation as before, because
the city still remained a part of the state. * * * The 23rd
section (of article 9 of the constitution) provides that
the city and county of St. Louis shall be independent of
each other. The city shall be exempt from all county
taxation. * * * The city, as enlarged, shall be entitled to
the same representation in the General Assembly, collect
the State revenues and perform all other functions in
relation to the State, in the same manner as if it were a
county as in this Constitution defined; and the residue
of the county shall remain a legal county of the State of
Missouri, under the name of the county of St. Louis.
* * * The phraseology of this section is highly significant
and would seem to be conclusive of the question under
discussion. Throughout this provision the word 'city' is
undoubtedly used in contradistinction to the word
'county.' The 'city' and the 'county' are to be independent of each other. If the city was to become a county
and the residue of the county remain such, why declare
that they should be independent of each other? Such a
declaration was entirely superfluous, if both were to be
counties. * * * It was the fact that the city was to be
detached from the county *without any county government*
being provided for it, and that fact only, which made it
necessary to declare that the city and the county were to
be independent of each other. 'The city shall be exempt
from all county taxation;' that is, the city shall be separated from, and independent of, the county, and shall be

exempted from all county taxation. * * * Again, if the city, as enlarged, was still a county * * * why provide that it should be entitled to the same representation (in the General Assembly) 'as if it were a county?' If a county, representation was already secured it by the second section of article 4 (which provides that counties shall have certain representation in the General Assembly). * * * We think that the manifest purpose of the scheme of separation was to detach the territory comprised within the enlarged limits of the city of St. Louis from the county of St. Louis, leaving it *a city proper divested of all county government.*"

It must follow, then, that since the City of St. Louis was "divested of all county government" it could not in any sense be a county, and it could not have any county officers. That is common sense. In the *McKee* case (69 Mo. 504), decided in 1879, while it was held that the laws providing for one constable in each ward of the city prevailed over an ordinance providing for three constables for two wards that had been consolidated for that purpose, yet the court said: "The language of those (sections 23 and 25 of article IX) and other sections that might be cited, is totally inconsistent with the idea that the city of St. Louis is one of the counties of the State. *State v. Walsh, ante,* 408. Would a general law with reference to the several counties of the State apply to the city of St. Louis? We think not.''

These decisions completely explode the theory announced in the *Finn* case that the City of St. Louis is a county. It can have no officers other than those provided for by the charter, so long as that charter designates the city officers who shall perform those functions required by the constitution and the laws to be performed within its boundaries. When those functions are thus performed by city officers the ''general laws of the state relating to persons and property and regulating the administration of justice,'' spoken of by the court in the *Walsh* case, *supra,* are just as fully enforced as if done by county officers.

As stated by the California and the Colorado courts, only in case the charter fails to provide for the performance of such functions may the legislature designate what officers shall perform them.

This leads to the proper construction to be given to section 25 of article IX of the constitution which reads: "Notwithstanding the provisions of this article, the General Assembly shall have the same power over the city and county of St. Louis that it has over other cities and counties of this State." It has already been pointed out that the word "county" therein used applies solely to the outside territory which retained the name of the county of St. Louis. What, then, is the power that the General Assembly shall have over the city? The courts, as already shown, have held that the requirement that the charter, the "organic law" of the city, shall be "in harmony with and subject to the laws," is of a very limited character. The courts also have held that this section 25 does not actually grant to the General Assembly the broad power which its language denotes since that would destroy the home rule power in the city which the framers of the constitution intended it should have. And so, as has been seen, the courts early decided that the city has full power to say what officers it shall have and to designate what ones of its city officers should perform those essential duties toward the state ordinarily performed in cities and counties, and that the power of the General Assembly is limited to general laws prescribing what shall be done by these city officers as to carrying out state policies, and not otherwise.

In the *Mason* case, *supra*, the court said: "County functions are to be performed by the city authorities, acting for the state, where it is not otherwise expressly provided. It is *'the city enlarged'* which is to 'collect the state revenue, and *perform all the functions in relation to the state* in the same *manner* as if it were a county' etc. As *the city* is to do these things, *it is necessary to do them through its own officers,* and it is necessary to do them 'in the same manner' as if it were a county. This is a part of the scheme furnished by the Constitution itself, and, of course, *superior to all laws, special and general.* * * * The power is given, not merely to provide for the government of the city, *but the city is required to say by what city officers the county functions shall be performed,* where the Constitution does not, in terms or by necessary implication, otherwise provide. For instance, the state revenue within the city is to be collected. It is to be *collected by the city officers; by what city officers it was clearly within the power of the freeholders to provide* as it was within their power to provide who should collect the city revenue."

And in the next year the supreme court in the *Walsh* case, *supra,* said: "We think that the manifest purpose of the scheme of separation was to detach the territory comprised within the enlarged limits of the city of St. Louis from the county of St. Louis, thereby leaving it a city proper divested of all county government, *the functions in relation to the State previously performed therein by the county government being transferred to the government of the city.*" In the *Powers* case (68 Mo. 320), decided in 1878, the court said: "That as the city government, authorized by the constitution, for the city of St. Louis, is entirely different in its organization from that of the counties, and as the duty of collecting the state revenue, which devolved upon the county of St. Louis under the general law, was thereafter to be performed by the city of St. Louis, *it became necessary to provide in the charter the requisite municipal agencies* for the performance of that duty. *Proper officers were to be designated, the mode of their selection prescribed, and the duties which were previously performed by the officials designated in the general law were, by express enactment, to be imposed upon them.*". Again, in the *Hoblitzelle* case (15 Mo. App. 441), decided in 1884, the court said: "Harmony with the general laws may require that a particular duty, as the appointing of judges and clerks of elections, shall be discharged *by some one. But beyond this, all is mere detail in structure and machinery, which the constitution wisely left to the framers of the charter.*" And again in the *Dorr* case (145 Mo. 466), decided in 1898, the court said: "The charter of the city (besides regulating its local affairs) contained many provisions to define the mode in which the city should perform many essential governmental duties toward the State 'as if it were a county' (Sec. 23). The city was practically put in the position of a county for the purposes of executing the functions of government in that locality. *As those functions were to be performed by city officers, the scheme and charter undertook, in the first instance, to prescribe how and by whom, those duties should be performed.*"

The whole sum and substance of the power of the legislature is tersely stated by the supreme court in the *Walsh* case, *supra,* where it said: "Of course the general laws of the state *relating to persons and property and regulating the administration of justice* remained in force after the separation as before, because the city remained a part of the State." That measured the power of supervision left in the legislature. It could enact general laws for the protection of persons and property, both civil and criminal, and regulating the administration of justice in the courts. The sovereignty of the state was thus preserved. The state is properly interested only that such laws be enforced. It is in accord with the genius of our democratic institutions that local officers elected by the people, and not appointed as in an autocracy by the head of the state, should enforce those laws. And, what difference can it make to the state what officers enforce the state laws, so long only as they are enforced? How does that derogate in the least the sovereignty of the state? It is true, of course, that it interferes with the patronage and power of the machine politicians who are always looking for power and pelf.

And that was the sensible, logical and legal definition of the limited power of the legislature over the City of St. Louis. In Chapter XVI the decisions of the supreme court of California have been noted to the same effect concerning the City and County of San Francisco, and in Chapter XVIII concerning the City and County of Denver is a reference to the *Cassiday* case (50 Colo. 503) in which the court forcefully declared that so long as the charter provides the agencies which shall discharge county functions within the city no interference with the sovereignty of the state arises, and pertinently inquired: "How, possibly, can the fact that different agencies than those provided for other counties are in this territory to perform governmental duties, when all such functions are carefully preserved and their discharge provided for, be held in any manner to affect state government?"

Under these decisions above noted the City of St. Louis was empowered to conduct its own affairs, to determine what officers it would have, to combine and consolidate offices in order to simplify its government under such officers as would result in the greatest efficiency and economy, without legislative interference, subject only that the charter should designate which of its officers should perform the functions required by the state to be performed in the exercise of its sovereignty. This would leave the city to elect all its officers at the spring election and thus be separated from state politics at the fall election, so that its affairs would receive that single attention which makes for better conduct of city government, and home rule would be made effective as was intended. And it would also have kept all employees and appointees in the public service within the city under the merit system.

But the crafty politicians, urged not by civic patriotism but actuated by a consuming desire for patronage and power, came burrowing in. In 1861 the Democrats in possession of the state legislature had enacted a law creating a board of police commissioners for the City of

St. Louis which, at that time, was a Republican strong-hold. (Chapter VI.) That board was made appointive by the governor who was a Democrat. It is evident that this was done purely for political purposes and not for the better government of the city. At the time the scheme and charter were framed the board of freeholders was of the opinion that to permit the continuance of this situation was not in accord with the principle and practice of home rule. However, they feared delay in the courts might ensue if the new charter should provide for a local police department under the control of the city, and so the charter provided that "no system of police shall be established or maintained other than the present metropolitan system as long as the same is established by law." The majority of the members of the board of freeholders consisted of Democrats. This may partially explain its action in this important matter. The governor was then, and generally has been, a Democrat. Whether these political conditions influenced the board of freeholders to leave the power over the city police in the hands of the governor instead of placing it in the hands of the city as should rightfully have been done, is a question. However, the weak-kneed conduct of that board was simply to admit the camel into the Arab's tent.

Here comes an interesting sequence. There had been a political revolution in the city which had resulted in unseating the Democrat who was then mayor and in the installation of an Independent in his place. As his successor William Ewing, a Republican, was elected mayor in 1881. Under the then charter he was empowered to appoint the judges and clerks of election. In 1883 the legislature was controlled by Democrats. Evidently they smelled the political flesh-pots, for they enacted, and a Democrat as governor signed, a law creating the office of recorder of voters for the City of St. Louis to be appointed by the governor with full power over the registration of voters, the appointment of all judges and clerks of elections, and the supervision of all elections to

be held in the city. For a special *city* election to be held
in that year the mayor, under authority of the charter,
appointed the judges and clerks. The recorder of voters
appointed by the governor also appointed judges and
clerks. In the *Ewing* case (15 Mo. App. 441) the court
held that the constitution gave to the city the right to
name all of its officers and that the mayor had the right,
under the charter, to make such appointments. Undoubtedly that decision was right, especially as the election was one at which no judicial or state officer was to
be elected. It was strictly local in its character and in
no way affected the state. However, on appeal to the
supreme court, that decision was reversed, (85 Mo. 64).
It may be only a coincidence that the members of the
supreme court, and the governor and the legislature, at
that time were Democrats or controlled by them, and
that the mayor of the City of St. Louis was a Republican.
In any event the control of the election machinery of that
great city was a political asset of no little importance.

That decision was predicated upon the theory of the
sovereign power of the state. Now what about this
doctrine of state sovereignty to be exercised by the legislature? It seems to depend altogether upon the brand
of state sovereignty in Missouri as to what is to be protected by autocratic control. In *State v. City*, 264 U. S.
472, the supreme court of the United States declared that:
"The power of eminent domain is an attribute of sovereignty." In *Kansas City v. Oil Co.*, 140 Mo. 458, the
supreme court of the state of Missouri held that "the
power of condemnation is an attribute of state sovereignty and is not inherent in a municipality." Nevertheless, that court further held that, despite any action by
the legislature, *this attribute of sovereignty was vested
in that city directly by the provisions of the constitution
which gave it the power to frame its home rule charter.*
The court said: "It is not pretended that this power is
inherent in a municipality created by the state. It must
be conferred by the state. * * * Sec. 16 of Art. IX of the

Constitution of 1875 provides that 'any city having a population of more than 100,000 inhabitants may frame a charter for its own government consistent with and subject to the laws of this state.' * * * No limitation is placed on the character of the charter except that it shall always be in harmony with the Constitution and laws of the state. *The charter derives the power of condemnation directly from the organic law of the state in such terms.* * * * The authorities cited by the learned counsel for defendant as to the necessity of a grant of power have no application to a city charter, which derives the power of condemnation of lands for public purposes directly from the organic law of the state in such unequivocal terms. It is not a matter of inference, but a direct grant of power. * * * *The power was conferred by the people of the state, and it was not in the power of the legislature to curtail it.*"

Note well the statement of the court that under section 16 of article 9 of the constitution the people of Kansas City were empowered to frame a charter to be the organic law for their own government in harmony with and subject to the constitution and the laws of the state; that such charter derives the power of condemnation *directly* from the organic law of the state in such *unequivocal* terms, and that this power was conferred by the people of the state and that it was not in the power of the legislature to curtail it. Then read the provisions of sections 20, 22 and 23 of that same article of the constitution (Appendix—6) which empowered the people of the City of St. Louis to frame a charter to be their organic law for their own government in harmony with and subject to the constitution and laws of the state. Then ask yourself this question: If the attribute of state sovereignty as to the exercise of the important power of eminent domain by which private property may be taken from its owner against his will is unequivocably vested in a city by these provisions of the constitution granting it home rule, then why is not the attribute of sovereignty over its own elections and the registration of its voters and over its police and issuance of saloon licenses like-wise vested unequivocally in it by the same constitution freed from "the power of the legislature to curtail it."? Is it because that as to elections and the police and the saloon licenses there is great political power and pat-ronage, while in matters of condemnation there is none? That court even went so far in the *Seehorn* case (246 Mo. 541) as to hold that the city, under its vested attribute of sovereignty, was empowered by the home rule provi-sions of the constitution to create by charter a *municipal* court and to vest in it jurisdiction in condemnation cases, although the statute gives to the circuit courts in the other counties that jurisdiction.

The camel had nosed further into the Arab's tent. It always selected the most comfortable and enjoyable part of the tent. The party in power in the state had thus secured control of the election machinery in the City of St. Louis, and that control is still exercised by a board of election commissioners composed of four mem-bers appointed by the governor. Added thereto was the appointment by the governor of a police board for that city. Further completing political domination of that city by the state house crowd the legislature in 1893 cre-ated the office of excise commissioner to be appointed by the governor with power over saloon and other licenses in the City of St. Louis, with the resultant political pres-tige and campaign revenue connected therewith. Why were the two largest cities of the state, St. Louis and Kansas City, picked out for this deprivation of their rightful powers of self-government? They were the only home-rule cities in the state supposedly safeguarded by the provisions of the constitution of 1875. And yet they were dragged down to the lowest level of autocratic domination. Everyone knows what these measures mean in political patronage and power and campaign revenue and graft for the party in control of the state administra-tion.

These were some of the gradual steps of the camel into the Arab's tent. The room that was left was not overlooked. In 1905 the legislature had enacted a law which provided that in each county there be elected a collector of revenue at the general fall election. Notwithstanding the direct holding of the supreme court that in the City of St. Louis there was and could not be any county officer and that all revenues were to be collected by the city collector, when a vacancy occurred in that office the governor promptly appointed a successor to fill it. That appointment was sustained in the *Koeln* case (270 Mo. 174) in which the court cavalierly disregarded not only the constitution but also its former decisions and without warrant declared that its opinion did not conflict with its rulings in the *Mason* case and in the *Walsh* case, *supra*. In the first place the constitution did not provide for a single state officer for the City of St. Louis, and in the second place the *Walsh* case specifically held that the constitution had left it "divested of all county government." Furthermore the constitution plainly provided that "*the city* shall collect the state revenue," and the *Mason* case directly held that the state revenue within the city was to be "collected by the *city officers;* by what city officers it was clearly within the powers of the freeholders to provide," while the *Walsh* case clearly stated that the city in collecting the state revenue "can act only through the instrumentality of its own officers." By what right, then, did the legislature and the court deprive the people of that city of their constitutional power? Was it based on law, or was it just another political decision? Finally in the *Dwyer* case (343 Mo. 973) decided in 1938, the supreme court, for like reasons, held that a vacancy in the office of city treasurer must be filled by the governor. Even the legislature seems to have reached the conclusion that this constant wrongful devolution of power on the governor in municipal affairs in the City of St. Louis had become nauseating for in 1939 it enacted a law (p. 486) which provides that now when such vacancy occurs it shall be filled by the mayor. Not only have these encroachments by the legislature upon the rightful powers and liberties of the people of the City of St. Louis, vested in them by the constitution of their state, been aided and abetted by the supreme court, but it has assiduously whittled away many of the rightful prerogatives of that people by limiting their home rule power to "municipal affairs," which that court and no one else has ever defined but which is left to the guess of the court in each individual case. It brings strong reminder of the subservient courts of Charles II which wantonly forfeited the charter of London and of other English boroughs, noted in Chapter II. However, there the court administered the *coup de grace* but in Missouri the court has weakened its victim by successive blows.

The action of the court in picking up city officers and making them county or state officers, by its *ipse dixit,* necessitates their election at the time of the general state election in the fall and thus thrusts them into state politics instead of being elected with all other city officers at the municipal spring election. This prevents systematic budgeting of city finances and militates against arrangement of the city government into proper departments with the reduced number of officers properly needed in the public service. It completely blocks the city from placing the so-called county officers under civil service, to the great delight of the politicians.

Mr. E. H. Wayman, city conselor of the City of St. Louis, writes: "We have had to be very diligent in guarding the city's rights, not only in litigation, but also against pressure groups who have some particular scheme or hobby they desire to have enacted, without stopping to think where the money is coming from to administer it. When they meet with no success at the hands of the city administration, they rush to the legislature for the enactment of a law to 'enable' the city to do the things they want to have done, and we have always had to

oppose these efforts upon the ground that all the enabling the city needs is found in its charter.''

The people of St. Louis scored a tremendous advance
when they secured inclusion in the constitution of 1875
of the provisions intended to give them true home rule,
to place in their hands the unrestricted power to declare
what officers they should have, their terms of office and
their compensation, thus making effective the consolidation of city and county government planned and hoped
for. Unfortunately, from the causes referred to in this
chapter, there has been a steady recession without anything effective having been done to regain the ground
lost.

There was a gleam of hope in 1924 when the constitution was amended empowering the City of St. Louis and
the county of St. Louis to consolidate into one legal subdivision under the municipal government of the City of
St. Louis. That amendment provided for the election by
the city and by the county of a board of freeholders to
prepare a scheme for such consolidation to be submitted
to the voters of the city and of the county. It was provided that, if the scheme thus prepared were adopted by
the voters, it should ''become the organic law of the
territory therein defined, and shall *take the place of and
supersede all law,* charter, provisions and ordinances
inconsistent therewith relating to said territory.'' (Appendix—7.) Had such scheme been adopted it is clear
that its provisions would have taken the place of and
have superseded ''all law inconsistent therewith.'' The
result would have been that the consolidated city and
county would thus have been freed from the interference
of the legislature and of the courts which had been so
baleful in its effects. The proposed scheme was defeated
at an election held October 26, 1926. The vote in the city
was 54,558 for to 8,097 against, but in the county the
vote was 10,772 for to 21,049 against. Since a majority
vote in the county as well as in the city was required it
lost. The politicians of both parties in St. Louis county

fought the proposition. Those in office did not want to lose their places at the public crib. Those of the opposite party did not want to lose the chance of getting to that crib at some future election. So they combined their forces for ulterior purposes to defeat a meritorious measure. It was most unfortunate that the framers of that amendment did not specifically provide therein that the charter of the City of St. Louis and all amendments thereto then existing or thereafter adopted "shall supersede all laws of the state inconsistent therewith" and thus have emancipated the city itself from the present overlordship exercised by the legislature and by the courts.

Another abortive attempt was made in 1930 to alleviate this situation. An amendment to the constitution was submitted to the people of the state which would have authorized the creation of a new "City of Greater St. Louis." It was proposed that it exercise control over the city and also of the outside county, but only with respect to such matters as planning, sewers, major traffic arteries, parks, institutions, traffic and police. The county government was to be abolished, but all existing municipalities, including the City of St. Louis, were to retain their separate corporate existence. The plan was lamely copied after that of New York City with a sort of hybrid borough system. The amendment was defeated by a vote of 218,381 for to 375,718 against.

The 1876 charter of the City of St. Louis stood practically intact for thirty-eight years. In 1902 the constitution was amended authorizing the charter to provide "for a chief executive and at least one house of legislation to be elected by general ticket," thus giving the city the option of a unicameral council instead of the bicameral system which was theretofore required. It was not until 1914 that a new charter was adopted. It provided for twenty-eight aldermen to be nominated one from each ward but to be elected by city-wide vote. Elections for municipal officers are held in April of odd-numbered years. The mayor, comptroller and fourteen aldermen are chosen for four-year terms. At the intervening city election held two years later the president of the board of aldermen and the other fourteen aldermen are chosen. This staggering of terms is in line with the short ballot principle. All are elected by city-wide vote. The mayor has a seat and a voice in the board of aldermen and may introduce ordinances, but he has no vote. He appoints the assessor, supply commissioner, register, city counselor, city marshal, city court judges, clerk of the city courts, president of the board of public service, director of public utilities, director of streets and sewers, director of public welfare and director of public safety. The board of public service consists of the president of that board, the director of public utilities, the director of streets and sewers, the director of public welfare and the director of public safety. The department of finance consists of the comptroller, and the assessment, collection, treasury and supply divisions. The board of estimate and apportionment consists of the mayor, comptroller and president of the board of aldermen. Its duties include the preparation of an estimate of receipts and requirements of each department annually and it shall submit the same together with a bill which it recommends appropriating the amounts deemed necessary for the use of each department, board, and office for the current fiscal year and a bill establishing the city tax rates for that year, to be passed upon by the council. The efficiency board (civil service) consists of three members, one appointed each year by the mayor for a three-year term, no more than two of whom shall be adherents of the same political party. Franchises may be granted by ordinance but may be offered and sold at public sale by order of the board of aldermen. Provision is made for the exercise of the power of condemnation of private property for public use, and for the procedure to be followed in the city court. The charter provides that: "The board of aldermen may by ordinance, adopted by vote of two-

thirds of all the members, on the recommendation of the
board of estimate and apportionment, discontinue any
division established by the charter, create new or additional divisions, and determine, combine and distribute
the functions and duties of divisions, officers and em-
ployes.'' But as we have seen, under the court decisions,
this does not apply to county officers and employees.

The charter also provided that the collector and the
treasurer should be appointed by the mayor. But the
supreme court later held them to be county or state officers under the state sovereignty subterfuge hereinbefore
noted, so that now they must be elected at the time of the
general state election. At the same time there are elected
the sheriff, constables, circuit attorney, prosecuting attorney, circuit judges and circuit clerk, judges and clerk
of court of criminal correction, judge of probate court,
justices of the peace, recorder of deeds, public administrator, and coroner. The election commissioners, the
police commissioners and the register of elections are
appointed by the governor, as has already been noted.
The charter provides for the initiative, the referendum
and the recall.

The City of St. Louis started out splendidly on the
way to real autonomy with one set of officials to perform
both city and county functions, with the power to consolidate and coordinate offices and simplify the form of
its government, and thus reduce the cost. Unhappily the
legislature and the courts have marred that future by
foisting so-called ''state officers'' upon the city, and thus
have largely defeated ''Home Rule'' and the other benefits expected.

In preceding pages it has been shown that the City
and County of San Francisco, when it had found itself
hampered by court decisions or by lack of power, has
caused the constitution of California to be amended many
times in order to give its people untrammelled control
of a complete ''city-county consolidated'' under one set
of officers with ''Home Rule.'' And in succeeding pages

it will be shown that the City and County of Denver, when a political decision of the supreme court of Colorado for a time destroyed the benefits of the constitution giving "Home Rule" to the city and the right to a complete city-county consolidation with one set of officers, patiently held its righteous wrath for six years during which time the recreant judges on that court were retired to private life, and their successors then declared the former opinion of that court to be wrong, incomprehensible and not the law and so set it aside and restored to Denver her rightful powers. With these examples before her eyes, St. Louis has tried sporadically but feebly and unsuccessfully to right the wrongs that have taken away from that city her rightful powers. Perhaps she will yet arouse herself to vigorous action and throw off the yoke by emulating the example thus set by California and Colorado.

Very recently the people of that great city have evidenced an awakened public interest in the deplorable conditions under which its government is handicapped in conducting its business. In 1938, pursuant to an ordinance of the board of aldermen, Mayor Dickmann appointed an advisory committee with Mr. Sidney Maestre as chairman to conduct a city survey and audit. Appropriations were later made under which the committee obtained the services of the governmental research institute of that city under Mr. L. W. Childress as chairman, whose officers and trustees comprise twenty-five public spirited citizens. A very exhaustive survey was made of conditions, a thorough examination of the provisions of the charter was had, and attention was given to interference occasioned by governor appointed officers and the nullifying decisions of the courts. On February 20, 1941, a printed report of 318 pages was filed with the mayor. Criticism is made therein of the dispersion of local government powers among different governing authorities, the division of authority and responsibility among the agencies of government, the illogical grouping of functions within and among the agencies, the confusion of legislative and executive functions, the complexity and inconsistency in the forms of agencies, the inappropriate functions and excessive number of boards and commissions, the election of numerous officers not of representative character, and the disunity and lack of coordination in the process of administration. Following these criticisms a plan of reorganization is proposed. Already we have noted at page 117 the condemnation in that report of state interference by boards appointed by the governor and of the nullifying attitude of the courts toward home rule and city-county consolidation intended by the constitution. That report there touches the spot of the underlying trouble. It may well be that it may arouse the people of St. Louis to carry on this work to their final liberation from legislative and judicial domination and a return to the principles and practices of self-government.

CHAPTER XVIII.

THE CITY AND COUNTY OF DENVER
(1902)

The City and County of Denver is the only city-county consolidated which at its inception sprang into complete consolidated form. It was created in 1902 by an *amendment to the state constitution* which prescribed that its powers and duties be performed by one set of officers. Werba and Grunewald in their "Making Milwaukee Mightier" say: "Of all the cities where some form of city and county consolidation has been effected, Denver affords the best example." (p. 65.) Judge Justin Miller, now of the court of appeals of the District of Columbia, in his report to the Durham (N. C.) chamber of commerce in 1933, said: "This is generally cited as the outstanding example of successful city-county consolidation. The results are eminently satisfactory."

Denver lies in the shadow of the Rocky Mountains, at the west end of that vast plain once marked on our early geographies as the "Great American Desert." But that was a misnomer. Its wide spaces were carpeted with nutritious buffalo grass which supported great herds of buffalo and antelope hunted by the Indians, and it has only been in recent years that greedy white men have ruthlessly torn up that precious sod and turned much of that region into the desolate "dust bowl." Among the early explorers who visited the vicinity of Denver were Major Zebulon Pike in 1806 for whom Pike's peak is named and Stephen Long in 1820 for whom

Long's peak is named, — both peaks standing at an elevation of over 14,000 feet in the front range of the Rockies.

But it was not until 1849, during the "gold rush" to California, that members of some of the parties bound there stopped at the site of Denver for the purpose of panning gold from the sands of Cherry Creek. In 1858 two Iowa companies settled in what was then called Auraria, later called West Denver. In that same year a company of Kansans settled in what was first called St. Charles, but at once they changed the name to Denver in honor of General James W. Denver the then governor of the Territory of Kansas. That territory stretched from the west line of the state of Missouri to the summit of the Rocky Mountains. Kansas paid no attention to these Denver settlers and in 1859 washed its hands of them by fixing its western boundary line as it is today— one hundred and sixty miles east of Denver. In 1861 this western remnant of Kansas, together with portions of the then territories of New Mexico, Utah and Nebraska, were created into the Territory of Colorado, and in 1876 it was admitted to the Union as a state.

On November 7, 1861, the territorial legislature had passed an act incorporating the city of Denver, under a special charter. This charter was saved in the schedule of the constitution adopted in 1876 and it was surrendered only when the consolidated City and County of Denver was created by constitutional amendment in 1902. During the intervening years the city had always been regarded as a special subject of legislation, separate and distinct from municipalities organized under the general laws. Nearly every session of the legislature amended this charter or enacted a new one. The city thus became the football of the political party in power at the state capitol for the time being. To make matters worse, the notorious "Robber Seventh" General Assembly amended the charter in 1889 so as to provide for a board of public works whose members were made appointive by the governor. It was claimed at the time that this was done to "protect the city against itself." But that was not the real reason. It was done to subject the city to greater control by the political party in power at the capitol. That board was given absolute power over all public improvements, streets and thoroughfares, the issuance of building permits, and other like matters, with its horde of political henchmen who owed allegiance only to the governor. In 1891 the legislature went still further by amending the charter so as to provide for a fire and police board whose members were also made appointive by the governor. That board was given absolute power over the fire department and the police department, and it was vested with the power to issue and revoke saloon licenses. This added great numbers to the army of political henchmen who also owed allegiance only to the governor. This alien domination rode rough shod over the people of the city. It was sheer usurpation. The legislature had no rightful power to create those boards. As to the board of public works the constitution specifically forbade the delegation to any special commission of the power to make, supervise or interfere with any municipal improvement. But the Colorado supreme court blandly held that the board of public works was "a department of the city government," notwithstanding the fact that it was appointed by the governor and that the city had no hand in its creation nor in prescribing its duties. The supreme court, evidently with tongue in cheek, held further that "the right of local government in cities and towns is generally a matter pertaining to the policy or wisdom of legislation, rather than a question of constitutional construction," whatever that meant except that the governor was left with his political power over the city unhampered and unimpaired. In addition, the legislature in the charter framed by it gerrymandered the wards so as to assure the governor and his party the control of the city council.

The City of Denver had thus been reduced to a position of political serfdom. So intolerable had conditions become that its people started a strong agitation for "Home Rule." The first step taken to overthrow the domination of the state-house gang was the organization of a citizens party and the election of a non-partisan mayor in 1895. He was reelected in 1897 but when he came up again for re-election in 1899 he was counted out by the ballot box stuffers and election fixers. This brazen effrontery aroused to vigorous life the demand that boss rule should be overthrown and that the people be restored to their right of self government. There was also strong criticism of the way county affairs were managed. It was felt that the county officers expended an unfair amount of the taxes on the territory outside of the city. Charges were made that the county was extravagant, and at times corrupt, in its expenditures. Judge Ben B. Lindsey, then on the county bench and later famous as judge of the Denver juvenile court, unearthed shocking graft at the hands of the board of county commissioners. The people of the city determined to put a stop to these conditions. Another cause of irritation was the situation as to the public schools. At first Denver constituted one school district organized in 1874. By reason of annexations of outside territory from time to time, four other school districts organized under the general law had come into the city, while two other school districts were partly within the city. Repeated efforts were made by the five districts wholly within the city to consolidate so as to equalize the burdens of taxation, centralize school management under a uniform system, and save expense. These attempts failed since the courts held that only by an amendment of the constitution could such consolidation be effected, because the special charter of the old district stood in the way. (23 Colo. 499 and 26 Colo. 136.) Another cause of deepseated dissatisfaction was that the city council had the power to grant franchises to public utility corporations. It was felt, and charged openly, that these franchises were too often granted as the result of corrupt bargaining.

In 1898 Thomas S. McMurray, the then mayor, called a charter convention to consider amendments to the city charter in order to correct some of these evils. However, disruptive influences of special interests finally caused enough of the convention members to stay away from the meetings so that a quorum could not be had and nothing constructive was accomplished. In 1899 an abortive attempt was made in the legislature to do something. A bill prepared by Mr. J. Warner Mills, with whom the author collaborated, was introduced but its constitutionality was questioned. In the case of *In Re House Bill No. 496*, 26 Colo. 182, decided in 1889, it is stated that its purpose was "for the consolidation of the City of Denver and the County of Arapahoe" by an amendment of Article XVIII of the Constitution entitled "Miscellaneous." The court was asked to pass on its constitutionality under a provision of the constitution permitting that procedure, but it refused to do so because the bill had not been reported out of committee and so did not fall within the constitutional requirement. Nothing further was done at that session of the legislature.

When the next legislature met in 1901 the people of Denver had become so thoroughly aroused that they had elected members of that body who were earnestly in favor of "Home Rule" and also of separating the city from its county. On the first day of the session the author of this book, as a member of the state senate, introduced a bill for an amendment to the constitution by adding a new article thereto to be known as Article XX creating the City and County of Denver. Instead of renewing the impracticable and probably unconstitutional plan to consolidate the City of Denver and the County of Arapahoe which stretched its length 160 miles from the Kansas line to the foothills of the Rocky Mountains, the author alone wrote an entirely new bill, commonly called the "Rush Bill," which provided that the

City of Denver and the six contiguous towns of Argo, Berkely, Elyria, Globeville, Montclair and Valverde, be separated from the county and be consolidated into a new political entity as "a single body politic and corporate," under the name of the "City and County of Denver."

The leading newspapers of the city and of the state, the civic and business organizations and the women's clubs, rallied to its support. It bore the endorsement of every political party. The people throughout the state had become tired of having the time of the legislature taken up with quarrels over the Denver charter and were disgusted with the political chicanery that entered into amendments thereto. On the other hand the public utility corporations and the special interests and their powerful newspaper allies fought the measure viciously. After a bitter struggle the legislature, by a handsome majority, voted to submit the amendment to the people, and the electors at the general state election in November, 1902, adopted it as a part of the constitution by a vote of 59,750 for, to 25,767 against. It received at the polls more votes than had theretofore been cast for any other amendment submitted to the people.

It was provided therein that the new city and county "shall own, possess and hold all property, real and personal, theretofore owned, possessed or held by the said City of Denver and by such included corporations, and also all property, real and personal, theretofore owned, possessed or held by the county of Arapahoe, and shall assume, manage and dispose of all trusts in any way connected therewith; shall succeed to all the rights and liabilities, and shall acquire all benefits, and shall assume and pay all bonds, obligations and indebtedness of said City of Denver and of said included municipal corporations and of the county of Arapahoe." (See Appendix— 26 for this Article XX in full.)

The widest power concerning public utilities was given it as follows: "It shall have power, within or without its territorial limits, to construct, condemn and

purchase, acquire, lease, add to, maintain, conduct and
operate, water works, light plants, power plants, transportation systems, heating plants, and any other public
utilities or works or ways local in use and extent, in
whole or in part, and everything required therefor, for
the use of said city and county and the inhabitants
thereof, and any such systems, plants, or works or ways,
or any contracts in relation to or connection with either,
that may exist and which said city and county may desire
to purchase, in whole or in part, the same or any part
thereof may be purchased by said city and county, which
may enforce such purchase by proceedings as in taking
land for public use by right of eminent domain, and shall
have the power to issue bonds upon the vote of the tax
paying electors, at any special or general election, in any
amount necessary to carry out any of said powers or
purposes, as may by the charter be provided.''

In this connection it is to be noted that early in the
history of the new city-county the contention was raised
in the *Hallett* case (34 Colo. 393), decided in 1905, that
the specific mention of the foregoing powers excluded the
exercise of implied powers. The court denied this contention and said: ''It was intended to confer not only
powers specifically mentioned, but to bestow upon the
people of Denver *every power possessed by the legislature*
in the making of a charter for Denver.''

Full provision was made in the amendment for the
automatic extension of the boundaries of the city and
county to accommodate its future growth as follows:
''The general annexation and consolidation statutes of
the state shall apply to the City and County of Denver
to the same extent and in the same manner that they
would apply to the City of Denver if it were not merged,
as in this amendment provided, into the City and County
of Denver. Any contiguous town, city or territory hereafter annexed to or consolidated with the City and County
of Denver, under any of the laws of this state, in whatsoever county the same may be at the time, shall be de-

tached *per se* from such county and become a municipal
and territorial part of the City and County of Denver,
together with all property thereunto belonging.'' Thus
was forestalled the difficulty encountered by St. Louis
and San Francisco in enlarging their boundaries. It
was further provided that ''the City and County of Denver shall alone always constitute one judicial district of
the state.''

Specific provision was made for the performance
within the city-county of the acts and duties generally
performed by county officers as follows: ''The officers of
the City and County of Denver shall be such as by appointment or election may be provided for by the charter;
and the jurisdiction, term of office, duties and qualifications of all such officers shall be such as in the charter
may be provided; *but every charter shall designate the
officers who shall, respectively, perform the acts and
duties required of county officers to be done by the constitution or by the general law, as far as applicable.*''

This last clause was purposely framed and included
so that the City and County of Denver should have but
one set of officers. It specifically kept this new city-county consolidated within the legitimate control of the
state, by providing that the acts and duties required of
county officers to be done by the constitution or by the
general law of the state were to be performed by such
officers as the charter should designate. It was intended
thus to escape from the troubles which we have seen had
been heaped on the cities of Philadelphia and St. Louis,
and, for a while, on the city of San Francisco, by the decisions of the courts. But it will presently be seen how
a corruptly constituted court in Colorado, for a time,
overrode this plain mandate of its constitution.

The provisions for transfer of government were as
follows: ''Immediately upon the canvass of the vote
showing the adoption of this amendment, it shall be the
duty of the governor of the state to issue his proclamation accordingly (which he did on December 1, 1902),

and thereupon the City of Denver, and all municipal
corporations and that part of the county of Arapahoe
within the boundaries of said city, shall merge into the
City and County of Denver, and the terms of office of all
officers of the City of Denver and of all included municipalities and of the county of Arapahoe shall terminate;
except, that the then mayor, auditor, engineer, council
(which shall perform the duties of a board of county
commissioners), police magistrate, chief of police and
boards, of the City of Denver shall become, respectively,
said officers of the City and County of Denver, and said
engineer shall be ex-officio surveyor, and said chief of
police shall be ex-officio sheriff of the City and County of
Denver; and the then clerk and ex-officio recorder, treasurer, assessor and coroner of the county of Arapahoe,
and the justices of the peace and constables holding
office within the City of Denver, shall become, respectively, said officers of the City and County of Denver, and
the district attorney shall be ex-officio attorney of the
City and County of Denver. The foregoing officers shall
hold the said offices as above specified only until their
successors are duly elected and qualified as herein provided for; except that the then district judges, county
judge and district attorney shall serve their full terms,
respectively, for which elected.''

It was further provided that: ''The police and firemen of the City of Denver, except the chief of police as
such, shall continue severally as the police and firemen
of the City and County of Denver until they are severally
discharged under such civil service regulations as shall
be provided by the charter; and every charter shall provide that the department of fire and police and the department of public utilities and works shall be under
such civil service regulations as in said charter shall be
provided.''

It was also provided that the charter and ordinances
of the City of Denver should, for the time being only and
until a new charter was adopted, and as far as applicable,

be the charter and ordinances of the City and County of
Denver, but that its people were "vested with and they
shall always have the *exclusive* power in the making,
altering, revising and amending their charter or to adopt
a new charter, or to adopt any measure" and that "it
shall be competent for qualified electors in number not
less than five per cent of the next preceding gubernatorial
vote in said city and county to petition the council for
any measure, or charter amendment, or for a charter
convention" which the council is required to submit to a
vote of the qualified electors at the next general election
not held within thirty days after such petition is filed,
and that whenever such petition is signed by qualified
electors in number not less than ten per cent of such
gubernatorial vote, with a request for a special election,
the council shall submit it at a special election to be held
not less than thirty nor more than sixty days from the
date of filing the petition; provided that any question
so submitted at a special election shall not again be submitted at a special election within two years thereafter.
At the time of such submission any alternative article or
proposition may be presented for the choice of the voters
and may be voted on separately without prejudice to
others. If adopted, such measure, charter amendment or
new charter, is to be published once in the official newspaper and the clerk of the city-county shall certify two
copies thereof and file the same with the secretary of
state and "the same shall go into effect from the date of
such filing," and "no charter, charter amendment or
measure adopted or defeated under the provisions of this
amendment shall be amended, repealed or revived, except
by petition and electoral vote."

It will be noted that the "exclusive power" in the
making and amending of the charter of the city-county is
vested in its people; that the legislature is thus deprived
of all power concerning the same; that as soon as they
are approved by the electors and have been published
and copies have been filed with the secretary of state they

immediately are in full force and effect. To make doubly sure that there be no outside interference it was further provided that no adopted or defeated charter, charter amendment or measure can be amended, repealed or revived "except by petition and electoral vote."

Here was a marked departure, an advance, from the rule which we have seen was laid down by Judge Cooley that "the state may *mould* local institutions according to its views of policy and expedience," as theretofore exercised. Previous to the adoption of this amendment in 1902 that power of the state had been lodged in and was exercised by the legislature. But the people of the state, *who are the state,* thereby divested the legislature of that power and delegated it to and vested it in the people of the City and County of Denver, freed from any power of the legislature to interfere therewith. Absolute "Home Rule" was thus assured. Complete power was given them to say in their charter, to be framed and adopted by them alone, what officers they should have to perform both city functions and county functions, their terms of office, their compensation, the times and manner of their election, and the duties they were severally to perform. There were to be no county officers as such, but it was provided that "every charter shall designate the officers who shall, respectively, perform the acts and duties required of county officers to be done by the constitution or by the general law, as far as applicable", in addition to their other duties as officers of the city-county.

To prevent further trafficking in public utility franchises it was provided that: "No franchise relating to any street, alley or public place of the said city and county shall be granted except upon vote of the qualified taxpaying electors, and the question of its being granted shall be submitted to such vote upon deposit with the treasurer of the expense (to be determined by said treasurer) of such submission by the applicant for said franchise." Within four years after the adoption of this amendment to the constitution two franchises were thus granted under the terms of which the city was to receive annual payments totalling approximately $2,500,-000 during a twenty-year term, and the citizens were given reduced rates for service, as against the old system where the city got nothing and all money paid went into the pockets of the members of the city council.

When the author of this book drafted the provision in Article XX that franchises could be granted only on the vote of the taxpaying electors he had not anticipated that bogus tax receipts would be resorted to by franchise seekers. In 1906 the Denver Gas & Electric Company and the Denver Tramway Company applied for the above mentioned franchises. The election returns showed that the latter was granted its franchise by about 500 votes while the former received a majority of but 100 votes for its franchise, — so strong was public sentiment against their former records. It was found that the gas company had contacted J. Cook, Jr., who owned a thousand vacant lots on which the taxes were a few cents each. The company then paid the taxes on them and caused a tax receipt for each lot to be issued severally to the employees of the company, thus arming them with fraudulent evidence of being taxpaying electors to be presented to the election officials. Under the presidency of Henry L. Doherty a school of his employees was held under the tutelage of Clare N. Stannard and Frank W. Frueauff, officers of the company, to instruct these employees how to use these bogus tax receipts on election day. Stannard and Frueauff disappeared after the election. The author of this book brought a contest in the court presided over by Judge Ben B. Lindsey to set aside the election returns. Subpoenas were served on Henry L. Doherty, J. Cook, Jr,. Fred'k A. Williams, chairman of the Republican party, and William T. Davoren, chairman of the Democratic party, to disclose what part, if any, they had taken in the perpetration of these election frauds. Each of them re-

fused to be sworn and Judge Lindsey promptly sent them
to the county jail for contempt of court. But the supreme
court, two of whose members were there as the result of
the "Theft Of A State" (Appendix—1) and the majority
of whom joined in the notorious *Johnson* decision hereinafter discussed, liberated them. The treasurer who
had issued the bogus tax receipts died shortly afterward
from humiliation at having been a corporation dupe in
that shameful proceeding.

And finally provision was made for the consolidation
of all the school districts and parts of districts within
the city and county into one district, under one board of
education, subject to the general laws of the state, the
property of all to become the property of the consolidated
district but the then indebtedness of each to be paid by
taxes on the property located within it.

Some have criticized the amendment because of the
details included in it. Ordinarily a constitution and
amendments thereto should be concise. But when the
author drew Article XX he had in mind the holding of
the supreme court in the school consolidation cases and
in sustaining the act of the legislature creating a board
of public works for the city under a strained construction
of the constitution. Therefore, in order that the court
might not find any cause to interfere, plain and specific
provisions were included as to property rights and liabilities, for additional powers to be exercised by the new
city-county, what officers were to take over its government and what their powers and functions were to be, for
the free exercise of the right of "Home Rule" and for
the consolidation of the school districts. If any of these
had been left to future action of the legislature it would
have been dangerous. Even with all the care taken to
precisely cover all these matters the supreme court did
interfere, as we shall see. But that interference was
overcome and today the City and County of Denver
exemplifies the fullest exercise of the right of self-
government in any city in this country and perhaps in

the world, unhampered by any action of the legislature, with absolute power to determine what officers it shall have, their jurisdiction, terms and compensation, and that there shall be only one set of officials. By embedding these things in the constitution itself it was made as certain as possible that they should never be interfered with.

Immediately upon the amendment going into effect in 1902 its beneficial results became apparent. Taxes were materially reduced, the dual set of officers was eliminated, official responsibility was fixed, conflict in authority was obviated and the governmental operations were simplified. William B. Guthrie, Professor of Government and Sociology at the College of the City of New York, in a paper read by him in 1917 before the National Municipal League, said: "The Denver experiment has clearly pointed out the way of boldly grappling with the problem by creating an artificial county and city area coterminous in extent and power. * * * It has markedly shortened the ballot, * * * lessened partisan influence by abolishing jarring officials in city and county, has effected a large saving in the operation of the government in the area involved, has removed duplications, concentrated the control of substantially identical transactions joining economy to efficiency, and has removed a serious obstacle to municipal home rule by lessening the chance of conflict in county areas where the functions are state and those deemed to be municipal were certain to clash." In the same year he made an estimate of the relative expenses before and after consolidation. His figures showed a total expenditure of the county administrative offices to have been $679,100 in 1911, when the second consolidation took effect after the *Cassiday* case, while the 1917 appropriations for the administration of those same functions were but $476,600 or a reduction of about one-third in the cost of operation. The then chairman of the Denver chamber of commerce tax expenditure committee, R. B. Mayo, said: "It is impossible to make an accurate statement of the savings resulting from consolidation,

because we are too far away from the time when city
and county were separated. But if we were to go back to
the old separate city and county governments and place
another government on top of our present government,
we would add, in my opinion, to our present costs just
about the cost of that additional layer of government.
Our present form is so much better that an additional
layer would be sheer waste.''

According to the United States census of 1900 the
population of the City of Denver was 133,858, and that
of the six included towns was 5,807, or a total of 135,665
for the new city-county consolidated. Its area thus constituted was and still is fifty-four square miles. The
population of the remaining portion of the former county
was 13,350, and its area was 842 square miles. The remaining western sixty miles of the old county was divided
in the middle, the northern half was created into the
county of Adams and the southern half was created into
the county of Arapahoe. The eastern one hundred miles
of the old county was also divided in the middle and
attached to the several contiguous counties lying to the
north and to the south of it.

Unfortunately, despite all the care in drafting the
constitutional amendment, the new city-county was beset
at its very beginning with controversy. It had to run
the gauntlet of the courts. There arose a bitter contest
at once between the forces in favor of government by the
people on the one hand and the reactionary political
forces allied to the utility corporations seeking to hold in
subjection the inhabitants of that city. It is worth while
to note the lengths to which they went to achieve their
ends and how at the last they lost out in an epochal struggle. The consolidated City and County of Denver sprang
into being upon proclamation of the governor on December 2, 1902. However, certain of the old officers refused
to surrender their offices to their successors specifically
named in the constitutional amendment. The city treasurer was one of them. Thereupon the county treasurer,

thus named as his successor, instituted a quo warranto action against him, in the case of the *People, ex rel. vs. Sours,* 31 Colo. 369. The respondent contended that there were fatal irregularities in the submission of the amendment by the legislature; that it wrongfully took the property of the county and of the six included municipalities from them without due process of law; that it amended more than six articles of the constitution in violation of the constitutional prohibition against submitting more than six amendments at one election; that it destroyed state sovereignty by eliminating county officers as such and by providing that their duties and functions might be devolved on officers to be designated in the charter, and claimed that this cut the city and county loose from the state and created it into "an *imperium in imperio*" with an unrepublican form of government. But the supreme court, on April 2, 1903, denied all these contentions and held the amendment to be valid. It was squarely held that the people of the state had absolute right to vest in the City and County of Denver full power to say what officers they should have, their terms, how elected or appointed, and that the state was not interested in the persons who were to perform county functions so long as the charter provided that they should be performed by officers of the city-county. The court aptly said: "No reason is apparent why there should be two treasurers to handle funds raised by taxation; or why there should be two bodies having control of the streets and alleys and bridges of the city and county to keep them in repair; or why there should be two boards in control of city and county property, or why there should be two attorneys, one to represent the city and one the county; or why there should be two boards within the territory to levy taxes, one to make a levy for city purposes and one for county purposes. The people in their sovereign capacity, said that there should be one set of officers." The court further held that the amendment did not cut the city-county loose from the

state, and that it did not result in an un-republican form
of government. Like decision on the same questions
was rendered on the same day by Judge Marshall of the
United States Circuit Court sitting at Denver in the
Watts case quoted from in the *Cassiday* case (50 Colo.
503) and in the dissenting opinion in the *Johnson* case
(34 Colo. 143,165.).

Pursuant to the provisions of the constitutional
amendment the first charter convention was elected and
a charter was framed by it in 1903. It was a model
charter. It was simple and concise. It provided for a
short ballot. It was framed to protect the people. But
the politicians and certain public utility corporations
did not like it, and so it was defeated by brazen election
frauds. A second charter convention was elected and
the charter framed by it was adopted by the electors in
1904, and in the same year officers were elected thereunder. That charter convention was unable to escape
very far from the pattern set by the first charter which
had been defeated.

The new government functioned smoothly until the
fall of 1904, when the politicians concluded that there
should be more offices and more officers. So both political parties nominated a full ticket to fill the former
county offices. The Republicans won. At the same election the Democrats by a majority of over 9,000 votes
elected as governor Alva Adams, thrice governor, whose
brother, William H. Adams, has also been thrice governor, and whose son, Alva B. Adams is now the United
States Senator from Colorado. As the result of that
election the Democrats had the majority in the state
senate, but the Republicans had the majority in the
lower house. Mark well this divided control of the legislature. There flowed from it the most amazing con-
sequences. At that same election an amendment to the
constitution was adopted abolishing the court of appeals
and transferring its two members, whose terms were not
to expire for two years or more, to the supreme court,

and it provided that the incoming governor should appoint two additional members of that court, subject to confirmation by the senate, thus increasing its membership from three to seven. Of the three members on the supreme bench one was a Democrat, one was a Republican, and one was elected as a Populist. Of the two being transferred from the court of appeals one was a Republican and one was a Democrat. It will be evident that the governor's two appointees would determine the political complexion of the newly constituted supreme court.

And now occurred a most astounding theft of the legislative, executive and judicial branches of an entire state without a parallel in history. (See Appendix—1.) Briefly, the state canvassing board unlawfully went behind the election returns properly certified by two Republican county clerks, overturned those returns so as to unseat two Democratic senators and place on the senate roster two Republicans in their stead, thus giving the Republicans a majority in the senate. A contest was then brought before the legislature against the newly elected governor. It was heard by this fraudulently created senate majority sitting in joint session with the house, and by a strictly partisan vote Governor Adams was unseated. However, his opponent was seated but for a single day when his pre-arranged resignation was filed and the Republican lieutenant governor was installed in his place. This vicarious governor, thus unlawfully elevated to that high office, proceeded to nominate two reactionary lawyers as the two additional supreme court judges, thus placing that court in the hands of those who had engineered this scandalous deal.

Thus was completed the theft of the state senate and the governorship, and thus was the supreme court packed and its control stolen. Before that court, thus constituted, came the *Johnson* case (34 Colo. 143), decided in 1905, to determine whether those persons allegedly elected as county officers at the preceding fall election were entitled to take office. And that court promptly

decided in their favor on the astonishing ground that
unless the City and County of Denver had two sets of
officers, one for the city and one for the county, it would
have "an unrepublican form of government in violation
of the constitution of the United States." As one wag
said: "The supreme court decided that in order for the
city-county to have a republican form of government it
was necessary that it have a full set of Republican county
officers."

Professor McBain of Columbia University in his
book, *supra,* (pp. 510-511) says that the decision in the
Johnson case "shamelessly warped" Mr. Justice Steele's
opinion in the *Sours* case so as to use it as *stare decisis*
in unwarranted support of its "well-nigh incredible"
decision based on "the utter sophistication of the reasoning of the court" with an "obvious lack of logic" in the
"somewhat muddle-headed opinion that was handed
down by the court, speaking through Mr. Justice Maxwell." With that statement concerning the *Johnson*
case this author heartily agrees. The character of that
unfortunate decision was undoubtedly due to the fact
that Mr. Justice Maxwell had neither experience nor
ability in the practice of the law. In Leadville he had a
mediocre practice which he coupled with running an abstract office. As a reward for his political activities in
behalf of corporate interests he was appointed to the
court of appeals by Governor Peabody and the constitutional amendment enlarging the supreme court slid him
into membership in that court together with George W.
Bailey and Luther M. Goddard as the result of the fraudulent "Theft Of A State" mentioned in Exhibit—1.
At the next election of members of that court in 1908
they were promptly and properly relegated to private
life and to political oblivion by the people of the state.

In that case the court embraced the fond delusion
that Article XX violated certain provisions of the constitution theretofore existing and that this made it unconstitutional. Every lawyer, even the veriest tyro, well

knows that the latest in enactment, whether it be a statute or an amendment of the constitution, prevails. If
there be a conflict then that which theretofore existed is
thus displaced. Furthermore, section 8 of Article XX
specifically provided that: "Anything in the constitution
of this state in conflict or inconsistent with the provisions
of this amendment is hereby declared to be inapplicable to
the matters and things by this amendment covered and
provided for." That was the latest declaration of the
sovereign people of the state in their constitution framed
by them and any self-respecting court would have heeded
and obeyed it which its members had solemnly sworn to
do. That court in the *Johnson* case went so far as to
hold that lacking county officers the city-county was cut
loose from the state, in the face of the specific requirement
in Article XX that "every charter shall designate the
officers who shall, respectively, perform the acts and
duties required of county officers to be done by the constitution or by the general law, as far as applicable."
Mr. Justice Steele, in a dissenting opinion joined in by
Mr. Justice Gunter who also wrote a dissenting opinion
in a companion case, with dignified restraint clearly restated the rule in the *Sours* case, and six years later that
court made these dissenting opinions the prevailing
opinion in the *Cassiday* case which declared them to be
"convincing, exhaustive, and constitutional" and condemned in scathing terms the *Johnson* case.

As a result of the decision in that case all the Democratic city officers performing county functions were
ousted. This caused a storm of criticism and resentment
among the people of the city-county. But they were left
helpless through betrayal by their own supreme court.
When United States Senator Thomas M. Patterson in
his *Rocky Mountain News* and *Denver Times* boldly
published the truth and pilloried the recalcitrant members of the supreme court at the bar of public opinion he
was promptly cited for contempt of court and, when he
offered to prove the truth of what he had published, he

was fined the sum of one thousand dollars. (35 Colo. 253.)

The people of the state were humiliated and enraged. They had done all that they could do by amending their constitution. Under the supreme court decision any further amendment would be useless. So they swallowed their wrath and bided their time. As the terms of the judges of the supreme court expired they were promptly retired to private life until five of the seven members of that court were men thus obtained who respected the constitution of their state which they had sworn to support.

As a result of the double set of officials foisted upon the city and county by the *Johnson* case the expenses of government mounted and taxes likewise increased. The business interests and the property owners complained bitterly. The general desire was to have the government restored to the plan clearly outlined in Article XX. So, in 1911, at the urgent request of the people of the city-county, the case of the *People vs. Cassiday,* 50 Colo. 503, was filed as an original proceeding in quo warranto in the supreme court in which it was sought to overturn the decision in the *Johnson* case, on the ground that it was wrong in principle and false in law. Five out of the seven justices of the supreme court agreed with that contention. In its decision the court, in commenting on the *Johnson* case, said: "That case was determined upon the broad proposition that the people of the whole state could not amend their Constitution so as to permit the people of the consolidated body known as the City and County of Denver, by their charter, to name agencies, other than those already provided by the Constitution and general laws, to discharge, within that territory, governmental duties relating to state and county affairs. * * * All that Article XX purports to do relative to the county offices is to provide that the people of the City and County of Denver, through their charter, shall designate the agencies which are to discharge the respective duties and functions which pertain to them. * * * How, possibly, can the fact that different agencies than those provided for other counties of the state are in this territory to perform governmental duties, when all such functions are carefully preserved and their discharge provided for, be held in any manner to affect state government? What federal inhibition is invaded because officers so designated may be chosen in the early spring-time rather than in the autumn, that they serve for four years rather than two, that they are designated by one official title instead of another, or that one set of officers is named to discharge the duties in that territory pertaining to both local and governmental affairs, since all such governmental acts and duties are retained intact therein and are to be fully performed?''

The court then, with vibrant denunciation and biting sarcasm, said: ''Until the ingenuity and invention of the human intellect shall have conceived and formulated— which it has not yet done—some sound, even plausible reason for the conclusions reached in the *Johnson* case, that Article XX provides for the City and County of Denver a government unrepublican in form, that decision must remain, as it is now, wholly unaccountable and incomprehensible. * * * It is clear that the warrant of authority, given to the people of the City and County of Denver, to merely designate the agency by which governmental duties therein shall be discharged, is not obnoxious to any provision of the enabling act or of the federal Constitution, and therefore it may be, and has been, lawfully done. * * * We find nothing in it subversive of the state government or repugnant to the Constitution of the United States. * * * What is the meaning of the language, 'Every charter shall designate the officers who shall, respectively, perform the acts and duties required of county officers to be done by the Constitution or by the general law, as far as applicable,' if it does not mean just what is says? It must mean that, or it means nothing. The language is plain and positive; it is without a trace of ambiguity. It is a part of the Constitution. It is so plain that construction is unnecessary. * * * No case has been cited, and we confidently assert that none can be found, which shows that it is not competent for a fixed governmental duty to be performed by an agent designated for that purpose of a local subdivision of the state. The meaning of this provision is clear, its terms are unambiguous, the mandate is positive.''

The court then, in speaking of the contention that the city-county must have two sets of officers, said: ''It is also concluded in that *(Johnson)* opinion that, because the county still exists, it follows inevitably that county officers *eo nomine* must also exist. By this course of reasoning, the express provisions of section 2 of Article XX are nullified, and the fact lost sight of that a county may exist without regard to the particular name borne by the agencies performing governmental duties therein, and without regard to the precise method of the selection of those agencies. The people of the whole state, by constitutional provision, so clear, so plain, so certain that it interprets itself, have provided that the duties in that territory, relating to both local affairs and governmental matters of state and county concern, shall be performed by a single set of officers who are to discharge double duties. We further conclude that, in the City and County of Denver, * * * there are no county officers and can be no county officers, purely as such.''

The supreme court of Colorado thus dispelled the fog that seemed to have enshrouded the judicial mind in other states, where, as we have seen in Pennsylvania and in Missouri, and for a time in New York and in California, opinions grounded neither on law nor in reason had blocked progress in self-government. In virile terms the Colorado court sustained the right of the people in their constitution to create a city into a city-county consolidated, with one set of officers. It boldly and for the first time properly announced that in such new entity there are no county officers as such and by analogy that there are no city officers; that its officers are for an entirely different type of government, original in aspect and *sui generis* in character. They are officers of the city-county consolidated, which is described in the constitution itself as "a *single* body politic and corporate."

However, that court which had thus marked out so clearly the path to be followed soon swerved from it in two later cases in which it chased the delusion that there is both a city and a county in the City and County of Denver, — a duality impossible in the face of the declaration in the constitution that it is a "single" body politic and corporate. In the *Hilts* case (52 Colo. 382), decided in 1912, the court held that a tax levy for county purposes in the city-county must be made under the general law instead of under the charter, notwithstanding the provision in section 4 of Article XX that "the city council shall have power to fix the rate of taxation on property each year for city and county purposes." In the *Mauff* case (52 Colo. 562) the court held that in a conflict between state law and the charter concerning elections the former prevailed. But in that same year the people, upon an initiative petition, amended section 6 of Article XX so as to provide that cities under "Home Rule" charters shall have "power to legislate upon, provide, regulate and control * * * all matters pertaining to municipal elections" and for the assessment of property for municipal taxation and the levy and collection of taxes thereon for municipal purposes, and said: "All provisions of the charters of the City and County of Denver and the Cities of Pueblo, Colorado Springs and Grand Junction, as heretofore certified to and filed with the secretary of state * * * are hereby ratified, affirmed and validated as of their date." In the *Prevost* case (55 Colo. 199), decided in 1913 the court said that by the adoption of that amendment the people of the state had "declared in terms that municipal elections were local and municipal matters upon which the people of municipalities had the power to legislate." And in the *Sabin* case (75 Colo. 545), decided in 1924, the court held that the mayor of the City and County of Denver was empowered by its charter to appoint a public trustee, although he is a county officer.

It seems clear, under the language of the constitution and under these court decisions, that the City and County of Denver is a "single body politic and corporate," with one set of officers to perform both city and county functions, provided that every charter shall designate the officers who shall, respectively, perform the acts and duties required of county officers to be done by the constitution or by the general law, as far as applicable. All that the legislature may do is to pass general laws prescribing what acts and duties county officers must perform, but in no event has it any power to authorize the governor or any other person to name a single one of such officers. That was the deliberate purpose of the author in drafting Article XX and so as to leave to the legislature that limited power necessary only to the proper exercise of the sovereign power of the state. As the result of the decision in the *Cassiday* case restoring one set of officers the expense of government again fell and taxes decreased. The people are content and would not think of returning to the old dual system.

The present charter, with slight amendment was adopted by vote of the city and county in 1914. No charter elsewhere provides for a shorter ballot. The elective officers for four-year terms are the mayor, the auditor, and two members of the election commission, one of whom is to be elected in the middle of the term of the other. The council consists of nine members, each elected from his district for a two-year term. So that at any election the greatest number of officers the electors are required to vote for in any councilmanic district are but four—the mayor, the auditor, one member of the election commission and one member of the council, and at the election held in the middle of the mayor's term but two, —one member of the election commission and one member of the council. This makes a short ballot and prevents confusion of the voters.

The district court of the City and County of Denver
selects and appoints the three members of the civil service commission, not more than two of whom shall be adherents of the same political party. This has resulted in
a high type of civil service commission.

The mayor appoints all other officers, and all the
members of all boards and commissions. The executive
departments of the city and county are but five: Improvements and Parks, Revenue, Law, Safety and Excise,
Health and Charity. The managers of these five departments constitute the mayor's cabinet which, acting with
the mayor, is given the power to "formulate the general
administrative policies of the city and county, and each
manager and officer in his department, shall be responsible for and have full power to carry out such policies."
The president of the council, the manager of improvements and parks, and the manager of revenue, constitute
the board of equalization, with power over the equalization, reduction, abatement and rebate of general taxes
vested by law in the board of county commissioners in the
counties of the state. Provision is made for the performance of county functions as follows:

County Administrative Offices and Functions	Performed By— Under Consolidation
Five County Commissioners . .	President of City Council, Manager of Revenue and Manager of Improvement and Parks
County General Hospital	Manager of Health and Charity
County Coroner and Poor Relief .	Manager of Health and Charity
County Surveyor	Manager of Improvements and Parks
County Roads and Bridges . . .	Manager of Improvements and Parks
Sheriff and County Jail	Manager of Safety and Excise
County Treasurer	Manager of Revenue
County Assessor	Manager of Revenue
County Clerk and Recorder . .	Clerk of City and County
County Attorney	City and County Attorney

The Manager of Safety and Excise appoints the
chief of police. The clerk, superintendent of schools, and
the justices of the peace are appointed by the mayor who
designates one of the latter to act as police magistrate.
The justices of the peace appoint the constables. Here
is a really simplified form of government.

The charter under the exclusive power vested in the city-county by the constitution provides a complete method for framing and amending the charter, for initiating and referring ordinances, for the direct primary, and also for the preferential ballot by which the voter may express his first, second and third choice for the candidates for any office.

Thus all the implements of self-government, obtained through the years of struggle described in preceding pages, are provided in their fullest extent in the charter of the City and County of Denver and are now enjoyed by its people. No other city in the world has a government so simple in form, so systematic in its organization, so free from overlapping functions, so economical in operation, and so responsive to its electors.

For nearly forty years the people of the City and County of Denver have enjoyed these benefits and no attempt has ever been made by them to revert to the old discarded system of a dual government with a set of county officers in addition to those for the city. If experience and satisfaction with results mean what they should the example there offered gives quite conclusive evidence to be considered by public officials of other cities interested in providing for their people a simplified and less costly form of government.

Mayor Benjamin F. Stapleton has been in the public service of the City and County of Denver for a large part of the last thirty-five years. During that period he has held the office of police magistrate, 1904-1915; postmaster, 1915-1921; mayor of the City and County of Denver, 1923-1931; auditor of the state of Colorado, 1931-1935; again mayor since June, 1935. He was re-elected in 1939. On October 13, 1939, he wrote the author as follows:

"With respect to the consolidated city and county government for Denver, for which the 'Rush Bill' laid the original foundation, from my experience it is the most satisfactory form of government that has so far been presented. Paradoxically, as it may seem, this form of government, as in force at this time, is at once both exceptionally democratic and centralized. Democratic in that the people have the first and last word to say with respect to the making and amending the charter. In the exercise of that authority, they have reserved unto themselves the right of the initiative, the referendum and the recall. In these respects the government of Denver seems to be exceptionally democratic. On the other hand, under the exercise of the authority conferred upon them by the 'Rush Bill' the people have cast the whole burden of responsibility for the enactment of ordinances on the city council, and for the administration of the government and for its management they have conferred, by charter, all authority upon the mayor, the members of his cabinet and his appointees, for all of whom he is held responsible to the people. In this respect the government of the City and County of Denver would seem to be very much centralized. Since Denver is a city and county, the boundary line and the people are identical, and between the city and the county there are no conflicting interests. The result is that one set of officials not only can, and actually do, perform all of the functions of the two governments at virtually the cost of one. The simplicity and far reaching effect of the provisions of the constitutional amendment have focused national and international attention upon them. Judging from the inquiries received from foreign countries, as well as from municipalities throughout America, it would seem that the Consolidated City and County government of Denver stands out as one to be studied, especially when civic matters are being considered by other cities. The people of Denver would never consent to the old dual system of city and county government, with its conflicts of jurisdiction, its double expense of administration, and its cumbersome ballot.''

CHAPTER XIX.

THE CITY AND COUNTY OF HONOLULU
(1907)

The City and County of Honolulu, in the Territory of Hawaii, is the latest creation of a city-county consolidated in this country. Its early history is interesting and recently it has become our westernmost naval defense.

The Hawaiian Islands were first known to white men in 1542, but no settlement was made by them until more than two hundred years later. In 1778 Captain James Cook visited the islands on one of his famous voyages and gave them the name of the Sandwich Islands. In 1840 a constitution was adopted by the natives, under a feudalistic form of government. Six years later feudalism was abolished. In 1852 an elective legislature and full suffrage were established. Attempts of the reigning family to restrict or to overturn these rights brought on a revolution which resulted in the declaration by the people of a republic on July 4, 1894. In 1898 the islands were annexed to the United States, and in 1900 they were created into the Territory of Hawaii. Like all territories it is subject to the control of Congress and its governor is appointed by the President. However, it has its own elective legislature and its own elective local officers. The Organic Act of June 14, 1900, provided for the division of the territory into counties. After an unsuccessful attempt by the legislature in 1903 to thus organize the territory, it passed an act in 1905 creating four counties, each of the principal islands being made a county. There was great objection to this act and after the new county officers had been elected the supreme court held it to be unconstitutional in an action of *quo warranto* against the board of supervisors filed by the Territory of Hawaii. Municipal government had been advocated since 1848. Upon the defeat of the county act by the court public sentiment became pronounced in favor of a city-county consolidated form of government. As a result, in 1907 the legislature enacted a law creating the City and County of Honolulu and it was approved by the governor. Its population as given by the 1940 United States census is 258,256, with an area of about 600 square miles.

That act provided, among other things, that "all that portion of the Territory commonly known as the island of Oahu, and all other islands in the Territory not included in any county and the waters adjacent thereto, shall be and is constituted a city and county by the name of "City and County of Honolulu." The act declared that the city and county is a municipal corporation and has vested in it all the powers usually exercised by a city and by a county. It provides that the consolidated city and county shall enjoy all the property, rights of property, rights of action, and all rights, privileges and powers of every nature and description of the county of Oahu, and was declared to be the successor of said county.

The officers provided for the new consolidated city and county were as follows: a mayor, a board of supervisors of seven members, a sheriff who is *ex officio* coroner, a city and county clerk who is *ex officio* clerk of the board of supervisors, a treasurer, an auditor, a public prosecutor, and a city and county attorney. All are elected for two-year terms, except the public prosecutor and the city and county attorney who are appointed by the mayor for a like term subject to removal by the attorney general with the approval of the governor. The city and county clerk performs the duties of registering the electors.

The mayor, with the approval of the board of supervisors, appoints the civil service commission of three members, no more than two of whom shall be members of the same political party. The mayor also, with the approval of the board of supervisors, appoints a police commission of five members "all of whom shall not belong to the same political party at the time of their appointment." But the initial members of that commission were appointed by the governor with terms of office designated by him so that one member would serve for one year, one for two years, one for three years, one for four years, and one for five years, and at the expiration thereof the mayor was to appoint successors for two-year terms. The police commission appoints the chief of police who, in turn, appoints all policemen. The five members of the board of water supply were appointed in the first instance by the governor, with a like arrangement of terms, and it was provided that their successors be appointed by the mayor with the approval of the board of supervisors. The park board, the chief engineer of the road department, the building inspector, and the chief of the fire department, are also appointed by the mayor subject to like confirmation.

The legislature has the sole power of making and amending the charter of the city and county, subject to the governor's veto. In 1937 the legislature authorized the appointment by the mayor of a charter revision committee. That committee, after many public hearings held by it, submitted its report to the legislature and, based thereon, some changes were made in the charter but none of major importance. There was some agitation for a commission form of government but it did not have enough support to commend itself to the charter revision committee.

The controller's annual report for the year ending December 31, 1939, shows a very economical conduct of the affairs of the city-county. The general expenditures for the legislative, executive and judicial departments (including the courts), for fire and police and other protection to property, health and sanitation, highway and street lighting, charities, hospitals and corrections, recreation, playgrounds and parks, pensions, interest and sinking fund requirements on warrants and bonds, and miscellaneous including such items as workman's compensation, damage claims, fidelity bond premiums, totaled $4,147,245, or but $15.67 per capita, while the cost of the police department (included in that total) was only $484,783, or but $1.88 per capita. It is not believed that anything like such a fine showing in economical operation can be shown by any city in this country having the dual form of government.

In the thirty-four years during which the people of the City and County of Honolulu have enjoyed the benefits of the city-county consolidated, they have been satisfied with the results and no attempt has been made to change back to the old system.

CHAPTER XX.

RESULTS OF CITY-COUNTY CONSOLIDATED

It must have been noted in the preceding pages that one of the underlying reasons for the separation of a city from its county is the disparity between the requirements of an urban population and that of a rural community. The former must have a large police force, great sanitary sewers, a well staffed health department, a fire department, an engineering department, great paved thoroughfares to accommodate a congested traffic, all at enormous expense that must be met by the taxpayers of the city, while rural communities require but few of these facilities and such expenditures. Furthermore, the manner and method of living is very different and is much simpler in the country. Rural communities chafe under the domination of the large city and complain of tax burdens imposed upon them to carry on governmental and judicial functions from which they receive but comparatively little benefit. There is, and cannot be, any real homogeneity between these two diverse elements of population.

We have seen how these fundamental differences between the urban and the rural population naturally brought about the separation of the City of Baltimore, the City of St. Louis, the City and County of San Francisco and the City and County of Denver from their respective counties. As a result the rural part of the former county enjoyed a simpler and less expensive form of government best suited to its needs. On the other

hand the urban part of the former county was thus
enabled to govern itself without harassment by conflict
between the demands of the rural residents and those of
the city, with the result that the latter was enabled to
conduct its own business in its own way and to expend
its revenues for its own use in the manner that served its
people best. That was the basic reason for the creation
of the "counties of cities" and of the "county boroughs"
in England, Scotland and Wales and of the creation of
the city-county consolidated in America. That purpose
was a laudable one and had it not been interfered with
reprehensibly by the politicians and by the courts all
would have been well. However, that interference did
not discredit the plan itself for the results achieved where
the plan was unhampered make it clear that it has been
of great and lasting benefit. Wherever such interference
has not reared its objectionable head the result of city-
county consolidated form of government has been a great
improvement and the people under it are satisfied. That
result alone should be proof enough of its desirability
and of its benefits.

It is well to recall that early in English history, cities
as they grew into importance in trade and industry and
in population insisted that they be created into "counties
of cities" separated geographically from their former
county and be empowered to perform both city and
county functions. More than eight hundred years of
experience by these early examples of the city-county
consolidated and by those which were later created from
time to time has demonstrated that conflicting interests
were thus eliminated which formerly had caused friction
between the city and its county, that responsibility was
fixed in a single elective body instead of having it distributed among several, with a resultant lowering of cost
to the taxpayers. It will be remembered too that in 1888
a great number of county boroughs were created in England and Wales, now eighty-eight in number, and that
there are one hundred and eighty-four Royal and Parlia-

mentary Burghs of the same type in Scotland, not separated geographically from their counties but standing
apart from them for all purposes of local government, as
completely as the several counties stand apart from each
other.

So satisfactory have the results been as to this city-
county consolidated form of government that not one of
the two hundred and seventy-two in England, Scotland
and Wales has ever reverted to the old dual system. Sir
Harry G. Pritchard, of Westminster, England, Secretary
of the Association of Municipal Corporations, and William A. Robson, noted English writer, both testify that
this consolidated form of municipal government works
so well that no thought is given to changing it. (pp. 69-70.)

In America the result of city-county consolidation
has given universal satisfaction to the people of those
cities having that form of government, even in the partial stage and more so in the completed form. In cities
like Boston and St. Paul where consolidation is only partial their people would welcome its extension. The more
complete its form the greater is the satisfaction.

For two hundred and twenty-eight years the cities
of Virginia, separated from their respective counties,
now numbering twenty-four by the addition of a new one
within the year, have enjoyed entire independence from
any county and they are satisfied. (pp. 205-6.)   New
York, during the past two hundred and eleven years has
gradually increased the consolidation of city and county
functions under its city government and is so well satisfied with the result that it is striving for complete
consolidation. (p. 227.)   New Orleans, coterminous with
its parish for a hundred and thirty-six years, has operated under a form of government approximating that of
the city-county consolidated and would not forego its
advantages. (p. 238.)   Baltimore, for ninety years, has
been separated from its county and performs both city
and county functions, without any thought of returning
to the dual system. (p. 248.)   Philadelphia consolidated

with its county for eighty-seven years, has operated under an almost complete form of city-county consolidated and is striving to make it one hundred per cent. (pp. 260 and 263.) San Francisco, separated from its county for the last eighty-five years, has been a city-county consolidated during that time and its people would not consider changing their simplified and economical form of government back to that discarded by them. (p. 238.) St. Louis, separated from its county for sixty-five years, performs both city and county functions and is determined to make more complete its city-county consolidation. (pp. 325-6.) Denver, separated from its county during the last thirty-nine years with slight interruption caused by a lawless court, has enjoyed an absolute city-county consolidated form of government and would not consider a return to the old system which it had endured under two sets of officers. (p. 254.) Honolulu, consolidated with its county as the latest addition to the ranks of the city-county consolidated in this country, has had that form of government for thirty-four years and there is no agitation for a change. Washington, D. C., created by Act of Congress one hundred and fifty-one years ago, has a consolidated form of government that operates efficiently and economically.

These nine important cities, running from the City of New York to the City and County of Honolulu, and adding thereto the twenty-four Virginia cities, together have a total population of 14,204,470. The fact that they have remained contentedly under a city-county consolidated form of government for so many years speaks strongly as to its advantages.

Furthermore, the creation of a city-county consolidated has always resulted in lowering the cost of government. It takes less to feed one set of officers than it takes to feed two. In the chapter on Philadelphia it is pointed out that the police cost for the new city-county including the entire county was much less than before. (p. 255.)

In the chapter on San Francisco on the authority of Hittell it is stated that in the year before consolidation the expense of separate city and county had been $2,646,000, as against but $353,000 by the consolidated city-county. (p. 270.) In the chapter on St. Louis it is pointed out that the tax rate was reduced at once from $3.42 to $2.80 on the hundred, and that "anticipation" bonds in the sum of $1,550,000 outstanding in 1875 because of lack of funds were quickly reduced to $350,000. (pp. 299-300.) In the chapter on Denver is quoted the statement by Professor Guthrie that consolidation had reduced the cost of government one-third and the report of Mr. Mayo that the expense of a useless layer of government was saved. (pp. 339-340.)

Bringing this picture down to date, the official reports of expenditures during the last fiscal year in the City of New York, the City of Philadelphia, the City of Baltimore, the City of New Orleans, the City of St. Louis, the City and County of San Francisco, the City and County of Denver, the City and County of Honolulu, and the City of Washington, which fall within the definition of the city-county consolidated, show a total of $692,369,-924, excluding schools, public utilities and assessments for public improvements, or $51.54 per capita for a total population of 13,434,353. Contrast that with the reports, on the same basis, from the seventeen other largest cities in this country, reaching from Boston and Chicago to Los Angeles and Seattle, showing a total expenditure of $766,538,521, or $56.42 per capita for a total population of 13,587,479. In arriving at the latter expenditure the county taxes paid by the people of these cities used for the performance of county functions was added to what they pay for the performance of their city functions in order to make proper comparison with cities of the city-county consolidated type which pay for the performance of both functions out of their revenues.

It is interesting to note the result of this comparison. The difference in population between the nine cities of the city-county consolidated type and that of the other seventeen cities is only 153,126. But the difference in cost of their government was $74,168,597!

In a few places a hybrid form of city-county consolidation has been attempted by devolving upon county officers the performance of certain city functions. But this has been found quite unsatisfactory. It opened the door to favoritism, political influence, inefficiency and waste, as has been pointed out on page 185.

In many of the large cities in this country, not now having the benefit of the city-county consolidated form of government, futile movements have been sponsored to create a so-called "Metropolitan District" under a sort of consolidated system of municipal government. In the first place there is an irreconcilable difference of opinion among its sponsors as to what should constitute the territorial limits of such district. Some advocate that it be limited to a city and its adjoining municipalities. Others are obsessed with dreams of grandeur and would include great stretches of territory regardless of homogeneity of population in an effort to create the "Greater City" of so-and-so. There is no agreement upon a fundamental definition of a "Metropolitan Area". That being the case, all such movements have disintegrated because of lack of cooperative effort, with the possible exception of the city of Philadelphia and New York City, —but in the latter the territory included was decidedly urban in character and did not include rural communities.

In the next place every scheme for creating a metropolitan area into a city-county consolidated form of municipal government necessitated the inclusion of many smaller municipalities. Their opposition to this has been very pronounced. They did not propose to lose their political lives, their civic ideals, the exercise of the right of local self-government, and their community identity. At once this aroused the bitter antagonism of the people of the municipalities proposed to be absorbed by the larger city. In California and in some other states the

constitution forbids forcible annexation by act of the
legislature, and requires the affirmative vote of the people of the municipality proposed to be annexed. Experience has shown that it is extremely difficult to obtain
such vote especially where several small municipalities
are affected. Many examples exist where the voters have
defeated such proposals. An attempt was made to create the City of Boston and a so-called metropolitan area
into a city-county consolidated system of government
but it came to naught. An attempt was made to create
the City of Chicago and Cook county with its many included municipalities into a city-county consolidated
but it was unsuccessful. An attempt to create the City
of Pittsburgh and Allegheny county with its included
municipalities into a city-county consolidated failed. The
same fate befell the attempt to consolidate the City of
Oakland and Alameda county with its included municipalities. All such attempts are usually bound to fail.

The experience of the centuries shows that the only
successful way to gain the benefits of the city-county consolidated form of government is to create a city itself
into that form by separating it from its county. In
Virginia the twenty-four cities of this type have populations running from 3,942 to 193,042. In Scotland twenty-
two are under 2,000. In England new county boroughs
must have at least a population of 75,000. In America,
outside of the Virginia cities, the populations vary from
7,454,955 in the City of New York to 258,256 in the City
and County of Honolulu.

In creating a city-county consolidated, whatever its
population, its success cannot be assured unless it is
given full power of home rule with the right of designating all its officers without interference by either the courts
or the legislature.

It is the considered opinion of the author, speaking
generally, that a city in this country having a population
of 100,000 or more will best serve the interests of its
people by separating itself from its county and creating

itself into a city-county consolidated form of government with home rule powers. It may thus attend to its business in the way its people wish and may expend its revenues for their benefit under officers of their own choosing. Overlordship will be no more and waste caused by conflict in authority under the dual system will be at an end. The City and County of San Francisco and the City and County of Denver furnish the best examples in this country of successful operation of this form of government. The Denver example is the better of the two.

CHAPTER XXI.

APPENDICES

1. The Theft Of A State (1904-1905)

In Chapter XVIII, entitled "The City and County of Denver," the statement is made in connection with events in Colorado in 1904-1905 vitally affecting city-county consolidation in that city, as follows: "And now occurred the most astounding theft of the legislative, executive and judicial branches of an entire state without a parallel in history."

It would seem that so sweeping a charge should be supported by a statement of the facts upon which it is based. I was there and had a direct part in trying to stop that theft. Therefore, I feel that I am competent to speak.

On December 2, 1902, Article XX of the constitution of Colorado, adopted by the people as an amendment thereto at the election in the month preceding, went into effect. By its specific provisions, (Appendix—26), the terms of all officers of the City of Denver and of all included municipalities and of the county of Arapahoe were terminated, and in their stead one set of officers to perform both city and county duties and functions was named therein. This was done by the people of the state in their sovereign capacity. Not only did they abolish county officers, as such, but they further provided in that amendment of the constitution that "every charter shall designate the officers who shall, respectively, perform the acts and duties required of county officers to be done by the constitution or by the general law, as far as applicable." The people in that amendment named the first single set of officers for the new city and county, and that provision therein for continuing one set of officers certainly left no ground for the existence of county officers as such, for their existence would destroy the very consolidation intended.

At the 1902 general state election the Republicans elected the entire state ticket, including a judge of the supreme court and those state officers who comprised the state canvassing

board.   When *People ex rel. v. Sours,* 31 Colo. 369, came before
the supreme court in the early part of 1903 that court then
had three members as follows: Judge Robert W. Steele, a
progressive Democrat, Judge John Campbell, a rock-ribbed,
reactionary Republican, and Judge William H. Gabbert, elected
as a Populist.   Judge Steele wrote an opinion sustaining the
constitutionality of Article XX.   Judge Campbell wrote an
opinion holding that part of the constitution to be unconstitutional.   While the case was still under submission it was reported to me by Judge Ben B. Lindsey, the celebrated judge
of the Denver juvenile court, on reliable information received
by him, that Judge Gabbert seemed to be impressed by the
recent Republican victory in the state and that he was debat-
ing whether or not he should get into the Republican band-
wagon so as to be re-elected, and that he had prepared a ten-
tative opinion concurring in that written by Judge Campbell.
That would have been the end of "Home Rule for Denver."
Literally, the issue lay in the lap of the gods.   Fortunately,
Judge Gabbert, after further consideration of the case felt he
would stultify himself as a lawyer and as a judge to concur in
the Campbell opinion and so he wrote an opinion concurring
in the main with that of Judge Steele.

But the germ in Judge Gabbert's mind about getting into
the Republican party grew.   By the time of the state election
in 1904 he had joined that party.   At that election the voters
of the state approved an amendment to the constitution which
abolished the court of appeals then consisting of three judges,
the term of one expiring with that year, and provided that the
other two, Judge Julius C. Gunter, a Democrat, and Judge
John M. Maxwell, a Republican, should be transferred to the
supreme court, and that two additional members of that court
be appointed by the newly elected governor, subject to confirmation by the state senate, thus making its members seven.
It will be noted that before the appointment of these two new
members the political complexion of the supreme court was
three Republicans and two Democrats, and that its future political complexion would depend upon which party elected the
governor and was in control of the state senate.

At the election in 1904 the certified returns showed that
Alva Adams, the Democratic candidate, twice before governor,
had been elected the incoming governor, and that the Democrats had elected a majority of the senate.   That meant that
the two new judges to be appointed on the supreme court
would be Democrats, and thus the political complexion of that
court would be Democratic.   And here is where the theft of
the state began.   The first step was to steal two seats in the

senate, and thus get a majority. Charles B. Ward, a Democrat, with whom I had finished a four-year term in the senate, was up for re-election in Boulder county. Dr. Michael Beshoar was the Democratic candidate for senator in Las Animas county. Both were returned elected. No power but the senate itself could change those returns. For section 10 of article V of the constitution provided that "each house (of the legislature) shall judge the election and qualifications of its members." Now note how this mandate of the constitution was ruthlessly violated by the conspirators.

Section 7758 of the Compiled Laws of Colorado provided that the county clerk in each county should take to his assistance two justices of the peace of his county, one of whom shall be of a different political party than himself, and that they shall canvass the vote cast in his county, and that he shall make an abstract thereof and transmit it to the secretary of state. Section 7763, of said Laws, provided that the governor, secretary of state, auditor, treasurer and attorney general "shall canvass the *abstracts* of votes cast in the different counties of the state for electors of president, judges of the supreme and district courts, for district attorneys, and for senators and representatives." Section 1165, of said Laws, provides that the board of state canvassers thus constituted shall meet on the 25th day after the election and proceed to canvass the votes and the result shall be certified by the secretary of state and furnish to each house a list of the members elected thereto.

The county clerk of Boulder county was a staunch Republican. He took to his assistance one Republican justice of the peace and one Democratic justice of the peace to canvass the vote cast in that county. They found that Senator Ward had been re-elected to the senate as shown by the returns. The county clerk made an abstract of the vote accordingly and filed it with the secretary of state. The county clerk of Las Animas county was also a staunch Republican. He took to his assistance one Republican justice of the peace and one Democratic justice of the peace. They found that Dr. Beshoar had been elected to the senate as shown by the returns. The county clerk made an abstract of the vote accordingly and filed it with the secretary of state.

The state canvassing board, all of its members being Republicans, met on November 27, 1904. Note the limitation on its powers not only by the constitution but by the statutes above quoted, and also by the courts. The supreme court in *People ex rel. v. County Commissioners,* 6 Colo. 202, 209, decided in 1882, said: "The general rule is that the powers of canvassers are ministerial, involving simply the labor of counting the votes returned, and determining who has received the highest number. They have a quasi judicial power to determine whether the papers transmitted to them are genuine election returns, *but they have no judicial power to reject votes polled.''* Again, in *Kindel v. Le Bert,* 23 Colo. 385, 398, decided in 1897, that court said: ''The only power conferred, and the only duty required of the canvassing board in relation to the canvass, is *to count the votes based upon the canvass made by the election judges,* and to give certificates to those receiving a majority of the votes thus ascertained. *The canvassing board cannot go beyond or behind the returns, or reject votes, or otherwise inquire into the validity or conduct of the election.* Upon the proposition that such duties are, in no sense, judicial, the authorities are uniform.''

It came to my attention that the state board of canvassers was violating the constitution and the statutes and was flouting the decisions of the supreme court. I found that it was receiving and considering *ex parte* affidavits of ''Tom, Dick and Harry'' for the purpose of going behind the returns and to reject votes that had been cast at the election and to inquire into the validity of the election. The time was too short to apply to the district court for a writ of mandate to compel the state board of canvassers to obey the plain letter of the law. Under the constitution the supreme court was authorized to take original jurisdiction in such cases. So, I prepared and filed with the clerk of that court a petition for a writ of mandate and prayed that the court take original jurisdiction in view of the imminence of the wrong about to be committed. That court held up that petition for one month, and until the last day in which the state canvassing board could act, and then refused to take original jurisdiction. I had prepared a like petition for presentation to the district court in the event of such denial. I quickly presented it to Judge Samuel L. Carpenter of the latter court and he immediately granted the writ. I took that writ to the office of the secretary of state where the state board of canvassers was holding its closing session and found its members locked in his office. I pounded on the door but no answer came. I shouted the contents of the writ through the key-hole but there was no response. As I went down the capitol steps I was told by a friend that the supreme court wanted to see me. Then, for the first time, I learned with bewildered astonishment that not only had the supreme court refused to take jurisdiction of the matter but that it had issued an order forbidding any court to take jurisdiction to stop the theft that was going on in the capitol. Immediately I went to the court room of the supreme court where a hearing in another matter was in progress. When it ended I said to the court that I had been informed that it wanted to see me, and that accordingly I had come. Chief Justice Gabbert seemed at a loss what to say, so Judge Campbell leaned over and whispered to him and Judge Gabbert then ordered that I show cause why I should not be held in contempt of court for having disobeyed its order. The time given was unconcionably short, but I prepared and filed an answer in which I set up that since the court had refused to take jurisdiction clearly it had no power to make an order in a matter over which it had divested itself of all jurisdiction, and further set up that the order was in violation of the constitution and of the statutes and was against the court's own decisions. Evidently the court did not relish the position in which it had placed itself as an accessory to the theft of the state senate, for it immediately washed its hands of it so far as it could by referring the matter to the grievance committee of the Colorado Bar Association. On March 18, 1905, that committee reported that the court had no jurisdiction to issue the order and two days thereafter the court dismissed the proceedings. The records of the court do not show that the order in question was ever entered at all. The court evidently was too ashamed of its part in the theft to have its permanent records disclose it.

In the meantime the state board of canvassers had reversed the vote for Ward and Beshoar and had certified that their Republican opponents had been elected, thus giving that party a majority in the senate. That party had elected a majority in the house of representatives, so that it then had a majority in the legislature. The next step was to get rid of Governor Adams who had been elected by a majority over Governor Peabody by more than nine thousand votes. So a contest was filed before the legislature by Peabody. The legislature found that some election frauds had been committed but with blind partisanship the Republicans wantonly threw out scores of election returns from normally strong Democratic precincts in their entirety and thus illegally disfranchised thousands of voters in their mad desire to complete the second step in the theft of the state. So they voted to unseat Adams and to put Peabody in his place. But here occurred one of the most remarkable pieces of political chicanery ever perpetrated. The Republican bosses feared that Peabody, if he were governor, would not appoint the two corporation and reactionary judges whom they desired appointed to fill up the supreme bench. So they compelled Peabody to sign his resignation and abdication in advance, and place it in the hands of W. S. Boynton, Republican state chairman, before they would vote to seat him, to take effect within twenty-four hours after the vote would be taken. He signed, the vote was taken, he was made governor for a day, his resignation and abdication was accepted, and the lieutenant-governor, Jesse F. McDonald, a reactionary Republican, was proclaimed as governor.

The senate and the governorship had been stolen. The next step of the conspirators was to get the supreme court into their clutches. Immediately McDonald sent in to the senate for confirmation his nominations of George W. Bailey from Ft. Collins and Judge Luther M. Goddard of Denver, the latter of whom had formerly been on the supreme bench. Bailey was a hard shell Republican satisfactory to the corporations, but they had their doubts about Goddard. The senate was in executive session. At the doors, in communication with their lieutenants inside, were the attorneys of the great railroad and public utility corporations. I was there listening and watching what was going on. It was brazen. It was shameless. The corporation lawyers sent in word to hold up the confirmation until they reported. I heard them openly say that they would go out to Goddard's home and see if "the old man was right." They went. When they came back they passed the word to the senate obediently waiting that both nominees were satisfactory and when the word was received they were confirmed.

The theft of an entire state, the legislative, the executive and the judicial branches of the state of Colorado, had been consummated. No blacker page in political history will be found. It was that supreme court, so conceived in infamy and damned by the general public, that quickly thereafter rendered the amazing decision in 1905 in *State ex rel. v. Johnson,* 34 Colo. 143, that the City and County of Denver did not have a republican form of government unless it had a Republican set of county officers in addition to its city officers,—a decision about which that same court six years later, in *State ex rel. v. Cassiday,* 50 Colo. 503, said: "That decision must remain, as it is now, wholly unaccountable and incomprehensible." That was a softer impeachment than to disclose the theft which brought it about.

THE AUTHOR.

(Pages in *italics* refer to this book)

2. Michigan Constitution (1850)—Art. X, Sec. 2

The legislature may organize any city into a separate county, when it has attained a population of twenty thousand inhabitants, without reference to geographical extent, when a majority of the electors of the county in which such city may be situated, voting thereon, shall be in favor of a separate organization. *(180)*

3. Michigan Amendment (1908)—Art. VIII, Sec. 2

Whenever any city has attained a population of one hundred thousand inhabitants, the legislature may organize it into a separate county without reference to geographical extent, if a majority of the electors of such city and of the remainder of the county in which such city may be situated voting on the question shall each determine in favor of organizing said city into a separate county. *(180)*

4. Minnesota Constitution (1858)—Art. XI, Sec. 2

The legislature may organize any city into a separate county, when it has attained a population of twenty thousand inhabitants, without reference to geographical extent, when a majority of the electors of the county in which such city may be situated, voting thereon, shall be in favor of a separate organization. *(180)*

5. Missouri Constitution (1875)—Art. IX, Sec. 15

In all counties having a city therein containing over one hundred thousand inhabitants, the city and county government thereof may be consolidated in such manner as may be provided by law. *(181)*

6. Missouri Constitution (1875)—Art. IX, Secs. 20, 23 and 25

Sec. 20. The City of St. Louis may extend its limits so as to embrace the parts now without its boundaries and other convenient and contiguous territory, and frame a charter for the government of the city thus enlarged, upon the following conditions, that is to say: The council of the city and the county court of the county of St. Louis shall, at the request of the mayor of the city of St. Louis, meet in joint session and order an election to be held as provided for general elections, by the qualified voters of the city and county, of a board of thirteen freeholders of such city and county whose duty shall be to propose a scheme for the enlargement and definition of the boundaries of the city, the reorganization of the government of the county, the adjustment of the relations between the city thus enlarged and the residue of St. Louis county, and the government of the city thus enlarged, by a charter in harmony with and subject to the Constitution and laws of Missouri, which shall, among other things, provide for a chief executive and two houses of legislation, one of which shall be signed in duplicate by said board or a majority of them, and one of them returned to the mayor of the city and the other to the presiding justice of the county court within ninety days after the election of such board. Within thirty days thereafter the city council and the county court shall submit such scheme to the qualified voters of the whole county, and such charter to the qualified voters of the city so enlarged, at an election to be held not later than twenty nor more than thirty days after the order therefor, and if a majority of such qualified voters, voting at such election, shall ratify such scheme and charter, then such scheme shall become the organic law of the county and city, and such charter the organic law of the city, and at the end of sixty days thereafter shall take the place of and supersede the charter of St. Louis, and all amendments thereof, and all special laws relating to St. Louis county inconsistent with such scheme.

Sec. 21.   A copy of such scheme and charter, with a certificate thereto appended, signed by the mayor and authenticated by the seal of the city, and also signed by the presiding justice of the county court and authenticated by the seal of the county, setting forth the submission of such scheme and charter to the qualified voters of such county and city, and its ratification by them, shall be made in duplicate, one of which shall be deposited in the office of the Secretary of State, and the other, after being recorded in the office of the recorder of deeds of St. Louis county, shall be deposited among the archives of the city, and thereafter all courts shall take judicial notice thereof.

Sec. 22.   The charter so ratified may be amended by proposals therefor submitted by the lawmaking authorities of the city to the qualified voters thereof, at a special or general election * * and accepted by three-fifths of the qualified voters voting for or against each of said amendments so submitted; and the lawmaking authorities of such city may order an election by the qualified electors of the city of a board of thirteen freeholders of such city to prepare a new charter for such city, which said charter shall be in harmony with and subject to the Constitution and laws of the state, and shall provide, among other things, for a chief executive and at least one house of legislation to be elected by general ticket. Said revised charter shall be submitted to the qualified voters of such city * * and if a majority of such qualified voters voting at such election ratify such charter, the said charter shall become the organic law of such city, and sixty days thereafter shall take effect and supersede the charter of said city and all special laws inconsistent therewith. (As amended in 1902.)

Sec. 23.   Such charter and amendments shall always be in harmony with and subject to the Constitution and laws of Missouri, except only that provision may be made for the graduation of the rate of taxation for city purposes in the portions of the city which are added thereto by the proposed enlargement of its boundaries.   In the adjustment of the relations between the city and the county, the city shall take upon itself the entire park tax; and in consideration of the city becoming the proprietor of all county buildings and the property within its enlarged limits, it shall assume the whole of the existing county debt, and thereafter the city and county of St. Louis shall be independent of each other.   The city shall be exempted from all county taxation. The judges of the county court shall be elected by the qualified voters outside of the city. The city, as enlarged, shall be entitled to the same representation in the General Assembly, collect the state revenue and perform all other functions in relation to the State, in the same manner as if it were a county as in this Constitution defined; and the residue of the county shall remain a legal county of the State of Missouri, under the name of the County of St. Louis.

Sec. 25. Notwithstanding the provisions of this article, the General Assembly shall have the same power over the city and county of St. Louis that it has over other cities and counties of this State. *(145, 181)*

7. Missouri Amendment (1924)—Art. IX, Sec. 26

The people of the city of St. Louis and the county of St. Louis shall have power (1) to consolidate the territories and governments of said city and county into one legal subdivision under the municipal government of St. Louis; or (2) to extend the territorial boundaries of the county so as to embrace the territory within the city and reorganize and consolidate the governments of said city and county, and adjust their relations as thus united, and thereafter said city may extend its limits in the manner provided by Article 22, chapter 38, Revised Statutes, 1929, or as may otherwise be provided by law; or (3) to enlarge the present or future limits of said city by annexing thereto part of the territory of said county, and to confer upon said city exclusive jurisdiction of the territory so annexed to said city. * * the mayor and the judges of the circuit court of the city and the judges of the circuit, probate and county courts of the county shall appoint a board of freeholders consisting of eighteen members, nine of whom shall be electors of said city and nine electors of said county. * * It shall be the duty of said board of freeholders to prepare and propose a scheme for the consolidation of said city and county, or the inclusion within the county of the territory within the city, or the annexation to said city of part of the county, and to adjust all other matters and issues that may be necessary to effect either of said purposes. The scheme shall be signed in duplicate by said board or a majority of them. * * Within thirty days thereafter, said election officials shall cause separate elections to be held in said city and county. * * Any such scheme shall not be submitted oftener than once in five years. If a majority of the voters of the city and a majority of the voters of the county voting at said separate elections shall ratify said scheme, then, at such time as shall be prescribed therein, the same shall become the organic law of the territory therein defined, and shall take the place and supersede *all laws,* charters, provisions and ordinances inconsistent therewith relating to said territory. *(321)*

8. California Constitution (1879)—Art XI, Sec 7

City and county governments may be merged and consolidated into one municipal government, with one set of officers, and may be incorporated under general laws provided for the incorporation and organization of corporations for municipal purposes The provisions of this Constitution applicable to cities, and also those applicable to counties, so far as not inconsistent or not prohibited to cities, shall be applicable to such consolidated government * * *(146)*

(NOTE: The many amendments to the Constitution of California are too voluminous and repetitious to justify reproduction. Verbatim portions, relating to city and county, are given. The material changes in the various amendments are indicated by italics, or marked "New.")

9. California Constitution (1879)—Art. XI, Sec. 8

Any city containing a population of more than one hundred thousand inhabitants may frame a charter for its own government, consistent with and subject to the Constitution and laws of this state, by causing a board of fifteen freeholders, who shall have been for at least five years qualified electors thereof, to be elected by the qualified voters of such city, at any general or special election, * * to prepare and propose a charter for such city * * it shall be submitted to the qualified electors of such city at a general or special election, and if a majority of such qualified electors voting thereat shall ratify the same, it shall thereafter be submitted to the legislature for its approval or rejection as a whole, without power of alteration or amendment, and if approved by a majority vote of the members elected to each house, it shall become the charter of such city, or if such city be consolidated with a county, then of such city and county, and shall become the organic law thereof, and supersede any existing charter and all amendments thereof, and all special laws inconsistent with such charter. * * The charter so ratified may be amended at intervals of not less than two years, by proposals therefor submitted by legislative authority of the city, to the qualified voters thereof at a general or special election, * * and ratified by at least three-fifths of the qualified electors voting thereat, and approved by the legislature as herein provided for the approval of the charter. In submitting any such charter, or amendment thereto, any alternative article or proposition may be presented for the choice of voters, and may be voted on separately without prejudice to others. *(145)*

10. California Constitution (1879)—Art. XI, Sec. 6

* * cities and towns heretofore or hereafter organized, and all charters thereof framed or adopted by authority of this Constitution, shall be subject to and controlled by general laws.

11. California Amendment (1887)—Art. XI, Sec. 8

Any city, *or consolidated city or county,* containing a population of more than one hundred thousand inhabitants may frame a charter for its own government, consistent with and subject to the Constitution and laws of the state. *(146)*

12. California Amendment (1892)—Art. XI, Sec. 8

Any city containing a population of more than *three thousand five hundred inhabitants* may frame a charter for its own government, consistent with and subject to the Constitution and laws of this state; * * approval (of such charter) may be made by *concurrent resolution* by a majority vote of the members elected to each house (of the legislature), it shall become the charter of such city, or if such city be consolidated with a county, then of such city and county, and shall become the organic law thereof, and supersede any existing charter and all amendments thereof, and *all laws* inconsistent with such charter. *(146)*

13. California Amendment (1896)—Art. XI, Sec. 6

* * all charters, *except in municipal affairs,* shall be subject to and controlled by general laws. *(146)*

14. California Amendment (1896)—Art XI, Sec. 8½

It shall be competent, in all charters framed under the authority given by section eight of article eleven of this Constitution, to provide, in addition to those provisions allowable by this Constitution and by the laws of the state, as follows:

1. For the constitution, regulation, government, and jurisdiction of police courts, and for the manner in which, the times at which, and the terms for which the judges of such courts shall be elected or appointed, and for the qualifications and compensation of said judges and of their clerks and attaches.

2. For the manner in which, the times at which, and the terms for which the members of boards of education shall be elected or appointed, for their qualifications, compensation and removal, and for the number which shall constitute any of such boards.

3. For the manner in which, the times at which, and the terms for which the members of the boards of police commissioners shall be elected or appointed; and for the constitution, regulation, compensation, and government of such boards and of the municipal police force.

4. For the manner in which and the times at which any municipal election shall be held and the result thereof determined; for the manner in which, the times at which, and the terms for which the members of all boards of elections shall be elected or appointed, and for the constitution, regulation, compensation and government of such boards, and of their clerks and attaches; and for all expenses incident to the holding of any election. Where a city and county government has been merged and consolidated into one municipal government, it shall also be competent in any charter framed under said section eight of said article eleven, to provide for the *manner in which, the times at which, and the terms for which the several county officers shall be elected or appointed, for their compensation, and for the number of deputies that each shall have, and for the compensation payable to each of such deputies.* (All the foregoing is new.) *(146)*

15. California Amendment (1902)—Art. XI, Sec. 8

Whenever fifteen per cent of the qualified voters of the city shall petition the legislative authority thereof to submit any proposed amendment or amendments to said charter to the qualified voters thereof for approval, the legislative authority thereof must submit the same. (New.) *(147)*

16. California Amendment (1906)—Art. XI, Sec. 8

Any city containing a population of more than three thousand five hundred inhabitants may frame a charter for its own government * * or, having framed such a charter, *may frame a new one. (147)*

17. California Amendment (1911)—Art XI, Sec. 8½

Where a city and county government has been merged and consolidated into one municipal government, it shall also be competent, in any charter framed under said section eight of said article eleven, or by *amendment* thereto, to provide for the manner in which, the times at which and the terms for which the several county *and municipal* officers and employees *whose compensation is paid by such city and county, excepting judges of the superior court,* shall be elected or appointed, *and for their recall and removal,* and for their compensation, and for the number of deputies, *clerks and other employees* that each shall have, and for the compensation, *method of appointment, qualifications, tenure of office and removal of such deputies, clerks and other employees. All provisions of any charter of any such consolidated city and county heretofore adopted, and amendments thereto, which are in accordance herewith, are hereby confirmed and declared valid.* (Italicized parts new.) *(147)*

18. California Amendment (1911)—Art. XI, Sec. 8

Sec. 8. Said board of freeholders may be so elected in pursuance of an ordinance adopted by a vote of *two-thirds* of all the members of the council, or other legislative body, of such city, * * or in pursuance of a (fifteen per cent) petition of qualified electors of said city, as hereinafter provided. * * It shall be competent in any charter framed by any city under the authority given in this section, or by amendment to such charter, to provide, in addition to those provisions allowed by this Constitution and by the laws of the state, *for the establishment of a borough system of government for the whole or any part of the territory of such city, by which one or more districts may be created therein, which districts shall be known as boroughs, and which shall exercise such special municipal powers as may be granted by such charter, and for the organization, regulation, government and jurisdiction of such boroughs.* (Note: This section was amended in 1922 by adding: "provided, however, that after the creation of any such borough, the powers thereof shall not be modified, amended or abridged in any manner, without the consent of a majority of the qualified electors of such borough voting at a regular or special election.") *(147)*

19. California Amendment (1911)—Art. XI, Sec. 7½

Any county may frame a charter for its own government consistent with and subject to the Constitution (or, having framed such a charter, may frame a new one,) relating to the matters hereinafter in this section specified, and none other, by causing a board of fifteen freeholders * * to be elected * * in pursuance of an ordinance adopted by the vote of three-fifths of all the members of the board of supervisors of such county * * for the purpose of preparing and proposing a charter for said county, or in pursuance of a petition signed by fifteen per centum of the qualified electors of said county * * praying for the election of (such) board. * * (The charter so framed, approved by the electors and ratified by the legislature) shall become the charter of such county and shall become the organic law thereof relative to the matters therein provided, and super-sede any existing charter framed under the provisions of this section, and all amendments thereof, and shall supersede all laws inconsistent with such charter relative to the matters provided in such charter. * * The charter, so ratified, may be amended by proposals submitted by the board of supervisors * * or (upon) a petition signed by ten per centum of the qualified electors of the county. (Note: It also declared that all charters shall provide, for the times at which and the terms for which all county officers may be elected or appointed, their compensation and removal, the number of justices of the peace and constables for each township and the number of such judges and other officers of inferior courts as may be pro-vided by the constitution or general law, for their election or appointment and their compensation, for consolidation and segregation of county offices, for the appointment and number of assistants, deputies, attaches and other persons to be employed in the several offices of the county and pre-scribing and regulating their powers, duties, qualifications and compensa-tion, including game wardens and probation officers. Officers made elective by the charter were required to be nominated and elected in the manner provided by general law. It was provided that this section shall not be applicable to any county that is consolidated with a city, of which there is none at this time. The City and County of San Francisco was not consolidated with its county, — it was separated therefrom. Note further: In 1918 the constitution was amended by adding a new section 7½a to article XI, which provided that any county *organized under the general law* and having a population of two hundred thousand inhabitants or over, and having within its territorial boundaries one or more incorpo-rated cities or towns, may frame a charter for a consolidated city and county government. But that section has not been used because counties having that population, as a general rule, are not "organized under the general law" but frame their charters under section 7½ of said article which does not provide for a consolidated city and county government.) *(147)*

20. California Amendment (1914)—Art. XI, Sec. 6

Cities and towns organized under charters * * * may *amend* their charters so as to become empowered to make and enforce all laws and regulations *in respect to municipal affairs,* subject only to the restrictions and limitations provided in their several charters, and in respect to other matters they shall be subject to and controlled by general laws. Cities

and towns heretofore or hereafter organized by authority of this Constitution may, by charter provision or amendment, *provide for the performance by county officers of certain of their municipal functions,* whenever
the discharge of such municipal functions by county officers is authorized
by general laws or by the provisions of a county charter framed and
adopted by authority of this Constitution. *(147)*

21. California Amendment (1914)—Art. XI, Sec. 8

Any city or city and county containing a population of more than
three thousand five hundred inhabitants * * * may form a charter for its
own government, consistent with and subject to this Constitution * * *
(which) shall become the organic law of such city or city and county, and
supersede any existing charter and *all laws* inconsistent therewith. *(148)*

22. California Amendment (1914)—Art. XI, Sec. 8½

It shall be competent in any charter framed in accordance with the
provisions of this section, or section eight of this article, for any city or
consolidated city and county, and plenary authority is hereby granted,
subject only to the provisions of this article, to provide therein or by
amendment thereto, the manner in which, the method by which, the times
at which, and the terms for which the several county and municipal officers
and employees whose compensation is paid by such city or city and
county, excepting judges of the superior court, shall be elected or appointed, and for their recall and removal, and for their compensation, and
for the number of deputies, clerks and other employees that each shall
have, and for the compensation, method of appointment, qualifications,
tenure of office and removal of such deputies, clerks and other employees.
All provisions of any charter of any such city or consolidated city and
county heretofore adopted, and amendments thereto, which are in accordance herewith, are hereby confirmed and declared valid.

It shall be competent in any charter or amendment thereof, which
shall hereafter be framed under the authority given by section eight of
this article, by any city having a population in excess of fifty thousand
ascertained as prescribed by said section eight, to provide for the separation of said city from the county of which it has heretofore been a part
and the formation of such city into a consolidated city and county to be
governed by said charter, and to have the combined powers of a city and
county, as provided in this Constitution for consolidated city and county
government, and further to prescribe in said charter the date for the beginning of the official existence of said consolidated city and county.

It shall be competent for any such city, not having already consolidated as a city and county to hereafter frame, in the manner prescribed
in section eight of this article, a charter providing for a city and county
government, in which charter there shall be prescribed territorial boundaries which may include contiguous territory not included in such city,
which territory, however, must be included in the county within which
such city is located.

If no additional territory is proposed to be added, then, upon the consent of the separation of any such city from the county in which it is located, being given by a majority of the qualified electors voting thereon in such county and upon the ratification of such charter by a majority of the qualified electors voting thereon in such city, and the approval thereof by the legislature, as prescribed in section eight of this article, said charter shall be deemed adopted and upon the date fixed therein said city shall be and become a consolidated city and county. (The laws of 1939 provide that when such charter or amendment is adopted by a city the county board of supervisors shall, at the next general election, submit to the voters of the county the question of separation of the city from the county.)

(If additional territory, consisting of unincorporated area or of one or more cities or towns, is proposed to be added, then separate affirmative votes of each must first be had, and such annexation may extend into an adjoining county subject to a majority vote of its electors.)

The legislature shall provide for the formation of one or more counties from the portion or portions of a county or counties remaining after the formation of or annexation to a consolidated city and county, or for the transfer of such portion or portions of such original county or counties to adjoining counties. But such transfer to an adjoining county shall only be made after approval by a majority vote of the qualified electors voting thereon in such territory proposed to be so transferred.

The provisions of section two of this article (concerning establishment of new counties and county boundaries), and also those provisions of section three of this article which refer to the passing of any county line within five miles of the existing boundary of a city or town in which a county seat of any county proposed to be divided is situated, shall not apply to the formation of, nor to the extension of the territory of such consolidated cities and counties, nor to the formation of new counties, nor to the annexation of existing counties, as herein specified.

Any city and county formed under this section shall have the right, if it so desires, to be designated by the official name of the city initiating the consolidation as it existed immediately prior to its adoption of a charter providing for a consolidated city and county government, except that such city and county shall be known under the style of a city and county. (All the foregoing is new.) *(148, 149, 182)*

23. California Amendment (1922)—Art. XI, Sec. 8

Such charter * * * shall become the organic law of such city or city and county, and supersede any existing charter *and all laws* inconsistent therewith. * * * The charter of any city or city and county may be amended by proposals therefor submitted by the legislative body of the city on its own motion or on petition signed by fifteen per cent of the registered electors, or both. *(148)*

24. Wyoming Constitution (1889)—Art. XIV, Sec. 6

Whenever practicable the legislature may, and wherever the same can be done without detriment to the public service, shall consolidate offices in state, county and municipalities, respectively, and wherever so consolidated, the duties of such office shall be performed under an ex-officio title. *(186)*

25. Montana Constitution (1889)—Art. XVI, Sec. 7

The legislative assembly may, by general or special law, provide any plan, kind, manner or form of municipal government for counties, or counties and cities and towns, or cities and towns, and, whenever deemed necessary or advisable, may abolish city or town government and unite, consolidate or merge cities and towns and county into one municipal government, and any limitations in this Constitution, notwithstanding, may designate the name, fix and prescribe the number, designation, terms, qualifications, method of appointment, election or removal of the officers thereof, define their duties and fix penalties for the violation thereof, and fix and define boundaries of the territory so governed, and may provide for the discontinuance of such form of government when deemed advisable; provided, however, that no form of government permitted in this section shall be adopted or discontinued until after it is submitted to the qualified electors in the territory affected and by them approved. *(186)*

26. Colorado Amendment (1902)—Art. XX

Sec. 1. The municipal corporation known as the City of Denver, and all municipal corporations and that part of the quasi-municipal corporation known as the County of Arapahoe, in the State of Colorado, included within the exterior boundaries of the said City of Denver as the same shall be bounded when the amendment takes effect, are hereby consolidated and are hereby declared to be a single body politic and corporate, by the name of the "City and County of Denver." By that name said corporation shall have perpetual succession, and shall own, possess and hold all property, real and personal, theretofore owned, possessed or held by the said City of Denver, and by such included municipal corporations, and also all property, real and personal, theretofore owned, possessed or held by the said County of Arapahoe, and shall assume, manage and dispose of all trusts in any way connected therewith; shall succeed to all the rights and liabilities, and shall acquire all benefits and shall assume and pay all bonds, obligations and indebtedness of said City of Denver and of said included municipal corporations and of the County of Arapahoe; by that name may sue and defend, plead and be impleaded, in all courts and places, and in all matters and proceedings; may have and use a common seal and alter the same at pleasure; may purchase, receive, hold and enjoy, or sell and dispose of, real and personal property; may receive bequests, gifts and donations of all kinds of property, in fee simple, or in trust for public, charitable or other purposes; and do all things and acts necessary to carry out the purposes of such gifts, bequests and donations, with power to manage, sell, lease or otherwise dispose of the same in accordance with the terms of the gift, bequest or trust; shall have the power, within or without its territorial limits, to construct, condemn and purchase, purchase, acquire, lease, add to, maintain, conduct and operate, water works, light plants, power plants, transportation systems, heating plants, and any other public utilities or works or ways local in use and extent, in whole or in part, and everything required therefor, for the use of said city and county and the inhabitants thereof, and any such systems, plants or works or ways, or any contracts in relation or connection with either, that may exist and which said city and county may desire to purchase, in whole or in part, the same or any part thereof may be purchased by said city and county which may enforce such purchase by proceedings at law as in taking land for public use by right of eminent domain, and shall have the power to issue bonds upon the vote of the taxpaying electors, at any special or general election, in any amount necessary to carry out any of said powers or purposes, as may by the charter be provided.

The general annexation and consolidation statutes of the state shall apply to the City and County of Denver to the same extent and in the same manner that they would apply to the City of Denver if it were not merged, as in this amendment provided, into the City and County of Denver. Any contiguous town, city or territory hereafter annexed to or consolidated with the City and County of Denver, under any of the laws of this state, in whatsoever county the same may be at the time, shall be detached per se from such other county and become a municipal and territorial part of the City and County of Denver, together with all property thereunto belonging.

The City and County of Denver shall alone always constitute one judicial district of the state.

Sec. 2. The officers of the city and county of Denver shall be such as by appointment or election may be provided for by the charter; and the jurisdiction, term of office, duties and qualifications of all such officers shall be such as in the charter may be provided; but every charter shall designate the officers who shall, respectively, perform the acts and duties required of county officers to be done by the constitution or by the general law, as far as applicable. If any officer of said City and County of Denver shall receive any compensation whatever, he or she shall receive the same as a stated salary, the amount of which shall be fixed by the charter, and paid out of the treasury of the city and county of Denver in equal monthly payments.

Sec. 3. Immediately upon the canvass of the vote showing the adoption of this amendment, it shall be the duty of the governor of the state to issue his proclamation accordingly, and thereupon the City of Denver, and all municipal corporations and that part of the County of Arapahoe within the boundaries of said city, shall merge into the City and County of Denver, and the terms of office of all officers of the City of Denver and of all included municipalities and of the County of Arapahoe shall terminate; except, that the then mayor, auditor, engineer, council (which shall perform the duties of a board of county commissioners), police magistrate, chief of police and boards, of the City of Denver shall become, respectively, said officers of the City and County of Denver, and said engineer shall be ex-officio surveyor and said chief of police shall be ex-officio sheriff of the City and County of Denver; and the then clerk and ex-officio recorder, treasurer, assessor and coroner of the County of Arapahoe, and the justices of the peace and constables holding office within the City of Denver, shall become, respectively, said officers of the City and County of Denver, and the district attorney shall also be ex-officio attorney of the City and County of Denver. The foregoing officers shall hold the said offices as above specified only until their successors are duly elected and qualified as herein provided for; except that the then district judges, county judge and district attorney, shall serve their full terms, respectively, for which elected. The police and firemen of the City of Denver, except the chief of police as such, shall continue severally as the police and firemen of the City and County of Denver until they are severally discharged under such civil service regulations as shall be provided by the charter; and every charter shall provide that the department of fire and police and the department of public utilities and works, shall be under such civil servcie regulations as in said charter shall be provided.

Sec. 4. The charter and ordinances of the City of Denver as the same shall exist when this amendment takes effect, shall, for the time being only, and as far as applicable, be the charter and ordinances of the City and County of Denver; but the people of the City and County of Denver are hereby vested with and they shall always have the exclusive power in the making, altering, revising or amending their charter, and, within ten days after the proclamation of the Governor announcing the adoption of this amendment the council of the City and County of Denver shall, by ordinance, call a special election, to be conducted as provided by law, of the qualified electors in said City and County of Denver, for the election of twenty-one taxpayers who shall have been qualified electors within the limits thereof for at least five years, who shall constitute a charter convention to frame a charter for said city and county in harmony with this amendment. Immediately upon completion, the charter so framed, with a prefatory synopsis, shall be signed by the officers and members of the convention and delivered to the clerk of said city and county, who shall publish the same in full, with his official certification, in the official newspaper of said city and county, three times, and a week apart, the first publication being with the call for a special election, at which the qualified electors of said city and county shall by vote express their approval or rejection of the said charter. If the said charter shall be approved by a majority of those voting thereon, then two copies thereof (together with the vote for and against) duly certified by the said clerk, shall, within ten days after such vote is taken, be filed with the secretary of state, and shall thereupon become and be the charter of the City and County of Denver. But if the said charter be rejected, then, within thirty days thereafter, twenty-one members of a new charter convention shall be elected at a special election to be called as above in said city and county, and they shall proceed as above to frame a charter, which shall in like manner and to the like end be published and submitted to a vote of said voters for their approval or rejection. If again rejected, the procedure herein designated shall be repeated (each special election for members of a new charter convention being within thirty days after each rejection) until a charter is finally approved by a majority of those voting thereon, and certified (together with the vote for and against) to the secretary of state as aforesaid, whereupon it shall become the charter of the said City and County of Denver and shall become the organic law thereof, and supersede any existing charters and amendments thereof. The members of each of said charter conventions shall be elected at large; and they shall complete their labors within sixty days after their respective election.

Every ordinance for a special election of charter convention members shall fix the time and place where the convention shall be held, and shall specify the compensation, if any, to be paid the officers and members thereof, allowing no compensation in case of non-attendance or tardy attendance, and shall fix the time when the vote shall be taken on the proposed charter, to be not less than thirty days nor more than sixty days after its delivery to the clerk. The charter shall make proper provision for continuing, amending or repealing the ordinances of the City and County of Denver.

All expenses of charter conventions shall be paid out of the treasury upon the order of the president and secretary thereof. The expenses of elections for charter conventions and of charter votes shall be paid out of the treasury upon the order of the council.

No franchise relating to any street, alley or public place of the said city and county shall be granted except upon the vote of the qualified taxpaying electors, and the question of its being granted shall be submitted to such vote upon deposit with the treasurer of the expense (to be determined by said treasurer) of such submission by the applicant for said franchise. The council shall have power to fix the rate of taxation on property each year for city and county purposes.

Sec. 5. The citizens of the City and County of Denver shall have the exclusive power to amend their charter or to adopt a new charter, or to adopt any measure as herein provided.

It shall be competent for qualified electors in number not less than five per cent of the next preceding gubernatorial vote in said city and county to petition the council for any measure, or charter amendment, or for a charter convention. The council shall submit the same to a vote of the qualified electors at the next general election not held within thirty days after such petition is filed; whenever such petition is signd by qualified electors in number not less than ten per cent of the next preceding gubernatorial vote in said city and county, with a request for a special election, the council shall submit it at a special election to be held not less than thirty nor more than sixty days from the date of filing the petition; Provided, That any question so submitted at a special election shall not again be submitted at a special election within two years thereafter. In submitting any such charter, charter amendment or measure, any alternative article or proposition may be presented for the choice of the voters, and may be voted on separately without prejudice to others. Whenever the question of a charter convention is carried by a majority of those voting thereon, a charter convention shall be called through a special election ordinance as provided in section four (4) hereof, and the same shall be constituted and held and the proposed charter submitted to a vote of the qualified electors, approved or rejected, and all expenses paid, as in said section provided.

The clerk of the city and county shall publish, with his official certification, for three times, a week apart, in the official newspaper, the first publication to be with his call for the election, general or special, the full text of any charter, charter amendment, measure, or proposal for a charter convention, or alternative article or proposition, which is to be submitted to the voters. Within ten days following the vote the said clerk shall publish once in said newspaper the full text of any charter, charter amendment, measure, or proposal for a charter convention, or alternative article or proposition, which shall have been approved by a majority of those voting thereon, and he shall file with the secretary of state two copies thereof (with the vote for and against) officially certified by him, and the same shall go into effect from the date of such filing. He shall also certify to the secretary of state, with the vote for and against, two copies of every defeated alternative article or proposition, charter, charter amendment, measure or proposal for a charter convention. Each charter shall also provide for a reference, upon proper petition therefor, of measures passed by the council to a vote of the qualified electors, and for the initiative by the qualified electors of such ordinances, as they may by petition request.

The signatures to petitions in this amendment mentioned need not all be on one paper. Nothing herein or elsewhere shall prevent the council, if it sees fit, from adopting automatic vote registers for use at elections and references.

No charter, charter amendment or measure adopted or defeated under the provisions of this amendment shall be amended, repealed or revived, except by petition and electoral vote. And no such charter, charter amendment or measure shall diminish the tax rate for state purposes fixed by act of the General Assembly, or interfere in any wise with the collection of state taxes.

Sec. 6. Cities of the first and second class in this state, are hereby empowered to propose for submission to a vote of the qualified electors, proposals for charter conventions and to hold the same, and to amend any such charter, with the same force and in the same manner and have the same power, as near as may be, as set out in sections four (4) and five (5) hereof, with full power as to real and personal property and public utilities, works or ways, as set out in section one (1) of this amendment.

Sec. 7. The City and County of Dnever shall alone always constitute one school district, to be known as District No. 1, but its conduct, affairs and business shall be in the hands of a board of education consisting of such numbers, elected in such manner as the general school laws of the state shall provide, and until the first election under said laws of a full board of education which shall be had at the first election held after the adoption of this amendment, all the directors of school district No. 1, and the respective presidents of the school boards of school districts Nos. 2, 7, 17 and 21, at the time this amendment takes effect, shall act as such board of education, and all districts or special charters now existing are hereby abolished.

The said board of education shall perform all the acts and duties required to be performed for said districts by the general laws of the state. Except as inconsistent with this amendment, the general school laws of the state, shall, unless the context evinces a contrary intent, be held to extend and apply to the said "District No. 1."

Upon the annexation of any contiguous municipality which shall include a school district or districts or any part of a district, said school district or districts or any part of a district, said school district or districts or parts shall be merged in said "District No. 1," which shall then own all the property thereof, real and personal, located within the boundaries of such annexed municipality, and shall assume and pay all the bonds, obligations and indebtedness of each of the said included school districts, and a proper proportion of those partially included districts;

Provided, however, That the indebtedness, both principal and interest, which any school district may be under at the time when it becomes a part, by this amendment or by annexation, of said "District No. 1," shall be paid by said school district so owing the same by a special tax to be fixed and certified by the board of education to the council which shall levy the same upon the property within the boundaries of such district, respectively, as the same existed at the time such district becomes a part of said "Dsitrict No. 1," and in case of partially included districts such tax shall be equitably apportioned upon the several parts thereof.

Sec. 8. Anything in the Constitution of this state in conflict or inconsistent with the provisions of this amendment is hereby declared to be inapplicable to the matters and things by this amendment covered and provided for. *(151, 181)*

(This amendment was commonly called the "Rush Bill" from the name of its author, who is the author of this book.)

27. Colorado Amendment (1912)—Art. XX, Sec. 6

The people of each city and town in this state, having a population of two thousand inhabitants as determined by the last preceding census

* * and the ciitzens thereof, shall have the powers set out in sections 1, 4 and 5 of this article, and all other powers necessary, requisite or proper for the government and administration of its local and municipal matters, including power to legislate upon, provide, regulate, conduct and control: the creation and terms of municipal offices, agencies and employments; the definition, regulation and alteration of the powers, duties, qualifications and terms of tenure of all municipal officers, agents and employees; the creation of police courts * * the jurisdiction, powers and duties thereof, and the election of police magistrates therefor; all matters pertaining to municipal elections * * (and) the registration of voters; the issuance, refunding and liquidation of all kinds of municipal obligations; the consolidation of water and park districts; the assessment of property for municipal taxation and the levy and collection of taxes thereon; the imposition, enforcement and collection of fines and penalties for the violation of any charter provision. The existing charters of the City and County of Denver and the cities of Pueblo, Colorado Springs and Grand Junction were ratified, affirmed and validated as of their date. *(151)*

28. Georgia Amendment (1924)—Art. XI, Sec. 2-a

The General Assembly shall have the power to consolidate and combine all governmental functions and powers now vested in and exercised by cities and municipalities having a population of more than 52,900 according to the Federal census of 1920, with the governmental functions and powers now vested in and exercised by the authorities of the county in which such cities or municipalities are situated; to create, designate, and give a name to political subdivisions composed of the entire area of such county; to vest in and confer upon such subdivisions such authority and power as may be conferred upon municipalities or counties, or both, under existing laws; to establish any and all offices now existing under the charters of such municipalities and also to abolish the offices of tax collector and tax receiver in any such counties; to create new offices, for the purpose of exercising and carrying out the powers to be vested in such political subdivisions, and powers and duties formerly appertaining to such offices so abolished and the powers and duties formerly exercised by such counties and such municipalities, all without regard to the uniformity of the powers, duties and compensation appertaining to the offices so created, in other municipalities, other counties, or other political subdivisions hereby authorized; to divide such political subdivisions into districts; to fix a maximum rate of ad valorem taxation to be levied by authority of such political subdivision, within the various districts, without regard to the uniformity of the rate; also to consolidate and combine any and all school systems and school districts now existing in any such cities or municipalities and counties into one system covering the entire area of the county to be governed and controlled under the provisions of the act creating the political subdivision hereby authorized, regardless of the method of control of schools or school systems in other counties or municipalities. The powers herein granted shall not be extended to cities, municipalities or towns, and cities and towns, and municipalities, the corporate limits of which are included within more than one county; nor shall said powers herein granted be extended to the counties in which cities, or towns, municipalities, and cities and towns, and municipalities are located. * * This provision of the Constitution shall not be construed to empower the General Assembly to create new counties, nor to affect or change the representation of any county in the General Assembly. Nor shall it be construed to authorize the General Assembly to abolish the offices of clerk of the superior court, ordinary, sheriff or coroner in any of the counties affected by this paragraph, said offices being expressly hereby reserved. The General Assembly shall not change or abolish any county nor the name thereof which may be affected thereby; and in naming the consolidated subdivisions in each case the names of the municipality or municipalities and of the county shall be combined so as to preserve them. The General Assembly shall create such political subdivisions by special act or law relating to a particular subdivision, but no such act or law shall have any force or effect until the same shall have been ratified by a vote of a majority of the qualified voters voting at a special election in such county, * * provided, however, that the people within the corporate limits of municipalities affected and the people of the county affected outside of the corporate limits shall vote separately; and before the act shall go into effect a majority of those voting in the municipalities separately, if more than one municipality is affected, and a majority of those voting outside of said municipality or municipalities, shall vote in favor of said act. *(187)*

29. Ohio Amendment (1933)—Art. X, Sec. 2

Any county may frame and adopt and amend a charter, and such charter may provide for the concurrent or exclusive exercise by the county, in all or in part of its area, of all or any of designated powers vested by the constitution or laws of Ohio in municipalities; it may provide for the organization of the county as a municipal corporation; and in such case it may provide for the succession of the county to the rights, properties and obligations of municipalities and townships therein incident to the municipal power so vested in the county, and for the division of the county into districts for purposes of administration or of taxation or both. No charter or amendment vesting any municipal powers in the county shall become effective, unless it shall have been approved by a majority of those voting thereon (1) in the county, (2) in the largest municipality, (3) in the county outside such municipality, and (4) in each of the majority of the combined total of municipalities and townships in the county (not including within any township any part of its area lying within a municipality.) Every such charter shall provide for the form of government of the county and shall determine which of its officers shall be elected and the manner of their election. It shall provide for the exercise of all powers vested in, and the performance of all duties imposed upon counties and county officers. *(189)*

30.   Florida Amendment (1934)—Art. VIII, Sec. 9

The Legislature shall have power to establish, alter or abolish, a municipal corporation to be known as the City of Jacksonville, extending territorially throughout the present limits of Duval County, in the place of any or all county, district, municipal and local governments, boards, bodies and officers, constitutional or statutory, legislative, executive, judicial, or administrative, and shall prescribe the jurisdiction, powers, duties and functions of such municipal corporation, its legislative, executive, judicial and administrative departments and its boards, bodies and officers; to divide the territory included in such municipality into subordinate districts, and to prescribe a just and reasonable system of taxation for such municipality and district; and to fix the liability of such municipality and districts.   Bonded and other indebtedness, existing at the time of the establishment of such municipality, shall be enforceable only against property theretofore taxable therefor.   The Legislature shall, from time to time, determine what portion of said municipality is a rural area, and a homestead in such rural area shall not be limited as if in a city or town.   Such municipality may exercise all the powers of a municipal corporation and shall also be recognized as one of the legal political divisions of the State with the duties and obligations of a county and shall be entitled to all the powers, rights and privileges, including representation in the State Legislature, which would accrue to it if it were a county.   All property of Duval County and of the municipalities in said county shall vest in such municipal corporation when established as herein provided.   The offices of Clerk of the Circuit Court and Sheriff shall not be abolished but the Legislature may prescribe the time when, and the method by which, such offices shall be filled and the compensation to be paid to such officers and may vest in them additional powers and duties.   No county office shall be abolished or consolidated with another office without making provision for the performance of all State duties now or hereafter prescribed by law to be performed by such county officer.   Nothing contained herein shall affect Section 20 of Article III of the Constitution of the State of Florida, except as to such provisions therein as relate to regulating the jurisdiction and duties of any class of officers, to summoning and impanelling grand and petit jurors, to assessing and collecting taxes for county purposes and to regulating the fees and compensation of county officers.   No law authorizing the establishing or abolishing of such municipal corporation pursuant to this section, shall become operative or effective until approved by a majority of the qualified electors participating in an election held in said County, but so long as such municipal corporation exists under this Section the Legislature may amend or extend the law authorizing the same without referendum to the qualified voters unless the Legislative act providing for such amendment or extension shall provide for such referendum.

(Note: In 1936 an amendment was adopted as section 10 of said article in identical language with the foregoing, except that it applied to the City of Key West and the County of Monroe.) *(189-190)*

31. New York Amendment (1935)—Art. X, Sec. 2

In the counties in the City of New York the City of New York is hereby vested with the power from time to time by local law, to abolish the office of any county officer other than judges, clerks of counties, and district attorneys, and to assign any and all functions of such officers to city officers, courts, or clerks, and to prescribe the powers, duties, qualifications, number, mode of selection and removal, terms of office and compensation of the persons holding such offices and the employees therein, and to assign to city officers any powers or duties of clerks of counties not assigned by this constitution. * * The legislature shall not pass any law affecting such matters in relation to such officers in the City of New York except on a message from the governor declaring that an emergency exists and the concurrence of two-thirds of the members of each house of the legislature, but existing laws regarding each such office shall continue in force and may be amended or repealed by the legislature as heretofore until the power herein granted to the city has been exercised with respect to that office. Elective county officers in office at the time this article, as so amended, takes effect, shall continue in office until the end of the terms for which they were elected." (Note: In 1938 this section was amended by adding thereto the following: "The provisions of this article shall not prevent the legislature from passing general or special laws prescribing or affecting powers and duties of such city officers or such courts or clerks to whom or which functions of such county officers shall have been assigned, in so far as such powers or duties embrace subjects not relative to property, affair or government of such city." This section was then renumbered as section 8 of Article IX.) *(191)*

---

32. PROPOSED LOS ANGELES COUNTY CHARTER AMENDMENT FOR MANAGER

There is hereby created a certification board which shall consist of the chief executive officer of each of the following institutions: University of California at Los Angeles, University of Southern California, California Institute of Technology, Loyola University of Los Angeles, Occidental College, Claremont Colleges, Whittier College, and their respective successors in office. The certification board shall, by a majority vote of all its members, select a list of names of five persons whom it deems best fitted to be members of the civil service commission, and shall submit such list to the board of supervisors, which board shall, by a majority vote of all its members forthwith appoint from said list three members who shall constitute the civil service commission. The members of the civil service commission shall classify their terms of office by lot so that one member shall serve until June 30, 1940, one member until June 30, 1942, and one member until June 30, 1944, or until their respective successors are appointed and qualify. Their respective successors shall each serve for a term of six years, unless sooner removed for cause. Any vacancy resulting from the expiration of the term of any member from any other cause shall be filled by the certification board submitting to the board of supervisors the names of two more persons than the number of vacancies to be filled, whereupon the board shall make its appointments in the manner hereinabove provided. The commission shall elect one of its members president.

The office of manager is hereby created. He shall serve for a term of seven years. He shall be appointed by the board of supervisors as provided in this section. He shall be a citizen of the United States and shall devote his entire time to the duties of his office. He shall receive a salary to be fixed by the board of supervisors in an amount not less than the highest salary being paid to any elective or appointive officer in the county service, and payable in equal monthly installments.

With all reasonable speed after this section becomes effective, the civil service commission, appointed as hereinabove provided, shall make a careful study of the men in the United States best qualified from the standpoint of character, executive ability, experience, and availability, to become manager, and shall then invite them to become applicants for that office without competitive examination, and shall select three persons whom the commission deems best fitted to be manager. The names of the persons so selected shall be certified to the board of supervisors, who shall forthwith appoint as manager one of the persons so certified. The manager may be removed by a four-fifths vote of the board of supervsiors after verified charges in writing have been preferred against him by said board or a member thereof and a public hearing had thereon by said board, with the right on the part of the manager to testify, present evidence, and be represented by counsel. A vacancy in the office of manager shall be filled in the manner above set forth. If the office of manager shall become vacant from any cause, the board of supervisors shall appoint an acting manager to serve as manager until such vacancy is filled, as provided in this section; provided, however, that no person shall serve as acting manager for more than ninety days.

The manager shall be the chief administrative officer of the county, and shall have and exercise administrative supervision over all the functions of the county, except as otherwise provided in this charter. (Generally speaking the powers and duties of the manager were to enforce county ordinances, attend all meetings of the board of supervsiors and make reports thereto, appoint all appointive county officers and assign them their duties, remove and transfer officers and employees, subject to civil service, consolidate into departments under a single head the various administrative duties and functions of the county, have charge of all county buildings and grounds and assign quarters and equipment for the use of all departments under his supervision, and prepare and submit an annual budget to the board of supervisors.) *(86)*

LEGAL AUTHORITIES AND CASES

(Pages in this book are shown in parentheses)

Charters of the 13 Original Colonies (74-76)
Constitutions of the 48 States
Codes and Statutes thereof and of Hawaii
Magna Charta (33, 35, 59, 127)
Reform Bill of 1832 (England) (43, 47, 54, 61)
Municipal Corporations Act of 1835 (England) (43, 44, 54, 55, 61, 194)
Local Government Act of 1888 (England) (54, 55, 56, 194)
Local Government Act of 1929 (England) (55)
Charters of American Cities-Counties:

> City of New York (155, 208, 209, 212, 214-223); City of New Orleans (235-237); City of Baltimore (154, 245-248); City of Philadelphia (155, 259, 262-264); City and County of San Francisco (143-149, 273, 274, 275, 278-280, 283-287); City of St. Louis (143-145, 292-296, 303-306, 308, 311-315, 317, 318, 320); City and County of Denver (150, 328, 332, 335-336, 342, 349-352); Independent Cities of Virginia (Henning's Statutes at Large); City and County of Honolulu (Statutes, Territory of Hawaii)

Corpus Juris, Vol. 59, Classification of Cities (168)
CYC, Vol. 36, Classification of Cities (168)
Corpus Juris, Vol. 43, Municipal Corporations (121)
Adler v. Degan, 251 N. Y. 467 (218, 219, 220)
Anderson v. Lewis, 29 Cal. App. 24 (277)
Arms v. City, 314 Ill. 316 (136)
Attorney General v. Board, 58 Mich. 213 (138)
Bernard v. Chicago, 316 Ill 519 (136)
Blanchard v. Hartwell, 131 Cal. 263 (146)
Bissett v. Town, 87 W. Va. 127 (136)
Board v. Heister, 37 N. Y. 661 (98)
Budd v. Hancock, 66 N. J. L. 133 (169)
Campbell v. City, 155 Ind. 186 (109)
Carrithers v. City, 126 Ky. 769 (128)
Chicago Terminal v. City, 220 Ill. 310 (136)
City v. Horton, 22 R. I. 196 (111, 131)
City v. Murphy, 313 Ill. 98 (136)
City v. Society, 24 N. J. L. 385 (121)

State ex rel v. Field, 99 Mo. 352 (306)
State ex rel. v. Finn, 8 Mo. App. 341 (299, 307, 308, 310)
State ex rel. v. Fox, 158 Ind. 126 (109, 132)
State ex rel. v. Hunter, 38 Kan. 578 (107, 110, 111, 120)
State ex rel. v. Kennedy, 60 Neb. 300 (105)
State ex rel. v. Koeln, 270 Mo. 174 (319)
State ex rel. v. Koslem, 130 Ind. 434 (107, 108, 120, 132)
State ex rel. v. Krause, 130 O. St. 455 (189)
State ex rel. v. Mason, 153 Mo. 23 (112)
State ex rel. v. Mason, 4 Mo. App. 377 (307, 308, 311, 319)
State ex rel. v. McKee, 69 Mo. 504 (310)
State ex rel. v. Moores, 55 Neb. 480 (103, 105, 112)
State ex rel. v. Parsons, 40 N. J. L. 1 (168)
State ex rel. v. Police Com'rs, 184 Mo. 109 (301)
State ex rel. v. Powers, 68 Mo. 320 (312)
State ex rel. v. Seavey, 22 Neb. 454 (105, 107)
State ex rel. v. Seehorn, 246 Mo. 541 (318)
State ex rel. v. Smith, 44 O. St. 348 (104, 120)
State ex rel. v. St .Louis, 34 Mo. 546 (100, 106, 111)
State ex rel. v. St. Louis, 319 Mo. 497 (295)
State ex rel. v. Sutton, 3 Mo. App. 388 (295)
State ex rel. v. Walsh, 69 Mo. 408 (167, 294, 305, 306, 309, 310, 319)
State v. City, 264 U. S. 472 (316)
State v. Dannenberg, 150 N. C. 799 (136)
State v. Parker, 116 Ia. 96 (20)
State v. Ray, 131 N. C. 814 (136)
St. Louis v. Western Union, 149 U. S. 465 (304)
Staude v. Commissioners, 61 Cal. 313 (273)
Taggart v. Commonwealth, 102 Pa. St. 354 (256, 308)
Telephone Co. v. City, 226 Fed. 82 *(136)*
Thompson v. City, 113 Ky. 540 *(129)*
Williams v. City, 36 Cal. App. 133 *(146)*

BIBLIOGRAPHY

(Pages where quoted shown in italics)

ADAMS, JAMES TRUSLOW,
>March of Democracy—(New York—1933)
>History of New England—(Boston—1927)
>Epic of America—(New York—1933)

ADAMS, HERBERT S., Studies in Historical and Political Science—
>(Baltimore—1884)

ALLISON, E. P., and PENROSE, BOISE, History of Municipal Development—
>(Philadelphia—1887)

AMERICANA, THE, Great Britain (41)

AMERICANA, THE, Municipal Corporations by Maltbie (135)

ANDERSON, WILLIAM, Local Government and Finance—(Minneapolis—1935)

ASH, MARK, The Greater New York Charter—(New York—1925, supplement—1936)

AULT, FREDERICK C., History of Municipal Government in St. Louis—
>(St. Louis—1938)

BALLARD, A., British Borough Charters—1042-1216—(Cambridge, Eng.—
>1913)

BANCROFT, GEORGE, History of the United States—(Little Browne & Co.,
>Boston—1834-74) (73)

BEARD, CHARLES A., and MARY R., Rise of American Civilization—(New
>York—1927)

BOLLES, A. S., Pennsylvania Province and State—(Philadelphia—1899)

BONNER, WILLIAM T., New York, The World Metropolis—(New York—1924)

BREASTED, JAMES HENRY, The Conquest of Civilization—(New York—1916)
>(20)

BRUCE, P. A., Institutional History of Virginia in the 17th Century—
>(New York—1910)

CAESAR, Commentaries on the Gallic War—(25)

CHANNING, EDWARD, Town and County Government in the English Colonies
>—(Baltimore—1884)

CHITWOOD, O. P., History of Colonial America—(New York—1931)

CLARKE, JOHN J., Local Government of the United Kingdom—
>(London—1933)

DYSART, THOMAS N., Municipal Integration—(St. Louis Daily Record—
>1940)

EATON, AMASA M., *Right of Local Self-Government*—(13 and 14 Harvard
    Law Review: 25 American Bar Association Reports—
    1902)

FAIRLIE, JOHN and KNIER, CHARLES M., *County Government and Municipal
                    Administration*—(New York—1930)

FINER, HERMAN, *English Local Government*—(Methuen & Co., London—
    1933) *(28, 35, 63, 66, 122, 135)*
    in *A Century of Municipal Progress*—G. Allen & Unwin
    London—1936 *(55)*

GILBERTSON, HENRY S., *The County*—(New York—1917)

GREEN, JOHN RICHARD, *Short History of the English People*—(Harper &
                    Bros, New York—1889) *(26, 28, 34)*

GRIFFITH, E. S., *History of American City Government,* Colonial Period—
    (New York—1938)
    *Modern Development of Local Government in Great Brit-
    ain and the United States*—(Oxford, Eng.—1927)

GUTHRIE, W. B., *City and County of Denver*—(Address National Municipal
    League—1917) *(340)*

HALEVY, ELIE, in *A Century of Municipal Progress*—(London—1936) *(53)*

HALL, CLAYTON C., *Baltimore, Its History and Its People*—(New York—
    1912)

HAMMOND, J. L., in *A Century of Municipal Progress*—(London—1936)

HART, SIR WM. E. and WM. O., *An Introduction to Local Government Law
                    and Administration*—(Butterworth & Co.,
                    London—1931) *(68)*

HITTELL, THEODORE H., *A History of California*—(San Francisco—1878)
                    (270) (Quoted by Percy V. Long, noted below)

ILLINOIS *Constitutional Convention Report Bulletin No. 11* (1920) *(210)*

JENNINGS, W. IVOR, *Principles of Local Government Law*—(New York—
    1931)

KING, CLYDE L., *History of the Government of Denver*—(Denver—1911)

KNIER, CHARLES M., *Illustrative Materials in Municipal Governmental
                    Administration*—(New York—1939)

KRESSLING, FRANCIS V., *San Francisco Charter of 1931*—(San Francisco—
    1931) *(284)*

LABAREE, L. W., *Royal Instructions to British Colonial Governors*—(New
                    York—1935)

LASKI, JENNINGS, HAMMOND and ROBSON, *A Century of Municipal Progress*
                    —(London—1936)

LINDSEY, BEN B., *The Beast,* pp. 237-250—(New York—1910)

LIVES OF LORD CHANCELLORS, Vol. 44, pp. 316, 319 *(39)*

LODGE, HENRY CABOT, *A Short History of the English Colonies in America*
                    —(New York—1881)

LOEB, ISADOR, *Government of the St. Louis Metropolis.* (Nat. Munic. Review,
    June 1930) *(291)*

LONG, PERCY V., *Consolidated City and County of San Francisco*—(Proceedings American Political Science Association—1911)

MAITLAND, F. W., *Constitutional History of England*—(Cambridge, Eng.—1913)

MALTBIE, M. R., *English Local Government of Today*—(New York—1897)

McBAIN, HOWARD LEE, *Law and Practice of Municipal Home Rule*—Columbia Univ. Press, New York—1916) *(301, 303, 345)*

MAYO, R. B., *Report to Denver Chamber of Commerce (340)*

MERRIAM, CHARLES E., *The Government of the Metropolitan Region of Chicago*—(Chicago—1933)

MILLER, JUSTIN, *Report to Durham Chamber of Commerce (327)*

MUNRO, WILLIAM B., *Municipal Administration*—(Macmillan Co.—1934) *(33, 42, 116)*

Government of European Cities—(Macmillan Co.—1917) *(31)*

NELSON, ARTHUR E., *City-County Consolidation* (Address Nat. Munic. League, 1923) *(180)*

NEW YORK, *Charter Revision Committee Report*—(New York—1936)

NEW YORK, *Report of Board of Statutory Consolidation*—(Albany—1937)

O'CALLAGHAN, E. B., *Documents Relative to Colonial History of the State of New York*—(Albany—1850)

OSGOOD, HERBERT L., *American Colonies in the 17th Century*—(New York—1904)

PHILLIPS, CATHERINE COFFIN, *Portsmouth Plaza*—(San Francisco—1932)

PINCHBECK, RAYMOND B., *City-County Separation in Virginia*—(Nat. Munic. Review—July 1940) *(206)*

PRESTON, HOWARD W., *Documents Illustrative of American History*—(New York—1886)

ROYAL COMMISSION, FIRST REPORT, *Local Government and Constitution and Extension of County Boroughs*—(London—1888) *(62)*

ROYAL COMMISSION, *Report on Extension of County Boroughs* (London—1925) *(65)*

ROBSON, WILLAM A., *The Development of Local Government*—(G. Allen & Unwin Co., London—1931) *(70)*

SATURDAY EVENING POST, *Editorial on New York Election (227)*

SHEPPARD, S. S. and MOAK, L. L., *New Orleans Leads in Consolidation*—(Nat. Munic. Review, Nov. 1940) *(238)*

SMITH, ALFRED E., *San Francisco: A Pioneer in the Consolidation Movement*—(Nat. Munic. Review, March 1941)

SPENCER, EDWARD, *100th Anniversary of Settlement of Baltimore*—(Baltimore—1881)

STODDARD, HENRY L., *It Costs to be President*—(Harper & Bros., New York—1938) *(74)*

STOKES, I. N., *The Iconography of Manhattan Island*—(New York—1915)

STUDENSKI, PAUL, *Government of Metropolitan Areas in the United States*—
(National Munic. League—1930) *(291)*

TACITUS, *Germania (25)*

TANZER, LAWRENCE A., *New York City Charter, Its Source and History*—
(New York—1937)

TAYLOR, W. R. L., *City of Norfolk*—(Nat. Munic. Review, Nov. 1936)

THORPE, F. N., *Colonial Charters and State Constitutions*—(Gov't Ptg. Office,
Washington—1898)

TUTHILL, FRANKLIN, *History of California*—(San Francisco—1866)

YOUNG, T. P., *Scheme for Separation and City Government in St. Louis*—

WEBB, SIDNEY and BEATRICE, *English Local Government*—(London—1908)

WELLS, H. G., *Outline of History*—(Macmillan Co., New York—1924) *(20,
21)*

WERBA, ARTHUR M., and GRUNEWALD, JOHN L., *Making Milwaukee
Mightier* (Milwaukee—1929) *(327)*

WHITE, LEONARD, *The City Manager*—(University of Chicago Press—1927)
(84)

WILSON, WOODROW, *The State*—(Boston—1898) *(27, 66)*

WOODWARD, WILLIAM E., *New American History*—(London—1938)

THOSE WHO HAVE HELPED

(Offices noted were those held when help was furnished)

ALEXANDER, MARION G., Research Clk. Atty. Gen., Concord, N. H.

ALEXANDER, W. E., Chief Clk. Sec. of State, Denver, Colo.

AMBLER, GORDON B., Mayor, Richmond, Va.

ANNEAR, THOMAS, State Auditor, Denver, Colo.

AULT, FREDERICK C., Acting Librarian Munic. Ref. Lib., St. Louis, Mo.

BAKER, MORRIS A., Ass't. City Solicitor, Baltimore Md.

BECK, CLARENCE V., Attorney General, Topeka, Kan.

BENNETT, MARK L., City Attorney, Topeka, Kan.

BICKFORD, J. V., Mayor, Hampton, Va.

BITTNER, FRANK, County Auditor, Milwaukee, Wis.

BLUME, G. C., Mayor, Jacksonville, Fla.

BOETCHER, WALTER C., Mayor, Indianapolis, Ind.

BOHANNAN, J. GORDON, Attorney, Petersburg, Va.

BOOKER, J. W., Mayor, Martinsville, Va.

BOIZELLE, WM., Ass't. City Attorney, New Orleans, La.

BOYD, HAROLD J., Controller, San Francisco, Cal.

BROOKS, T. A., Administrative Officer, San Francisco, Cal.

BRENNON, L. C., City Clerk, Portsmouth, Va.

BROWN, DWIGHT H., Secretary of State, Jefferson City, Mo.

BURINGTON, DON W., Ass't. Atty. Gen., Des Moines, Ia.

BURNS, FRANCIS P., City Attorney, New Orleans, La.

BURTON, HAROLD H., Mayor, Cleveland, Ohio.

CARMICHAEL, DONALD S., Department of Law, Cleveland, Ohio.

CARSON, JOSEPH K., JR., Mayor, Portland, Ore.

CAVE, JESS S., Com'r Public Finance, New Orleans, La.

COGHLAN, RALPH, Editor Editorial Page *St. Louis Post Dispatch.*

CONRAD, BRYAN, Ass't. Director Va. Conservation Com., Richmond, Va.

CONROY, THOMAS J., Ass't. Atty. Gen., Hartford, Conn.

CONWAY, JOE, Attorney General, Phoenix, Ariz.

CORBELL, JOHN D., City Clerk, Norfolk, Va.

CRANE, C. S., Mayor, Honolulu, T. H.

CUNNINGHAM, CHAS. L., Dep. Controller, St. Louis, Mo.

CUNNINGHAM, JOSEPH M., Dep. Controller, New York City.

CURTIS, ARTHUR E., Director of Finance, San Francisco, Cal.

DABAGH, THOMAS S., Librarian (and assistants) Law Lib., Los Angeles, Cal.

DABNEY, VIRGINIUS, Editor *Times-Dispatch,* Richmond, Va.

DALEY, RICHARD J., Dep. County Comptroller, Chicago, Ill.

DANIEL, JOHN M., Attorney General, Columbia, S. C.

DAVIES, AUDREY M., Librarian Institute Public Adm'n., New York City.

DAVIES, JOHN L., City Attorney, Columbus, Ohio.

DAVIS, FRANK M., Comptroller, Buffalo, N. Y.

DAVIS, J. JAMES, Mayor, So. Norfolk, Va.

DAYTON, KENNETH, Director of the Budget, New York City.

DESHA, JOHN R., Dep. City Atty., Honolulu, T. H.

DIAMOND, DAVID, Corporation Counsel, Buffalo, N. Y.

DICK, CHRISTIAN, Librarian (and assistants) U.S.C. Lib., Los Angeles, Cal.

DICKMANN, BERNARD F., Mayor, St. Louis, Mo.

DILLARD, A. FLEET, Ass't. Director Statutory Research, Richmond, Va.

DIRKS, HERBERT, Dep. Atty. Gen, Indianapolis, Ind.

DODDS, PAUL R., banker, 7th and Grand, Los Angeles, Cal.

DOVELL, ASHTON, City Attorney, Williamsburg, Va.

DOYLE, W. J., City Clerk, Boston, Mass.

DREWRY, R. F., Ass't. Atty. Gen., Pierre, S. Dak.

DUFFY, HERBERT S., Attorney General, Columbus, Ohio.

DYKSTRA, DR. CLARENCE A., President University of Wisconsin.

EDWARDS, HORACE H., City Attorney, Richmond, Va.

EGGER, ROWLAND, Director of Budget, Governor's Office, Richmond, Va.

ELLS, H. P., Secy. Commission of Efficiency, Toledo, Ohio.

ENGEL, GEO., Auditor General, Detroit, Mich.

ERETH, FRED W., Dep. City Comptroller, Rochester, N. Y.

ERICKSON, DAVID J., Dep. Atty. Gen., St. Paul, Minn.

FALLIN, HERBERT, Budget Director, Baltimore, Md.

FALLON, WILLIAM H., Mayor, St. Paul, Minn.

FARQUEHAR, SAMUEL T., Univ. of Cal., Berkeley, Cal.

FARRELL, EUGENE S., Acting City Auditor, Newark, N. J.

FARRIES, G. COE, Ass't. City Solicitor, Philadelphia, Pa.

FERNANDEZ, A. M., Ass't. Atty. Gen., Santa Fe, N. Mex.

FLACK, DR. HORACE E., Director Legislative Ref., Baltimore, Md.

FOGG, SANFORD L., Dep. Atty. Gen., Augusta, Me.
FOX, CHARLES J., City Auditor, Boston, Mass.
FREY, EDWARD R., City Controller, Pittsburgh, Pa.
FRIZZELL, E. G., City Auditor, Danville, Va.
GEHAN, MARK H., Mayor, St. Paul, Minn.
GRAY, R. A., Secretary of State, Tallahassee, Fla.
GRAYSON, SPENCE M., City Attorney, Savannah, Ga.
GREEN, P. WARREN, Attorney General, Trenton, N. J.
GRIFFITH, ALFRED H., Mayor, Buena Vista, Va.
GUCKENBERGER, GEORGE, County Auditor, Cincinnati, Ohio.
HALL, WILMER L., State Librarian, Richmond, Va.
HALL, W. L., City Manager, Staunton, Va.
HAMILTON, G. W., Attorney General, Olympia, Wash.
HARPER, ELLEN R., Director Research, Alexandria, Va.
HARRIS, R. S., Comptroller, Lynchburg, Va.
HATCHETT, JOSEPH M., City Manager, Petersburg, Va.
HAYDEN, CLYDE, County Attorney, Hamilton, Mont.
HELLMAN, FLORENCE S., Library of Congress, Washington, D. C.
HERDMAN, GUY H., Ass't. Atty Gen., Frankfort, Ky.
HILLIARD, BENJAMIN C., Chief Justice Supreme Court, Denver, Colo.
HOAN, DANIEL W., Mayor, Milwaukee, Wis.
HODES, BARNET, Corporation Counsel, Chicago, Ill.
HOLLINGSWORTH, JOSEPHINE, Librarian (& assistants) Munic. Ref. Lib., L. A.
HOUSTON, L. J., JR., City Manager, Fredericksburg, Va.
HUDSON, JUDGE GRANT L., Denver, Colo.
HUNTER, W. P., City Manager, Roanoke, Va.
JACKSON, HOWARD W., Mayor, Baltimore, Md.
JACOBS, JOHN HALL, Librarian Public Library, New Orleans, La.
JONES, C. V., City Attorney, Durham, N. Car.
JONES, H. O., City Attorney, Americus, Ga.
JONES, HOWARD P., National Munic. League, New York City.
JONES, LAWRENCE C., Attorney General, Montpelier, Vt.
JOHNSON, J. HARRY, Ass't. Atty. Gen., Oklahoma City, Okla.
KEEFE, A. J., Dep. City Comptroller, Chicago, Ill.
KERNER, OTTO, Attorney General, Springfield, Ill.
KLOS, JAMES A., County Controller, Rochester, N. Y.
KNIGHT, EDWARD H., Corporation Counsel, Indianapolis, Ind.
KNOX, ALLISON S., Chief City Accountant, Cleveland, Ohio.
KNOX, ROY A., Director of Budget and Efficiency, Los Angeles, Cal.
LANGLIE, ARTHUR B., Mayor, Seattle, Wash.
LAZARUS, REUBEN A., Counsel Bd. Statutory Consol., New York City.
LEE, RAY E., Attorney General, Cheyenne, Wyo.
LINDSEY, JUDGE BEN B., Los Angeles, Cal.
LINDSEY, JOHN R., Director Finance, Louisville, Ky.
LINK, GEO. M., Secy. Bd. Estimate & Taxation, Minneapolis, Minn.
LOWERY, JOSEPH M., County Auditor, Los Angeles.

MAESTRI, ROBERT S., Mayor, New Orleans, La.
MATHEWS, W. T., Dep. Atty. Gen., Carson City, Nev.
MacGREGOR, FRANK S., 49 E. 33rd St., New York City.
MAYNARD, ELIJAH W., City Attorney, Macon, Ga.
McGOLDRICK, JOHN D., Comptroller, New York City.
McNICHOLS, WM. H., Auditor, Denver, Colo.
MEISEL, A. L., City Manager, Williamsburg, Va.
MILES, CLARENCE G., City Attorney, Lincoln, Neb.
MILLER, JUDGE JUSTIN, Washington, D. C.
MONTGOMERY, J. H., JR., Ass't. City Atty., Richmond, Va.
MOORE, GUY W., Chief Ass't. Corporation Counsel, Detroit, Mich.
MOORE, J. HAMPTON, Mayor, Philadelphia, Pa.
MORRIS, NEWBOLD, President of the Council, New York City.
MUNRO, DR. WILLIAM B., Cal. Institute of Technology, Pasadena, Cal.
NELSON, ARTHUR E., Ex-Mayor, St. Paul, Minn.
NYE, BARLOW, Ass't. Atty. Gen., Lincoln, Neb.
O'TOOLE, JOHN J., City Attorney, San Francisco, Cal.
PARKMAN, HENRY, JR., Corporation Counsel, Boston, Mass.
PELHAM, BENJ. B., County Accountant, Detroit, Mich.
PHILLIPS, HARRY, Ass't. Atty. Gen., Nashville, Tenn.
PIATT, W. H. H., Attorney, Kansas City, Mo.
PINCHBECK, DR. RAYMOND B., Chm'n, Com. Co. Gov't. Univ. of Richmond,
    Richmond, Va.
PRITCHARD, SIR HARRY G., Sec. Ass'n. Munc. Corp's., Westminster, England.
PROFFITT, CHARLES G., Columbia University, New York City.
RANKIN, REBECCA B., Librarian Munic. Ref. Library, New York City.
RENTZ, FRANK A., Attorney General, Madison, Wis.
REX, FREDERICK, Librarian Munic. Ref. Library, Chicago, Ill.
RICE, JOHN D., Dep. Atty. Gen., Salt Lake City, Utah.
RINEHART, ANITA, Librarian Munic. Service, Louisville, Ky.
ROBERTS, LOUIS L., City Attorney, Evansville, Ind.
ROSSI, ANGELO J., Mayor, San Francisco, Cal.
ROWE, CHAS. L., Ass't. Atty. Gen., Montgomery, Ala.
SAVAGE, J. C., City Attorney, Atlanta, Ga.
SCHOCK, HIRAM, Ass't. City Solicitor, Pittsburgh, Pa.
SCHOLTZ, JOSEPH D., Mayor, Louisville, Ky.
SCULLY, CORNELIUS D., Mayor, Pittsburgh, Pa.
SHARFSIN, JOSEPH, City Solicitor, Philadelphia, Pa.
SHOUP, DR. EARL L., Western Reserve Univ., Cleveland, Ohio.
SNELL, EARL, Secretary of State, Salem, Ore.
STAPLES, ABRAM P., Attorney General, Richmond, Va.
START, ROY C., Mayor, Toledo, Ohio.
STAPLETON, BENJAMIN F., Mayor, Denver, Colo.
STOUT, WESLEY W., Editor *Saturday Evening Post,* Philadelphia, Pa.
STERRETT, F. F., City Treasurer, Buena Vista, Va.
STEWART, JAMES GARFIELD, Mayor, Cincinnati, Ohio.

STREEPEY, JOHN P., Ass't. Atty Gen., Little Rock, Ark.

SULLIVAN, JEREMIAH A., City Solicitor, Newport, R. I.

SWAN, ROBERT A., Legal Secy. Law Officers Dept. Royal Courts of Justice, London, England.

SWEM, E. G., Librarian College of William and Mary, Williamsburg, Va.

TAYLOR, W. R. L., Mayor, Norfolk, Va.

THOMAS, W. C., City Comptroller, Seattle, Wash.

THOMPSON, JAMES H., Dep. Atty. Gen., Harrisburg, Pa.

THOMPSON, S. C., Chief City Accountant, Philadelphia.

TILLOTSON, B. F., Ass't. Atty. Gen., Bismarck, N. Dak.

TITUS, DR. CHARLES H., Univ. of Cal., Los Angeles, Cal.

TOBIN, BENJAMIN J., Acting Dep. Auditor General, Detroit, Mich.

TUCKER, EDWARD M., Attorney, Hamilton, Mont.

TURNER, O. J., City Comptroller, Minneapolis, Minn.

UHL, RAYMOND, Acting Director, Bureau Pub. Admn., Charlottesville, Va.

UPHAM, R. B., City Comptroller, Chicago, Ill.

URNER, HENRY, City Auditor, Cincinnati, Ohio.

VAN WINKLE, I. H., Attorney General, Salem. Ore.

WALLERSTEIN, MORTON L., Exec. Secy. League Va. Munic., Richmond, Va.

WALMSLEY, T. SEMMES, Mayor, New Orleans, La.

WARREN, ALTHEA, Librarian (and assistants) Public Lib., Los Angeles.

WASHBURN, H. L., County Auditor, Houston, Tex.

WAYMAN, EDGAR H., City Counselor, St. Louis, Mo.

WETTACH, ROBERT H., Ass't. Atty. Gen., Raleigh, N. Car.

WENDT, WM. H., City Comptroller, Milwaukee, Wis.

WHITE, A. H., Clerk Supreme Court, Denver, Colo.

WHITE, DR. ROBERT C., City Comptroller, Philadelphia, Pa.

WHITE, WILLIAM ALLEN, Editor *Emporia Gazette,* Emporia, Kan.

WILENTZ, DAVID T., Attorney General, Trenton, N. J.

WILLIS, JAMES H., Ass't. City Atty., Birmingham, Ala.

WITHERSPOON, JOHN H., Chief Ass't. Corp. Counsel, Detroit, Mich.

WOOD, J. D., Mayor, Norflok, Va.

WOODBURY, W. R., City Manager, Harrisonburg, Va.

ZANGERLE, JOHN A., County Auditor, Cleveland, Ohio.

INDEX